Gender, Ireland,
and Cultural Change

Routledge Studies in Twentieth-Century Literature

First published 2010
by Routledge
711 Third Avenue, New York, NY 10017

Simultaneously published in the UK
by Routledge
2 Park Square, Milton Park, Abingdon, Oxon, OX14 4RN

Routledge is an imprint of the Taylor & Francis Group, an informa business

First issued in paperback 2011

Typeset in Sabon by IBT Global.

Library of Congress Cataloging-in-Publication Data
Meaney, Gerardine, 1962–
    Gender, Ireland and cultural change : race, sex and nation / by Gerardine Meaney.
       p. cm. — (Routledge studies in twentieth-century literature ; 13)
    Includes bibliographical references and index.
    1. English literature—Irish authors—History and criticism.   2. English literature—Women authors—History and criticism.   3. Feminism and literature—Ireland—History—20th century.   4. Nationalism and literature—Ireland—History—20th century.   5. Nationalism and feminism—Ireland—History—20th century.   6. Race in literature.   7. Sex role in literature.   8. National characteristics, Irish, in literature.   9. Ireland—In literature.   10. Ireland—In popular culture.   I. Title.
    PR8733.M43 2010
    820.9'9415—dc22
    2009041538

ISBN10: 0-415-95790-7 (hbk)
ISBN10: 0-415-89647-9 (pbk)
ISBN10: 0-203-85958-8 (ebk)

ISBN13: 978-0-415-95790-8 (hbk)
ISBN13: 978-0-415-89647-4 (pbk)
ISBN13: 978-0-203-85958-2 (ebk)

Gender, Ireland, and Cultural Change

Race, Sex, and Nation

Gerardine Meaney

Routledge
Taylor & Francis Group
New York   London

Contents

Acknowledgments

This book derives from more than a decade of researching, teaching and writing. Several chapters and sections of chapters have been previously published and many have been rehearsed and refined by conference presentations, as invited and uninvited contributions to a broad range of debates in Irish studies. Consequently I have benefitted enormously from a very broad range of editors, colleagues, collaborators, students, librarians, conference organizers, readers and audiences who have commented on aspects of this work as it has circulated and developed over the years and who facilitated that development. I would like to particularly thank Moynagh Sullivan for years of debate on the themes of this book and to thank Moynagh, Anne Mulhall and Wanda Balzano for the opportunity to contribute to key volumes in the re-invention of Irish studies in the last few years, which re-ignited a then dormant writing project. The research projects in which I have been involved since 2003 have all informed this work in various ways. I have had the benefit of working with a group of extraordinarily intellectually generous historians, Maria Luddy, Mary O'Dowd and Bernadette Whelan. The interdisciplinary context of our collaborations has had a crucial role in the development of this book, on the one hand deepening my understanding of historical forces and archival sources and on the other liberating me from a rigid chronology. Needless to say both the interpretations of the historical record and the temporal discontinuities remain my responsibility. I would like to particularly acknowledge Emma Radley, Anne Mulhall, Caroline Magennis and Jim McPherson's work on the Women on Modern Irish Cutlure Database, Maria Luddy's monumental work in organizing the database project and Rob O'Toole's in providing technical support: the material in the database has fed into Chapters 1, 3 and 4 in a variety of ways. Thanks also to Maria Luddy, Leeane Lane, Emma Radley and Clara Cullen for the ongoing discussion of Rosamond Jacob and her extraordinary diaries. And yet more thanks to Emma for many Žižek conversations which bear fruit in Chapter 5. Diane Negra initially emboldened me to venture into television studies. Clair Wills and the London Irish Studies Seminar invited me to talk about Brenton, Ireland and spies at a crucial juncture and their feedback was invaluable. I am very grateful to Elizabeth

Cullingford and Cheryl Herr for their active support and stimulating ideas over the last number of years and to Seamus Deane for reading and commenting on an earlier version of this book. Eibhear Walshe encouraged the exploration of Hollywood action movies in the hallowed halls of the Royal Irish Academy and has been an important influence on the discussions of Kate O'Brien in this volume. Thanks to Cinta Ramblado and Auxilliadora Perez for the context of debates around gender and memory in Ireland and Spain in which to reconsider Dortohy Macardle's fiction, Marjorie Howes for the valuable editorial feedback on 'The Sons of Cuchulainn', James Smith for the opportunity to engage with his pioneering work on representations of the Magdalen Asylums, Michael O'Rourke for his response to the Thurston paper at *Theories*, Anne Fogarty for her comments on Thurston and Lawless, Tony Roche for his comments on Kate O'Brien and a great seminar in which to sort out my ideas on Joyce and Penelope, Declan Kiberd for always thought provoking arguments, Ailbhe Smyth for starting so many of these debates, Christopher Murray for his response to the initial conference paper on Antigone, Alan Sinfield for the benefit of his editoral insights on 'Penelope, or Myths Unravelling' and especially to the editors of *Women: A Cultural Review*, particularly Helen Carr, for an international feminist forum in which to test ideas over many years. Caroline Magennis's invitation to address the conference on Irish masculinities in Belfast in 2010 finally brought this journey to an end and thanks to her and to Pat Coughlan, Tina O'Toole, and Piaras Mac Einri for their positive input. Karen Corrigan and Frank Phelan have helped out and encouraged personally and professionally from the beginning. My thanks also to John Geary and Bernie Quinn for their encouragement at a vital moment.

I wish to gratefully acknowledge the following agencies and institutions whose research support has been crucial: the IRCHSS for its support for the 'Inventing and Reinventing the Irish Woman Project'; the HEA for its support for the North-South 'Women in Public and Cultural Life' project; the AHRC, UK and the University of Warwick for the establishment and development of the 'Women in Modern Irish Culture Database'; HEA (PRTLI4), the Humanities Institute of Ireland UCD and the School of History at the University of Warwick for starting grants for work on the Diaries of Rosamond Jacob.

Behind all these projects is the *Field Day Anthology of Irish Writing*, volumes 4 and 5. My ongoing thanks are due to Angela Bourke, Maria Luddy, Margaret McCurtain, Mairin Ni Dhonnchadha, Mary O'Dowd, Clair Wills and Seamus Deane for the stimulus of that collaboration. As always in acknowledging the anthology, I remember the contribution of Siobhan Kilfeather to debates about sexuality and gender in Irish Studies.

I am particularly appreciative of the institutional support of UCD for this research through the award of a President's Fellowship in 2004 and sabbatical leave in 2008. I am very grateful for the practical and intellectual support of the Humanities Institute of Ireland at UCD and of Marc Caball and Valerie Norton in particular. Mary Daly, originally as Director of the HII and then as College Principal, has been most helpful in supporting my research for this book. In the School of English, Drama and Film Anne Mulhall, Danielle Clarke and Emma Radley have been great colleagues in developing courses which have been based on and fed into this research over the last few years.

The staff of the National Library of Ireland, British Library and of the James Joyce Library at UCD have been unfailingly helpful and interested over the years. Lexy Howe at Kudos kindly provided me with a copy of a relevant episode of *Spooks*.

I have been tremendously fortunate in the quality of postgraduate and postdoctoral students and researchers among whom I have had the opportunity to work over the last decade. I would particularly like to thank Claire Bracken, Dervila Layden, Aintzane Legareta Mentxaka, Jenny O'Connor, Jenny Knell, Sarah O'Connor and Emma Radley for the opportunity to share their intellectual journeys, which has very much enriched my own while writing this book. Teaching the M.A class in Gender, Sexuality and Culture has been a great way of exploring ideas over the last two years and I am grateful to them and to a wide range of undergraduate students for the opportunity to discuss, test out and get the benefit of their responses to ideas and texts.

My thanks to Erica Wetter and Elizabeth Levine at Routledge. The last stage of production of this book depended on the kindness—and endless patience—of a virtual stranger, Michael Watters of Integrated Book Technology, who got me through through proofing and indexing at a difficult time by the power of his goodwill.

Gerry Dowling has, as always, kept me going, kept me thinking and kept me sane. Because this is a book about change, written by a woman living through economic, social, political and personal change, I like to think it is engaged in remembering the past to imagine the future. My mother, May, whom I was gradually losing as I finished this, taught me by example that change is in our own hands and the future can be made very different from the past. The changeable future she gave me now belongs to my daughters, Ciara and Grainne, and their infinite potential. And so this book is for all four of them, who map out for me how much is possible.

Previous versions of chapters 1, 2, 3 and 4 have been published in part or in full in the following forms: 'Race, Sex and Nation', *The Irish Review*, Feminist Theory Special Issue, Autumn 2007; 'The Sons of Cuchulainn: Violence, the Family and Irish Canons', *Eire Ireland*, Summer 2006; 'Dark Imaginings and White Anxieties: the Gothic Republic' in *'Unmarried' Mothers in Twentieth-Century Ireland: Cultural Reflections*, ed. Cinta Ramblado Minero, Edwin Mellen Press, 2006; 'Kate O'Brien' in *The UCD Aesthetic*, ed. Anthony Roche, New Island Press, 2005, pp. 76–86; 'Regendering Modernism: The Woman Artist in Irish Women's Fiction', *Women: A Cultural Review*, Vol.15, no.1, Spring 2004, pp. 67–92; 'Penelope, or, Myths Unravelling: Writing, Orality and Abjection in *Ulysses*,' *Textual*

Practice Vol. 14, no.3, Winter 2000, pp. 519–29; 'Decadence, Degeneration and Revolting Aesthetics: The Fiction of Emily Lawless and Katherine Cecil Thurston', *Colby Quarterly*, Vol. 36, no.2, June 2000, pp. 157–76; 'Landscapes of Desire: Women and Ireland on Film', *Women: a cultural review*, Vol. 9, no. 3, Nov 1998, pp. 238–251; 'Territory and Transgression: History, Nationality and Sexuality in Kate O'Brien's Fiction', *Irish Journal of Feminist Studies*, Vol. 2, issue 2, Dec 1997, pp. 77–93. Chapter 7, 'The Devil's Own Patriot Games: Ireland and the Hollywood Action Thriller,' was previosuly published in *Representing the Troubles*, eds. Eibhear Walshe and Brian Cliff, Four Courts Press, 2004, pp. 79–92 is reproduced with permission of Four Courts Press. Chapter 8 was previously published as 'Not Irish Enough? Masculinity and Ethnicity in *The Wire* and *Rescue Me*' in *Postmodernism and Irish Popular Culture*, eds. Wanda Balzano, Anne Mulhall, Moynagh Sullivan, Palgrave Macmillan, 2007 and is reproduced with permission of Palgrave Macmillan. 'The Woman with Child' from *The Transitory House* by Freda Laughton, published by Jonathan Cape is reprinted by permission of The Random House Group Ltd.

Introduction

In an interview at the time of the publication of her 2007 novel, *Foolish Mortals*, Jennifer Johnston commented on the historical range of her novels, "I seem to be writing a sort of history of Ireland, starting at the beginning of the century and coming up to date. It's not deliberate, I didn't set out to do that."[1] Johnston began her career with novels exploring the impact of World War I and indirectly that of the Northern Irish conflict. *Foolish Mortals* was her "Celtic Tiger" novel, tracing the socially and emotionally complex lives of a twenty-first-century Dublin family. Johnston's fictional "history of Ireland" has dealt with major historical events, though usually from the perspective of characters marginal to those events. However, her primary focus has been on the fabric of ordinary lives, on the changing social, psychological and emotional habits, norms and crises of Irish lives lived, for the most part, rather quietly. While her fiction began chronicling decaying big houses shipwrecked by history, her milieu has predominantly been the small house novel. For this reason it is useful to begin an account of cultural change in Ireland with two scenes from her novels, thirty years apart, both domestic and family scenes that indicate a great deal about the public world outside. In Irish fiction and in Johnston's novels in particular, the domestic and familial are vortices of economic and political forces, philosophical and psychological intensities. Her families are allegories of the nation in general and very particular in their miseries—and joys. In *Shadows on Our Skin*, published in 1977, the Logan family sit down to their tea in Derry:

> "Five were lifted last night." As Brendan spoke he worked at a piece of bread on his place with a finger until it turned into a terrible grey, inedible lump.
> They were sitting as the perfect family should sit in apparent peace around the table. The mother poured golden tea from a large tin pot.
> "They ask for it," she said, lifting a flowered cup and passing it to the father across the table. He grunted.
> Anyone coming in now, Joe thought to himself, would think how nice. How lovely. That's what they'd think.[2]

The Logans are a foursquare, normal family, neatly divided into two Oedipal triangles. The father is an alcoholic, trading on the myth of his heroism in an unidentified IRA campaign. His compulsively house-proud wife works at the local bakery, the only one of her family productively employed. The eldest son, Brendan, has returned from England, joined the IRA and begun to find that armed struggle is not quite what his father's stories might have led him to believe. Characteristically for the 1970s, all of this is filtered through the consciousness of the youngest son, Joe, a schoolboy who writes poetry and sets the whole narrative in motion with his friendship and doomed infatuation for a young English teacher from Wicklow. A family argument here is a political row and vice versa:

> "You never used to talk like you do now, Mam."
> "Quit it, Brendan. Does it not enter your head that there's a rare difference between sitting round and listening to a bunch of old men telling their hero stories and what is happening now. I've learned a bit more sense. I see only sadness. So much for the heroes."
> "If Ireland were free . . . "
> "Words."
> "The Tans in their big Crossley tender . . . " sang the father in his tired voice.
> "Words. Words. Words. God. If I'd've had the guts I'd've left you. To drown in your words. I've no doubt that in forty years time, or in fifty maybe, you'll be doing the same thing as he is now."[3]

There is no safe boundary here between the domestic and political, nor between the mythic and the realistic. The novel's title is taken from a song by the Celtic rock band, Horslips, who recorded a concept album in 1973 called *The Tain*, based on the stories of the *Táin Bó Cúailnge*. The song, "Time to Kill," is the last on the album: "Now we've got time to kill. Kill the shadows on our skin. / Kill the fear that grows within. Killing time, my friend." Horslips both works within and criticizes the heroic tradition of *The Tain*. The sleeve notes quote W.B. Yeats's view on the figures of Irish mythology: "We Irish should keep these personages in our hearts, for they lived in the places where we ride and go marketing, and sometimes they have met one another on the hills that cast their shadows upon our doors at evening."[4] The shadows of the past in "Killing Time" are not connected with life (riding, marketing and meeting) as they are in Yeats's remarks, but with death. In *Shadows On Our Skin* the song fascinates Joe and the novel references the heroic sacrifice of Cuchulainn and the female allegorical figure for Ireland in the name of the teacher, Kathleen. In Johnston's novel it is the female protagonist who becomes the target of ritual violence and a disastrous excess of immature love when Brendan falls in love with her and a jealous Joe blurts out that her fiancé is in the British army. Unlike Cuchulainn, Kathleen not only survives but offers Joe a different legacy, offering him as a parting gift her copy of *A Golden Treasury of Verse*, inscribed: "Kathleen Doherty is my name / Ireland is my nation / Wicklow is my dwelling place / And heaven's my destination." Kathleen has somewhere to go and she is capable of constructing a different future for herself and others.

In marked contrast to the tragic structure of the family in *Shadows on Our Skin*, the family in *Foolish Mortals*, published in 2007, is comically amorphous. This time the title comes from *A Midsummer's Night Dream*:

PUCK.   Shall we their fond pageant see?
            Lord, what fools these mortals be!
OBERON.   Stand aside: the noise they make
            Will cause Demetrius to awake.
PUCK.   Then will two at once woo one;
            That must needs be sport alone;
            And those things do best please me
            That befal preposterously.[5]

Things befall quite preposterously at times in *Foolish Mortals*, a carnivalesque novel that uses amnesia as one of its central narrative devices. In contrast to the Logans' nuclear square, the shape of the O'Connor family defies linear description. Turning up for Christmas dinner as the novel draws to a conclusion are Tash, "the head of the family," painter, mother to Henry and George; Stephanie, writer, ex-wife of Henry, beloved of George, mother to Donough and Ciara; Henry, publisher, amnesiac, father; George, Henry's brother and Stephanie's lover; Jeremy, Henry's lover, brother to Henry's dead second wife; Ciara, Henry and Stephanie's daughter; Donough, Henry and Stephanie's son; and Brendan, Donough's lover. In contrast to the Logans this group is defined by the intricacies of love and desire and consequently it has a very tenuous grip on the past. Henry lives in a perpetual present: "Words spin in my head, like fishes in a pond, small colored fishes, and you put your hand to grasp one and it is gone, a flash of gold or green and it dives into the depths and your hand is left empty; they brush your fingers, teasing, gold and red, silver, blue and green, but you have not the dexterity to catch one."[6] In a constant internal dialogue with himself, Henry asks, "But why do you want to remember those words? I don't remember, I just remember their importance in my life."[7] The novel defies expectation by leaving Henry with no more than edited highlights of his past: his forgetting is associated with his belatedly learning to live. "How can I continue to live without my past?"[8] he asks, but he does continue, loves and even thrives. In this respect he represents a version of twenty-first-century Ireland. Another version shadows and overshadows him, however. His mother, Tash, once a prodigious artist, forgets how to paint and quite quickly ceases to be:

> She [Stephanie] stood for a moment in the hall; Christmas was all around her, holly, ivy, mistletoe hanging from the lamp above her head; candles flickered on the mantlepiece, deep bronze chrysanthemums were on the table, the smell of food and the sounds of laughter . . . a chord on the piano, a moment's silence and then Tash's voice. "Somewhere over the . . . " The others backing her. "Rainbow, way up high." La la la la. "There's a land that I dreamed of . . . "[9]

Tash has this one glorious final moment center stage: Stephanie, who is herself a writer, has set the scene quite deliberately, staging a traditional Christmas for this very untraditional family. Her mother-in-law derails this attempt to stabilize the new order through continuity with past ritual. Neither family nor history is predictable and death disrupts the celebration of life. Tash "was the diva. They all stood and watched her with awe, waiting for the high note. . . . She stopped and looked round, keeping them in suspense. For a split second she looked puzzled. 'I?' She fell backwards."[10] Tash is an unusual figure of female authority in Johnston's fiction. She is a creative force rather than a maternal presence and her dramatic death, which saves her from a no longer livable life, is appropriate and even funny:

> Carnivalistic laughter likewise is directed . . . towards a shift of authorities and truths, a shift of world orders. Laughter embraces both poles of change, it deals with the very process of change, with crisis itself. Combined in the act of carnival laughter are death and rebirth, negation (a smirk) and affirmation (rejoicing laughter). This is profoundly universal laughter, a laughter that contains a whole outlook on the world.[11]

Stephanie's postmodern utopia is not achieved, but rebirth of a sort occurs. "Tomorrow. And tomorrow. 'The fucking dinner,' she thought. 'All that work and stress. We'll eat it cold tomorrow and we'll open our untimely presents tomorrow.'"[12] Comparing the two family meals in Johnston's novels, thirty years apart, shows fiction in which history is written neither in terms of a linear narrative of progress nor dreary ideological stasis, but as a series of junctures of loss and life, beginning and endings, impossibilities imagined and untimely events.

This study of cultural change is itself untimely. It was written as Ireland was slipping, almost imperceptibly at first, from the almost utopia of *Foolish Mortals*, a byword for economic development, to an exemplary case of the perils of overconfident capitalism. It was written at a point where the radical extent of changes in attitudes to such basic and primal areas of experience as sexuality and children obscured their rapidity. The very prevalence of images of how dreadful the Irish past was (such as *Angela's Ashes*, *Song for a Raggy Boy*, *The Magdalene Sisters*) made it seem incredibly remote. And the rapidity of change obscured the depth of continuity. The drearily familiar concatenation of motherhood, nation, referenda and paranoia erupted periodically at crisis points around issues of sexuality, sovereignty and, eventually, race. The narrative of rapid national progress was dependent on suppression of the evidence of the persistence of structures of conformity, domination and exclusion at the heart of Irish society and culture. Retrospectively, I can see that this book and significant change in my practice of feminist criticism have been shaped by two ongoing processes in Irish cultural, social and political life. One is the impact of the dramatic shift from emigration to immigration in the last decade, which has been a cultural liberation but also produced a xenophobic backlash in politics and policy that is all the more insidious for being almost unconscious. The results of the 2004 referendum were a shock to the cultural system that fractured any remaining complacency about racial politics in Ireland. Over 80 percent of the Irish electorate voted to revoke the automatic right of citizenship to all children born on the island of Ireland and to restrict citizenship on the basis of kinship and ethnicity. This massive majority was at radical odds with the artistic celebration and external perception of Ireland's vibrant new multiculturalism. It revealed a substratum of intense conservatism and potential racism, just as a succession of referenda on abortion in the preceding decades had revealed a substratum of misogyny. A substantial section of the first chapter of this book was published under the title "Race, Sex and Nation" in response to an invitation from Moynagh Sullivan to revisit, in the light of these developments, the analysis of "sex and nation" that had informed my work on Irish women's writing in the 1990s. Sections of Chapters 2, 4 and 7 were written and published before the referendum, but hopefully are set in a new framework by the reevaluation of the relationships between gender, nation and race prompted by it.

The second process is outside the focus of this book, but has inevitably impacted on its analysis of Irish culture. The accumulating evidence over the last decade of the scale of the institutionalization, degradation and casual torture of children by religious orders acting with the active collusion and support of the state in Ireland between 1930 and 1980 culminated in the publication of the Ryan Report in 2009. The terrible seeping sense of horror with which many in Ireland responded to the revelation of the systemic nature of the physical, emotional and sexual abuse and economic exploitation of children in "care" and of women unfortunate enough to be caught in the Magdalene laundry system has been deepened by the uncanny sense that this story was already known. The nature of that knowledge and the price of suppressing it are dealt with in detail in Chapter 3. Any evaluation of nationalism in the Irish context has to be conditioned at this stage by an understanding of the kind of state it produced and what that state and its dominant church were capable of perpetrating. This book draws on the insights of postcolonial criticism, but it is also informed by unease at the way in which a crude political variant of a postcolonial understanding of Irish history has become a recurrent alibi when the state seeks to avoid responsibility for either the Irish past or present. This reached an apotheosis when several government ministers, responding to the Ryan Report, used the excuse that the industrial school system was inherited from Britain. Former minister Michael Woods insisted, in an extraordinary radio interview defending the deal that effectively gave the Catholic Church a state indemnity against compensation claims by victims of abuse while in its care, that the benign intentions of the founder of the Christian Brothers had been undermined by the directives of the British state school system, which at the time demanded that corporal punishment be imposed. The documentary maker and activist Mary Raftery touched a political nerve when she pointed out (also in a radio interview) the unpalatable fact that the establishment of an independent Irish state meant that vulnerable Irish children did not benefit from the reform of these systems until decades later than their English counterparts. Child abuse is not a uniquely Irish problem, though the Ryan Report indicates the systematic scale of it was unique to Irish conditions. Postcolonial states sometimes go through long and painful periods of adjustment where the insecurities of the state are visited upon its more vulnerable citizens in the form of native oppressions replacing imperial ones. A considerable number even resort to pitiless theocracy. One of the more pressing tasks for postcolonial theory in Ireland is to critically analyze the toxic potential in the synergy of nationalist and religious certainties, to move on from insistence on the potential for gloriously complex and hybrid identities in pre-state Irish nationalism to consider why this potential was unfulfilled and how the crippling ideological mix of national and religious fervor produced the history it did.

While this book is informed by postmodern and particularly psychoanalytical feminism, this is tempered by an emphasis on material social and political conditions that have required an ongoing dialogue with historical research. In some respects my approach to the relationship between cultural production and social structures is Gramscian, tracing extended processes of cultural negotiation through a variety of thematic areas. The organization of the material thematically rather than chronologically is informed by this approach. Because the focus of this book is on change from a feminist perspective, it is concerned with cultural processes and social movements that have impacted on the most intimate experiences and the most deeply held senses of identity. Consequently, that Gramscian structure is inadequate without the benefit of psychoanalytic criticism. One of the insights I have gained from working on interdisciplinary research teams is the value of bringing different methodologies and even epistemologies to bear on the same material, but also the redundancy of divorcing textual analysis from historical understanding in seeking to understand cultural change. In the Irish case, the extent to which that history has been hidden requires attention to ongoing historical research on everything from the design of rural cottages to infanticide.[13] Maria Luddy has observed that her "investigation into the history of prostitution in Ireland," for example, problematizes the image of Irish purity maintained by successful repression, "and suggests that resistance to the Catholic Church's teaching on celibacy and sexual continence . . . was far more common than generally believed."[14] Historical sources are sometimes hard to find for an understanding of intimate areas of human experience, especially where those experiences have been formed in resistance to the dominant ideology of the time. As the process of locating and analyzing these sources proceeds, a chance for a dynamic partnership between cultural and social history has opened up in Irish studies. Deepika Bahri argues that literature can treat as fiction what cannot be admitted as fact, even by the participants. Consequently, it can explore the repressed in any given culture and can sometimes be a privileged point of insight into history.[15] The literary manifestations of the official gendering of Irish national identity and of resistance to those official identities offer such a point of insight, but only when tempered by an understanding of the material grounding of both. Cultural criticism and cultural history need to be predicated on an understanding of the role of the socio-symbolic order in the production of gender roles *and* an awareness of the way in which those roles were played by historical men and women, real bodies, lived lives.

This book finds itself in a series of studies of "Twentieth-Century Literature" and substantial tracts of it do engage with the twentieth-century novel in particular. However, it engages with a broad range of texts not normally included in the category of literature. These are predominantly narrative fiction, in film and television form, but occasionally also folk songs, ballads, documentaries and even devotional literature. Poetry and painting figure occasionally, but the focus is on the stories we tell ourselves and have told about us and that enable us to imagine who we are, whatever we mean by "we." The organization of material in the following chapters is determined by an understanding of culture as a complex fabric where multiple forms, revered and derided texts, past and present, writing and reading, are interwoven. Cultural definitions and generic boundaries shift and change, canonical certainties are reevaluated. Tradition is not constituted by a monumental array of great works, still less a procession of great men, but by what the present needs from the past. That need requires from the critic both analysis and circumspection. "Virgin Mother Ireland," the first chapter in the part on "Race, Women and Nation," is an exercise in such analysis and proposes that the relationship between gender and national identity in Ireland is exemplary of the transition from insurgent to state nationalisms, but that it is also structured by an understanding of the national in racial terms. The second chapter, "Landscapes of Desire," focuses on film and the way in which a gendered construction of national identity and in particular the allegorical configuration of Ireland as Mother Ireland or fair Hibernia persisted throughout the twentieth century. The concluding chapter in this part focuses on Maud Gonne and Augusta Gregory's short plays and Dorothy Macardle's gothic fiction to examine the relationship between feminism and nationalism in the literary revival and in the post-independence southern state. It also outlines the suppression and persistence of dissent from the dominant social and sexual order and the ways in which the ghosts of the new Ireland's "illegitimate" subjects began to haunt its legitimizers.

The part on "Writing, Bodies, Canons" is predominantly, but not exclusively, concerned with literature, with decadence, modernism and postmodernism and with the relationship between sexual and aesthetic freedoms. Several key chapters here are devoted to novels by Irish women writers and all of it is informed by the project of feminist recovery of the vast array of work by Irish women that challenge the prevailing definitions of Irish writing. The volume of writing by Irish women would indicate that neither the construction of the myth of the writer as spokesman for his tribe, nor the configuration of the canon in national and masculine terms, nor even the symbolic function of women in nationalism were in any way disabling for the production of work in a very diverse set of genres and media by a very large number of women. The Women in Modern Irish Culture Database had by 2008 identified work by 9,334 women, who between them had produced 14,131 books, 16,212 articles, 651 films and 320 plays between 1800 and 2005. If Irish women were a subaltern group, the subaltern spoke long, loud and often. Their silence has been a construct of literary criticism and history and of a very narrowly defined canon, not a historical reality. While the analysis of twentieth-century fiction and drama here tries to do justice to the extent and compexity of women's cultural expression, the overall focus is on gender, that binary system in which the masculine term is too often taken for granted. So Joyce is set beside Kate O'Brien, but also Emily Lawless, Katherine Cecil Thurston and Rosamond Jacob. Yeats, Synge and Deevy's plays are juxtaposed with Jim Sheridan and Johnny Gogan's films. This diverse company is illuminating for all parties. Running through these chapters is a concern to reevaluate the history of Irish literature in the context of what we are rediscovering about its diversity and the social contexts in which it was written. The extended discussion of the role of Joyce's work in the configuration of contemporary Irish literary criticism and the field of Irish cultural studies is concerned to move beyond the fetishization of modernism and the Revival, on the one hand, and the trauma of the famine and the authenticity of folk culture on the other.

The ubiquity of images of Irish masculinity in early twenty-first-century popular culture has already attracted considerable critical comment.[16] The concluding part of this book, "Race, Masculinity and Popular Culture," seeks to set these images in context and to examine them as part of the project of other national identity formations. It identifies and analyzes the signification of Ireland in a globalized world of images. This part begins with a chapter examining the representation of the Northern Irish conflict in Hollywood action thrillers and then maps out the role of Irish-American masculinities in US television drama. The concluding chapter is primarily concerned with the representation of Ireland in contemporary English culture, specifically in the work of Howard Brenton, but sets this work in a context derived from Trollope and Stoker. Beginning with an extended analysis of the representation of Ireland in feminine terms, it seems appropriate to end with a discussion of the role that Irishness plays in the construction and differentiation of national identities in masculine terms and masculinities in national terms. Any analysis of gender, culture and Ireland must perforce analyze the role of nationalism, but in the chapters that follow I have sought to present the national as a category demanding explanation rather than an explanatory category. Perhaps that task is easier now that Irish nationalism has itself undergone significant cultural change. The last three decades have seen significant reconfigurations of the political landscape. The two largest political parties still derive from the old Civil War treaty split, but it is twenty years since either has been able to form a one-party government. Stability has depended on the formation of coalitions with small parties ranging from the right-wing Progressive Democrats to the environmentalist Green party. The third largest party, Labour, has been an intermittant partner in government since the late 1940s and its left of center, social democratic influence has been a persistent agent of legislative changes that have had profound social effects, although it is almost invisible in most mainstream Irish Studies accounts of Irish politics. Nationalism in Ireland as in most Western states remains a pervasive political discourse, but is only part of the picture. The increasingly complex body politic has lurched awkwardly from center right to center left and back again during the last twenty years of rapidly accelerating social and economic transformation. One of the many features that all nationalisms have in common is their conviction of their national uniqueness. Unease in Ireland about fuller integration into the European Union is perhaps rooted in the dawning anxiety that Irish uniqueness has become increasingly implausible, a commodity sold to too many tourists to retain an innate value.

Two different but related images adorn the cover of Tom Inglis's study of the impact of globalization on Irish culture and society, *Global Ireland: Same Difference*. The Virgin Mother and Barbie are strikingly juxtaposed in a design that illuminates the way in which gender has been constructed in critical accounts of Ireland's rapid cultural and social changes. Explicit in the contiguity of these images is a high degree of pessimism about the extent to which the radical changes in women's position in Ireland has brought about liberation. Implicit is the symbolic configuration of the state of the nation through images of women. Both of the images on the cover of *Global Ireland* are images of images: they are photographs of a statue and a doll but also refractions of centuries of representation of female purity and commodified sexuality. In stark contrast, the introduction to Inglis's book is almost uniquely honest in contemporary Irish Studies about the subjective experiences that shape its sociological perspective and consequently individual women figure strongly. Yet the paradigm of representing Ireland in terms of iconic femininity remains. Neither Virgin Mary nor Barbie is an image that originated in Ireland: if these images represent the meaning of Irishness it was always already globalized. It is not simply that these are mythic images to be countered by a more authentic history. They are both representative of dominant ideologies of gender and both remain powerful. Myths are part of history, produced by and producing it. Yet a fascination with these images runs the danger of assuming their ubiquitous power, rendering invisible the history of resistance to the dominant ideology of gender in Ireland and once again rendering masculinity invisible as if it were somehow unproblematic, unmarked by ideology. This is not the tenor of *Global Ireland*, but it is a very strong tendency within Irish cultural studies where the work of feminist and queer theory tends to be partitioned from the mainstream, often coexisting within the same academic institutions but publishing and presenting research in parallel universes. There is a notable imbalance of citation between these two, with the margins perforce debating ideas and texts in the mainstream without reciprocity. This is extraordinarily striking in Joe Cleary's widely praised study, *Outrageous Fortune*, for example, which argues that feminism has joined revisionism and postcolonialism as an institutionalized critical practice in Ireland, but cites no Irish feminist criticism. In contrast, the historian R.F. Foster appears to endorse the claim made by Mary Robinson in 1971 that the Irish Women's Liberation Movement constituted "the only radical force in the stagnant pool of Irish life" at the time[17] and to credit feminism as a major force for social change. Foster's discussion of feminism is, however, as no more than one aspect of the decline of the influence of the Catholic Church, and he recruits evidence of women's increased freedoms to his argument against the "Begrudgers," those who at the height of Ireland's prosperity were nostalgic for a romanticized past, "less prosperous, certainly, less enlightened, possibly, but kinder, more ethical and less barbarous than the times in which we now live."[18] It seems likely that economic decline will rapidly bring about a decline in such nostalgia, but it will also create problems for the liberal feminism that became mainstream on the basis that women's participation in the workforce and consumer spending power were a force for economic development. It is significant that one of the emergency cost-cutting measures introduced by the Irish government at the height of its financial crisis in 2009 was a reduction in tax relief for childcare. Foster's account does not map the extent to which Catholic social teaching retained a residual hold on both attitudes and legislation in relation to women's rights in Ireland. The apparent ambivalence about European integration in Ireland in the twenty-first century is problematic given the extent to which recourse to the European courts was a necessity for both women's and gay rights groups in bringing about precisely the changes Foster lauds. The extent to which national referenda have manifested this unease in a desire to reassert control, over women, migration or the structures and borders of an expanding Europe, should strike a warning note.

If the Virgin Mary and Barbie have one striking thing in common, it is their combination of white face and golden hair. The critique of Ireland as a racial state and the study of the formation of Irishness as a white identity have emerged most strongly from sociology in Ireland, but it is a very rapidly expanding force linked to the emergence of a new Irish cultural studies. It is notable that in the first major collection of critical essays on contemporary Irish popular culture, *Irish Postmodernisms and Popular Culture*,[19] almost half of all the essays are concerned with race and almost all are concerned with gender and/or "quare theory." According to Cleary:

> The proper business of any critical theory is not to validate a pregiven political position, whether to the left or right. It is, rather, to track the matrix of oppressive and emancipatory forces at work in every period of modernity, and indeed to be attentive to how even the most emancipatory developments can sometimes collude with or be commandeered by the regressive.[20]

Feminist criticism, queer theory and migration studies will always be improper by this definition and their impropriety in the field of Irish cultural criticism is compounded by their attention to how even the most regressive developments can be countered by emancipatory strategies. Moreover, all tend to be part of a broad coalition of social movements for social and cultural change. This coalition is not always strong, confident or successful, rarely organized and never unified, but it does exist and it is defined by an orientation toward present struggles and future possibilities beyond the academy, at odds with the orientation toward the past that has come to define postcolonialism as well as revisionism in Irish Studies. At its best it can upset all "pre-given" political positions and is concerned to track oppression, but more concerned to change consciousness. From Mary Wollstonecraft to Judith Butler, feminism has promulgated the idea that a change in the material of culture can bring about a change in material conditions. The movement that declared the personal is political has a particular commitment to changing the way in which the respective roles of women and men are imagined and, once imagined, felt. Feminism is much criticized for being a movement of the Enlightenment, of modernity, of the West, but among the multiplicity of positions embraced by the term *feminism* there has been a sometimes submerged but always persistent critique of Reason's excesses, an occasional bracing antidote to the romanticization of tradition and a sustained and sometimes anguished debate about the relative claims of community and the rights of individuals and groups of women, for whom a break with tradition can be a matter of basic survival.

The focus of the opening chapters of this book is on the construction of Irish uniqueness and the consequences of that construction for the regulation of gender roles, sexuality, artistic expression and any manifestation of difference or dissent. That focus also reveals the extent to which the carapace of Irish national uniqueness concealed inner tensions, the rapidity with which the cracks (already more than evident when Johnston's Logan family sat down to their uncomfortable tea in 1977) proceeded to create fractures in the whole edifice and the fact that residual chunks of it remain standing.

Part I

Race, Women, and Nation

1 Virgin Mother Ireland

FEMINISMS AND NATIONALISMS

If "all nationalisms are gendered,"[1] the Mother Ireland trope merely indicates the operation of a fundamental structuring principle recognizable in both official and insurgent nationalisms. It is one instance of the structural interdependence of gender and national identities. "The hegemonic process of constructing a nationalist ideology depends upon distinguishing between self and other, us and them, in the creation of a common (shared) identity; women as symbol, men as agents of the nation, colonized space as feminine, colonial power as masculine."[2] Miroslav Hroch argued in the 1990s with regard to both the then resurgent Eastern European nationalisms and to nineteenth-century nationalisms that:

> Identification with the national group . . . includes . . . the construction of a personalized image of the nation. The glorious past of this personality comes to be lived as part of the individual memory of each citizen, its defeats resented as failures that still touch them. One result of such personalization is that people will regard their nation—that is, themselves—as a single body in a more than metaphorical sense. If any distress befalls a small part of the nation, it can be felt throughout it, and if any branch of the ethnic group—even one living far from the "mother-nation"—is threatened with assimilation, the members of the personalized nation may treat it as an amputation of the national body.[3]

If the nation is experienced as "a body," then the body in Western culture is primarily figured as and through the female body. The systematic violation of individual women's bodies in a way that understands itself as destroying both an organic community and an abstract nation is a horrific validation of Hroch's analysis of the new nationalisms in this respect. According to Anne McClintock:

> All too often in male nationalisms, *gender difference* between women and men serves to symbolically define the limits of national difference

and power between *men*. Excluded from direct action as national citizens, women are subsumed symbolically into the national body politic as its boundary and metaphoric limit.[4]

Women are obviously crucial to national expansion and consolidation in their role as biological reproducers of the members of national collectivities, but something more complex than the desire to see the nation's population expand is at stake. Peggy Watson offers an explanation that would indicate why certain nationalisms seem more prone and some less prone to obsession with control of women through and as mediums of reproduction. Watson offers an example with striking parallels to Ireland. She recounts a response from an unnamed member of the post-communist Polish senate that:

> The reason for concentrating on the abortion issue at the expense of other pressing problems was simply because it was regarded as something which *could* be done . . . the regulation of women was seen as an area which required action, but also one where power could readily be exercised, whereas the economy engendered feelings of powerlessness . . . Attempting to legislate against the right to abortion in effect serves both to institutionalize the power of men, and to legitimate this power by providing a platform for new, more radical and "modernized" definitions of women as *exclusively* grounded in domesticity.[5]

A range of legislative measures to promote just such ends occurred in newly independent southern Ireland after 1922, culminating in the delineation of women's social function within the home in Article 41.2 of the 1937 constitution. The elision of women's role as activists into idealized passivity and symbolic status is again characteristic of the transition from national movement to state authority internationally. (The analogy with Poland is another reminder that the conjunction of white faces and histories of colonization and migration is not nearly as unusual as Irish cultural theory has sometimes made it seem.) Gender resurfaced as an area where reassurance could be sought against political violence, mass unemployment and rapid social change in the 1980s, a decade characterized in the Republic of Ireland by bitter constitutional campaigns to control the domains of reproduction and the family and ferocious divisions over sexual, familial and religious values.[6]

It might be assumed that the emergence of a prosperous post–Celtic Tiger Ireland would have eliminated the need for this kind of policing of the internal border constituted by women's bodies. In some regards that has been the case. In most important respects, however, the work of national scapegoat has simply been outsourced, as so much other domestic labor, onto immigrant women. The ease with which popular hysteria about pregnant migrants "flooding" Irish maternity hospitals with their nonnational babies could be translated into 80 percent electoral support for a constitutional amendment limiting Irish citizenship on the basis of ethnicity and affiliations of kinship and blood indicates that racism was never a marginal factor in Irish political life nor a specific historical response to the numbers of actual migrants arriving in Ireland in the late nineties. It was and is now constitutionally enshrined as a structural principle in national identity. Liberal appeals for Irish sympathy with immigrants on the basis that previous generations of Irish emigrants shared their experience ignore the extent to which the Irish cultivated, traded in and still exploit the valuable commodity of their white identity both abroad and at home. Kingsley's cry of horror that Irish white chimpanzees were so much worse than black African ones is perhaps too much quoted for a reason. It obscures the extent to which subsequent generations of Irish have been able to trade on their difference from the Africans with whom Kingsley's racist perceptions were more comfortable. The Victorian parlor game that Luke Gibbons so influentially described halted, like Kingsley, at the one point in the map of the British Empire where the natives were white.[7] Far from subverting racial hierarchies, the existence of liminally white groups has always been a functioning part of the racist system. Colonized or ethnically distinct whites such as the Irish and Scottish provided the British Empire with a highly expendable soldiery and an army of civil servants to deploy around the empire in the nineteenth century. As the Irish emigrated to the US, they progressively "became white"[8] without at all disconcerting racist structures. (The way in which certain kinds of white ethnicities such as Irish and Polish function in the construction and control of working-class identity in the US is an increasing area of study.[9]) Long overdue, as studies of Irish emigration develop, is a thorough analysis of the way in which the experience of Irish emigrants abroad had an impact on how the Irish who remained at home viewed themselves, particularly in relation to race. It is certainly the case that a highly racialized and rigidly gendered identity was promulgated by both church and state in Ireland as true Irishness.

GENDER AND THE CONSTRUCTION OF WHITENESS

Without rehearsing in detail well-known arguments, it may be useful to summarize. The psychodynamic of colonial and postcolonial identity often produces in the formerly colonized a desire to assert a rigid and confined masculine identity, against the colonizers stereotype of their subjects as feminine, wild and ungovernable. This masculine identity then emerges at the state level as a regulation of "our" women, an imposition of a very definite feminine identity as guarantor to the precarious masculinity of the new state. The specific role of the Irish Catholic Church in this maelstrom of economic, political, social and psychological forces is rather more than one among a number of regulatory institutions. It is after all sometimes very difficult to ascertain where church began and state ended in regard to the institutionalization of individuals, public health and education, for example. The fissure between whiteness and the colonial (not typically white) historical experience of Ireland was traditionally concealed by radiant images of Ireland itself in terms of what Richard Dyer calls "the supreme exemplar of . . . feminine whiteness," the Virgin Mary.[10]

Dyer's work on whiteness is very suggestive in the Irish context, though his own analysis is primarily of whiteness in imperial and postimperial cultures. Dyer's work on the function of white women in colonial culture and of liminally white groups and the porous boundaries of white identity is particularly relevant. I want to put forward an argument here that the centrality of Mariology in Irish Catholicism and the extent to which issues of reproduction and sexuality dominated public debates and anxieties around modernization while sharing many of the general characteristics of the gendering of national identity outlined earlier are in the Irish case also powerfully linked to residual anxieties around race and Ireland's postcolonial position as a white European nation.

National identities are structured by the binary of them and us, insiders and outsiders, natives and foreigners. Irish nationalism may have had within it the potential for all kinds of hybrid, liberationist, adulterated and inclusive versions of Irish identity. However, the dominant ideology of state and nation was for most of the twentieth century extraordinarily narrow and exclusive. Bryan Fanning has documented the "othering" of Protestants, Jews and Travellers as part of the process of state nationalism in the Republic of Ireland.[11] The dominance of the postcolonial–revisionist debate in the formation of Irish Studies and the analyses it produced of Irish nationalism have long outlived their usefulness. Both sides of the debate have obscured the role of whiteness in the construction of Irish identity as well as the relationship between gender and race in that construction.

Postcolonial theory offered feminist critique in Ireland a vital way of understanding sexual conservatism, the relationship of the Catholic Church and the state and the gendering of national identity as elements that it shared with a wide variety of postcolonial cultures. Postcolonialism remains part of the context in which "non-national women were made central to the racial configuration of 21st century global Ireland, illustrating not only orchestrated moral panics about 'floods of refugees', but also the positioning of sexually active women as a danger to the state and 'the nation.'"[12] However, as the sociologist and theorist of race Ronit Lentin points out:

> To date, theorizing Irishness as white privilege has been hampered by legacies of racialisation of Irishness as structured by anti-Irish racism in Ireland and abroad. However, Ireland's new position as topping the Globalisation Index, its status symbol as the locus of "cool" culture, and its privileged position within an ever-expanding European Community calls for the understanding of Irishness as white supremacy.

Whiteness works best when it remains a hidden part of the normative social order.[13]

The emerging field of "whiteness" studies offers a necessary development that illuminates the extent to which race performed a key function in the construction and policing of Irish identity throughout the twentieth century and of the origins of contemporary social and institutional racism in Ireland. It is vital to deconstruct the binary of colonizer and colonized, agency and victimization, pure and hybrid, and acknowledge the extent to which complex processes of accommodation, resistance and opportunism have shaped the concept of "Irishness."

The promulgation of the image of the Virgin Mary as "Queen of Ireland"[14] is on one level just another permutation of the Virgin–Whore dichotomy at the heart of Western culture's representation of women. That dichotomy acquired a very particular paranoid intensity in twentieth-century Ireland, however, which is linked to both the history of colonialism and the compensatory urge to promote an essential Irishness that was purer—in effect whiter—than other European races. In this context, the relationship between images of the Blessed Virgin and Mother Ireland is important, not least because the veneration of the former was shadowed by disappointment in the latter. Tracing the evolution of "visual Marianism" in Ireland, art historian John Turpin has argued that "Marianism was a badge of national identity" sponsored by the post-independence southern state as well as the Catholic Church.[15] The influence of French Catholicism on the development of Marian devotion in Ireland is well documented; in effect the image of the Virgin Mother imported from France in the nineteenth century was already highly politicized, an anti-Marianne and an instrument of anti-Enlightenment, counterrevolutionary propaganda. Ultimately highly compatible with romantic nationalism, the cross-fertilization of this image with that of "Mother Ireland" helped dislocate the traditions of radical republicanism from insurgent nationalism in nineteenth-century Ireland. In the post-independence southern state this fusion of national and religious iconography became a lynchpin of the ideology of race and gender.

THE DISEMBODIED MOTHER

The conflation of images of Mother Ireland and Virgin Mary in Irish populist Catholic nationalism deployed the Virgin Mother's status as epitome of whiteness as a guarantee of Irish (racial) purity. This function could only be performed if the maternal body was idealized out of existence, or at least out of representation. The peculiar stillness and singularly unmaternal figures of the Virgin Mary that predominate in Irish churches and grottoes only become apparent by contrast with the expressive faces and rounded bodies prevalent in Andalucian ones, for example. This refusal to countenance any representation of the mother's body as origin of life was paralleled by the predominance of images of the Virgin Mary as mother of an adult son, usually Jesus in the mode of the Sacred Heart, and in general in visions, icons and statues that represented her after her assumption, that is to say after her disembodiment. Yeats, in the cultural nationalist journal, *Samhain*, identified the trend toward curiously lifeless images and the centrality of the images of an impersonal virgin in this process as early as 1905, which would indicate that it was already implicit in Catholic nationalism in the late nineteenth century:

> A Galway convent a little time ago refused a fine design for stained glass sent from Miss Sarah Purser's studio, because of the personal life in the faces and in the attitudes, which seemed to them ugly, perhaps even impious. They sent to Miss Purser an insipid German chromolithograph, full of faces without expression or dignity, and gestures without personal distinction, and Miss Purser, doubtless because her enterprise was too new, too anxious for success, to reject any order, has carried out this ignoble design in glass of beautiful color and quality. Let us suppose that Meister Stefan were to paint in Ireland to-day that exquisite Madonna of his, with her lattice of roses; a great deal that is said of our plays would be said of that picture. Why select for his model a little girl selling newspapers in the streets, why slander with that miserable little body the Mother of God?[16]

Irish censorship was extraordinarily sensitive in excising all references to childbirth from the films it cut, including even comic scenes of fathers pacing hospital waiting rooms. Even the liberal journal *The Bell* found itself at the center of a storm of controversy when it published Freda Laughton's poem, "The Woman with Child" in 1945:

> How am I held within a tranquil shell,
> As if I too were close within a womb,
> I too enfolded as I fold the child.
> As the tight bud enwraps the pleated leaf,
> The blossom furled like an enfolded fan,
> So life enfolds me as I fold my flower.
> As water lies within a lovely bowl,
> I lie within my life, and life again
> Lies folded fast within my living cell.
> The apple waxes at the blossom's root,
> And like the moon I mellow to the round
> Full circle of my being, till I too
> Am ripe with living and my fruit is grown.
> Then break the shell of life. We shall be born,
> My child and I together, to the sun.[17]

The Bell's editorial view of Laughton was overwhelmingly positive: it announced in the same issue that she had won the competition for the best poem published in *The Bell* in 1944 for "When You Were with Me."[18] A short article by Valentin Iremonger praised "the exactness of her visual imagination."[19] "Whatever sort of building she eventually raises, the foundations are being well laid . . . her verse has a sensuous and imaginative quality that raises it above the level of realism."[20] Iremonger was in no doubt about Laughton's canonical potential, comparing her to Spinoza and Pope, as well as Tennyson and Arnold:

> How far or in what direction she is likely to develop it is yet too early to say. Certainly she is one of the few poets to-day who are worth watching, who have a strong individual talent, and a distinct flavor of their own. Her ultimate importance will depend on whether what are as yet barely opinions will crystallize into an attitude to life. In the meantime, I look forward with more than usual interest to her first book.[21]

Laughton's work insists her gender is part of her poetic identity, but this is regarded as a strength: like most good female poets, she shows a strong intellectual bent but still does not forget that "there is danger in utterly forgetting / The setting of fine jewels, / The subtle arrangement of the perfumed bouquet, / The studied mosaic of the harem" (ibid., 250).

This appraisal of Laughton did not go unchallenged. The "Public Opinion" section of *The Bell* some months later, in August 1945, included a long letter from Patricia K. Harrison that criticized Laughton's work for her alliteration and her use of metaphor, but above all for being "sensuous": "In these poems there is sensuousness for the sake of sensuousness, and not real imagination; compare 'Mary, his espoused wife, being great with child,' with 'Like the moon I mellow to the round Full circle of my being.'"[22] Unusually (but not uniquely) this particular public opinion was felt to require an editorial answer provided by poetry editor Geoffrey Taylor. Taylor replies in considerable detail to Miss Harrison's "dogmatic and capricious" technical statements about poetry, then concludes, "But what Miss Harrison seems most to object to is 'sensuousness.' Let her remember Milton and Keats." This storm among the teacups of Irish literature's back pages neatly illustrates the difficulties of this terrain for the woman poet: Laughton is attacked for her implied impropriety on the one hand, but even when lavishly praised for the sensuousness of her work, admonished to beware her "intellectual bent" on the other. More than that, however, Harrison's odd letter indicates how immediately any representation of pregnancy provoked Mariological analogy. The contrast between the mother as active subject, "I mellow," and passive vessel, "being great," is crude but instructive.[23] *The Bell*'s championship of Laughton's work indicates it understood feminine self-representation as part of its modernizing project even if it characterized that self-representation in terms of jewels, bouquets and harems. The controversy marks one of a number of points where the self-conscious project of cultural change in *The Bell* coalesced with an eruption of the female body into mainstream literary discourse.[24]

THE FOREIGNER WITHIN

One of the central projects of this book is an analysis of the derealization of motherhood in the ideology of the southern Irish state, the often-violent rejection and repression of the maternal body as such and the extent to which that body became a specter, haunting national consciousness. That specter functioned in true gothic fashion, I will argue, as an indicator of the culture's paranoia, a paranoia that sought to exclude the sexual, maternal, nurturing, ever-hungry body, but also anything that threatened the nation's white identity. Motherhood was overtly idealized and venerated in its social and religious aspects, but also ruthlessly demonized if it occurred outside the legalities and control of church and state. This duality is, of course, not specifically Irish. It was long the dominant construction of motherhood in Western culture. However, it acquired a specific, local form in the context of an insecure postcolonial state in the aftermath of civil war, unable to realize economic independence to match its political freedom. The reasons for the intensity with which sexuality and especially reproduction were patrolled in the Irish context remain debated. The long-term impact of the trauma of the famine is obviously crucial. The landholding practices that became widespread in the nineteenth century to guard against recurrence of that famine—which ensured a persistent pattern of low rates of marriage, late marriages and emigration until late into the twentieth century—obviously required a high level of sexual repression to be sustainable. As Mary Daly makes clear in her study of twentieth-century Irish demography,[25] this pattern was not unique to Ireland in the late nineteenth century:

> Although no other European country experienced a catastrophe of the order of the Great Famine, other countries and regions in Europe did experience many of the same aspects of the late nineteenth century population story—heavy emigration, late marriages, a high rate of permanent celibacy, and a declining rural population. But until recently, very few accounts of Irish emigration have noted, for example, that Britain was also a country of emigrants or that Germany, the Scandinavian countries, and Italy experienced a significant volume of emigration at some stage during the nineteenth century.[26]

What was unusual about the Irish case was the longevity of the interlinked pattern of emigration, postponement of marriage and celibacy. Maria

Luddy's groundbreaking study of prostitution and Irish society offers a very detailed account of the way in which prostitution, venereal disease and eventually all forms of unregulated female sexuality came to be identified in nationalist discourse with the presence of the British army in Ireland, the complicity of early twentieth-century Irish feminism in this construction and the widely held belief that all such problems would simply leave when the British army did.[27] The use of the term *amateur prostitute* to describe sexually active single women is indicative of attitudes. Luddy examines the particular ignominy in which nationalism came to hold the "separation" women, in receipt of government allowances while their husbands or sons served in the British army in World War I. These women were seen to combine infidelity to the nation, independent means and the opportunity for unregulated sexuality. Intriguingly, Luddy identifies instances of violent conflict between the separation women and Sinn Fein supporters toward the end of World War I. Clair Wills has noted the resurgence of this complex of associations during World War II and the moral panic surrounding the combination of the arrival in Northern Ireland of American soldiers and of young women from rural Ireland to take up factory work.[28]

Daly's account of the way in which the problem of population decline was viewed in the post-independence southern state offers an important insight into the relationship between gender roles, family life and an understanding of the nation in racial terms in the ideology of that state. She quotes the Reverend Patrick Noonan, a speaker at the Muintir na Tire rural week in 1946: "Unless immediate and drastic measures are taken, the Irish race will either disappear altogether or continue to survive as an enervated minority in a planted country."[29] Clair Wills has recently noted the persistence of eugenicist ideas about population in Ireland into the 1950s,[30] and Daly traces them through official discourse in the 1930s. Irish understanding of its culture and history as unique and self-defining is typical of romantic nationalisms in general: the extrapolation of that uniqueness in racial terms was typical of a particular and particularly terrible phase of European nationalism that was largely confined to violent rhetoric in Ireland. Noonan's rantings that "great numbers of aliens"[31] were buying up the best land in Ireland (inexplicably vacated by emigrants) at a time when there was no substantial immigration may represent an extreme form of nationalist paranoia, but paranoia about the stability of the boundaries between the declining race at home and the wider world was very much part of the mainstream of Irish political culture between the 1930s and 1950s. Some of this fear was by the 1950s grounded in the isolation of a neutral country during and after the Second World War.[32] Much of this anxiety was focused on emigration, however. As Daly points out, the new state's attempts to "save rural Ireland" appeared to contribute to its decline. Its attempts to discourage migration suffered from the same circular logic; despite moral alarms about the threat to the morality of young Irish women who emigrated unaccompanied to Britain, and attempts by Archbishop McQuaid to prevent such emigration or at least closely monitor the women who left, the influence of Catholic social teaching made it impossible to impose age restrictions on emigration as many of the teenage girls who went to Britain looking for work did so with parental encouragement:

> A disproportionate amount of the material on emigrant welfare concerns women. Whereas men were generally treated as adults who were capable of fending for themselves, it was commonly believed that women needed protection. This concern reflects the great importance that was attached to sexual morality and the need to ensure that Irish women would continue to be suitable mothers to the next generation of Irish Catholic children . . . By the 1960s the focus of emigrant welfare broadened to include the homeless, former industrial school pupils and men who had been discharged from psychiatric hospitals.[33]

Far from Ireland being flooded by marauding aliens and their influences, the most alienated and damaged Irish were exported. Contrary to the picture painted by the Catholic clergy in Ireland of young women emigrants to England running "terrible risks" of being trapped into "houses of ill fame, and very often terrible tragedies follow," welfare agencies in England, some of them also Catholic, were preoccupied with the influx of the group that came to be designated "pfi," pregnant from Ireland.[34] Emigration was a much more common and attractive option for an Irish single mother than the regimes of mother and baby homes and Magdalene asylums in Ireland until the 1980s: thereafter a related stream of pregnant women traveling to England for abortion, still prohibited in Ireland, continued to flow.

THE VIRGIN MARY, QUEEN OF IRELAND

A highly racialized discourse of nationality was prevalent in popular Catholic devotional literature in twentieth-century Ireland that promulgated the idea of a special link between Ireland and the Virgin Mother. Most existing histories of Mariology focus on high art. For example, Kristeva suggests that in the Renaissance figures of the Madonna and child we see the emergence of a secular humanist sensibility, the new ego-centered, rational, masculine subject consecrated in the Christ child but also grounded in his very human relationship with his adoring mother.[35] This is not the type of image of the Virgin Mary that predominated in popular Mariology in twentieth-century Ireland. The images that appear to have been most popular were in statue form, Mary as apparition, with raised hands, sometimes standing on the stars, sometimes crushing the serpent and, particularly, the picture of the Immaculate Heart of Mary juxtaposed with the Sacred Heart of Jesus. This latter image is preserved in the names of numerous churches and religious institutions including a religious order in both Ireland and the

US. The refusal to countenance any representation of the mother's body as origin of life was paralleled by the predominance of images of the Virgin Mary as mother of an adult son, usually Jesus in the mode of the Sacred Heart, and in general in visions, icons and statues that represented her after her assumption, that is to say after her disembodiment.

At the zenith of Catholic influence in the southern Irish state, Pope Pius XI's address to the Eucharistic Congress of 1932 spoke of the "The Virgin Mary, Queen of Ireland." A survey of Mariological devotional literature, religious souvenirs and Episcopal pronouncements indicates Pope Pius was not indulging in metaphorical flourishes. The concept of a special relationship between Ireland and the Virgin Mary was heavily promoted in the early decades of southern independence. Reverend James Cassidy was a notable contributor to the genre of quasi-historical Mariological literature. In his 1933 book, *The Old Love of the Blessed Virgin Mary, Queen of Ireland*, he remarks on the prevalence of pictures of the Holy Family in Irish households of the time. (17) In this devotion he finds "an echo of what must have been a marked devotion of ancient Ireland, devotion of the family to the Mother of the Holy family." (17) Cassidy's reasons for assuming such a devotion "must have been" widespread echo rather chillingly over the intervening decades: "To such a devotion, Ireland would naturally lend itself, for the constant tribal scrutiny of family life encouraged the preservation of those domestic virtues which are the fundamental props of wholesome nationhood." (18) The naturalization of tribal surveillance over the family is essential for Cassidy to "the preservation of moral beauty," (18) but it is also an intrinsic part of Irish identity. (35) The modernity of the dogma of the Immaculate Conception does not at all trouble Cassidy's identification of Mary's immaculacy with ancient, pure Irish identity: he suggests that a version of the doctrine could be found in the eighth-century writings of St. Colgu. The circularity of Cassidy's mythmaking is an object lesson in the promulgation of ideology. Praising a "typically Celtic tribute to Mary (26)," Cassidy remarks:

> The rugged humility of the tribesman and the chivalry of the holy warrior seek hand in hand the protection and ideal leadership of a great Queen in whom they see a fount of spiritual fortitude and a mighty inspiration. Its note of child-like familiarity and trustfulness tell of the ease with which the Irish have always lived in the world of the supernatural. What race could express to Mary the desire for eternal life in words of more trusting and loving simplicity than the writer uses here. Heaven for him meant the "visit" of a child to its Mother. Of that "visit" he felt assured, just because she was such a Mother and he had such a vivid sense of his child-like right to her maternal solicitude. (28)

A twentieth-century theological construction of Mary is rendered timeless by reference to an ancient Celtic past and the purity and continuity of the Irish nation validated by the attribution to it of devotion to a changeless icon of feminine purity. Cassidy's book is indicative of a strong trend in Irish Catholic publications where purported histories of devotion to Mary are also politically charged appropriations of Celticism for Catholic nationalism. "The Irish people, too, have always seemed dowered with a genius for domesticity. In ancient Ireland, as in the Ireland of today, all roads seemed to lead to the hearth and the home. The result was an exceptionally wholesome family life that leavened the entire nation. This devotion to the principles of home life explains the unusual moral rectitude of Irish maidenhood." (56) In this formulation, Ireland was a nation that defined itself primarily in terms of its women precisely because they were scarcely there, immaterial, "the true Gael saw a more fundamental support of national life in the luminous ideal of womanhood than in the more material service of the country's manhood." (56)

Cassidy ends his book by calling Mary "great Queen of Eire,"(60–61) "the greatest queen Ireland ever knew, or ever can know, the Immaculate Mother of God." (61) Not all accounts of Mariological devotion in ancient Ireland were quite so haphazard with historical fact as Cassidy's. Concannon's *The Queen of Ireland: An Historical Account of Ireland's Devotion to the Blessed Virgin*, for example, praises the Irish role in the promulgation of the doctrine of the Immaculate Conception, thus at least acknowledging that both the doctrine and the Irish have a history that intervened between ancient Celts and 1922.

While the pictures of the disembodied mother as ideal may have disappeared, her cultural impact has not. An echo of this arose in the controversy over the EU-wide advertising campaign to promote voting in the last European Parliamentary elections. The advertisement naturalized the EU by embodying it as a nurturing woman, the good white mother offering herself freely (as opposed to impregnable Fortress Europe). The attempt to produce a transnational form of identity falls back here on the devices of the nation in order to attract affiliation. The opening image of a baby trying to choose between its mother's bare breasts was apparently considered offensive only by Ireland and Britain. The British response was to airbrush out the nipples, the Irish initially at least to simply not show the ad. (Irish exclusion of the maternal body in this instance reduced the English response to eccentricity.)

The popular reaction overrode civil service squeamishness through sheer derision—though the laughter might have been more convincing did Ireland not have one of the lowest rates of breast-feeding in the world. The EU advertisement controversy and the low rates of breast-feeding are both indicative of residual unease around the maternal body in action. Indeed the willingness of women from other cultures to breast-feed at least in front of other women has been constructed as an intercultural "problem," particularly in rural Ireland. The problem of the maternal body as a body has a very specific history in the construction of white, gendered, Irish identity.

The contemporary perception of Catholicism as an atavism that Ireland has outgrown ignores its specifically modernizing project in Ireland, promulgating regulation, bureaucracy and integration within the global/universal church. This is modernization that understood itself in terms of achievement of an essential and ancient national destiny and identity, but fully utilized twentieth-century industrial and media production to promulgate that identity. John Turpin's work on visual Marianism in Ireland points out the importance of mass manufacture of objects of devotion in its popularization. The material culture of popular Catholic devotion in Ireland was a point of intersection with the modern marketplace, not its antithesis. This is not so very different from the alliance of the GAA, Guinness, Bank of Ireland and ancient Irish myth in a series of sponsorship deals. The ensuing advertisement campaigns prove the endless plasticity of Cuchulainn in their promotion of the Celtic Tiger's trinity of questionable banking practice, beer and competitive sport in the holy spirit of high-end technical innovation as expressions of true Irish identity. The combination of the Giant's Causeway and CGI is the contemporary correlative of the industrialization of devotion. And both produce images of Ireland that are both racial and gendered.

ARE WE POST-POSTCOLONIAL YET?

Irish critics sometimes react with hurt and bewilderment at the skepticism about Ireland's postcolonial status expressed by critics for whom the conjunction of postcolonial and white is highly suspect. The extent of Irish filiation to the late Edward Said's foundational model of postcolonial critique is in part accounted for by his understanding of Yeats and Joyce as paradigmatically postcolonial modernists. Vincent Cheng gives a highly illuminating account of the antipathy he experienced in the American academy for his work on a dead white male, no matter how colonized the Dublin of Joyce's upbringing. Cheng's use of Joyce as an emblem of inauthenticity and a useful resource for the construction of all sorts of cosmopolitan, migrant, hyphenated and intercultural identities is a highly attractive alternative to those elements in Irish cultural criticism that regard Irishness as a privileged category for the understanding of Joyce's project. Cheng's warning that "the search for genuine and authentic native voices will serve only to provide us with a feel-good liberal and multicultural glow—while in actuality merely recycling tokenism and nostalgia"[36] is salutary. Cheng's analysis draws heavily on Declan Kiberd's *Inventing Ireland*. Yet Kiberd's speculation, "who is to say that the latest group of arriving Nigerians might not" become "more Irish than the Irish themselves,"[37] is predicated on the kind of "authenticity without risk" that Cheng critiques. Kiberd is very much to be commended for addressing the issue of racism directly in his recent work. However, there are limitations implicit in a paradigm where there still exists something called "a people" that must be "secure in its national philosophy" before it can deal confidently and fairly with others. Kiberd's essay lauds hybridity, not least because it assumes Irishness as the ultimate hybrid identity, infinitely capacious and assimilative and already so post-colonial that it need never be challenged and changed by the experience of Nigerian immigrants. The identification of Nigerian immigrants and Norman invaders hardly needs to be deconstructed: the sense of a foreign threat the nation must contain seriously threatens the liberal impulse. Kiberd's recruitment of the legacy of Irish missionaries and Bob Geldof to the argument (that argument again) that Ireland is not racist obfuscates completely the extent to which the discourse of missionary Ireland mimicked colonial stereotypes, this time casting the Irish as the bringers of civilization and salvation to the barbarian "black babies." (The assimilation of the lyricist of "Banana Republic" to the postcolonial nation as inheritor of that tradition would, if it were tenable, certainly add weight to the argument that the "Make Poverty History" campaign is more about assuaging the affluent world's guilt than solving Africa's problems.)

The danger to postcolonial critique now in Ireland is that it will be co-opted to a discourse of the authentic and native, sometimes called shared history. In short, the danger is that the history of the nation will once again become an alibi for the depredations of the state. The relationship between nation and state is an unresolved tension within Irish postcolonial theory. As Colin Graham acutely observes, the case made by David Lloyd and Carol Coulter for an affiliation between nationalism and feminism in the Irish context depends on the elimination of the hyphenated relation of the nation-state.[38] The economic disjunction between the two parts of the island of Ireland is the elephant in postcolonial theory's sitting room. In Sean O' Reilly's *The Swing of Things*,[39] the released republican prisoner and his Russian immigrant neighbor are (almost) equally marginal to contemporary Dublin. They sit silently over a pint, not talking about their past. Their status is of course different. One has an unquestioned right to stay, the possibility of a Trinity degree and of access to insider status, even if his history ultimately precludes achievement of this. The Derry laborers in the city's construction industry living like the other migrants in hostels, the "wife and wains" back home, are a closer parallel. O'Reilly's novel is interesting in that it marks one of the very few attempts to write a contemporary Dublin novel within the paradigms of Irish postmodernist fiction and it posits its northern protagonist (an odd amalgam of Leopold Bloom and Stephen Dedalus) as an insider/outsider. It is a position that might usefully be explored in contemporary theory, lest the north become the south's token of authentic historical trauma, another alibi.

THE POSTCOLONIAL GIRL

Of course, the position of the insider/outsider, of the bifurcated other within, is one that is already well articulated in Irish cultural theory. It is the position of feminist analysis, of queer theory, of groups whose marginality is romanticized into silence. Postcolonial theory in Ireland has been highly resistant to being "differenced" from within. Declan Kiberd's *The Irish Writer and the World* quotes extensively from Julia Kristeva's *Strangers to Ourselves* in its concluding essay on multiculturalism, but includes no extended engagement with any Irish women writers. There are interesting parallels in the first issue of the *Field Day Review*, which reads almost as an elegy for the critical paradigms with which its key contributors have changed the face of Irish Studies in the last two decades. (The histories of racism and immigration feature fairly obliquely in Cormac O'Grada's article on "Dublin's Jewish Immigrants of a Century Ago.") The text of the review essays is relatively familiar to anyone working in Irish Studies, with many essays based on lectures delivered to the Notre Dame summer seminar. It is significant that the only really paradigm-affecting piece is an elegy, Seamus Deane's essay on Edward Said, and that this is the only place where the radical shifts in cultural theory post-9/11 and the Afghan and Iraq invasions surface, however fleetingly.

As in *The Irish Writer and the World*, the literary writing of Irish women is absent, though there are a couple of scholarly essays by women. Images of women are not absent, however, and the inclusion of (one) woman artist's work is of particular significance. It is on the visual dimension of the volume that I want to concentrate, for it suggests the challenges that Irish Studies glimpses at its windows. The high production values of the review mark it as a product of a particularly well-endowed corner of the global academic marketplace. The first thing to strike the casual flicker through is the contrasting preponderance of photographic images of past poverty. There is an emigrant narrative inscribed here, but it is too easy to dismiss it as an Irish-American narrative of sepia rags to well-designed riches. For the volume visually disrupts its own coordinates and it does so through the construction of a feminine gaze directed beyond its project. The front cover is folded over, with only one figure from Bert Hardy's[40] original picture of Willie Cullen and his family apparent. This part is a little girl, her back to the photographer, who is looking out of the window. When the cover is fully extended, her younger sister becomes the center of the composition, looking up at her father who returns her look with great affection. The caption tells us this is a picture of Willie Cullen playing with his children, but it is only the smaller child who plays back. On the cover, the disengaged little girl is central but unreadable, her face turned in the opposite direction to our scrutiny.

The design offers the possibility of two overlapping interpretations. The most overt plane of meaning is that the new review, while representing the past, is conscious of another subject position, one oriented toward the future, the outside, the world beyond the little Cullen girl's window. This future-oriented Irish subject is constructed by the cover as feminine, nascent, yet to mature and still resistant to engagement and interpretation. It is the central enigma of the subject and critical perspective that this review celebrates and institutionalizes. The folding over of the photograph implies a further and autocritical impulse. The complete picture would place this feminine future within the framework of the domestic and the family. The design hides this possibility away, turning the picture of the nurturing father and the affectionate child into the lining of the image of feminine refusal. The review wears its unconscious on its sleeve, intensely desirous of an encounter with a feminine subject, insistent that such engagement is beyond its reach. But the little girls in the photograph would be women in their fifties now, women with lived lives beyond the photographic frame, their own mature perspective on the world beyond the window. The girls in the picture might be readable in terms of the definition of a (feminized) subaltern that Deane commends in Gayatri Spivak's writing:

> populations below the horizon for whom everything, even their liberation, had been already so spoken for that the effort was to enable these people—mostly women—to begin to speak and thereby create an alternative form of power to that which had silenced them.[41]

But what of the women the girls became and the generation they represent? Didn't they begin to speak, find their own alternative form of power? They belong to the generation of civil rights, women's liberation, of articulate women in all walks of life who engaged in a wide variety of political and artistic practices. They are far more than silent potential.

The rest of Bert Hardy's photographs of women, including a number where women and girls face the camera directly, form part of a sequence in the volume where they are heavily outnumbered by images of men engaged in work and politics. The female gaze continues to trouble the frame(work), however. Margaret Corcoran's series of paintings, *An Enquiry*, takes its title from Edmund Burke's *An Enquiry into the Origins of the Ideas of the Sublime and the Beautiful*. Two paintings from the series are included, both within the pages of Benedict Anderson's essay on globalization. The painting that figured prominently in Luke Gibbon's essay on the series, "Engendering the Sublime: Margaret Corcoran's *An Enquiry, An Enquiry VIII*," is included in small format. *An Enquiry VIII* rhymes with the front cover illustration, showing a woman again with her back to us, her attention turned to the painting in front of her (George Barrett's painting of Powerscourt Waterfall). The full page and dominant illustration of Corcoran's work is *An Enquiry I*, which features a young woman looking toward the viewer, turned away from Thomas Hickey's orientalist painting of an Indian woman. All the paintings in *An Enquiry* are set in the Milltown Rooms of the National Gallery of Ireland. These rooms contain the late eighteenth-century and early nineteenth-century paintings of the Irish School so that Corcoran's series is an interrogation of a canon of Irish painting as well as an exploration of Burke's aesthetics. Gibbons's article on Corcoran's work in *Circa*[42] effectively reads it as a feminist extension of Burke's project, even suggesting that Burke's emphasis on anticipation and identification as elements of the sublime aesthetic experience prefigures Laura Mulvey's analysis of the gendered nature of spectatorship in cinema. Corcoran's identification of her painting technique with Degas and Monet certainly supports Gibbons reading of her work in terms of modernist self-reflexive use of both framing and the gallery space. Yet this neat recruitment of *An Enquiry* to both Burkean aesthetics and modernist interrogations of tradition is undercut by *An Enquiry I*. The feminine subject here is not a good daughter who plays the game, nor simply a recalcitrant one who refuses to be read. Moreover, the differencing of the gaze in Corcoran's work exceeds the category of singular feminine intervention into an artistic practice and critical discourse conducted in exclusively masculine terms. The modern young woman who looks back at us from *An Enquiry I* does not block our gaze at the objectified "oriental" woman behind her, but she does interrupt it. She looks back, challenging our secure spectatorship position, blocking the secure binary identifications of active gaze and agency on the one hand, object of gaze and passivity on the other. In this painting to be looked at is to challenge that look, at least if you are the white woman in the foreground of the canvas, not the "other" woman in the background. The intervention of the female gazer poses a question before Hickey's portrait, "what do you think you are looking at?" This painting is much harder than *An Enquiry VIII* to read as straightforwardly Burkean for it insists on a pause before the onward rush of paint and emotion, forcing an internal dislocation in the position of subject and object rather than a synthesis of the two. *An Enquiry I* differences the role of painter and spectator and in the process differentiates itself from the Burkean sublime. There is a definite satirical edge to the portrayal of the female figure as art student, the painter framing her own position as copyist of the (minor) masters within the narrative of the series. That narrative is, of course, beyond the scope of selective reproductions to reproduce. However, it is worth noting that what gets lost in the transposition is the sense of movement that all commentators (including Gibbons) have identified as a major component of Corcoran's technique. The foregrounding of *An Enquiry I* precludes any simplistic reading of this in terms of a transition from object to subject of painting, because the contemporary female figure is remarkably still and sharp while it is the framed portrait behind that seems to promise movement and life. In this respect it echoes another woman's painting, one that thematically bears comparison with Corcoran's series. Moira Barry's *Self-Portrait in the Artist's Studio* (1920) is set within the privacy of the artist's studio rather than the national/public space of the National Gallery, but it also features a woman looking away from a variety of canvasses, over her shoulder, directly at the on-looker, in a pose which is uncannily close to the foreground young woman in *An Enquiry I*. The canvases behind Barry are, however, blank with one exception (which appears to be a still life) and only one is framed. Again the paintings are more fluid than the woman in front of them. Barry's self-portrait is a highly stylized work in a very traditional form, but it also uses the modernist techniques whose influence Corcoran acknowledges. *Self-Portrait in the Artist's Studio* is, like the paintings by Barrett and Hickey, owned by the National Gallery, but not part of the canon configured by the Milltown rooms. It was, however, exhibited as part of the 1987 exhibition of Irish Women Artists at the gallery and featured prominently in the published catalogue of that exhibition.

Juxtaposing the two paintings suggests a genealogy of women artists' relationship with both modernist and postmodernist painting. Both challenge the opposition of subject-object, inside-outside, framed-framing. The woman in Barry's *Self-Portrait* is an artist surrounded by the potentiality of her own painting, the blank canvases yet to be filled. She reminds us that women have not only been part of the history of art, but have an artistic history of speaking, looking and painting "for themselves." In *An Enquiry I* there are two women, one an acute observer of a tradition of painting that leaves her below its framed horizon, overshadowed by a beautiful image of female otherness. The second woman seems almost to be flowing out of focus, her gaze directed at an object we cannot identify. The double framing of her image—within Corcoran's painting of Hickey's painting—in important respects demystifies her. She becomes less a token of the exotic unknowable to be exchanged for the authenticity of the sublime and more a reminder of the structural limitations of the aesthetic.

An Enquiry suggests the postmodern, feminist artist can keep on moving through and beyond the limitations of a national and patriarchal culture, but will never have the luxurious fiction of really blank canvases to be filled. The Irish tradition behind her produces sublime and beautiful images of romantic landscape and racial stereotype—and Corcoran's series links the two in a way that exceeds Gibbons's description of its presentation of "the image itself as an enquiry into its own making."[43] The positioning of Corcoran's paintings in *Field Day Review* is highly significant, for it both cordons them off from the textual analysis of Ireland that dominates the volume and identifies them with the investigation of globalization in Benedict Anderson's essay. Irish Studies has been heavily invested in its own particularity, a particularity that seeks exception from the global system that produces it. Ireland is produced in turn by this discourse as a beautiful and disturbing original, rather in the manner of a modernist work of art. Irish literary criticism has a brilliant history—brilliant in the mode of a moving searchlight, providing blindingly clear illuminations of particular texts and times without ever offering the larger view that would show where exactly it itself is positioned. The inclusion of Corcoran's painting hints at a nascent awareness that race and gender will reconfigure the field. Perhaps it glimpses outside the window a landscape that includes Moira Barry, the adult woman the Cullen girls became, the books written out there, the cultural maps the new immigrants will produce, the possibility of a very differenced Ireland in the world.

2   Landscapes of Desire
Women and Ireland in Twentieth-Century Film

Irish cinema is not a national cinema in any conventional sense. Irish film-making has developed in a context where strong expectations of the appropriate content and style of films set in Ireland have been set by British and American predecessors. Perforce, much Irish filmmaking has internalized a sense of Ireland as primarily location; romantic, comic or tragic, but strange. The representation of land, gender and their interrelation has been crucial to Ireland's reception and reinvention of that constructed location. According to Dudley Andrew, "when it comes to cinema, Ireland makes an exemplary world stage, providing unexpected access to occluded aspects of globalization."[1] Both Luke Gibbons and Fidelma Farley have argued over the years for the relevance of Jameson's concept of postcolonial national allegory to an understanding of Irish cinema.[2] My concern here is to complement and complicate that analysis with a reading of Irish film's development in terms of the metaphoric gendering of Ireland, the eroticization of landscape and the fusion of melodrama and history in contemporary films set in Ireland. What follows, then, is not a comprehensive survey of the cinematic representation of Ireland. Rather it is an attempt to map its recurrent preoccupations and their evolution in the twentieth century. The feminist critique of Irish culture that emerged in the last three decades has largely understood itself as a demythologizing critique. This demythologizing process had two contrary, but not always incompatible, trends within it. The first countered the myth of "Mother Ireland" with the "reality" of women's lived experiences, through historical and social research, realist narrative and the assertion of an aesthetic of authenticity. The second major trend in this process concentrated on destabilizing myth from within, through parody, revision and reappropriation of the figures, forms and representations of women and could be described as postmodernist. These two trends within feminist critique of Irish culture can be usefully mapped onto similar trends within cultural criticism of Ireland's cinematic representation. The first corresponds to the once pervasive and still powerful resentment of such representation of Ireland as "untrue," the second to the more recent attempts to analyze the recurrent forms of constructing Ireland in cinema. Both feminist analysis of Irish culture at large and analysis of films set in Ireland have focused with an extraordinary intensity on the unstable metaphoric relation of Irish land to Irish identity, a preoccupation they share with a large body of Irish writing and filmmaking. According to Luke Gibbons, "Landscape has tended to play a leading role in Irish cinema, often upstaging both the main characters and narrative themes in the construction of Ireland on the screen."[3] While this usurpation has often threatened to swamp both narrative and character in fatalistic atavism, Gibbons insists that landscape in the Irish context is neither the opposite of meaning or history nor merely inscribed with them, but is productive of political significance and of disruptions in the naturalizing conventions of its representation. Gibbons's emphasis on the instability of oppositions between nature and culture, landscape and history is very much at odds with feminist criticism's analysis of the systematic fixing of just such an opposition through and as sexual opposition. "If the dominant discourse works to naturalise nationalist ideologies and culture, the feminine discourse works to denaturalise it, producing a space that must be filled, a problem of identity and position in the text."[4]

Yet landscape is simultaneously gendered (as feminine) and politicized in films set in Ireland. Panoramic introductions to Ireland as a scenic location are often concluded by a scene of political confrontation or a first view of the heroine, sometimes both at once. This metaphoric relation of woman and land can easily be mapped onto the "sovereignty goddess" tradition that remains a persistent aspect of Irish literary culture. Film, however, offers visual pleasure in landscape itself that allows it to dispense with the presence of a female figure and to assume an eroticized relation to land as such. The recurrent plot of a conflict over land also drew on a tradition of popular fiction and drama that is not always congruent with a simple Oedipal relation to land as "Mother Ireland." The representation of Irish land as scenery is indebted to Hollywood's construction of rural idyll and westward escape: the inescapable political and social significance of this particular land challenges that construction. This chapter looks at the problematic relation between landscape and gender, fantasy and politics, in films set in Ireland. My initial focus is on the way in which Irish women represent Ireland itself on-screen. The second part of the chapter analyzes the eroticization of Irish landscape in films set in Ireland, in the context of Irish visual culture generally. The concluding section maps the persistence of these modes of representing Ireland right up to the end of the twentieth century.

REFLECTIONS: WOMEN AND IRELAND ON-SCREEN

From the beginning the way in which Irish women were represented on-screen was intimately connected with the way Ireland itself was perceived. In effect, in looking at the representation of Irish women on-screen one is looking at the representation of Ireland as and in those women. This con-figuration of femininity and nationality is not unique. In many respects it was influenced and even produced by the neighboring figure of Britannia. The Victorians sometimes pictorially represented that stern and matronly lady as an elder sister or consoling aunt of poor, forlorn but beautiful Hibernia. Hibernia, fair, young, in difficulty if not on the verge of catastrophe, was a common figure in British representations of Ireland in the nineteenth century.[5] The influence of this representation or perhaps more accurately the same structure of representing Ireland in female form can be traced throughout the twentieth century in cinematic representations of Ireland.

One can see it in various guises in the "Colleen Bawn" films of the silent era. The original Colleen Bawn was Elly Hanley, a sixteen-year-old girl who was murdered after a fraudulent marriage to a minor local squire in 1819. By the time the story passed through Gerald Griffins 1829 novel *The Collegians*, through Dion Boucicault's stage version and an operetta, into film at the hands of the Kalem Company in 1911, it had developed a happy ending. Squire and tenantry are reconciled through the marriage of Eily O'Connor and her squire in this film version. *The Colleen Bawn*, directed by Sidney Olcott, became a prototype for the reconciliation-through-romance narratives that were to continue to offer images of a hopeful future for Ireland with dreary consistency throughout the twentieth century. In 1921 the Film Company of Ireland presented another Colleen Bawn narrative, directed by John MacDonagh. This was not based on the murder case, but used Colleen Bawn as a generic name for a fair and pure girl. Romance and marriage promised a reconciliation not of classes this time, but of Catholic and Protestant. (The film is very insistent that Willie is a proper, landed, honorable and cultured gentleman, so religious difference is not complicated by class difference.) *Willie Reilly and his Colleen Bawn* tells the story of love triumphing over extreme adversity as the Catholic Willie is dispossessed, framed for theft, convicted of abduction and sent into exile for seven years for the crime of loving the Protestant Helen Whitecraft. Helen, believing Willie dead, loses her reason in the course of all this and only his return restores her sanity. In response, her father is finally willing to be reconciled to an interdenominational marriage. The final image is of Willie, Helen and their daughter with the reconciled Mr. Whitecraft. In the Irish context, romance and reason are linked it seems. Willie restoring Helen's reason is heavy metaphorical weather for the restoration of harmony and sense to Hibernia through religious reconciliation.

The same pattern remains discernible in an otherwise disparate array of films made in and about Ireland and occasionally by Irish companies or directors throughout the 1930s, 1940s and 1950s. The British filmmakers, Launder and Gilliatt, reverted to the Victorian project of redeeming Hibernia from Irish excesses in *I See a Dark Stranger* (Individual Pictures, 1946). Deborah Kerr played Bridie Quilty, a young Irish woman enthralled by her late father's tales of war against England who, through a series of accidents and a strange identification with Roger Casement hinging on a German phrase book, becomes a German spy during World War II. She comes to see the error of her ways through her love for a British intelligence officer (Trevor Howard, no less). Their final reconciliation and marriage in England is carried off with at least a little knowing irony: Bridie storms out when she finds her new husband has booked her into the Cromwell Arms for the honeymoon.[6]

In general, however, the political relationships resolved as romantic relationships in these films became more complex from the end of the silent era onward. In *West of Kerry* (aka *The Islandman*, directed by Patrick Heale, Irish National Film Corporation, 1938) it is corrupt, urban, middle-class Dublin and the pure traditions and natural rhythms of life on the Blasket Islands that are united in the marriage of the main protagonists. Here, as was increasingly the case in these romantic narratives set in Ireland, the romance renews, regenerates or purifies a male partner who has been exhausted or corrupted by modern urban life. The woman personifies tradition and/or nature as well as Ireland. At this point the image of Hibernia has effectively been displaced by that of the wild Irish girl whose provenance dates back to Lady Morgan's 1806[7] novel of that name. From the 1940s on, a series of Irish and Irish-American actresses or actresses who played Irish roles played this wild Irish girl figure with varying emphasis on her rebelliousness, seductiveness, tragic potential, moral ambiguity and red or very dark hair. Kathleen Ryan, Siobhain McKenna and (oddly) Deborah Kerr[8] were prominent in the more serious treatments of this figure: Maureen O'Hara became the embodiment of its more attractive qualities.

Hungry Hill (directed by Brian Desmond Hurst, Two Cities, Britain, 1947) is not the best of these films by any means, but it usefully combines all their key elements. The character of Fanny Rosa is an immediately recognizable type of wild Irish girl, a quicksilver, difficult to possess heroine, a "wild bird." An early scene between her and one of the sons of the Big House shows her in peasant dress, very much at home in the natural landscape. She rejects his proposal, telling him she wants to travel. When he tries to embrace her, asking when he can see her again, she walks out of shot, answering, "I don't know. I might not like you tomorrow." Fanny Rosa's independence is tamed eventually in motherhood, but, excessively and disastrously devoted to her son, she almost causes the collapse of the family and the loss of the Big House itself. Yet it is Fanny Rosa's repudiation of hate and vengeance at the film's end that makes reconciliation and future stability possible. She is represented as bridging the gap between landlord and peasant, English and Irish: for example, integrating a formal ball with the *ceili* simultaneously going on in the grounds. At the film's end, Fanny Rosa stands between her Irish servant and English daughter-in-law when she forgives the man who is charged with her son's death. In *Hungry Hill* the wild Irish girl and suffering mother figures coalesce. Marriage as a way of reconciling political opposites is superseded by the image of a woman who, precisely because of her ambiguity, symbolizes the union of that which is rationally and politically irreconcilable.

In *Captain Boycott* (directed by Frank Launder, Individual Pictures, Britain, 1947) the romance plot again predominates, romance leading away from revolutionary mob violence toward civil society. This film is discussed in more detail in the next section, but it is worth noting here that the central couple represents the internal divisions of Irish society during the land war of the 1870s. Strikingly, despite the fact that it is British made, the only significant English character in the film is so far excluded from the final resolution as to need armed protection to leave the country. The context of domestic British politics in the immediate aftermath of World War II and Launder and Gilliatt's role in the production of wartime propaganda films that stressed communal solidarity were important factors here. Indeed, *Captain Boycott* is indicative of how important it is to remember that more is at stake in the representation of Ireland than attitudes to Ireland itself. Any foreign location can be used to examine, advocate or condemn at a safe distance practices or politics that would be much more controversial if set at home. Both *Captain Boycott* and *Hungry Hill* are at least as much about the understanding of class conflict and property in postwar Britain as they are about Ireland.

The Quiet Man (directed by John Ford, Republic, US, 1952) takes as its opening premise the redemptive qualities of traditional Ireland for those corrupted by American industrial society. The Irish setting is a fantasy one; its rural bliss and wise innocence associated both with nostalgia for childhood and with sexual fulfillment. In this respect, the film bears useful comparison with the treatment of Scotland in *Brigadoon*. But *The Quiet Man* is also a glorious parody of the "wild Irish girl" romantic subgenre. There has been much comment on the scene where Maureen O'Hara emerges from a misty landscape of Oedipal nostalgia just beyond John Wayne's mother's place. Its subversion of the codes of cinematic authenticity has been foregrounded by Gibbons.[9] Despite its parodic qualities, however, *The Quiet Man* remains the most commercially successful representation of the restoration of proper sexual order through love for a good old-fashioned Irish girl. Wayne regains the ability to fight, becoming a man again in a comic punch-up with O'Hara's brother from whom she insists he claim her traditional dowry. A seamless fusion is achieved between the exploitation of Ireland as a scene of romance, as an "other" place uncontaminated by decadent contemporary society, and 1950s Middle America's romance with the rural, natural and authentic.

A more effective deconstruction of the genre is effected in *This Other Eden*, one of a handful of films produced in Ireland in the 1950s by Emmett Dalton. These films were predominantly adaptations of Abbey plays, frequently and sometimes unjustly criticized for remaining too stagebound. *This Other Eden* was adapted from Louis Dalton's biting stage satire of post-independence southern Ireland and its relationship with the old adversary. It was unusual in having a woman director, Muriel Box. Fidelma Farley has produced a book-length study of the complexities of gender and national identities in this particular adaptation of Dalton. *This Other Eden* has all the classic ingredients of the politics and romance of Irish film; a wild Irish girl with two potential suitors, one Irish, one English; the shadow of past violence on the present and a dispute over property. On one level, it examines the repercussions for a small community when the illegitimate son of its great, dead hero, Carberry, threatens to break the hypocritical silence that has protected the dead patriot's reputation by denying his son's parentage. Intertwined with this narrative, however, is a comedy romance between Maire McRoarty and an Englishman, Crispin Brown (played with great gormless charm by Leslie Phillips) who wishes to return to what had been his family's home in the town before his father had been implicated in the assassination of Carberry by the British during the War of Independence.

The first encounter between Maire and Crispin occurs on a train traveling across distinctly mundane, markedly modern rural scenes. Crispin initially tries to speak Irish to Maire. The subsequent exchange between them mocks conventional ideas of national identity. When Maire mocks, "your command of the Irish language doesn't seem to be very extensive," he makes a great point of telling her he is in fact English, assuming that it is possible to mistake him for anything else. When she comments that this seems a good enough reason for speaking English, he counters that it is also a good reason for the Irish to speak Irish. There follows much confusion as to Maire's nationality: when she says there is not much Irish spoken where she comes from, he assumes she is a Dubliner, she claims to be from Birmingham. This elicits a lecture on her duties as an Englishwoman abroad and more comic confusion at his expense:

> "You may find the Irish hating you. In the past they have had every reason to. But always remember it's your duty not to hate them."
> "Sometimes I hate them very much."
> "Why that's terrible, you know, really terrible. You simply mustn't do it. Where Ireland is concerned it's for the English to remember and the Irish to forget."

Finally losing her temper when Crispin takes responsibility for Irish emigration, Maire exclaims that the Irish will do anything for Ireland but live in it:

> Don't you dare lecture me about the Irish. I'll hate them if I want to. I've every right to hate them. I'm Irish myself.

As the train passes across an increasingly scenic landscape, Ireland's more picturesque qualities are presented as products of English imagination.

Crispin's desire to settle in the "romantic, forlorn, so utterly Irish" house for sale in her hometown elicits Maire's warning, "Don't let them rob you." More thoroughly than in *John Bull's Other Island*, which it modernizes and reimagines, *This Other Eden* inverts and then subverts the traditional markers of English and Irish identity. Maire's identity in particular is seen as plastic and self-invented. Commenting on her effect on the English, she jokes, "All I had to do was plaster on a brogue an inch thick and they wanted me to go on talking forever." Mocking her abundance of English suitors she comments that the English are "not like the Irish with no romance in them." The audience sees repeated evidence of her ability to transform herself and control her surroundings, first in her dealings with Crispin, then with her father. Maire is an ambivalent figure, a returned emigrant and a better businesswoman than the standard wild Irish girl, too independent to play Hibernia plausibly. Given the choice of a decent Irish husband hand-picked by her father or return to Birmingham, she installs herself in the Big House as Crispin's wife. Though she has seemed thoroughly in charge of this relationship from the outset, the conclusion is rather bleakly in keeping with the traditions of Hibernia narratives. The disenchanted republican Clannery notes in wonderment that the English manage to come well out of everything. *This Other Eden* subverts the conventions of representing Ireland as Woman, but in the absence of a plausible alternative, can do no better than laugh at its own concluding capitulation to those conventions.

MOTHER IRELAND

Parallel to the image of Ireland as sweet, wild girl, the image of Ireland as suffering and nurturing mother recurs. The latter is not nearly as prevalent in film as it is in Irish literature, possibly because the romantic conventions of mainstream Hollywood do not accommodate it as easily. From the start, however, the figure of the suffering mother has a kind of iconic status, which though peripheral to the narrative can be crucial to the meaning attributed to that narrative. A scene from *Rory O'More*, released by the Kalem Company in 1911, showed Rory's mother weeping in the court when a sentence of death was passed on her rebel son. Though his sweetheart has previously figured strongly in the narrative, trying to divert the soldiers on his trail and assist his escape, in this scene of suffering the mother is foregrounded (the sweetheart is represented comforting her).

    The Informer was originally adapted from Liam O'Flaherty's novel in 1929, but remade with John Ford as director in 1935. Ford's version represents this suffering Irish mother as indistinguishable from the Mater Dolorosa of Catholic iconography. Mrs. McPhillip's house is invaded by Black and Tans and her son Frankie shot down, but she forgives the man who has informed against him and cost him his life. The equation of the mother here with both suffering motherland and with Christian values of forgiveness

is both melodramatic and powerful. Standing beneath an enormous cru-
cifix in the church where her son is laid out, she takes the role of Mary
as mediator between the sinner and his god, using the language of Christ
himself to the dying informer. "I forgive you, son, sure you didn't know
what you were doing. You didn't know what you were doing." Her forgive-
ness is powerless in this world, unfortunately, for he is already the victim
of a retaliatory shooting. "The organization" is not presented as killing the
informer to revenge her son, but as a pragmatic measure to protect itself.
Mrs. McPhillip embodies Ireland; she does not govern its realities.

Mother Ireland was not always a sweet old lady. In *Odd Man Out*
(directed by Carol Reed, Two Cities, Britain, 1947) old Granny hides a
revolver up her sleeve, confident that the raiding police will not search her.
In *Captain Boycott* old Mrs. Davin exhorts her son to fight, positively chor-
tles with glee when she finds him hiding a gun and vehemently expresses
her disgust when he turns his back on violence and supports the political and communal activities of the Land League. The image of the patriot
mother is often thus comically treated, her more threatening aspects incompatible with the mainstream film audiences' image of motherhood. Film
has tended to fuse that aspect of Mother Ireland that demands the blood
of her sons with sexuality, splitting the wild Irish girl and Mother Ireland
stereotypes neatly in two, with nurture and suffering on one side, sex and
violence on the other. This split is epitomized in the mother and daughter
characters, Molly and Maureen Fagan, in *The Gentle Gunman* (directed
by Basil Deardon, Ealing, Britain, 1952). The action revolves around the
men in the film, but at a key moment the focus moves to the two women
waiting for news at home. I want to talk about this episode in detail, since
it crystallizes film's representation of the relationship between Irish women
and political violence. An establishing shot tracks Maureen across the desolate landscape to her home as evening falls, associating her with nature,
darkness and restless energy. After a cut to her mother indoors, completely
still except for the motion of her rosary beads, we see Maureen moving
restlessly around the room. Maureen has already been presented as unnatu-
ral, unconcerned for her wounded brother and eager for her former lover,
Terry, to be shot as a traitor. In this scene her mother insists Terry will save
her son and outwit the IRA: "he's too good for them and for you." Molly
also tells her that he will take away Maureen's current lover, his younger
brother, "and then you'll be ready for another cheap thrill out of the next
poor lad that goes over the border with a gun in his pocket." As she says
this Molly stands up beside the lamp: her daughter moves closer to the fire.
When she finally admits she does not want Terry to die, she moves away
from the flames and into the foreground of the frame, previously occupied
by her mother. Standing behind her daughter and talking over her shoulder,
almost directly to the camera in a way that gives extraordinary authority
to her point of view, Molly gives her daughter no credit for this revelation:
"I'm thinking it's death itself you're in love with." Maureen flees upstairs,

leaving her mother in sole possession of the domestic space, the daughter destined for the desertion and loneliness her mother predicts.

Sexual and violent women like Maureen are the negative mirror image of Ireland as woman. For obvious political and historical reasons, they have featured much more frequently in British treatments of Ireland than American ones. Contemporary Irish filmmakers have a degree of fascination with this Irish version of the femme fatale, who has become rather more fatal as the image of the female terrorist has become the dominant media image of republican women. Jude in *The Crying Game* (directed by Neil Jordan, Palace Pictures/Channel Four Films, Britain, 1992), eventually gets her thrills from a more active role than that available to Maureen, but she is still presented as in love with death itself. The other stereotypes are equally persistent: Julia Roberts is an unlikely Hibernia, but there, filmed finally in a green coat, she is at the end of *Michael Collins* (directed by Neil Jordan, Warner Bros., Ireland, 1996) lamenting her fallen hero. *Some Mother's Son* (directed by Terry George, Hell's Kitchen, Ireland, 1996) complicates the image of the suffering republican mother: with its emphasis on the mother's perspective on the son's suffering, it is nonetheless in that tradition. In *The Field* (directed by Jim Sheridan, Granada, Britain, 1990) the legacy of a somewhat different tradition prevails. *The Field* explores the relation between a violent attachment to land and the gendering of landscape. As such it draws on a tradition of representing Ireland not through a woman, but as itself a feminine land and landscape.

LAND, LANDSCAPE AND DESIRE

It is easy to underestimate the power of a long-term association with the land, not just with a specific spot but with the span of it in memory and imagination, how it fills one's dreams.[10]

In the opening scenes of (the again usefully typical) *Hungry Hill*, many of the key elements in the treatment of Irish land and landscape in film are condensed. Behind the opening credits, a carriage moves across a landscape of spectacular mountain scenery. As the credits end, just as one expects a closer view of the vehicle and those in it, the carriage moves out of shot, so that the landscape briefly fills the screen. The scene then shifts, cutting to the mountain road where the carriage reemerges and then stops. The passenger, the local landowner, Mr. Broderick, gets out, walks up a small hill and then pauses, surveys the land with a distinctly proprietorial air and consults a variety of plans and maps. Broderick's antagonist, Morty Donovan, arrives, walking uphill into the shot, as if emerging from the earth itself. Donovan's presence is reinforced as sinister and occult when he asks, "How do you like the site for your new mine, Mr. Broderick?" Broderick is clearly perturbed that anyone knows his plans. This effect is strengthened when Donovan sneers, "the fairies it might have been told me." He then proceeds to curse the project, predicting it will bring only "trouble and sorrow" to the Brodericks and insisting "you should have asked permission of the hill itself." The difficulty of the Broderick family in having and holding its mining interests in the face of Irish sabotage and hostility is paralleled by the difficulty of its male descendants in getting the right woman and keeping her, outlined in the previous section. This kind of useful ambiguity is typical of the treatment of Irish land as landscape in cinema, particularly British and American cinema.[11] Ireland is presented as Romantic, anti-industrial and primeval and this is what is recognized in its landscape. That landscape is nonetheless unavoidably the site and symbol of political struggle, one of those far and away places where politics and history happen, but where conflict is safely attributed to the innate wildness of the natives. The narrative pattern that emerges is away from recognition of the politics of place toward the fantasy fusion of land and woman.

There are a whole series of scenes in films made in or about Ireland that reproduce the dynamics of *Hungry Hill*'s opening. Film seems particularly prone to that eroticization of landscape that comes to substitute for eroticized bodies in many aspects of Irish culture. It has been argued that this particular cultural formation stems from the sovereignty goddess tradition where the land of Ireland was both mother and either unattainable maiden or promiscuous consort of strangers. That tradition was reinforced by and quite deliberately revived for political purposes in response to a nineteenth-century colonial discourse that feminized the wild Irish until they seemed mere dreamy, destructive "Celts." Instead the new nationalism that emerged in the early twentieth century proclaimed them true sons of the motherland.[12] In Ireland then the eroticization of landscape developed out of the politics of place: the picture of a landscape is always marked by the history of land and specifically its ownership. I want to draw here on two articles that deal with the work of contemporary Irish painters, Catherine Nash's analysis of the work of Kathy Prendergast and Cheryl Herr's analysis of Micheal Farrell.[13] Both these articles expand into wide-ranging analysis of landscape and the body in Irish art and political culture and both were written at the time that Irish cinema was also reengaging with these themes. Nash points out that "the issue of land and land ownership is central to the colonial situation, but it is also important symbolically in the postcolonial context when identification with landscape and place is one of the prime sources of cultural identity."[14]

The two elements of the relation to landscape outlined by Nash are absolutely overt in the opening scenes of *Hungry Hill*, discussed earlier. Land dispute has been a frequent subject of narratives set in Ireland since the Ulster unionist Letitia McClintock published the anti-land league novel *A Boycotted Household* in 1881. Argument over land is a frequent plot device and it is almost always linked to a dispute over or with a woman.

Captain Boycott, released in the same year as *Hungry Hill*, opens in a remarkably similar way. Behind the credits, a coach moves against a backdrop of spectacular mountain scenery. The narrative begins with a sharp reminder of the conflict over this apparently sublime landscape. The coach stops to observe the retrieval of the body of the local bailiff from the boghole into which it has been dumped by discontented tenants. Again landscape dissolves into conflict over land and the land itself; in this case the bog seems to be aligned with the violent discontent of the local population. More immediately than in *Hungry Hill*, the conflict over land is associated with the romance that will resolve it. Inside the coach a sack of grain bursts, revealing the gun hidden within it. Anne Kilain, played by Kathleen Ryan, ties up the sack with her ribbon, concealing the gun and her knowledge of it. The association of grain, femininity and gun here associates sex, violence and the land in quite the opposite way to *The Gentle Gunman*. The scene prefigures not just the sexual union of Anne, who has come to the area seeking security for her family and ailing father by "grabbing"[15] the farm of an evicted tenant, with Hugh Davin (Stewart Granger), the film's strongest proponent of tenant rights. It also prefigures his associated turn away from violence. The film's ending presents Anne as a figure not just of resolution and reconciliation, but also of law and social stability. Davin, the future husband who will integrate her into the community, and the local priest, Alistair Sim, stand between her cottage and the mob, saying thus far and no farther. This can be seen as symbolic of the fate of the land reform movement itself, which stopped short of nationalization in favor of creating a class of property-holding small farmers who became the backbone of post-independence social and sexual conservatism. The consequence of that "moderation" is outlined in *The Field* where the violent attachment to land is presented both as a result of the history of colonization and the blight of postcolonial southern society. *The Field*, unlike the films of the 1940s, is heavily resistant to the presentation of Ireland as landscape and is careful to set up the land from the outset as the locus of intense territorial conflict within the local community. Having established this, it does feature a scene that parallels the openings of *Hungry Hill* and *Captain Boycott*. Bull McCabe travels in a cart with his son and his companion, Bird, across a scenic landscape to look down on "his" field with a proprietorial attachment that far exceeds that of Mr. Broderick for his hill. The terms of his admiration and possession are almost explicitly sexual:

> There she is. Jasus would you look at her boys . . . Our fathers' fathers' fathers' father dug that soil with their bare hands, built those walls. Our souls is buried down there and your sons' sons' sons' sons will take care of it, boy. Do you get my meaning? Guard it well.

This earthy intensity is contrasted to the sterile domesticity of the nonfunctional couple that disappears behind and is yet necessary as a link between all those lines of fathers and sons:

"Do you remember that linoleum the mother bought for that room a way back? Do you know how much it cost a square yard? 1 shilling and 6 pence a square foot, that's more than that field down there and linoleum wears out."

"And you'd have to go a long way to find cattle that would take to linoleum."

It is worth noting Cheryl Herr's comment that the body in Irish discourse always seems on the verge of reabsorbtion into the landscape: the dangerous body "has been scrutinised with an intensity that stills photographically" (1990, 6–7). The nice thing about a field as erotic object is that it isn't going anywhere. Herr develops her analysis of this pinning down, fixing and distancing from the body, which is a legacy of Victorian moralism, nationalist insistence on moral purity and, above all, the peculiarities of Irish Catholicism to argue that in the visual arts in Ireland "bodies are imaged as changeless . . . inert . . . masses on the verge of reabsorbtion into the landscape." In the visual economy of *The Field*, this reabsorbtion has occurred. But the narrative is quite clear that such reabsorbtion is, simply, madness and death. "While the need for a certain stillness remains projected onto the body, preferably the body of a woman or a landscape figured as female, the authorised centres of meaning in the society discover again and again that their own ability to move has been impeded."[16] The history of the land and its people offered a powerful motivation for that desire to still the body, for it is a history of famine ("those dead are all around us," the priest in *The Field* explains), emigration and poverty. Land, sexuality and their relation are, given that history, issues of bare survival. The son's choice of the rootless, sexual traveling woman in the film is catastrophic, but it is an assertion of fluid life over still survival. In the 1990s Irish filmmakers still seemed to be faced with the necessity of repeating the journey west in an attempt to awaken the still body of land, to move it out of the photographic into the cinematic. Herr argues that "in postcolonial literature the development or recovery of an effective relationship to place after dislocation or cultural denigration by the supposedly superior cultural and racial colonial power, becomes a means to overcome the sense of displacement and crisis of identity."[17] Such a relationship is also characteristic of postcolonial cinema. Some films, like *Into the West*, find at the end of the westward quest only the dead lost mother, though, a traveling woman herself and now a fluid sea creature, she sets her men in motion, on the road again. *Into the West*'s romanticization of the traveling community risks condemning them to definition as the rootless other of a too-settled nation.

December Bride (directed by Thaddeus O'Sullivan, Little Bird, Ireland, 1990), identifies an unpossessable woman with a land that can be "transversed, journeyed across, entered into, intimately known, gazed upon,"[18] but can only be owned fragilely, in spite of itself:

To problematize identity allows for a cultural use of ideas of landscape that can reject its use within colonialist discourse to stereotype the native as biologically linked to the natural landscape. Similarly a feminist use of ideas of landscape and place must confront the dangers of essentialism within ecofeminism and accounts which view women's relationship to landscape in terms of innate biological and psychological structures . . . The recognition of the constructed nature of identity allows landscape to be used as a source of identification without implying a fixed, natural and inherent identity.[19]

Joyriders (directed by Aisling Walsh, Little Bird, Britain, 1988) marked an interesting, flawed attempt to combine these projects in its story of a young urban woman's flight to the west coast and finally to a hill farm away from the brutality of deprived urban life. Initially disillusioned, finding sexual oppression and violence in her hoped-for haven, she finally accomplishes a real escape in the company of a young joyrider. The fantasy is in many ways a conventional romance and replicates the fantasy of the West as a site of fantasy's fulfillment (even if here a stolen car replaces the cart). The film ends with an unorthodox but recognizable "family." But though it is through a male vehicle, the woman here escapes her fixed place, steals her children back from the law and religion and acquires her sexuality and freedom, self-possession and a "proper" place to live. It has its limitations, but it does try to map out a landscape of female desire. In this regard this fairly low-key commercial film continues the project of *Maeve* (directed by Pat Murphy and John Davies, British Film Institute and RTE, Britain and Ireland, 1981), which, controversially, sought in its final scenes to appropriate the edge of Irish land—the broken Antrim coastline—to the representation of female community. Pointedly, a journey westward (from Derry to the Donegal coastline) in Margo Harkin's *Hush-A-Bye-Baby* (Derry Film and Video Workshop, Ireland, 1989) is simultaneously a move toward traditional Irish identity and the site of keenest desolation for the pregnant young protagonist. In *Snakes and Ladders* (directed by Trish MacAdam, Livia Films, Ireland, 1996), released at the beginning of the Celtic Tiger era, the trope is treated comically. One of the urban, hip young women at the film's center drives out into the countryside and is seduced by a slimy television personality, rural Ireland providing the scene of corruption in contrast to the urban world of nightclubs, pubs and flat dwellers that is the film's main location.

A DIFFERENT VIEW?

The preoccupations of Irish cinema by the end of the twentieth century appeared to be contrary to the tradition of representing Ireland as woman. Indeed, Irish film seemed about to overturn that image. This is particularly true of the work of Pat Murphy and Margo Harkin, the most influential Irish feminist filmmakers of the period. *Maeve* is centrally concerned with the collapse of feminine subjectivity into national emblem and the importance of the motherland trope in this process. Consciously engaging with the relation between women and motherland, Murphy's and Harkin's agendas as political filmmakers include an attempt to use film as a medium powerful enough to disturb and change the mythic relation between nation and woman. *Hush-A-Bye-Baby*'s closing montage of the Virgin Mary and a teenage girl secretly giving birth is a case in point. The controversial modeling of a scene in *Anne Devlin* on a classic *pietà*, with Anne in prison cradling her dead brother in her lap, invokes the fusion of Mother Ireland and Virgin Mother characteristic of the passive, suffering Irish mother on-screen since *Rory O'More* and *The Informer*. Anne Devlin is not passive, however, and her suffering is brought about by her own political activities. Her silence, in stark contrast to the laments of all the Mother Irelands, is powerful: the film's concluding voice-over insists it has saved many men from the gallows.

Despite such oppositional work, the images of woman as Ireland/Ireland as woman remained powerful and pervasive in 1990s Irish cinema. The new mirror being held up in the feminine image was to a violated, abused, confused, but more forceful Ireland. The now sexual, often pregnant, female body still suffered and still embodied the nation's suffering. This is true of the treatment of domestic violence in *Guiltrip* (directed by Gerry Stembridge, Temple, Ireland, 1995), of family life, or its negation, in the 1994 television drama *Family*, and in the linkage of sectarian violence and sexual abuse in *This is the Sea* (directed by Mary McGuckian, Pembridge, Ireland, 1996). Indicative perhaps of new optimism, or the increasing role of Irish filmmakers in making films set in Ireland, suffering was now frequently overcome or even eclipsed by the woman/nation's survival and strength. A whole series of "maternal narratives" from the eighties and nineties bear witness to this trend: *December Bride*, *The Playboys* (directed by Gillies McKinnon, Green Umbrella Films, Britain, 1992), Orla Walsh's short film *The Visit* (Roisin Rua Films, Ireland, 1992) and even *The Snapper* (directed by Stephen Frears, BBC, Britain, 1993). The reconciliation effected by these images is between "postnationalist Ireland," trying desperately to get past that "post," and that which nationalist Ireland denied. Instead of public, political discourse excluding private pleasure and pain, cinematically and televisually private pleasure and pain represented the state of the nation. In effect what was being played out was the tension between the modern, supposedly dynamic European state and its very different history. These tensions were represented and offered imaginative/imaginary resolution through images of increasingly articulate and independent women.

MELODRAMAS OF BESET NATIONHOOD

The practice, conscious or otherwise, of representing Ireland or its condition through female figures or heterosexual romance is one that those predecessors shared with the indigenous literature of Ireland. In effect it is one of a small number of tropes in filmmaking related to Ireland that have an almost identical meaning for both Irish and international audiences. In that context, the persistence of the trope is unsurprising. The implications of that persistence are not essentially negative for the depiction of women, as Murphy's and Harkin's work made clear in the 1980s. But blithe assumptions that Irish cinema has become too modern and sophisticated to reproduce the old myths might risk reproducing them unchallenged. At the end of the 1990s an increasing tendency to parody both the myths and their persistence was evident. Orla Walsh's short film, *Blessed Fruit* (Ireland, Roisin Rua, 1999), makes glorious fun of the conflation of sexuality and reproduction in Irish film. A young journalist, unsure of which of her glamorous liaisons is responsible for her possible pregnancy, takes somewhat skeptically to prayer on Christmas Eve. The film depicts the many possible outcomes she imagines to the situation. These are counterpointed with a contemporary Dublin version of the Annunciation: "Jasus, it was like the *X-Files*," exclaims a duped Joseph. Walsh has been an outspoken critic of the difficulties facing young women directors in accessing funds from the Irish Film Board and RTE, the state broadcasting station. The controversy she started in relation to funding allocations in 1998 was undoubtedly a factor in the increased percentage of women receiving funding in 1999 under the Short Cuts scheme, a key showcase for young directors and scriptwriters. Her film also raises the issue of the timidity in relation to sexual and religious content in most Irish films of the 1990s.

GENERIC MUTATIONS

Ordinary Decent Thrillers

Two kinds of narrative dominated mainstream feature production in and about Ireland at the end of the twentieth century. The first of these was the adaptation of the contemporary Hollywood thriller genre to the Irish context, as in *I Went Down* (directed by Paddy Breathnach, Ireland, Treasure Films, 1997) and *Ordinary Decent Criminal* (directed by Thaddeus O'Sullivan, Ireland, Little Bird, 2000). The former was enormously popular with young Irish audiences, for whom witty gangster films debunking traditional notions of Ireland are an unusual treat. The three films dealing with the life and times of Dublin criminal, Martin Cahill, map out the parameters of a new urban thriller genre. The Irish pastoral idyll has become outlaw territory, the Dublin mountains providing the criminals with the opportunity to elude pursuit and escape surveillance. The bad guys crucify traitors, but the good guys set up the hero for an IRA assassination. Only one of the three films represents a policeman who is not corrupt: *Vicious Circle* (directed by David Blair, BBC Northern Ireland,

Ireland, 1998), made as a television movie and then released in cinemas, is by far the most conventional cops and robbers story of the three. Despite the operation of the IRA as *deus ex machina* in the other two, John Boorman's *The General* (Ireland, Merlin Films, 1998) is the only one of the films to set Cahill's story firmly in the Ireland of his time. Violence in northern Ireland, corruption in the south and the persistent power and angry disenchantment with the Catholic Church are etched with powerful economy in the margins of the story: slum clearance, the life of the Dublin underclass and their casual disposal by authority figure prominently.

The fascination with the criminal master of the contemporary urban labyrinth signals the emergence of a new masculine narrative, emblematically modern, culturally hybrid, inconclusive. Unlike the older female allegories, these are neither national nor coherent narratives. The world of these films is that of the capital and its hinterland, mountains as amenities to urban dwellers, outlaw territory where the criminal gangs can evade modern surveillance equipment. The history they relate is fictionalized, disputed, uncertain. The makers of *Ordinary Decent Criminal* acknowledged the film was based on the factual Cahill, but his story was edited of its darker facets and the main character renamed. The conclusion shared by the other two, implying police connivance in Cahill's assassination, was strenuously denied by them and gave rise to major controversy in Ireland at the time of the release of Boorman's film. The unstable status of the Ireland they depict in the way Ireland is imagined is indicated by the ambiguity of the boundary between fact, legend and fiction in all three films.

Melodrama and Modernity

The second and most prolific strand in 1990s Irish filmmaking was a combination of family melodrama and "heritage" setting, representing a much more familiar Ireland, largely for the consumption of an international audience. Comic variations on this were an increasing tendency in the nineties and featured prominently in TV series set in Ireland, such as the BBC's *Ballykissangel* (1996–2001). Most of the films are set in the past: some, like *Ballykissangel*, *The Nephew* (directed by Eugene Brady, Ireland, Irish Dream Time, 1998) and *Waking Ned Devine* (directed by Kirk Jones, UK, Fox, 1999),[20] simply look like the past. This group is generally derided by Irish cultural critics. Situating current Irish filmmaking firmly in the context of economic globalization, Kevin Rockett has argued that: "These films, whether family dramas or not, are ostensibly dealing with social or political issues, but often lose sight of the broader critique of which they are capable due to the strictures imposed by Hollywood three-act dramaturgy."[21] As Rockett pointed out, these constraints are not a peculiarly Irish problem. The dissatisfaction evident among the southern Irish–based contributors to *Cineaste*'s 1999 review of Irish cinema with Irish film output was symptomatic of a wider unease at the end of the twentieth century. Ruth Barton contended that:

> A cycle of films dating from the early Nineties has presented audiences with a view of Ireland which is deeply nostalgic, rooted in pastoral values, and organised around a strong sense of community. Many of them are set in the past, others depict an Ireland of today which has little or no relationship with modernity. These heritage films are particularly regressive in terms of their gender politics.[22]

This is undoubtedly the case with regard to gender *roles*, but gender politics is often about the exposure of regressive structures and their persistence. Moreover, many of the contributors to *Cineaste* appear to assume that 1990s Irish films *succeed* in the construction of coherent narratives, conforming to generic expectations and the three-act structure and that they express an unproblematic nostalgia, naturalistically representing gender as primal and untouched by history. Again and again, however, these films are marked by incoherence, fissures in plausibility, motivation or point of view. In this regard they bear some affinity with the nineteenth-century Irish novel, which bequeathed its plots to the first Irish films and a problem with realism to the Irish cultural tradition. The difficulty of the "heritage" films in negotiating with the Hollywood conventions is perhaps inevitable given their ambition to feel the frisson of past repression, separate it safely from present reality and enjoy the scenery on the way. Moreover, the heritage that might expect to be celebrated seems inescapably fragile and dangerous, a contested space which is sometimes difficult to fix in time. While landscape continues to grandstand the narrative, the objects invested with nostalgia and reverence are not peasant craftworks, but the symbols of modernity; the motorbike in *The Playboys*, the radio in *Dancing at Lughnasa*, a television set in *Bogwoman* (directed by Tom Collins, Ireland, Hindsight Films Ltd., 1998). The latter film is an interesting indication of the way in which the conventions of historical melodrama can be transferred to an unfamiliar setting in a low-budget independent film, in an attempted fusion of "family drama" and "social or political issues," in a way that resists "the strictures imposed by Hollywood three-act dramaturgy."[23] The bogwoman of the title moves from the "bogland" (urban slang for countryside) of Donegal to the Bogside area of Derry city and the film is structured as a series of flashbacks when she revisits her old rural home and remembers the historical events in which she participated in the city. As in many recent Irish films modern mass communication media play a crucial role. This is often escapist, as in the cowboy films and comic books in *The Butcher Boy*. The glamour and attraction of imported American media is hardly surprising as Martin McLoone comments "in a culture which validates the afterlife more than the material world and which spends most of the time venerating the past and the dead."[24]

Paradoxically, however, modern media is portrayed in contemporary film as the means through which Ireland experiences its own history. A pre-credit sequence in *Bogwoman* uses news footage with a reconstructed voice-over to set the scene for those unfamiliar with the history of the Bogside. Thereafter the television news footage is integrated into the narrative: the protagonists are shown watching, reacting and experiencing it as part of their lives. In this way, television broaches the boundary between safe domestic space and the dangerous streets, a boundary that Maureen tries to maintain for most of the narrative. *Bogwoman*'s conclusion offers an extreme case of the breakdown of melodramatic convention in these films. Elsaesser's pivotal study of melodrama proposed that:

> The family melodrama . . . records the failure of the protagonist to act in a way that could shape the events and influence the emotional environment, let alone change the stifling social milieu. The world is closed, and the characters are acted upon. Melodrama confers on them a negative identity through suffering and the progressive self-immolation and disillusionment generally ends in resignation.[25]

The flashback sequences in *Bogwoman* end with Maureen joining the other Bogside women in the streets and helping to make Molotov cocktails. The concluding image and voice-over, however, are contemporary, showing Maureen in the ruins of her old rural home and expressing the desire for a new peace. In this instance the politics of the film is at odds and yet at home in the borrowed conventions. In the end, ideology, character and the film's plausibility are cracked open simultaneously.

The relation between form and content in these new Irish melodramas is regularly that between personal story and historical context. In *A Love Divided* (directed by Sydney McCartney, Ireland, Parallel Films, 1999) family and communal melodrama is itself the history that is retold. As the title indicates, the film is constructed as a Romeo and Juliet–style love story, an updating of the basic scenario in *Willie Reilly and His Colleen Bawn,* with love triumphing over sectarian adversity. These lovers are not teenagers, however, and the film begins, not ends, with their marriage. The plot is based on the Fethard-on-Sea boycott in 1957, when the dwindling Protestant population of a small Wexford village was subjected to ostracization and sometimes near ruin by their Catholic neighbors. At issue was the right of a mixed-marriage couple to send their children to a school of their choosing, without it being seen as contravening their pledge to raise the children of the marriage as Catholics. To this small nut of independent thinking an ecclesiastical hammer of extraordinary force was applied. The film portrays the central family not as an expression of the national or communal, but as the only locus of happiness available to the protagonists in opposition to community, church and nation. It is one of the very few Irish films to espouse the radical individualism that lurks in melodrama, yet its oppositional potential sinks without a trace in the lush, romantic, pastoral scene it so laboriously sets. The film is further burdened by a central implausibility. Having established the central couple as passionately devoted to each other, it must also present them as losing all trust and understanding of each other in a remarkably short period under clerical pressure, only to miraculously regain it under the influence of a benign Scotswoman and a little island scenery. While clergy, community and the law work to destroy them, modern media in the form of an interview by a sympathetic reporter brings them back together. The film visually obeys all the requirements of heritage cinema, even offering a domestic plenitude for which nostalgia is plausible, in contrast to the comfortless interiors that feature in so many of its counterparts. Dramatically, however, *A Love Divided* cannot offer a personal resolution to social conflict and so its happy ending is muted and unsatisfactory. The voice-over throughout and point of view of most of the narrative events is that of the wife. She concludes that her marriage was tried and found strong, her children "did us proud," but the village was never the same again. The resounding lack of social harmony with which the film ends is reinforced by the information that ultimately the children were homeschooled, attending neither the Protestant nor Catholic schools in the village. Were this outcome treated with pathos and heightened emotionalism, it could fit very well within the conventional frameworks of melodrama. Instead the audience is offered bitter irony in the form of a historical footnote, reporting that the Catholic Church finally apologized for its "petty pogrom in County Wexford"[26] in 1998.

"Melodrama is often used to describe tragedy that doesn't quite come off."[27] The heritage melodramas of the 1990s were not just commodities selling Ireland as an infusion of instant historical flavor to a contemporary global marketplace. The appeal of the form beyond the mainstream and the mainstream's increased interest in urban and contemporary settings are indicative that something more complex was at stake. The difficulty in reconciling the duplicate closing images of Maureen in *Bogwoman* and the uncertain resolution of *A Love Divided* indicates not the absence of melodrama, or drama in excess of its terms, but its very essence:

> Melodrama can . . . be seen as a contradictory nexus, in which certain determinations (social, physical, artistic) are brought together but in which the problem of the articulation of these determinations is not successfully resolved. The importance of melodrama . . . lies precisely in its ideological failure.[28]

The rapidity of political change in the 1990s made it harder and harder to make the old plots work as they once did: the prevalence for historical settings may owe something to this, but even there new structures and new attitudes emerged. Commercial considerations and the pragmatics of film funding ensured that films made in and about Ireland continued to employ the generic conventions of mainstream Hollywood production. Increasingly these included urban thrillers as well as period pieces. Irish audiences themselves now need these conventions as the conditions of narrative intelligibility. Like the television watchers, radio listeners and comic book readers of 1990s Irish film, that audience experiences its relation to Ireland and Irishness always already mediated. In film that mediation has occurred through the forms of globalized media corporations and those transposed from other, local cultural forms.

The genre achieved no great aesthetic or commercial achievement in 1990s Irish cinema, but it spawned a consummate antithesis, *The Butcher Boy*. "Melodrama is a dramatic narrative in which musical accompaniment marks the emotional effects": Jordan's film uses music to desensitize and generate ironic distance. History, in the form of the Cuban Missile Crisis, is global and fantastic, not local and realistic. The film returns too to the old dichotomy between the symbolic power and historical powerlessness of Irish motherhood. Jordan's casting of Sinead O'Connor, symbol of troubled modernity, as the apparitional Virgin Mary and animated model of the Colleen Bawn does more than parody. It posits a different relation to realism, heritage and history, drawing on magic realism, but also realizing in film both the gothic and poetic challenges to the constraints of realism definitive of the twentieth-century Irish novel. And it makes an image of a mobile Virgin a definitive, if ambiguous moment of Irish cinema. The adult Francie's reaction to the Virgin Mary's final apparition (dreading it) heralds a recurrence of his madness; it is emblematic of the critic's recoil from the cinematic recurrence of a nightmare Ireland of muck, misery and repression. That recoil has the energy of disavowal, the flip side of heritage film's fascination with the same territory. Both were symptomatic of the vortex of attraction and repulsion that characterized Celtic Tiger Ireland's relationship with its past.

3 Feminisms, Nationalisms, and Identities
Gender and Dissent

> She said, "They gave me of their best,
> They lived, they gave their lives for me;
> I tossed them to the howling waste,
> And flung them to the foaming sea."
> (Emily Lawless, "After Aughrim")

In 1998, in response to the Good Friday Agreement in Northern Ireland, the electorate of the Republic of Ireland voted in a referendum to relinquish its territorial claim on the whole island, previously enshrined in Articles 2 and 3 of the constitution. In effect this marked the end of the much commented on disjunction between law and reality in Ireland. That disjunction was both a result of a history of resistance to colonial law and of the post-independence southern state's institutionalization of aspiration rather than achievement as the condition of nationhood, most prominently in Articles 2 and 3. This sense of nationhood as a state yet to be achieved displaced dissent into the realms of metaphysics or designated it as alien, at odds with the Irish soul. When political violence in Northern Ireland began to threaten to destabilize the Republic, a gradual disengagement and occasional deconstruction of this version of the Irish nation moved from the intellectual margins to the "mainstream" understanding of history, in literature and in political institutions. For a long time, however, trading in "the exhausted fictions of the nation"[1] as poet Eavan Boland put it, was not an empty aesthetic exercise, but the form and content of political legitimation for the state. Modernist fiction made the disruption of that trade almost definitive of its relation to Ireland. The fact that the literature that could be assimilated to that legitimizing project became the central tradition of Irish poetry should not be surprising in the context of contemporary suspicion of the political motivation behind canon formation. Irish nationalism is not, at this stage, simply an insurgent or anti-imperialist nationalism. It has also been, since 1923, the dominant ideology of a state and the very disjunction between the idea of the state and the image of the nation was part of that state's defense mechanism against the consequences of partition. In an important essay in 1991, Clair Wills argued that "the motherland trope . . . in all its guises, is like a pin which connects sexual stereotyping with political and cultural domination of the Irish"[2]:

merely to assume the role and function of poet depends on a certain stance in relation to this trope of motherland. For the representation of the Irish land as a woman stolen, raped, possessed by the alien invader is not merely one mythic narrative among many but, in a literary context it is *the* myth . . . The trope functions not only as the means by which the poet can lament the loss of the land but also, through his linguistic embodiment of it, the means by which he may "repossess" it. The structure through which the poet obtains this mandate is complex, but its critical ingredient is an already poeticised (mythic) political discourse of the nation which enables the poet to act as spokesperson for his community—"public voice" of his mute and beleaguered "tribe."[3]

This understanding of the constriction of sexual and national identity that is a consequence of this trope has underpinned much feminist analysis of Irish's women writing in the interim. Its power to configure the role of the poet, in particular, has been a frequent object of analysis. More recently Moynagh Sullivan's work has illuminated the way in which this tradition has defined the grounds of intelligibility of Irish male writers, and the terms on which they are accorded canonical status. As Sullivan's work demonstrates, this is once again an Irish intensification of a more general tendency, this time in modernist poetics.

This chapter is primarily concerned with the relationship between gender and nation for women writing drama and fiction rather than poetry, but "*the* trope" figures prominently. As evidenced in the volume of entries in the Women in Modern Irish Culture Database and outlined in the Introduction to this book, the volume of writing by Irish women would indicate that the construction of the myth of the writer as spokesman for his tribe and the configuration of the canon in national and masculine terms were not in any way disabling for the *production* of work in a very diverse set of genres and media. Public awareness of the extent and quality of this writing was a relatively late development in Ireland, paradoxically stimulated by the furore over the very small number of works by women included in the *Field Day Anthology of Irish Writing*[4] in 1991. Eavan Boland had articulated the view of a generation of writers when she commented in 1989 that:

> Irish poetry was predominantly male. Here or there you found a small eloquence, like *After Aughrim* by Emily Lawless. Now and again, in discussion, you heard a woman's name. But the lived vocation, the craft witnessed by a human life—that was missing. And I missed it . . . The influence of absences should not be underestimated. Isolation itself can have a powerful effect in the life of a young writer.[5]

The difficulty of the woman writer in "looking back through her mothers" has been commented on by a succession of twentieth-century women writers, from Virginia Woolf to Alice Walker. These difficulties were compounded in the Irish case by the very overt role of the ideology of the nation in the construction of the canon. Again this is not unique: literary canons are consistently defined in national terms. Moreover, in Irish writing the role of modernist dissident from canons, nations and even gender formations was well established long before Boland wrote her essay. Despite this, Lawless's complex ironies, her possession of the voice of Mother Ireland in order to question the myth's endurance, by comparison with the dominant tradition, remain "small" things in the face of a tradition that still appeared monolithic at the end of the 1980s. Boland's assertion of the lack of female predecessors is all the more striking when one considers her role in Arlen House, still the only Irish publisher to have attempted to systematically republish full length work by women writers.[6] Admittedly, most of the writers reprinted were novelists, which may have indicated an unwillingness to challenge the poetic "tradition" or the influence of the foregrounding of the novel in feminist literary history elsewhere. It is striking that commenting in 2008, Marina Carr puts forward a similar perception of the dramatic tradition.[7] There is no shortage of literary foremothers for this generation of Irish women writers, but they offer a troubled genealogy. Partly this is because many of them are politically at odds with their successors. Lawless's relation with the national tradition is complicated, to say the least, by her staunch unionism. Many nationalist women writers participated wholeheartedly in the process Boland descried, whereby the nation turns its "losses to victories," "restates humiliations as triumphs"[8] and re-presents the myth of Mother Ireland. These writers, quite as much as those who are ironic or hostile toward nationalism, raise the problem of assuming either gender or nation to be constants for all (Irish) women across history. Mary Eva Kelly's "The Patriot Mother" violently and passionately affirms the mythos of Mother Ireland. The devouring mother demands and glories in the son's death and declaims:

> Dearer, far dearer, than ever to me,
> My darling you'll be on the brave gallows tree.[9]

This poem presents an extreme case of the relationship between first-generation feminism and the nation, both (inevitably in the context of nineteenth-century Ireland) defined in opposition to the state. Though identification with the nation is through a maternal figure, that identification offers participation in history and constitutes "the rejection . . . of the attributes traditionally considered feminine or maternal insofar as they are deemed incompatible with insertion in that history"[10]:

> oh, may the food from my bosom you drew
> In your veins turn to poison if you turn untrue.[11]

Mother Ireland as Lady Macbeth, the patriot mother unsexes herself in the same gesture as she becomes the mouthpiece of the nation. This woman's poem, in the very violence of its repudiation of a sentimental version of maternity, indicates both the intensity and ambivalence intrinsic to women's participation in national ideology. Despite the difficulties they encounter when attempting to stage their own historical agency or imagine themselves as citizens rather than symbols, nationalism obviously appeals to women. One reason for this may be identified in Benedict Anderson's commentary on the cult of the unknown soldier, where he links nationalism's concern with death and continuity to reproduction and to religion. "Nationalist imagining" in its concern with death "suggests a strong affinity with religious imagining":[12]

> Religious thought also responds to obscure intimations of immortality, generally by transforming fatality into continuity (karma, original sin, etc.). In this way it concerns itself with the links between the dead and the yet unborn, the mystery of re-generation. Who experiences their child's conception and birth without dimly apprehending a combined connectedness, fortuity and fatality in a language of "continuity"?[13]

Nationalism offers a public, historical significance to the domain of the private and familial, suturing the disjunction between those predominantly feminine spaces and public power. There are undoubted connections between religious and national imaginings of continuity and its imagining of the maternal, but while both speak (often) of death, birth is unspeakably abject. This economy that imagines continuity as a continuity of the dead is profoundly linked with the myth of the nation as Virgin Mother discussed in preceding chapters. The rest of this chapter looks at the attempts to stage women's role in the construction of the nation from within the nationalist imagination by Augusta Gregory and Maud Gonne; the haunting narrative of those who insist on being born beyond the borders of that imagination by Dorothy Macardle; and Kate O'Brien's vernacular modernist challenge to the continuity of the national-religious project.

THE IRONY OF SACRIFICE: GONNE, GREGORY AND ANTIGONE

As an instance of feminist thinking about women's ambivalent position in relation to nation and civil society, Luce Irigaray's critiques of Hegel's version of a gendered community of the nation indicates a fundamental shift in feminist analysis. In the 1974 essay, "The Eternal Irony of the Community" from her still influential *Speculum. De l'autre femme*, Irigaray maps the impossibility of women's position within the Hegelian community. *Sexes et parentés*, published in 1987, uses the same chapter of *The Phenomenology of Mind* to argue for "the necessity for sexuate rights."[14] Irigaray reverses the elision of state into nation. Despite Hegel's insistence that:

The ethical substance is . . . Absolute Spirit realized in the plurality of distinct consciousness definitely existing. It [this spirit] is the community . . . is spirit which is for itself, since it maintains itself by being reflected in the minds of the component individuals; and which is in itself or substance, since it preserves them within itself. Qua actual substance, that spirit is a Nation (Volk); qua concrete consciousness, it is the Citizens of the nation. This consciousness has its essential being in simple spirit, and is certain of itself in the actual realization of this spirit, in the entire nation; it has its truth there directly, not therefore in something unreal, but in a spirit which exists and makes itself felt.[15]

Irigaray makes no reference in either *Speculum* or *Sexes et parentés* to nationalism or nationality. She concentrates on the chapter in *The Phenomenology of Mind* on "The Ethical World: Law Human and Divine; Man and Woman." Hegel insists that mere sexual and kinship ties (to one's own wife/husband and children, for example) are not ethical, since they are not abstract. Hegel presents women's primary function in relation to the community and the nation, as well as to the individual men of her own family, not in terms of reproduction, but in terms of her role in giving meaning to death. Antigone is his implied role model. Because abstract and emptied of particularity, the dead are individual and universal in a way unavailable to the living:

The power which perpetrates on the conscious individual this wrong [death] of making him into a mere thing is "nature"; it is the universality not of the community, but the abstract universality of mere existence. . . . the consciousness of those who share the blood of the individual removes this wrong in such a way that what has happened becomes rather a work of their own doing, and hence bare existence . . . gets also to be something willed and thus an object of gratification.[16]

This rather problematically describes the plot of Augusta Gregory's *The Gaol Gate*, first performed in 1906. Gregory's short plays were bread-and-butter fare for the national theater she founded with Yeats and Synge. *The Gaol Gate* is in many ways paradigmatic of her best work; brilliantly brief, combining strong folkloric elements, fusing Christian and national symbolism with a real sense of tragedy. Interrogative irony is crucial to the play's structure. Two women, Mary Cahel and her daughter-in-law, Mary Cushin,[17] stand waiting outside the gaol gate at dawn. The son and husband respectively of the women, Denis Cahel, has been incarcerated within for some time and the two women have received a letter from the prison authorities. Neither can read and Mary Cahel has persuaded her daughter-in-law that it would be unwise to ask a literate neighbor for help, for the women fear Denis may have informed against the actual perpetrator of the agrarian outrage for which he is held. Instead they have walked through the night to the prison. When the gate is finally opened they find Denis was hanged the day before, refusing to implicate any of the actual participants in the crime. The play's structural irony depends on the exposition of the women's changing attitudes. Initially they dread the consequences for Denis and themselves if local rumor that he has turned informer prove true:

> MARY CAHEL. It is only among strangers, I am thinking, he could be hiding his story at all. It is best for him to go to America, where the people are as thick as grass.
> MARY CUSHIN. What way could he go to America and he having no means in his hand? There's himself and myself to make the voyage and the little one-een at home.
> MARY CAHEL. I would sooner to sell the holding than to ask the price paid for blood. There'll be money enough for the two of you to settle your debts and to go.
> MARY CUSHIN. And what would you yourself be doing and we to go over the sea? It is not among the neighbours you would wish to be ending your days.
> MARY CAHEL. I am thinking there is no one would know me in the workhouse at Ougherterard. I wonder could I go in there, and I not to give them my name?
> MARY CUSHIN. Ah, don't be talking foolishness. What way could I bring the child? Sure he's hardly out of the cradle; he'd be lost out there in the States.
> MARY CAHEL. I could bring him into the workhouse, I to give him some other name. You could send for him when you'd be settled or have some place of your own.[18]

At the prospect of such separation from her child, Mary Cushin changes the subject, "It is very cold at the dawn." This exchange between the two women makes abundantly clear how inappropriate theories of national community based on the identification of nation and state can be to insurgent nationalisms. Denis's (national) community demands of him complete refusal to participate in the institutions of the state. "Let the sergeant do his own business with no help from the neighbours at all," admonishes Mary Cahel when her more naive daughter-in-law argues there could be no harm in her husband naming names on the basis that "it's known to all the village it was Terry that fired the shot."[19] As the older woman knows well, the price of nonconformity is the loss of social existence. The best thing an informer can do is change his name and emigrate: the best his womenfolk can do is to lose his name in the anonymity of the workhouse or America. That telling the "truth" to save himself would make Denis very much less than a man is made clear when his mother assumes the exigencies of survival will require her to take and rename his son. The role of head of the family reverts to her and in that role she will deploy all of what McLouglin calls the "survival strategies" characteristic of the resilient pauper.[20]

Both women's tones and preoccupations change when the dawn brings the gatekeeper and news that Denis is actually dead, "Dead since the dawn of yesterday, and another man now in his cell" (359). Assuming he has died of the "great cold and a cough" (359) he had the night he was taken, his mother thinks his death a release for him. "There is lasting kindness in Heaven when no kindness is found upon earth. There will surely be mercy found for him, and not the hard judgement of men!" (359–60). The introduction of this religious dimension and the accumulation of dawn references and imagery prepare for the fusion of Christian and national symbolism in Denis's final transformation into hero. Meanwhile, his wife joins his mother in "keening" or lamenting him. The lament (*caoineadh*)[21] features prominently in *The Gaol Gate* and *Dawn*. By the end of the nineteenth century this was a collective, female, oral art, integral to women's function as professional mourners at wakes and funerals.[22]

The illiterate women in *The Gaol Gate* are faced, on the one hand, with an institutional power that sends a letter to tell them it intends to kill their son/husband and, on the other, with a community that they cannot trust to mediate for them with such power. "Myself and this woman have no learning. We were loth to trust any other one" (7). Their laments transform that linguistic impotence into narrative authority. The first lament for Denis Cahel is by his wife, still in ignorance of the full circumstances of his death. Particular to her own grief, it also makes clear the role played by the social necessities of survival in these women's concern for the manner of their man's dying and the good name he leaves after him. It is worth quoting in full:

MARY CUSHIN. (*Who has sunk on to the step before the door, rocking herself and keening.*) Oh, Denis, my heart is broken you to have died with the hard word upon you! My grief you to be alone now that spent so many nights in company! What way will I be going back through Gort and through Kilbecanty? The people will not be coming out keening you, they will say no prayer for the rest of your soul! What way will I be the Sunday and I going up the hill to the Mass? Every woman with her own comrade, and Mary Cushin to be walking her lone! What way will I be the Monday and the neighbours turning their heads from the house? The turf Denis cut lying on the bog, and no well-wisher to bring it to the hearth! What way will I be in the night time, and none but the dog calling after you? Two women to be mixing a cake, and not a man in the house to break it! What way will I sow the field, and no man to drive the furrow? The sheaf to be scattered before springtime that was brought together at the harvest. I would not begrudge you, Denis, and you leaving praises after you. The neighbours keening along with me would be better to me than an estate. But my grief your name to be

blackened in the time of the blackening of the rushes! Your name
never to rise up again in the growing time of the year! (360)

Denis has died twice, physically and socially, and his wife must sustain
the physical loss without the social support that would make it bearable.
A veritable Polynices, unmourned, unceremoniously buried in the prison
yard with "not one of his own there to follow after him at all" (361),
this is the nadir of Denis Cahel's reputation in the play. From this point,
however, it is revived, for the information that he has received a prison
burial brings the final revelation that he was indeed hanged and that those
neighbors guilty of the crime arrested with him were freed. At this point,
as McDiarmid and Waters point out, "the two Marys of Galway inscribe
the death of the male victim with meaning."[23] Mary Cahel's triumphant
lament for her son on hearing this news integrates the women at last
into the linguistic community and transforms poor chesty harmless Denis
("my poor Denis never handled a gun in his life" [357]) into Christ and
Cuchulainn in one:

> Are there any people in the streets at all till I call on them to come
> hither? Did they ever hear in Galway such a thing to be done, a man to
> die for his neighbour?
>   Tell it out in the streets for the people to hear, Denis Cahel from
> Slieve Echtge is dead. It was Denis Cahel from Daire-caol that died in
> the place of his neighbour!
>   It is he was young and comely and strong, the best reaper and the
> best hurler. It was not a little thing for him to die, and he protecting his
> neighbour. (361–62)

The anonymous embarrassment is transformed into proud patriarch:

> Gather up, Mary Cushin, the clothes for your child; they'll be wanted
> by this one and that one. The boys crossing the sea in the springtime
> will be craving a thread for a memory. (362)

The lament tradition allowed ample scope for the airing of grievances
against the living in the context of praise for the dead. Mary Cahel's alienation from the opposing forces of state and national community resurface
in telling the tale that signifies a triumph over the maligning neighbors in
the course of claiming from them what is now again due to her and hers.
The worthlessness of those he has saved merely embellishes the grandeur
of his gesture:

> Pat Ruane was no good friend to him at all, but a foolish, wild compan-
> ion; it was Terry Fury knocked a gap in the wall and sent in the calves
> to our meadow.

Denis would not speak, he shut his mouth, he would never be an informer. It is no lies he would have said at all giving witness against Terry Fury. (362)

As the nature of his sacrifice is expounded, his mother expands its significance from neighborhood to region to nation:

> I will go through Gort and Kilbecanty and Druimdarod and Daroda; I will call to the people and the singers at the fairs to make a great praise for Denis!
> The child he left in the house that is shook, it is great will be his boast in his father! All Ireland will have a welcome before him, and all the people in Boston.
> I to stoop on a stick through half a hundred years, I will never be tired with praising, come hither, Mary Cushin, till we'll shout it through the roads, Denis Cahel died for his neighbour. (362)

The intoxicating mix of Christian symbolism with national tradition is enough to transform the grief of these two waiting Marys outside the gaol/tomb into exultant harbingers of national resurrection. While the Hegelian woman's function in relation to the nation and the dead is conscious it is also deeply impersonal. The first "false" lament for Denis as failure by his wife is far more personal than his mother's final lament for an abstract idea of a hero:

> The woman takes this dead being into her own place on his return into the self—a being that is universal, admittedly, but also singularly drained of strength, empty and yielded passively up to others.[24]

It is his "name" that is immortalized, but they are the linguistic and narrative community in which it lives and for whom it is "better . . . than an estate" (360). His reputation will be the capital from which they can derive the communal credit necessary for their survival. These then are pragmatic Antigones. The mediating function they fulfill between their man and death is, moreover, itself mediated. Gregory was an enthusiastic folklorist, but she was precisely that. Class, education and a highly developed cultural and political agenda interpose between her and these women she figures as the national community. Her transposition of the characteristic forms and tropes of the lament from the oral traditions of Galway to the Abbey Theatre *stages* the production of the "spirit which exists and makes itself felt" as the nation. That transposition effects an ironic interrogation of the process. For those whose bread and turf were not at stake in the realization of national spirit, Mary Cahel's combination of shrewdness, self-interest and linguistic adaptability might have seemed closer to the new nation of strong farmers, publicans and petit bourgeois poised on the verge of self-invention in 1906 than to an unchanging, peasant essence of Irishness. Gifted propagandist of heroism, the old woman is also close enough to the project that Gregory set herself in her Abbey plays to be read as an ambivalent author surrogate.

AN IRONIC DAWN

The irony of all this is that, in the end, it is Antigone who makes the sacrifice and is sacrificed, for unlike the man she buried, she has no possibility of rebirth. No one will perform the rites of passage for her, her relation with death is unmediated and her sacrifice of her self has meaning only because it is undertaken for another. It is private, not public:

> Hegel affirms that the brother is for the sister that possibility of recognition of which she is deprived as mother and wife, but does not state that the situation is reciprocal. This means that the brother has already been invested with a value for the sister that she cannot offer in return, except by dedicating herself to his cult after death.[25]

Maud Gonne's *Dawn* attempts to exceed this logic. The public and social sacrifice is made by a woman for a motherland that is, by kinship and blood, her own mother. She remains faithful when the sons desert. Brideen's nationalist resistance in *Dawn* is close to Irigaray's paradigm for feminist resistance:

> In these analyses of the family in relation to the state, Hegel explains that the daughter who remains faithful to the law relating to her mother must be excluded from the city, from society. She cannot be put to death by violence, but she must be put in prison, deprived of liberty, air, light, love, marriage, children . . . condemned to a slow and solitary death. The figure of this daughter is represented by Antigone.[26]

However, at the end Brideen's sacrifice is the means by which men are brought back to fidelity to motherland and to the revolutionary dawn. As Antoinette Quinn has pointed out, "disappointingly, in a play written for the Daughters of Erin,[27] it genders political activism as masculine."[28] Brideen, the faithful daughter, starves for Ireland. Her death shames the men into the proper exercise of their masculine role on behalf of the mother she loves more than they do. The play's curious tone, valorizing the dawn of resistance and yet unrelentingly dark in its substance, owes much to its roots in Gonne's firsthand experience of famine conditions as a relief worker in Mayo. Interestingly, for a woman whose capacity for self-dramatization became legendary, Gonne evacuates the role of middle-class activists and fund-raisers such as herself from the play, which "instead empowers the peasants themselves."[29] Herself a skilled propagandist, speaker and writer for the nationalist cause, Gonne nonetheless represents the daughter's fight for Mother Ireland as primarily a matter of bodily endurance.[30] While *Dawn* precedes the widespread use of the political hunger strike, it is impossible now to read its conversion of Brideen's victimization by famine to defiant choice of hunger and death before submission without reference to that tradition:

> hunger-strikers must persuade the people they fast against to take responsibility for their starvation . . . they force their antagonists to recognize that they are implicated in the hunger of their fellow beings. At the same time, though, the strikers turn their rage against their enemies upon themselves and immolate themselves in effigy. Their suicide is murder by proxy.[31]

Rewriting the Mayo famine of 1898 as political rebirth in the new century, *Dawn* both deploys and exceeds the strategy of the hunger strike. It is, after all, a text—the suffering bodies are remembered and represented, not actual. If Brideen is an Irish Antigone, she leads rather than follows her brother and husband into death, substituting her death for the sacrifice her brother and husband have failed to offer the mother.

> SEUMAS. (*rising*) Mother, forgive me for Brideen's sake. Let me, too, die for you. Dead Brideen shows me what I have to do. I have vengeance to take on the Stranger, for her, for Patrick, for my father, and I have vengeance, Mother, to take for all that you have suffered. (84)

The limitations of this are apparent in the play itself. The men promise, "By dead Brideen, we swear we will make Bride of the Sorrows Bride of the Victories" (84). Too late to save his sister, Seumas offers his mother the curious recompense of his own death also. Indeed, the revolution at hand is imagined not as a new life, but as solidarity with the dead, "The dead are speaking to us" (84). This is, of course, a classic Hegelian version of the nation as graveyard. As such the political significance of the faithful daughter's death collapses into familial pathos: "Being as she is, she does not achieve the enunciatory process of the discourse of History but remains its servant, deprived of self."[32] *Dawn* figures the nation's perpetuity in terms of its dead men. "She is with her father and Patrick in the dawn." Bride's lament for her daughter is rhetorical and stagey by comparison with the folk authenticity that Gregory can bring to the form:

> (*Child gathers branches of apple blossoms and Bride puts them in the dead woman's hand. Bride sings.*)
> It is dark the land is, and it's dark my heart is,
> But the red sun rises, when the hour-heart is come,

> O the red sun rises, and the dead rise, I can see them,
> And it's glad they are and proud.
> White Oscar is with them and my own boy,
> And Con who won the battles, and the lads who lost,
> They have bright swords with them that clash the battle welcome,
> A welcome to the red sun that rises with our luck. (82)

This bloodied sun rises on a repetition of the nation's past glories and the inglorious specter of deprivation is banished. Gonne's Antigone, then, "is the privileged place in which red blood and its semblance harmoniously (con)fuse with each other, though she herself has no rights to benefit from the process."[33]

Dawn indicates that in transitional periods women do not simply embody the nation, but articulate, activate and are agents of it. Gonne's later history indicates the dangers of that participation: assimilated to a myth, her substance emptied out to signify postcolonial disappointment and the rapid repudiation of the forces unleashed in the violence of the state's origins. Pat Murphy's film *Anne Devlin* offers a more recent exploration of this logic. Initially a traditional figure, Anne is first introduced in a visually striking sequence leading a group of women to retrieve and rebury the body of an executed rebel. Thereafter, however, she moves out of the traditional and familial context in which her political affiliations have developed to a chosen, self-defined activism. Her incarceration in Kilmainham gaol identifies her very closely with Antigone. She initially marks the passing of her time in prison by her menstrual cycle, but the dark and isolated confinement claustrophobically rendered within the film eventually suspends even that. Anne is not bloodily executed with the men she tries to protect by her silence, but "put in prison, deprived of liberty, air, light, love, marriage, children . . . condemned to a slow and solitary death."[34] Silence rather than action define her agency in history, though the complexity and nature of her own political commitment is much more fully realized than that of Brideen.[35] The film ends with a voice-over explanation of her eventual isolation and erasure from historical record as anything more than a loyal servant. Nationalism historically mobilizes women to attain a state, the nationalist origins of which predispose it to exercise power as power over, particularly, women.

FEMINISM AND NATIONALISM IN A NEW STATE

In 1924 a young woman called Dorothy Macardle published a collection of short stories she had written in prison, entitled *Earthbound*. Arrested from her classroom in a Dublin school for young ladies, Macardle was initially imprisoned for her activities in the War of Independence, after the treaty as a republican prisoner. Dismissed from her position as history teacher for her political activities, Macardle was to become a highly effective propagandist for the republican side in the Civil War and later for the Fianna Fáil party. She was publicly very closely associated with Eamon de Valera, but was seriously alienated by the antifeminist measures he enshrined in the 1937 constitution. "As the Constitution stands, I do not see how anyone holding advance views on the rights of women can support it . . . it is a tragic dilemma for those who have been loyal and ardent workers in the national cause."[36] A measure of her political significance and of her disillusion was given in Tim Pat Coogan's biography of de Valera: "For her to take issue with de Valera was akin to one of the four Gospel authors falling out with Christ."[37] Macardle's friends and associates at various stages included Gonne and a number of former suffrage activists, such as Rosamund Jacob and Hannah Sheehy-Skeffington. Like them she was a middle-class intellectual who had broken with the conventions of her class and gender in support of the nationalist cause.

Her stories in *Earthbound* are redolent of the desperation and bravado of the time. Their aim is frankly propagandist, the pages tedious with national heroics and dead heroes. One story, however, stands out. Read from a contemporary perspective, "The Portrait of Roisin Dhu" anticipates the feminist critique of Irish cultural nationalism by commentators such as Eavan Boland and Edna Longley.[38] An Irish rendering of a classic gothic tale, Macardle's story concerns a gifted artist, Hugo Blake, who persuades Nuala, a young countrywoman, to sit as his model for Roisin Dhu, i.e., Ireland. Described by the female narrator as "passionate, lonely,"[39] Blake, orphaned early, has substituted national for familial ties in a paradigmatic Oedipal displacement, "the anguish of pity and love he had had for his mother he gave to her country when he came home" (92). "The Portrait of Roisin Dhu," written while Macardle was in gaol, anticipates the feminist critique of nationalist mythologizing that would not be publicly aired until the 1980s. A young peasant woman models as Roisin Dhu for an obsessed artist and her life ebbs from her into his picture. She dies as it is completed. In order to become the image of Ireland, the individual woman is drained of life. The story plays the gothic scenario of Poe's "Oval Portrait" against the Irish nationalist tradition of figuring Ireland as a woman. In Poe's story an artist paints his beloved wife, oblivious to the life draining from her. At the point when his portrait is concluded, the woman dies. "The Portrait of Roisin Dhu" tells the same story: Blake is described as a "vampire" (93), stealing the soul from the landscapes he habitually paints. Nuala's brothers warn her, "'Tis not good to be put in a picture, it takes from you" (95). The time and place of its writing and the history of the Roisin Dhu image change, focus and specify Poe's story's meaning. Blake misquotes Mangan's "Dark Rosaleen":

> I could plough the blue air!
>   I could climb the high hills!
> O, I could kneel all night in prayer
> To heal your many ills! (97)[40]

Mangan's poem fuses the erotic and national as Blake and his painting fail to do:

> The Erne . . . at its highest flood.
> I dashed across unseen.
> For there was lightening in my blood,
> My Dark Rosaleen!
> My own Rosaleen!
> Oh! There was lightening in my blood,
> Red lightening lightened through my blood,
> My Dark Rosaleen![41]

The ambiguity is deliberate. Mangan and the cultural nationalist movement initiated and epitomized by *The Nation* newspaper in which the poem first appeared in 1846 strategically wed national and romantic sentiment. That fusion was both political cover and an inheritance from the Gaelic "Aisling" poets translated, imitated and transposed in *The Nation* into the forms of print capitalism. By contrast Blake's passion for his subject is ethereal: "No woman in the world, we said, had been Hugo's Roisin Dhu; no mortal face had troubled him when he painted that immortal dream— that ecstasy beyond fear, that splendour beyond anguish—that wild, sweet holiness of Ireland for which men die" (91). In Mangan's poem it is the lover of Dark Rosaleen who fades away. She herself is promised "health, and help, and hope" (all of this needs to be put in the context of the date of publication, the second year of the Great Famine). Like those who appreciate Blake's Roisin Dhu, the poet can see only one inevitable consummation for this love:

> O! The Erne shall run red
> With redundance of blood,
> The earth shall rock beneath our tread,
> And flames wrap hill and wood,
> And gun-peal, and slogan cry,
> Wake many a glen serene,
> Ere you shall fade, ere you shall die,
> My Dark Rosaleen!
> My own Rosaleen!
> The Judgement Hour must first be nigh,
> Ere you can fade, ere you can die,
> My Dark Rosaleen![42]

The point of "The Portrait of Roisin Dhu" is, of course, that the particular and individual woman, the particularity and individuality of women, is sacrificed to feed the timeless symbol. The impression of timelessness is absolutely necessary to the postulation of national identity as an immortal dream and to the production of an ecstasy beyond fear that induces men to die for nations. And timelessness and immortality can only be figured in that which has lost its history, its mortality, its self, and become pure representation. The story of Nuala's transformation into Roisin Dhu is almost a case study in mythmaking, emptying the signifier of history and singularity to embody the force of myth.

Macardle's story also cited a contemporary poet's work, one whose representative license must have affected her closely as a friend and associate of Gonne. Looking at Nuala, the narrator thinks: "'Those red lips with all their mournful pride' . . . Poems of Yeats were haunting me while I looked at her. But it was the beauty of one asleep, unaware of life or of sorrow or of love . . . the face of a woman whose light is hidden" (94). This Yeats quote in "The Portrait of Roisin Dhu" is from "The Rose of the World" from *The Rose*.[43] Gonne called this collection "wild and fascinatingly Irish"[44]: its relation to the Roisin Dhu or dark little rose of national sentiment is obvious, direct and so overdetermined and complicated by occultism and theosophy that it becomes something else. Like Mangan's poem, Yeats's "rose" is an object of romantic love as well as a national symbol. But in this case the rose is not any woman or everywoman, but a very particular woman, Maud Gonne, and a woman who deliberately cultivated the role. Gonne played Ireland, quite literally as Cathleen ni Houlihan in Yeats's play of that name, in 1902. Yeats was famously to worry, "did that play of mine send out / Certain men the English shot?"[45] Gonne's performance is still given some of the credit/blame.[46] Margaret Ward has persuasively argued that the views of women disenchanted with the new Ireland of the 1920s were stereotyped as hysterical and dismissed accordingly.[47] In order to take them seriously, however, one must do more than praise them simply for being public, active and political. The women who achieved prominence in Irish nationalism between 1900 and 1922 were predominantly though not exclusively middle-class intellectuals. Gonne, Milligan, Carberry, Markievicz, Sheehy-Skeffington and Jacob had varying views on and involvement in military action, but all are best remembered as propagandists and political activists: some initially in the suffrage and anti-conscription movements, all at a crucial period in the struggle for independence. Revolutionary epochs create breaches in the confining walls of gender, class and family: post-revolution the walls go back up again. These women did not simply reject the settlement of 1922. Many were involved in the women's peace committee's attempt to broker a truce between the opposing sides at the outbreak of the Civil War and it says much for their standing at the time that their delegation was received by both sides. They fared badly in the transition from state breaking to state making. Opposing a government bill to restrict women's access to civil service positions, Jenny Wyse-Power expressed frustration that: "No men in a fight for freedom ever had such loyal co-operation from their women as the men who compose the present Executive Council . . .

and these are the people who tell us that we are physically unfit."[48] It is indicative that these measures were introduced within a week of the treaty debates, so pressing was the issue of women's employment felt to be. Interestingly, Yeats and Oliver St. John Gogarty supported Wyse-Power against the government. Yeats in particular seems to have been surprised by the nature of the debate, but much impressed by the force of Wyse-Power's accusations.[49] The victory in the Senate of the opposition to the bill was surprising and untypical. The rhetoric of equality and entitlement had little long-term impact in an insecure emergent state seeking stability and respectability with all the fervor it had once devoted to liberation.

Macardle identified herself with that new state and remained in the political mainstream, unlike her increasingly marginalized contemporaries and associates, Gonne, Sheehy-Skeffington and Jacob, who became associated with single issues, particularly prisoners' rights. She continued to write popular gothic fiction and ghost stories as well as the mainstream historical and propagandist work for which she is remembered. Her fiction increasingly became a field of critical displacement for her unease with the state she helped form. Her dual role, as legitimizing historian and questioning storyteller, epitomized the "tragic dilemma for those who have been loyal and ardent workers in the national cause"[50] she shared with many political women of her generation. Intriguingly, *Fantastic Summer*[51] concerns an Italian gypsy woman who had fought as one of the local partisans but becomes demonized thereafter, feared for those very qualities that were admirable in wartime. So alienated does this woman become that eventually she takes on the role and power of a witch that the community's fear has created for her. The parallels with Ireland are complex, as were women's negotiations, accommodations and dissidence within the new regime. The hidden nature of Macardle's criticism of Irish society indicates a considerable degree of awareness and dissatisfaction with the restraints that the new nation-state put upon women. It also indicates that those restraints worked and that they did so both internally and externally. The nature and consequence of the repression consequent upon this restraint is played out frighteningly in Macardle's most popular novel, the appropriately named *Uneasy Freehold*.[52]

UNEASY FREEHOLD: MACARDLE'S REPUBLIC

If the Virgin Mary, Queen of Ireland, constituted the official version of Irish identity, this shining myth cast some strange shadows. The dichotomy between the public ideology of the state and the private costs paid for its maintenance are illuminated through the dichotomy in Macardle's work. The tension between Macardle's gothic writing and her other role as legitimizing historian of the southern Irish state and author of *The Irish*

Republic might be considered a case study in the return of the repressed. The former registers an unease with the latter that could not voice itself as public dissent. I want to develop these themes in a reading of the gothic fiction, specifically Macardle's 1924 short story "The Portrait of Roisin Dhu" and 1944 novel, *Uneasy Freehold* (published in the US as *The Uninvited*). In both of these texts a female presence is dematerialized but haunts both national culture and domestic security. The gothic becomes an arena where the reservations that Macardle held about the state she helped form and her own uneasy freehold within it could be explored. It is worth noting that where Macardle sought to express public and political dissent she did not merely have to contend with her own sense of loyalty to Ireland or Fianna Fáil. For example, her letter to the *Irish Press* protesting against the 1937 constitution (specifically its enshrinement of the primacy of women's "duties in the home" over employment or public duty) was not published by the paper for which she was a long-term reviewer.

Macardle remains best remembered for *The Irish Republic*,[53] which was published with an approving preface by de Valera in 1937, the same year as her letter protesting against de Valera's constitution was suppressed by the *Irish Press*. Macardle's own foreword to her history gives a fascinating insight into the Fianna Fáil view of the history of the period beginning Easter Monday 1916 and ending with "the Republican defeat seven years later":

> Whether the Irish Republic ever existed has been disputed not only by jurists and not only with words. For the Irish people the Republic was, for a few tense years, a living reality which dominated every aspect of their lives. Its existence was a fact of human history, if not of logic or law ... Its existence was of a kind very baffling to its enemies for the Republic was an invisible within a visible, an intangible within the tangible State.[54]

These opening remarks illuminate not just Macardle's historiographical project, but a very particular view of the idea of an Irish republic to which she and others of her generation held. The republic as aspiration, as a goal fought for in the period 1916–1922, had for Macardle an existence that baffled the logic and law of the British Empire, but that had also failed to be realized in the compromises, laws and implicitly even the new constitution that her own party promulgated. Her republic is the ghost of what might have been and Macardle's preface sheds some light on the somewhat laissez-faire attitude to state and law, including the concept of law as aspiration not regulation, that are sometimes attributed to twentieth-century Irish political culture. It is important not to romanticize this attitude, which eventually fueled amendments to the constitution prohibiting abortion while protecting the right to travel to where abortion was available, for example, and on the other hand facilitated the casual incarceration of individuals for minor social and sexual as well as political deviations from the norm for prolonged periods in the history of the southern state. The inmates of Magdalene laundries might have benefited enormously from a situation where the letter of the law held greater sway over the spirit of the nation.

Macardle's republic is a ghost, haunting the disappointed thirties. The state and society that she inhabited is itself, moreover, derealized in her formulation. Actuality is the pale shadow of a lost ideal. Parallel to this haunted history, Macardle also wrote in popular narrative form. In Macardle's gothic fiction the metaphors of haunting and derealization are rendered in narrative terms that are tremendously telling about what the Ireland of the 1940s knew and simultaneously refused to know about itself. Specifically I want to look at the way in which female bodies in this gothic fiction are fed upon by myth and how they are derealized until they become no more than a scent, a presence, a specter on the edge of consciousness, which renders the holding of home, land, cultural or political authority uneasy. In *Uneasy Freehold*, Roddy and Pamela Fitzgerald, brother and sister, take up residence in Cliff End in Devon, a house with a reputation for sinister disturbances that has been empty for six years. They haven't much money. London has not helped Pamela in particular to recover from the death of her father and the six years she spent nursing him. Roddy is described by his sister as "Bloomsburied" (31) and has a mildly broken heart after an entanglement with a rather heartless modern young woman. He is writing a history of British censorship with a view to contesting that censorship, but the book has stalled and he wants to get away from what he calls "snackbar writing" for magazines. The brother and sister are hungry for a sense of home. Pamela says, "think of it! To own soil and rocks and trees and a beach" (21) and Roddy looks forward to being "looked after again by Lizzie," a housekeeper who retains the aura of nanny and comes to Cliff End with them. On their arrival at what they intend to be a rural retreat, an immediate antagonism arises between Pamela and their landlord, Commander Brooke, which quickly develops on national lines that identify the Fitzgeralds with Ireland, Brooke with the most xenophobic element of the English gentry:

> "Is there a Celtic strain in North Devon," [Pamela] asked, "You would expect it, wouldn't you, here, between Cornwall and Wales?"
> "None!" [Brooke] replied rather sharply. "The Welsh are an entirely difference race." And an inferior one, his tone conveyed. (16)

Pamela is very proud to be named after the wife of the rebel Lord Edward Fitzgerald: Brooke's military rank reinforces his status as the opposite of Pamela's Irish rebel heritage. Telling the story of the original Pamela Fitzgerald to Commander Brooke and his granddaughter, Stella Meredith, Pamela comments, "I don't know any story more full of heroism and romance" (16). "I am afraid," the Commander answers stiffly, "that I am not well acquainted with Irish rebel history." Stella left Cliff End at the age of three, when her mother died, and hasn't been back since. She is delighted and startled by Pamela's remark that we should not be afraid of ghosts, they are simply spirits returned again to the place they love, but Commander Brooke is much angered by it. "'Really,' thought Roddy, 'I felt Pamela had not been fortunate in her choice of topics; Welshmen, ghosts and rebels did not appear to be among the old man's favourite themes'" (17). The novel's peculiar invocation of Irishness is typified by Roddy's description of the Irish housekeeper's Irish stew "hot, meaty, redolent of good flavours; but not for July" (28). This novel begins at least as a novel of summer awakening and it is as if Ireland is somehow at odds with that story. Yet Pamela's tale of her illustrious namesake foreshadows the ghost story that the novel becomes.

Initially Commander Brooke is comically stage-English, the kind of wildly prejudiced elderly male relative who bothers the heroines in the work of Jessica Mitford. Pamela, however, sees a much darker figure of patriarchal power in the old man. She observes that Stella "is not permitted to grow up" (17). "'It is hateful,' she said, 'to think of that child—losing such a mother; left to grow up with a heart-broken old man. I wonder whether she knows what happiness is'" (40). The lunch party Pamela and Roddy host for Brooke and Stella completely disintegrates when the latter starts nervously twisting her handkerchief and releases a strong flowery scent from it, which she calls "my scent" and of which the old man intensely disapproves (17). In a parallel to her own flowering again after her father's death, Pamela diagnoses Stella's "stunting" by her grandfather who is "good to her in his way" but represses any sign he thinks he sees of her father's irresponsible Welsh strain breaking out in her (22). The image of Stella as a flower recurs in the novel and is linked with this idea of underdevelopment. Rodney calls Stella a "strange child" (though we are told she is seventeen or eighteen) and remarks, "she made me think of a narcissus just breaking out of its sheath" (22). From the start, the house from which this strange flower has sprung has a haunting presence. When Roddy sits up writing a review of de la Mare's stories he is struck by the sense of an invisible presence inhabiting and bringing life to it: "The curious, living stillness, with a tremor of the invisible vibrating in it, that de la Mare creates in his stories, possessed the place; the sound from the sea was no more than the breathing of nature in her sleep; my lighted room floated alone in space" (22).

Macardle's preface to *The Irish Republic* indicates a preference for the ineffable, a sense that the invisible is somehow more real than the surface of things. In *Uneasy Freehold*, however, this sense of a presence beyond the ordinary becomes very gradually menacing. The atmosphere of the house is uncanny in the purest Freudian sense, "that class of the frightening which leads back to what is known of old and long familiar."[55] On her first visit to the house as an adult, Stella remarks, "It is very curious for me. . . . because I didn't think of it really as a house, as a live house, I mean, that people would eat in; I thought it was only a memory; a memory, and stone walls" (51). The novel invites a psychoanalytic and even psychotherapeutic reading. "We talked about dreams," Roddy recalls, "and I found myself propounding with more explicitness than I had achieved before, the theory that dreams are an abstraction of a repressed conflict, disguised in symbols borrowed from the happenings of the day" (52). The dream that is her only memory of the house allows Stella to recover from her childhood trauma. She dreams of her mother, Mary, turning out the light in her room. "'Please remember next time you dream that,' Pamela said firmly, 'that I am coming to light it again.'" Freud's reading of ghost stories led him to the conclusion that the ubiquitous haunted houses of these tales are the uncanny replicas of the mother's body—our dark, frightening, desirable, first home. If this is so, then Stella's return to and exorcism of Cliff End constitutes a successful therapy. She comes to occupy for herself the place of womanhood. Roddy asks his friend Judith, "how would you deal with these miseries out of the past?" Her answer is, "Simply by living in the house as you are living in it." Roddy concludes, "it would be strange if the vigour and content of the living could not banish the lingering sorrows of the dead" (87).

This psychoanalytic reading of the novel in terms of acknowledging buried trauma and recovering though understanding and loving support needs to be understood in the context of two other interpretative frameworks established in the novel. The first and initially the strongest is a critique of colonialism, with Stella as the victim of dispossession and oppression by Commander Brooke and his daughter Mary, who adopted her husband's illegitimate child, Stella, and took her from her natural mother. According to her grandfather, the trouble with Stella is that, "She is her father's daughter. She remembers him, that is the trouble. She resembles him physically. The influence of that strain in her is so potent that it has been my life's aim to break it down" (175). If a strain of Welsh artistry can get this reaction, what then are the implications of the darkness and strangeness attributed to Stella's Spanish mother? Stella's natural parentage makes her a subjugated native in her grandfather's home. The uncanny reversal where Roddy understands that he, not the ghosts, is an alien intruder supports this reading of the novel of as a critique of colonial attitudes:

> I was uneasy because I was eavesdropping there. It was an intrusion; this house was old; long before we were born it had its occupants, living and dying here. We were aliens and trespassers in their hereditary home. Now, I knew they were in possession of the house once more, their timelessness closing over our intrusion as water over a stone. (82)

Reversal and projection are, of course, cornerstones of gothic narrative. In particular, events and situations that cannot be acknowledged as part of one's own culture and society are often projected outward. So the sexual, social and political anxieties of the late eighteenth-century English household were safely projected onto medieval French and Italian castles during the first wave of popular gothic fiction. Similarly Sheridan Le Fanu's *Uncle Silas* is free to explore the paranoia and isolation of the beleaguered Anglo-Irish Big House by setting its story entirely in England. It is this specific device of Anglo-Irish gothic that Macardle also employs and that indicates a third way of reading *Uneasy Freehold*. The novel projects onto its cliff end between Cornwall and Wales that which cannot be acknowledged as an aspect of the uneasily and recently free state of Ireland. For if Commander Brooke is an icon of Englishness, the imagery surrounding his (un)dead daughter, Mary, invokes a very different mythology. Commander Brooke speaks of his daughter's "unstained, saintly spirit": "Mary was rock-crystal; as clear as spring-water; she never lied to me in her life" (174). So spiritual she is transparent, Mary is the prototypic good white woman. Lizzie, the Irish Catholic housekeeper, identifies her ghost as a terribly uncanny likeness of this feminine ideal: "All in white, she was, with long fair hair" (174). This is a horrific perfection: "Blue her eyes were, and terrible, as if she was looking down into Hell" (92). Roddy remarks, "it is too like the conventional apparition" (92), but the fair-haired, blue-eyed woman dressed in white is not a conventional figure of evil, but of spirituality and chastity. The local Irish Catholic priest unwittingly confirms that Mary's ghost is a version of the Virgin Mother after whom she is named as he protests this woman's only failing was to be too good for this world.[56] Asked by Roddy and Pamela why Mary allowed her husband's mistress to accompany and visit them, he attributes it to her "great magnanimity" and lack of "worldly wisdom" (97). When asked by Pamela if the ghost could be Mary, "The priest looked shocked. 'My daughter, Mary Meredith was not a heroine of melodrama. Mary was almost a saint'" (99).

While Mary is no heroine, she is a figure in the melodrama of Macardle's novel. Her purity and goodness are associated with a paralyzing cold. It is almost impossible to light a good fire in the studio, the room where her spirit is strongest (59). Lizzie describes how her look "went through me like a blast of ice" (92). As in "The Portrait of Roisin Dhu," to be the embodiment of an ideal is deathly. When Stella has almost been lured to her death by the spirit of Mary Meredith, Roddy thinks, "Oblivious of me, of her own life, of all human needs and impulses, she had given herself to this myth" (160).

In sharp contrast to the imagery surrounding Stella's social and legal mother, her natural mother, Carmel, is associated with darkness, the body and warmth. "Carmel's treasures" (190) are gaudy, fragile, "the insignia of a Spanish dancer" (191). Her "hair and eyes were dark" (191). The initial reaction of Pamela to the possibility that it is Carmel who is haunting the place and not Mary is "if it is Carmel who is haunting, I don't think I want to stay; I think I'm afraid" (186). The novel dismantles the horror genre conventions and social expectations that inform that sense of dread. His first glimpse of Meredith's first painting of Carmel leaves Roddy "stupe-fied": "this could not be Carmel! Even in early girlhood, Carmel would not have been like this; she would have had a dark, hard, audacious face" (197). This first picture is called "Dawn." Meredith's second painting of Carmel is called "The Artist's Model" and shows the same image, with, turning away from it "the same face and it had not aged; it was young still, but gaunt, haggard and hungry" (198). Gradually Roddy and Pamela realize the enor-mity of what has been done to Carmel by the artist and his saintly wife:

> "He painted that when she was sick in his house," Pamela's voice was appalled. . . . "He watched her face when she looked at it. He probably finished it with the help of what he saw then—finished it while she was dying."
> "And exhibited it," [Roddy] added, "when she was dead." (198)

If this is Stella's wild Celtic heritage it is just as destructive as the repressions of Brooke and Mary. Meredith continues to exist only through his paintings, however: it is the two women in his life whose presences cling to Cliff End. They remain not because of jealousy over their shared man, but to continue their battle for their shared daughter, Stella. The stern governess whom Mary put in charge of Stella's education, Miss Holloway, expresses disgust at Carmel's affection for the baby Stella: "The child had been weaned, she was sickly, she did nothing but cry. She had only to cry and Carmel would rush to dandle her, rock her, put a comforter in her mouth, cover her with kisses. These peasant girls never learn" (149–50). Miss Holloway's name identifies her with the women's prison in which Maud Gonne, Constance Markievicz and Hannah Sheehy-Skeffington, amongst others, were incar-cerated during the War of Independence. Miss Holloway's temporary incar-ceration of Stella in her nursing home at Commander Brooke's request can be read as part of the novel's anticolonial critique, identifying Stella with Ireland's struggles for self-determination. It also suggests the nature of the connection between colonialism and patriarchy as Stella's inconvenient and embarrassing search for an understanding of her lost mother is dismissed as a symptom of nervous instability.

This emphasis on mother–daughter and woman-to-woman relations is less a construction of a feminist genealogy, however, than a highly polar-ized construction of mothering in terms of warm nature on the one hand, cold discipline on the other. The novel's main polemical force is directed in favor of child rearing based on "delight" in children and against "that damned puritanical school" (115) that sees as the main task of child rearing and education "to make you different from what you are" (76). Stella's first intimation that two spirits, one malignant, one benign, are haunting the house is linked with her confused recollection of not being loved as a child: "I wasn't a lovable baby; Miss Holloway says I was cross and tiresome and never pretty at all, so I thought mother loved me a little bit just because she was good and did her duty" (162). Stella has a vague recollection of a different kind of maternal love that comes to the surface when she encounters Carmel's ghost. She senses this "is *really* loving, as if she—as if she delighted in me and wants my love, too. It was like that last night, at first" (162). Just as Mary had kept Carmel apart from her daughter while they lived, her spirit tries to freeze out her rival: "Then, suddenly, everything stopped. It was as if everything was a clock and the clock stopped dead . . . I woke with my heart jumping, and it was cold—it was the deadliest cold I have ever known" (162). Gradually it becomes apparent that there is a third ghost in this house, the crying, uncomforted child that Stella became as Mary's daughter. Stella's dream of her childhood proves to be the key to understanding the nature of the ghosts haunting Cliff End:

> "I am in a room alone in the dark. There is a black thing outside, clutching at me—perhaps it was that tree [outside the nursery window]. I am frightened in the dark and I cry. I cry for a long time and then somebody comes in. She leans over me and whispers some pretty words—I never know what they are, and then she lights a light. It is lovely and I am happy, but someone else comes and puts it out."
>   "And you cry again?" Pamela asked.
>   "Then I am too frightened to cry." (162)

The haunting sobbing of the lonely child ceases, Carmel's spirit achieves peace and Mary is finally defeated when the roles of mother and daughter are reversed. "What is the Spanish for 'mother?'" Stella asks (296):

> She [Stella] began with fragments of Spanish, little words, broken phrases; then phrases of English came. But neither the words nor the language mattered anything, there was such tenderness in her voice. It rose and fell, soft, persuasive, a little lyric of pity and love, as if a mother were comforting her child. "Madre mia, madre carissima," I heard . . . "Rest in peace," I heard her say gently. (298)

In her love for Roddy, Stella becomes Carmel's daughter: "There had been a dawn of wildness and freedom in Stella's eyes" (167). "Nature and life were on my side and Stella's now," Roddy concludes (304), acknowledging Carmel's role as life-force.

The parallels between the cruel separation of mother and child, the punitive treatment of children and the eventual confinement, emotional cruelty and neglect that may have caused Carmel's death in *Uneasy Freehold* and what we now know about conditions in Irish institutions dedicated to the myth of Mary is too striking to be coincidental. Yet the novel shares the ambiguities of gothic and of the republic Macardle helped make. It invites us to think, but it also allows us not to know. And while it may reverse the identifications, it leaves the polarities of good and bad mother, darkness and light, intact. When her vengeful nature is finally known, the once crystal clear Mary is described in terms of dark not white. Roddy refers to the "the dark web that Mary had woven" (304), for example. *Uneasy Freehold* is readable in very different ways depending on the extent of your insider knowledge. The novel ultimately raises the question of whether or not gothic subversions and displacements must inevitably reinstate the polarities and certainties that the narrative has brought into question.

CALL ME BY NAME

Macardle's novel maps out the contours of repression in 1940s Ireland and identifies that which is lost and caught in an eternal return to be the natural mother, the mother of the body, of nurture, rather than social convention and restraint. This is double-edged. Carmel, the unmarried mother, is an excess over the needs of home and adulthood who must be acknowledged and loved but also laid to rest for the daughter to awake into sexuality, freedom and her own place. I want to draw particular attention to the role of naming here. Carmel is finally released from the spirit world to the peace of the mortal body when her motherhood is acknowledged, when Stella calls to her "Madre mia" in her own language. That scene brings to mind a far more contemporary piece of art, *Call Me By My Name: Requiem for Remains Unknown*, an "extallation" by Gerard Mannix Flynn. *Call Me By My Name* commemorated 150 women buried in the Magdalene laundry in High Park in Drumcondra in Dublin, whose remains were exhumed and reburied in 1993. Many of the women were buried with no record of their name or legal acknowledgment of their death. The extallation was situated on the corner of Lesson Street and Stephen's Green in the city center in 2003, on the site of the first Magdalene laundry built in Dublin.[57] It differentiated itself from "installation" art by mapping that which was hidden and buried onto public exterior space. In a conjunction of text and monument, *Call Me By My Name* ruptured the boundaries between public and private; past and present; art, trial and politics. The extallation was far more than a memorial. It was in many ways the apotheosis of the immensely strong current in contemporary Irish culture, which is concerned to uncover the past and reshape what is understood by Irish history. It also resisted and exposed the equally strong desire to draw a sharp dividing line between that past and the present. *Call Me By My Name* doesn't need to ask where the bodies are buried, but it asks what the bodies mean. The bodies of the Magdalene women were privately exhumed so that the ironically named Sisters of Charity could sell the land in which they were buried. (The rising age, absence of new recruits and consequent cost of care of the members of religious orders was matched in the Celtic Tiger era by a prodigious rise in the value of their land and property in Dublin.) Consequently, these women's unnamed bodies signify a profoundly disturbing link between past abuse and current "development." The extallation was in a sense a second exhumation, a public one in a central city space that challenged passersby to "Remember, Remember Me." In a city where buildings and streets are heavily sprinkled with plagues announcing their connections with the famous names of history and literature, *Call Me By My Name* confounded and renewed the commemorative tradition in Irish culture, making the city own its erasure of these women and their lives and deaths. The extallation also reminds us that this erasure is not simply past. To paraphrase Judith Butler on Antigone, one might approach these ghostly women with "the question of whether the limit for which she stands, a limit for which no standing, no translatable representation is possible, is not precisely the trace of an alternate legality that haunts the conscious, public sphere as its scandalous figure."[58]

FOREIGN BODIES

In *Uneasy Freehold*, the location of warmth and nurture and possibility in the foreign mother, Carmel, is typical of a strand in Irish women's fiction whereby Spanish, French or Italian women are romanticized as emblems of different ways of being a woman, an artist or even sometimes a Catholic. The identification of the foreign and illicit sexuality in Macardle mirrors public policy in relation to censorship and regulation of dance halls and other social spaces in Ireland at the time, which in turn mirrors the ideology of national and sexual purity outlined in Chapter 1 of this volume. The identification of these qualities with good motherhood is quite contrary to the official ideology, however. The emphasis on the mother's scented body and on the superiority of natural affection over legally sanctioned relationships was in direct opposition to the idealization of suffering and desexualized maternity promulgated by church and state in the adulation of Mary. Stella remembers her childish fear of "a black thing outside, clutching at me." Gradually the novel reveals that the threat is not the black thing outside, but the perfectly white ideal within. As Bryan Fanning's 2002 study of *Racism and Social Change in the Republic of Ireland* pointed out, "Ireland was never immune from the racist ideologies that governed relations between the west and the rest, despite a history of colonial anti-Irish racism."[59] The nature of the overwhelming referendum victory of the 2004 constitutional restriction on citizenship rights indicated this was not only the case, but that racist ideology in Ireland has very specific contours derived from traditional associations of Irishness and purity that the Celtic Tiger considered itself to have long outgrown. The hysterical pictures painted by media and politicians of immigrant women overwhelming Dublin maternity hospitals indicate that paranoia about sex and race and their connection has found a new focus. The role of sexual scapegoat has been subcontracted to the immigrant women who take on so many jobs no longer acceptable for Irish citizens. There are still, it seems, illicit forms of maternity and Carmel's ghost haunts the bright new European republic, so eager to shed the gothic melodrama of its past.

TERRITORY AND TRANSGRESSION: HISTORY, NATIONALITY AND SEXUALITY IN KATE O'BRIEN'S FICTION

Kate O'Brien: Feminism and Modernism in Irish Fiction

Kate O'Brien's fiction can seem formally tame if one defines the Irish novel in Joycean terms. Irish women writing in the first decades after independence have suffered somewhat from a definition of Irish modernism too narrowly focused on Joyce and Yeats and of modernism in terms of those very specific Irish variants. It is a useful antidote to recollect Elizabeth Bowen's close association with Virginia Woolf and to consider how useful, if problematic, a resource the English tradition of "great women writers" might have been for Irish women novelists. O'Brien's *Mary Lavelle* has more than a hint of *Jane Eyre* in its plot and structure and O'Brien throughout her work is strenuous in asserting a common European culture. Her work demands to be read, but rarely is read, as simultaneously but distinctly Irish, modernist and feminist.[60] The construction and redefinition of identity, the problematics of language and history for the feminine subject and the relation of sexuality to politics are recurrent factors in her work. O'Brien's marginality is almost excessive; her best work was banned in Ireland for many years, she was prohibited from entering her second homeland, Spain, for most of the Franco years and her lesbian identity is an important but contentious issue in her work.[61] The woman-centered perspective from which Irish identity is examined in O'Brien's writing challenges the meaning of that identity. Prohibition and impossibility are the conditions of social existence in her fiction.[62] The novels are often ostensibly structured around the transgression or observation of a social or moral norm and the related choice between exile and homeland. These choices are rarely made, however. Taboos are legitimized and reinstated at the very moment of transgression. Exiles return to find they are no longer at home in the country they left or leave to find they have brought the confinement of home with them. Paradoxically it is the fiction's concern with the marginal and trangressive that empowers it to explore the socio-symbolic basis of twentieth-century Irish culture.

   The Ante-Room[63] is concerned, on the one hand, with charting the possibility of transgression and, on the other, with mapping the horizons of an intensely confined society. Like many of O'Brien's novels, it is located in a strictly limited geographical and social space. The novel is set over three days; the characters are physically almost static. Spatial confinement is intense and claustrophobic and comparable to that imposed on Ana de Mendoza in *That Lady*,[64] which, like *The Ante-Room*, is a historical novel. Ana refuses to repudiate her lover and is imprisoned by a jealous Phillip II of Spain in a space that is gradually decreased until she is effectively walled up alive. In *The Ante-Room* enclosure is domestic and considerably more comfortable, but the tantalizing glimpses of a freedom they cannot achieve torture the Mulqueen household as surely as the gradual erosion of her allotted space tortures Ana. Like her, the Mulqueen family waits for death as the only release possible to them. The Mulqueens also, however, occupy the ante-room to twentieth-century Irish history and their story is O'Brien's analysis of the elements that were to make that history, by 1934, appear a bitter anticlimax.

Identity, Sovereignty and the Maternal

The domestic enclosure of *The Ante-Room*[65] is a space dominated and defined by mother figures. The central relationship between Agnes Mulqueen and her brother-in-law, Vincent, is a failed Oedipal displacement. Vincent tells Agnes that when he dies he will think of her, but she replies that it will be of his mother (255), a tragicomically accurate prediction. Vincent's desire for Agnes and his eventual suicide are both attempts to retreat from the painful fragmentation and conflict of living into the complete satisfaction he only achieved in is boyhood relationship with his mother. He had sought to recapture this relationship and the secure selfhood it had given him through his marriage to Agnes's sister, Marie-Rose: "He thought that at her fire he would grow warm and confident enough to be himself, as he had been with his mother" (102). He does not comprehend that his projection of this fantasy onto his wife is an element in the failure of their marriage. Rather, he sees her difference from the image he seeks as a failure of imagination on his part: "This was a failure of the artist in him, the dreamer" (102).

The models of selfhood and of relationship to which Vincent aspires are defined by "the idealisation of primary narcissism,"[66] "the fantasy that is nurtured by the adult, man or woman, of a lost territory." That fantasy is a mainstay of socio-symbolic order, but to serve that purpose the loss of that territory of the maternal must be experienced and internalized. Vincent, however, consistently tries to deny that loss. He cannot accept that there is no one "to make everything alright."[67] The impossibility of attaining his ideal intensifies his desire for it. His wife's sister, Agnes, has the desirable qualities of being unattainable and separated from him for long periods and so subject to idealization. The idealized mother and the idealized Agnes blur into one image of perfection: "When I'm tired the two of you get mixed in my head" (255).

It is not only the feminine protagonist who is in danger of losing her identity in Vincent's world of images, however. When Agnes asks Vincent what his mother was like, he answers: "'A bit like me—I think—in her face. She was small of course.' He laughed. 'As little as you'" (254). In psychoanalytic terms, Vincent never successfully completes the process of self-identification described in the Lacanian mirror stage. He remains trapped in the Imaginary. Concomitant with his view of women as reflective surfaces, returning more or less satisfactory images of himself, is an acknowledged reliance on these women to give him his identity. Such an acknowledgment is utterly incompatible with attainment to a secure place in the symbolic order, the law of the Father, and with the social, cultural and sexual context of the novel.

The problem with the psychoanalytic reading of this text I have just outlined is that in an Irish context, particularly the historical context of the novel's setting, the desire to regain a lost territory has an immediate and specific political reality, not just as a national ideal, but also as the basis of economic development and survival. Vincent is a supporter of the Land League and its attempts to transfer landholding to tenant farmers. The intensity of the relationship between the political, psychological and philosophical stakes in the game of identity becomes apparent in the dispute between Vincent, Agnes, Marie-Rose and William Curran (a local doctor in love with Agnes) at the novel's center. Vincent argues that:

> "Nothing is fixed. Nothing is what it appeared a moment ago to be."
>
> "Then if I assume at this moment," said William Curran, "that you are a Catholic, an Irishman, a shipowner, a householder and a husband—am I wrong?" (126)

Here Curran offers Vincent his identity in classic patriarchal terms, defined so emphatically by his relation to property that there can be no doubt that his religion, nationality and wife are also possessions. As the two men move in on Agnes, she is the disputed territory between them. She is that which they wish to possess, but she is also the medium through which two other disputes are to be resolved. The philosophical dispute has been triggered by a discussion of the Land League, which both young men support in opposition to Agnes's father. The political discussion took place in the dining room after the ladies had withdrawn and they, and the reader of *The Ante-Room*, only hear the concluding comments. Agnes is thus excluded from the political discussion of the competing claims of legality and authority on the one hand and of "a good and natural idea" (125) on the other. She must, however, choose between just such rival claims, represented by Curran and Vincent. The dispute over Agnes is identified with a dispute over sovereignty and landholding and links the political discussion with the philosophical one. The attempt to redefine landholding becomes in turn identified with the men's competing attempts to define reality. Typically Vincent asks Agnes to define reality for him—"What do you think, Agnes?" (126)—and equally typically she offers a definition with which neither he nor Curran can agree: "For ordinary purposes I think there is [a status quo], in spite of everything" (126).

Agnes's intervention, however, suggests that land and reality may yet prove as intractable to both imagination and rationality as Agnes and Marie-Rose themselves. In the course of the conversation, the women challenge the philosophical positions of both men. While Curran is relatively unperturbed, Vincent's sense of self is eroded and the emphasis of his argument and thoughts shifts away from an autonomous, choosing "I" toward the unconscious, the feminine and "unreality" (127). First he repudiates Curran's "proper" definition of him and argues that his religion, nationality, house and wife are not his property, that on which he has imposed his name, but forces that impose names and an identity on him:

> "Take X," he said, "and stick those labels on him which you say you can read all over me—"
> "They're not labels," said the doctor, "they're you. They're X."
> "Poor X! Since he assumed some of these things of his own choice, and by thinking he'd perhaps like to, and since he can detach himself from those others he was born with, to think about them either with approval or dislike—how can they be he?" (127)

Agnes here intervenes to undermine the existential possibilities implicit in this position and push the argument to an unexpected conclusion:

> "So X is only himself in so far as he doesn't think?" asked Agnes.
> "Very likely."
> "All the easier to find a status quo," said William Curran, "since no-one thinks."
> "But I, for instance, think I think," said Marie-Rose, "and isn't that a kind of thinking?"
> "Not the kind, I hope, Mrs. O'Regan, that will prove to your husband that you aren't you." (127)

It is clear in Curran's response to Marie-Rose that the sexual, political and philosophical identities sought by the two men can be threatened by any kind of "thinking" on her part, since such thinking identifies her as a sexual, political and philosophical subject, rather than disputed object and field for the symbolic resolution of intractable political and national disputes. Consequently, the first direct address by one of the women to the other brings the discussion to an end.

Curran will be one of those to define the territorial and philosophical boundaries of the new Ireland. His response to Marie-Rose, his unwillingness to take her seriously, implies that those definitions will be fragile. The conservatism and dogmatism of the new Ireland will, like Curran's patronizing certainty, be rooted in insecurity. For Curran not only recognizes the connection between knowing who your wife is, knowing who you yourself are and what defines reality, he also aspires to marry Agnes (and there is an implication at the novel's conclusion that he may do so), whom he will certainly never know. Vincent, dispossessed of motherland, refuses to take up a position of masculine authority and colonize in his turn. Curran is willing to take up such a position, but in important ways it is not available to him. Despite the novel's nineteenth-century setting, these two men represent tendencies within Irish nationalism that the catalyst of the Treaty will polarize into the two parties to the Civil War of the immediate post-independence period. If it is Curran who inherits the new Ireland, that new state will always seem like a falsification of the ideal. Law and land will not be brought into alignment. Three years after the publication of *The Ante-Room*, the constitution of that state will offer a form of resolution of that dilemma: as discussed earlier Articles 2 and 3 made territorial claim on the whole island. A legality disjunct from reality will be part of the self-definition of the state. No armed attempt was ever made by the state to enforce this territorial claim and the primary architect of the constitution, Eamon de Valera, was quite capable of interning those who sought to enforce it by violent means. As in the argument between Curran and Vincent, this territorial contradiction is compensated for by rigorous and absolute claims within the constitution on the territory of the feminine that, as in *The Ante-Room*, becomes both symbol of sovereignty and threat to the state.

The Politics of Impossible Desire

In *The Ante-Room*, as Vincent and Agnes contemplate a scene known to the family as "Mother's view," Vincent makes plain that it is the presence of the object of his desire, not her absence, that he finds painful. Moreover, her presence implies his absence: "When I'm in Dublin, I manage most of the time to live a fantasy life," he said, "but here, when I see you, how real you are, with activities and plans that have nothing to do with me—that goes. And then there is nothing" (180). Impossibility is posited as not only the condition, but the very substance of desire. Vincent's attempts to persuade Agnes to go away with him are a final effort to breach this condition of impossibility and to escape the oscillations between presence and absence of the self and of the other to which his love subjects him. Agnes's resistance to this plan is in part a resistance to appropriation of herself into his idealization of her, in part an indication that impossibility is also the substance of her desire for him. The novel is one of unfulfilled desire, but also one where the feminine protagonist chooses the condition of desire itself rather than that fulfillment her lover sees as a possible salvation and she sees as a form of annihilation. According to Lacan:

> For the unconditional element of demand, desire substitutes the "absolute" condition: this condition unties the knot of that element in the

proof of love that is resistant to the satisfaction of a need. Thus desire is neither the appetite for satisfaction, nor the demand for love, but the difference that results from the subtraction of the first from the second.[68]

Agnes above all fears language's power to transform and exhaust her "dark imaginings," to eliminate their difference: "For her final fear was of words . . . Must all her hoard of misery be sloughed away?" (81–82). She fears to fulfill her desire, but she fears more that her desire will be uttered, confessed, codified, forgiven and so killed. Her "misery" is also her guarantee that she is more than X, a list of social attributes. It marks the extent to which she exceeds definition.

This insistence by both Agnes and Vincent on the identity of impossibility and desire can be read as an answer to Foucault's questions:

Why do we say, with so much passion and so much resentment against our most recent past, against our present and against ourselves, that we are repressed? By what spiral did we come to affirm that sex is negated? What led us to show, ostentatiously, that sex is something we hide, to say it is something we silence?[69]

These are questions pertinent to a significant range of Irish fiction. *The Ante-Room* is willing to address them. It presents repression as productive of desire and the prolongation of an unrealizable desire as the condition of Irish nationhood. The novel is not content with reproducing the circular relation of repression and desire in the specific context of the late nineteenth-century Irish Catholic middle classes, however. It does posit something outside that circle, though it will not or cannot identify it, particularly as an essential core of sexuality or self, nature or history. In *The Ante-Room* impossible desire posits the existence of the indefinable Real[70] and the ache of relationship to it. It is the particular achievement of the novel that this concern with the Real never develops into a consolatory or essentialist position. The Real is politicized, identified with subversion of social and sexual order. In pursuit of it, Agnes continues to resist appropriation to the maternal ideal Vincent seeks and the (related) virginal ideal her church exacts. She chooses a different identity for herself. This resistance, like that of Ana de Mendoza, exacts a huge price from the one who resists and offers no possibility of freedom. The perpetuation of impossible and ideal desire has quite contrary implications in the historical and psychological realms. Agnes, the disputed territory, has slipped out of definition and grasp, a "feminine" evasion that affirms her as a subject in her own right. A politics of impossible desire, based on negation and denial, is also a politics that annihilates its subject, however, and places its object (Agnes/Ireland/nationhood) outside history and beyond hope. Agnes is a stern antithesis to Mother Ireland, but also a territory with no future, always in the anteroom to history. She retains herself in excess of X at too high a price. In effect she is crushed between the forces of feminine self-identity and national self-determination. The feminine protagonist in this historical fiction is not offered a choice of different forms of liberation, but of different modes of oppression. And Agnes's choice means death for her lover and for the political subject who seeks to define himself in relation to her:

> "This is love—it hardly ever happens."
> She drooped, drew back from him.
> "You mean—it never happens."
> Her face had a look of death. (273)

Narcissism is perilously and paradoxically close to the death drives. The completeness Vincent seeks is deathly and his death is, for Vincent, a return to (his idealized version of) Mother: "Darling Mother. He pulled the trigger, his thoughts far off in boyhood" (306). This is very black humor at the expense of Oedipus's Irish descendents. O'Brien extends her grim parody of the family romance in her treatment of the other mother–son couple in the novel. Mrs. Mulqueen and Reggie, her only son, are locked in a grotesque inversion of "the idealisation of primary narcissism." Just as Vincent and his mother are finally united in death, Mrs. Mulqueen and Reggie are united in a deathly life. The mother, dying of cancer, and the son, syphilitic, "a large wreck of a man" (21), are repeatedly presented as living for each other. Their relationship keeps them locked alive in bodies that have disintegrated into rotting corpses. Reggie's "flesh uniformly red, was dry and flaky about his mouth and bulging neck, and sweaty on his forehead and hands" (21–22). Agnes sees her mother eventually as:

> A dying stranger . . . A corpse, the shadow of a corpse, breathing in heaviness and fear, a corpse made dreadful to the senses, and groaning in its half-dream, half-pang. (226)

Mrs. Mulqueen, who stays alive to protect Reggie from the reality of death, is, for him, the omnipotent mother of childhood and fairy tale, a Kali who controls life and death. For Agnes, she is "the utmost of abjection."[71]

HISTORY, NATIONALITY, SEXUALITY

Even qualified by the parodic ending, the closing off of possibility, choice and change at the conclusion of *The Ante-Room* seems to limit the possibilities for fiction as well as for the feminine protagonists. O'Brien's next novel, *Mary Lavelle*[72] effectively rewrites the scenario of *The Ante-Room*, in different historical and geographical circumstances, and comes to a very different conclusion. *Mary Lavelle*, like O'Brien's other Spanish novel, *That Lady*, and like *The Ante-Room*, is concerned with prohibited desire. It is also, however, a novel that poses the problem of the feminine subject's relation to history as one capable of redefinition. The two historical novels, *The Ante-Room* and *That Lady*, are concerned with women's exile from historical agency and their subjection to history. Second wave feminism tended to explore this problem for women in patriarchy in terms of the "castration or decapitation"[73] dilemma that crushed Agnes in *The Ante-Room*. Either a woman can succumb to exile from history, becoming the symbol of eternity, the bearer of natural forces and guarantee of life/guarantee against death, or she can participate in a history that denies that which exceeds the masculine terms of its own, linear formulation.

For an Irish woman writer of O'Brien's generation (she started college in Dublin in 1916, the year of the rising), this dilemma would have immediate relevance and a very specific formulation. The historian, Clíona Murphy, commenting on the relationship between the Irish women's suffrage movement and Irish nationalism, summarized: "Politicised women were forced to make a decision between their sex and their nation . . . some felt obliged to choose the latter."[74] Such decisions were if anything more pressing after the women's suffrage movement had been submerged by events and by the force of nationalism. In *The Land of Spices*, set during the period when the suffrage movement was at its strongest in Ireland, the potential artist, Anna Murphy, ponders the choice of political priorities available to her. These are personified by her constitutionalist nationalist father, the local priest (a supporter of Sinn Féin) and Miss Robertson, a women's suffrage activist who has been to prison for her activities:

> When her father quoted Tim Healy's witticisms at the Irish Bar, she foresaw that shafts of hers would one day hit more deeply and more amazingly. When Father Hogan talked contemptuously of the Irish Party, and expounded the political doctrines of Arthur Griffith, she pondered the value to herself of a patriot's career; and when she talked with Miss Robertson, she felt her own strong ability to out-Pankhurst Mrs. Pankhurst. (209)

This dazzling choice of causes and roles is in considerable contrast to *That Lady* and *The Ante-Room*, where the women at the novels' centers can only enact to its extreme conclusion a political and historical logic that produces, rather than is produced, by them. These wide variations in the formulation of women's relation to history do not follow any progressive or chronological pattern in O'Brien's fiction. Nor is it easy to classify the novels as more or less "optimistic" in this regard. Ana Mendoza resists tyranny, but that tyranny defines the terms in which she can express her resistance. She chooses prison rather than submission: to maintain her independence, she must lose her freedom. *That Lady*[75] is in part O'Brien's response to the Second World War, a parable of resistance to fascism. The form of Ana's resistance, however, is borrowed unchanged from the Irish nationalist tradition. The radical suffragist Hannah Sheehy-Skeffington is cited by Murphy: "The time may arise when the prison may be the only place of honour left to an honest man. Many a brave Irishman has proved the truth of the axiom in the past. It is now for Irish women to realize citizenship by becoming 'criminalised.'"[76] This suggests that at certain crisis points in Irish history both sexual and national identity have been allied in a transgressive relation to law, order and social authority.

Mary Lavelle[77] intersects with history on the basis of transgressing its laws. Despite the urgency of its concern with historical forces, it deals with situations and experiences roughly contemporary to its composition. To some extent the historical novel, since it deals with the past, is already committed to determinism. The subject of the historical novel is subject to history. *Mary Lavelle* looks back to the Irish War of Independence, but also forward to the Spanish Civil War. It "reads" history in a much more dynamic way. The novel plots the trajectory between two conflicts that are defined within the novel by their relationship to each other: "Amusedly once through the oration of a Basque nationalist she heard the names 'Arthur Griffiths' and 'Patrick Pearse'" (128). The executed Pearse, despite the amusement, is a grim enough prediction of what is to come for the Basque nationalists, but the mention of Griffiths offers other possibilities. Griffiths, the architect of the Ourselves Alone slogan of Sinn Féin, ironically provides a point of connection and recognition between insurgent nationalities. National identity is here relational rather than exclusionary and exceeds the binary polarity imposed by a history of colonization. Aintzane Legareta Mentxaka has undertaken an extensive study of the influence of the Basque country on O'Brien.[78]

Mary eventually learns that journeys do not end and that there is no going back: "afterwards she would take her godmother's hundred pounds and go away. That was all. That was the fruit of her journey to Spain" (344). Declan Kiberd has noted of O'Brien herself that "the price of crossing the border [between different codes and identities] for literary women was that few of them could ever hope to return."[79] The ending of *Mary Lavelle* is by no means pessimistic, however, for the novel is primarily concerned with gaining access to that dangerous borderline territory that O'Brien identifies as the proper place of poetry. The description of the bullfight at the center of *Mary Lavelle* is indicative of O'Brien's recurrent attempts to formulate an aesthetics that exceeded and challenged the dyadic formations of national and sexual identity that dominated cultural nationalism and insinuated themselves into Irish literary modernism. The artistic practice attributed to the bullfight by O'Brien is sublime[80] and modernist. It is political, but subversive of any political code, on the side of the political subject, not as citizen, but as deviant, subversive, more than X:

> Death, so strangely approached, so grotesquely given and taken, under the summer sky, for the amusement of nonentities, death made into

an elaborate play, for money and cheers, and exacting in the course of the show a variety of cruelties and dangers; death, asking for helpless victims as well as for the hazards of courage; death and pain, made comic, petty and relentless, for an afternoon's thrill . . . Here was madness, here was blunt brutality, here was money-making swagger—and all made into an eternal shape, a merciless beauty, by so brief a thing as attitude. Here—and Mary, to whose youth all knowledge was new, received this sudden piece of it as crippling pain—here was art in its least decent form, its least explainable or bearable. But art, unconcerned and lawless. (116–17)

The language of the bullfight recurs in the description of Mary and Juanito's lovemaking. The sexual and the aesthetic inhabit the same space in the text. Mary sheds virginity symbolic of her dispossession of herself and becomes a participant in, rather than an observer of, the play of life and death she identifies in the bullfight. As with the bullfight, there is no denial, no glossing over, of the death-dealing and painful aspects of this relation. Don Pablo, Juanito's father who is also fascinated with Mary, dies while they make love and Mary's choice of lover involves a rejection of Agatha Conlon who first brings Mary to the bullfight and as such initiates her into the possibility of transgression and freedom. Agatha herself is very much a participant in the economy of sexual impossibility, however, and Mary is angered by the forces that make the older woman repent of the "sin of love."[81] Sexual initiation also involves a painful defloration, to the dismay of most commentators, who deplore or dismiss the love scene: Mentxaka, who links it to Picasso's *Guernica*, is an exception. The text's emphasis on the willful nature of Mary's passion and her insistence on taking the sexual initiative make this impossible to characterize as masochistic surrender. It is too keen a reminder of the ambivalent boundaries of the female body. The hymen is more consistently part of a possessive patriarchal imagination than of the female body, however (Derrida notwithstanding), and it is the appropriation of her body to a symbolic function and the constraints on her sexuality that Mary herself is somewhat painfully violating.[82]

The subject is in process in this novel and the process is not concluded. Neither history nor ideology operate here as an inexorable logic. The law of impossibility is transgressed and the consequences of that transgression are deliberately left open. "The only way in which a writer can participate in history is by transgressing this abstraction through a process of reading-writing."[83] Kate O'Brien's novel of the Irish War of Independence and the Spanish Civil War is written in the space between them. *Mary Lavelle*'s relation to history is interrogatory and anachronic. It interrupts historical "progression" and situates itself in the pause between cause and effect where only possibility exists. Desire precipitates action, impossibility is breached and the effects of transgression are not contained by the logic of plot. The law of action and reaction, transgression and retribution, does not apply. One of the most interesting aspects of the novel is its assertion that feminine sexuality is political, is indeed the key to a different politics and another history. Mary's "adultery"[84] is a rejection of an Ireland that has not fulfilled the promise of independence. Moreover, it is crucial to the novel's engagement with the political future of Spain and of Europe as a whole. In the novel's concern with Ireland's relation to a broader European culture and politics, it marks both the integration of the new Ireland into that culture and the difference that remains. Moreover, both national and international identity are posited from the margins, through relation to the Basques, not the old colonizer or major centers of Europe. Since that relationship is, here and elsewhere, explored in terms of a feminine protagonist, O'Brien's fiction offers an unusually explicit account of the relationship between gender and territoriality and a putting into question of "the nation-space"[85] produced by such a relationship. According to Kristeva, "the poetic word, polyvalent and multi-determined, adheres to a logic exceeding that of codified discourse and fully comes into being only in the margin of recognised culture."[86] O'Brien's fiction tries, and sometimes fails, to exhaust "codified discourses"—of religion, gender, nationality, history. It repeatedly identifies that which exceeds X as the proper subject of fiction. Both *The Ante-Room* and *Mary Lavelle* are deeply engaged with the politics, particularly the sexual politics, of this excess and its containment. It is her exploration of the limit of the feminine's integration into and exclusion from political and symbolic structures that renders O'Brien's fiction of interest to contemporary feminism. Amongst other things, she explores the socio-symbolic bases of post-independence Irish society at a point when those bases were fragile and still in the process of establishing themselves. The sense of national identity as identity to itself has produced, but is untenable at, such moments of transition. It is not surprising then that *Mary Lavelle*, which seeks to explore the boundaries between identities and is concerned with the position of the internal foreigner, the woman, ends in the middle of a journey, on the border between two national territories, Spain and France, in an undefined and unoccupied space.

WOMEN AND NATIONALISM: SOME CONCLUSIONS

It is precisely because it does appear to have "red blood" in it that nationalism traditionally appeals to women. It is important to neither demonize nor romanticize women's involvement with nationalism and to remain attuned to the racial discourse always lurking within that of kinship. Red blood indicates violence as well as birth and kin, and Kristeva points out that women's disaffection from the symbolic always risks their violent repudiation of it.[87] Feminism began by asking for women to have access to the life of the nation-state. It may now be more concerned to change the basis of both nation and state, to effect a difference rather than achieve the "same" rights. Yet it remains important to understand the basis of the affiliations between women and nationalism, which historically has publicly operated in situations of national crisis, privately underpinned emergent nation and stable state. It is equally important to be aware of and challenge the sacrificial logic that structured that affiliation. To give Antigone a home above ground it would be necessary to relinquish "the privileged place in which red blood and its semblance harmoniously (con)fuse with each other."[88] The national body could no longer be a body to be possessed, but to be lived in. In her analysis of *Nations Without Nationalism*, Kristeva argues that:

> Foreign to the unisex commonality of man, everlasting irony of the community, as the sorrowful Hegel so aptly said, women today are called upon to share in the creation of new social groupings where by choice rather than an account of origin, through lucidity rather than fate, we shall try to assure our children living spaces that, within ever tenacious national and identity—forging traditions, will respect the strangeness of each person within a lay community.[89]

Such a utopian possibility can only be imagined if the relationship between gender and national identity is confronted in all its complexity. In the margins of the national project, women's writing might offer an "idea of continuity" different enough to assist the formation of such a community.

Part II
Writing, Bodies, Canons

4   Modernism and the Gender of Writing

DECADENCE, DEGENERATION AND REVOLTING AESTHETICS

The period from 1890 to 1910 was an important one in the development of the Irish novel, though fiction is frequently overlooked in the critical concentration on the more spectacular achievements of the theater and poetry of the time. Of particular significance was the development of fiction by Irish women fueled by the emergence of a self-consciously political feminism. This chapter seeks to situate key Irish modernist texts in the complex web of cultural production, reception and interpretation where their meanings were once negotiated, to highlight their entanglement in contemporary debates about the interrelationship of body and politics, artifice and identity and to trace their negotiations between the complex claims of gender, class and nation.

NEW WOMEN AND DECADENTS

A simple opposition between progressive and regressive cultural politics is not tenable in regard to women's writing of the late nineteenth and early twentieth centuries. Despite very considerable differences in style, subject matter and professed aesthetic aspirations, the New Woman writers were linked with the decadent movement by the conservative press as examples of cultural, national and sexual degeneracy. (Teresa Mangum notes that the two groups were regularly reviewed together under such titles as "Literary Degenerates" or "Sex in Modern Literature.") "The dark side of progress," the concept of degeneracy, blurred in lurid loathing the distinctions between internal threats to social and sexual order and the many other, external threats to European hegemony. Victorian England invested a great deal of moral authority in cultural activities proper to an empire convinced of its civilizing mission. Improper cultural activities, or those that challenged or mocked that tradition, were identified with political subversion. As Sandra Siegel commented in a key intervention:

So long as the words "civilization" and "masculine" were conceived as conceptual cognates, the New Woman was shocking and the new decadents were an "invention as terrible." The New Woman like her mirror image, the new decadent, who was always male, confused what was essential to her nature. She not only moved in the public sphere, but behaved like a man, even as the new decadents, in their self-absorption and inaction, behaved like women, lost their masculine vigor.[1]

Two key figures in the confusion of gender and culture so deplored were from a nation often cited as an example of degeneracy. The obvious one is Oscar Wilde; the lesser known was the writer who coined the term *New Woman*, Sarah Grand. By an act of self-invention that would surely have impressed Wilde, Grand constructed herself from her unpromising beginnings as Frances Elizabeth Clarke (later McFall), born in Donaghadee in 1854. Her early life is a little unclear. She went to England after her father's death to live as a poor relation, attended charity boarding schools that appear to have made Lowood look like a model for building self-esteem, eloped with an army surgeon, left him to pursue her career as a writer, became Sarah Grand, campaigned for women's suffrage on two continents and by the middle of her life had moved so far from the periphery to the center of English society as to marry the mayor of Bath.

Grand was one of a number of Irish women writers and women with Irish connections who played an important part in the development of the New Woman character in fiction and of sensational and decadent fiction. George Egerton (Mary Chavelita Dunne) and Katherine Cecil Thurston were similarly prominent exponents of this new fiction. Thurston, the most decadent, sensational and successful of the three, often dealt with Irish characters, but Irish characters abroad. (I will focus later on Thurston's final novel, *Max*, which features a woman artist.)

The woman artist, or potential artist, was an important figure in the increasingly self-reflexive fiction that these women produced. This marked an important shift from the work of earlier nineteenth-century women writers, who could not attribute "realistically" to their characters the same freedoms they themselves enjoyed as writers and earners. It also reflected and elaborated the intensified self-reflexive quality always associated with the juxtaposition of the terms "woman" and "writer." Neither the sensational nor the politically committed women writers of the period felt obliged to preface their work with disclaimers, apologies and self-defense, as the first women novelists had done. Yet their surrogates within their fiction are often themselves passionately defended and in turn offer impassioned pleas not only for general social and sexual, but also specific educational and artistic freedom for women. Thurston's Max/Maxine pleads for understanding from the lover she tries to reject:

I have power—power to think—power to achieve. And how do you think that power is to be developed? . . . Not by the giving of my soul into bondage—not by the submerging of myself in another being . . . Can't you understand? I left Russia to make a new life; I made myself a man, not for a whim, but as a symbol. Sex is only an accident, but the world has made man the independent creature—and I desired independence.[2]

Novels from the turn of the twentieth century that feature women artists tend to displace this self-reflexivity by making painters, not writers, the central protagonists. Part of the attraction must have been cultural continuity: the woman artist expanded what had been a feminine accomplishment, sketching, into an art and a profession. She epitomized the New Woman, since her advent was even more recent, modern and daring than the woman writer's, but she also seemed to epitomize the new century of possibility.

In representing women in such unconventional roles, these writers were part of the movement that shattered the narrative paradigms of the previous century and laid the foundation for modernism. The unconventionality was enough to render any distinction of purpose from the decadents invisible to conservative, popular opinion. Nor was that unconventionality confined to their fiction. Wilde was not the first celebrity writer by any means, but the combination of mass literacy, the popular press and the association of art and decadence made notoriety easier for some of his contemporaries in more ways than one. The newspaper coverage of Thurston's divorce was salacious and unkind, but it does not appear to have diminished her books' popularity. In an era of sensation fiction, sensational novelists were only to be expected.

Late twentieth-century feminism tended to go too far in producing an antithesis where contemporary reviewers saw identity. Elaine Showalter, in her introduction to the excellent anthology *Daughters of Decadence*, argues that:

> Women writers needed to rescue female sexuality from the decadents' image of romantically doomed prostitutes or devouring Venus flytraps, and represent female desire as a creative force in artistic imagination as well as in biological reproduction.[3]

In a related vein, critics such as Linda Dowling and Teresa Mangum have suggested that the New Women and decadents prefigure the alignment and conflict between feminism and postmodernism:

> For a feminist novelist, this suspicion (of the decadents) that language has no "meaning," that in fact the surfaces of language and the style of utterance are more "real" than the "content" of ideas one presumes to constitute in language must have posed then, as it does now, a profound

dilemma. [Grand's] Beth's quest for a form appropriate to women's experience thus becomes part of a larger dilemma for the writer, dilemma most forcibly rendered by the stylists who adamantly rejected the very notion of content.[4]

Moreover, there is some truth in Karl Beckson's comment in his exhaustive study of London's cultural life in the 1890s that:

> The image of the aggressive female, intent on emasculating the decadent Victorian male. . . . achieved its most strident expression in Wilde's Salomé (1893) and in Beardsley's illustrations for the English translation.[5]

Yet Wilde was a close friend of one of the wittiest New Woman writers, Ada Leverson, who remained staunchly loyal to him during his trial and wrote an appreciation of him in 1926. True, he called her the Sphinx, a linkage of the very modern with the eternal female similar to Salomé. Their relationship could even be considered characteristic of that between decadence and the New Woman: contradictory, often based on misunderstanding, but ultimately supportive in ways neither movement necessarily understood at the time. It is true the agendas of the two groups were different, one aiming at social reform, the other wishing to dissociate literary and "moral" values, but these are only directly contrary if viewed in very narrow terms. Irish critics, for example, always ascribe to Wilde a political and subversive aestheticism. (The ambiguity of the relation between "social decadence" and "artistic decadence" was, of course, deliberately cultivated by the artists themselves.)

The aesthetic values of the decadents and the New Woman writers also diverged, but certain key characteristics were common to both; narrative excess, stylistic experiment, sexual candor and self-reflexive analysis of art's function, however differently they might understand it. As Mangum's outline of Beth's dilemma indicates, women writers, in asserting their right to be both, tended toward self-reflection in art. Just as in the decadents' works, mirrors and portraits figure prominently in New Woman fiction: their pivotal roles in *Max* are exemplary. Above all, an examination of late nineteenth-century and early twentieth-century Irish women's fiction complicates the assumption that "the quest for a form appropriate to women's experience" can be mapped between the polarities of postmodern artificiality and nostalgia for an authentic expression always already lost to women.

THE ETHICS OF LITERARY FORGERY: EMILY LAWLESS

The vortex of forces, constituted by decadence, degeneracy and gender revolt, that shaped fin de siècle literature can be usefully explored in the work of an Irish woman writer notoriously difficult to categorize, Emily Lawless. A contributor to the prominent journal, *The Nineteenth Century*, Lawless's work was inevitably read by contemporaries in the context of the aesthetic and sexual politics of the time, as well as that of Irish politics and Home Rule, all of which were frequently debated in its pages. The high seriousness, moral tone and historical weight of her work appear to put her emphatically in the opposite camp to the decadents. She also appears to have opposed women's suffrage, though it is difficult now to read either her novel, *Grania*, or her biography of Maria Edgeworth as anything other than proto-feminist works.

Lawless's critical essay proposing an "ethics of literary forgery" began as a review of scholarly translations of ancient Irish manuscripts and speculating on the lierary forger:

> Supposing—I say supposing, because one may really suppose any-thing—that for once he did not fail—supposing that he succeeded in producing so ingenious an imitation, so steeped in the colors of his elected period, so discreet in its modifications, so slyly, delicately ar-chaic in all its details as to deceive the very elect—what then? Would his guilt be thereby lessened? On the contrary, it is clear that from our present point of view it would only be increased tenfold.
>
> And this is really the gist of the matter; so, for fear of any misun-derstanding, I had better repeat it. It is not a question as to whether we ever can succeed in such imitation, but as to whether we ought to wish or even to try to succeed. The point may appear to be one of the small-est possible importance, especially considering the infinitesimal value of most of such imitations, but it is not quite so small as may at first appear, and has decidedly larger bearings.
>
> For to write badly is after all only to prove oneself human; but to go about telling—worse, printing—lies is surely the very superfluity of naughtiness?[6]

A great deal is at stake for this Anglo-Irish novelist in this essay, for the claims of authenticity had already been used to disqualify her from com-mentary on Ireland and would be again. In "Forging a Tradition: Emily Lawless and the Irish Literary Canon," James Cahalan notes that *The Nation* newspaper accused her of looking down on her peasant charac-ters "from the pinnacle of her three-generation nobility" (28). Synge dis-missed *Grania* because "the real Aran spirit is not there," attributing her shortcomings as a chronicler of island life to her status as a lady.[7] Yeats, while acknowledging she had "in her the makings of a great book full of an avid and half spectral intensity," insisted her potential had thus far been stunted by her "imperfect sympathy with the Celtic nature"[8].

For Lawless as surely as for her decadent compatriots, artificiality was life giving and the demand for authenticity merely political prescription:

A good deal of talk goes on in these days about the Celtic spirit, but does any one really know what that spirit is? Has any one ever tracked it to its secret home; ascertained where it was born, and of what elements it was originally composed? If we look at it closely and quite dispassionately, is it not nearly as much a topographical as either a philological or an ethnological spirit? Certainly if "the breath of Celtic eloquence" is not also to some degree the breath of the Atlantic, I should be puzzled to define what it is. So soft, and so loud; so boisterous, and so heady; extremely enervating, according to some people's opinion, but Oh how subtly, how fascinatingly intoxicating, it is certainly not the property of any one creed, age, or condition of life, any more than it is of any one set of political convictions. We can only say of it that like other breaths it bloweth where it listeth. There is no necessary connection between it and the Clan-na-Gael, any more than there is between it and Landlords' Conferences or Diocesan Synods. Nay, may we not even go further? May we not say that a prosaic pure-bred East Briton—the child of two incredulous Bible-reading parents—may in time grow positively Celtic in spirit if only he will surrender himself absolutely to these influences; if only he will fling away his miserable reason, and refuse from this day forward to disbelieve anything, especially anything that strikes him as absolutely impossible?

And is not the converse proposition at least equally true? May not a very Celt of the Celts—an O or a Mac into whose veins no minim of Saxon blood has ever entered since the Creation—become so unCelt-like in his inner man, so be-Saxonised if one may use the phrase, in the atmosphere of caucuses and committee rooms; so appallingly practical, so depressingly hardheaded, nay—if the corruption be carried far enough—actually so logical, that at last, as a Celt, he cannot, strictly speaking, be said to have any existence at all?[9]

The logic of Lawless's aesthetic argument leads her into direct conflict with the presumption of racial essence, just as her excursion into literary history led her into conflict with such presumptions in relation to gender. Richard Lovell Edgeworth, an embodiment in every possible respect of the institution of patriarchy, is her regular target in her biography of Maria Edgeworth:

a more benevolent embodiment of the principle of autocracy has perhaps never flourished since that institution was introduced upon a much-ruled planet.

It was the very benevolence of [t]his autocratic standpoint which made it impossible for him to believe that any one belonging to him—especially a mere daughter, a member of the less important half of his enormous brood—could fail to be the better for carrying on her little pursuits under his direct eye, and subject in every detail to his approval or disapproval. That he was in essentials one of the best-intentioned of fathers is certain, yet few bad, few merely indifferent fathers, have inflicted upon a gifted son or daughter worse injuries, from an intellectual point of view, than he did.[10]

Ironic reversal is a central part of Lawless's critical arsenal against the surveillance of the arbiters of authenticity, morality and nationality in fiction, but in important respects she herself was the victim of a counterreversal. While she maps the allure of identity as artifice, her work shows the intractable force of belief in "real" "historical" "character."

(New) Woman of Aran

Lawless's work makes clear precisely what was at stake in negotiating the complex relationship between gender and national identity. This is nowhere more apparent than in the contrast between her progressive views on gender and retrogressive ones on land reform. *Granía* (1892)[11] indicates how the habit of figuring Ireland in feminine terms could complicate writing firmly opposed to nationalist politics and how the habits of imperialist perception could ensnare progressive, feminist thinking. The novel tells the story of a spirited young woman who cannot fit into peasant society on one of the Aran Islands. Though she possesses characteristics of the New Woman, Granía's integrity and independence are consistently represented in the novel as more true to the spirit of the place and the history of its people than the conventional lives of those around her.

> To her Inishmaan was much more than home, much more than a place she lived in, it was practically the world and she wished for no bigger, hardly for any more prosperous, one. It was not merely her own holding and cabin, but every inch of it that was in this peculiar sense hers. It belonged to her as the rock on which it has been born belongs to the young seamew. She had grown to it, and it had grown to her. She was part of it, and it was part of her. (1:103)

Her name, Granía O'Malley, identifies Lawless's protagonist with the legendary Gaelic woman chieftain. Granía refuses to learn English and is passionately attached to her home island of Inishmaan and her intensely religious invalid sister, Honor. Throughout the novel there is a tension between the representation of Granía herself as proto-feminist heroine and doomed epitome of a traditional Irish identity.

Though identified with the island, she does not belong to the island community, an alienation identified as part of her inheritance from her mainland mother: "In her neighbours' eyes she was a 'Foreigner,' just as her mother had been a foreigner before her" (1:104). Reviewers at the time in both Ireland and the US comment on a Spanish intensity that is both Granía's inheritance from the west of Ireland's turbulent history and responsible for her distance from the conventional mind-set of those around her. In contrast, a reviewer in *Athenaeum* commented that "Granía, heroic in her failings as in her strength, and Honor, the pale saint, are beautiful types of Irish womanhood." Essentially Irish and essentially foreign, Granía embodies the island and so, paradoxically, makes it strange and feminine. This familiar logic is ultimately obstructed in Lawless's version, however, for Granía cannot be possessed.

In a key scene, Granía sees in a wretched cottage where she takes shelter the fate in store for her if she marries Murdough Blake, despite her love for him. It is worth quoting at length, not least because Granía is still difficult to access and Lawless's prose must at some stage be allowed to speak for itself:

> Presently the door of the nearest cabin opened, and a woman came out, carrying a pail in her hand. She came directly towards Granía, who sat still on her stone under the pelting rain and watched her. She was a terribly emaciated-looking creature, evidently not long out of bed, though it was now getting to the afternoon. She seemed almost too weak, indeed, to stand, much less to walk. As she came up to the stranger she gazed at her with a look of dull indifference, either from ill-health or habitual misery; set her pail under the pipe in the bank through which the stream ran, and, when it was filled, turned and went back, staggering under its weight, towards the door of her cabin again.
>
> With an instinct of helpfulness Granía sprang up and ran after her, took the pail from her hands and carried it for her to the door. The woman stared a little, but said nothing. Some half-naked, hungry-looking children were playing around the entrance, and through these she pushed her way with a weary, dragging step. Then, as if for the first time observing the rain, turned and beckoned Granía to follow her indoors.
>
> Dull as it had been outside, entering the cabin was like going into a cellar. There was hardly a spark of fire. That red glow, which rarely fails in any Irish home, however miserable, was all but out; a pale, sickly glimmer hung about the edges of some charred sods of turf, but that was all.
>
> A heavy, stertorous breathing coming from a distant corner attracted Granía's attention, and, looking closely, she could just distinguish a man lying there at full length. A glance showed that he was dead drunk, too drunk to move, though not too drunk, as presently became apparent, to maunder out a string of incoherent abuse, which he directed at his wife without pause, meaning, or intermission, as she moved about the cabin. One of the brood of squalid children—too well used, evidently, to the phenomenon to heed it—ventured within reach of his arm, whereupon he struck an aimless blow at it, less with the

intention apparently of hurting it, than from a vague impulse of asserting himself by doing something to somebody. He was very lamentably drunk and probably not for the first, or the first hundredth, time.

The woman indifferently drew the child away and sent it to play with the other children in the gutter outside. Then having set the black pot upon the fire, she squatted down on her heels beside it, heedless, apparently, of the fact that there was not a chance of its boiling in its present state, and taking no heed either of her visitor or of her husband, who continued to maunder out more or less indifferent curses from his corner. (1:115–18)

There is no doubt that the current generation of Irish students respond to *Granía*—when it is made available to them—with a great sense of approbation, as a realism that they missed in the more canonical texts in their course. I am conscious in situating the text in relation to the discourse of degeneracy of potentially stifling that response. But the text's hospitality to the revolt against the national past of young Irish women is both relevant and part of the way in which it must be read at the beginning of the twenty-first century. This pleasure of identification with the text's repudiation of usually romanticized Irish peasant life and the aura of illicit knowledge it possesses because of its noncanonical status are part of the meanings that have accrued to *Granía* since its publication, not distortions to be stripped away for a clearer historical view.

The distaste for maternity and its identification with a death of the self rather than the advent of life is evident in much nineteenth-century writing by women. Here the repugnance is intensified by the poverty, violence and despair of the family life portrayed. It is a bracing antidote to the idealization of Aran and the West, metonymic of "authentic" Ireland, made all the more effective by the metaphoric relation of Granía herself to the place. (The novel is titled for her, subtitled "The Story of an Island.")

For Granía it is a moment of radical disillusion. She sees her future self in the woman before her, but more disturbingly the handsome Murdough, already fond of drink, in the wreck of a man. In effect, this scene reverses the novel's one great moment of exaltation, when out in the boat with Murdough she realizes she loves him:

She did not know yet what it was, but it was a revelation in its way—a revelation as new and as strange as that other revelation two days before in the boat, only that it was exactly the reverse of it. A new idea, a new impression, was again at work within her, only this time it was a new idea, a new impression upon the intolerableness of life, its unspeakable hopelessness, its misery, its dread unfathomable dismalness. Why should people go on living so? she thought. Why should they go on living at all, indeed? Why, above all, should they marry and bring more wretched creatures into the world, if this was to be the way of it? (118–19)

It is a highly unusual scene. Even in the 1890s such dark thoughts were rarely attributed to sympathetic heroines and we might expect the disgusted rejection of romantic love and maternity to have shocked contemporary readers. The largely admiring contemporary reviews indicate that this was not the case, however. Lawless's hardworking peasant woman occupies a different relation to both feminine roles than that of the standard middle-class heroine. Granía herself is in many regards the antithesis of the degeneracy of those around her. She is also the representative of a doomed race: her linguistic purity and integrity of national character are anachronistic. The doubling, whereby the islanders are both atavistic throwbacks and symbols of contemporary decay, is paralleled in Granía, who is a woman of the present and distant past with no future at all. Her revolt against motherhood is also revulsion against breeding a degenerate race. Greenslade, for example, cites W.E. Henley's denunciation of "abysmal fecundity" in 1892, the year of Granía's publication, as a feared attribute of those least "fit" to breed.[12] The narrative's distaste for the other peasant characters is epitomized by the reference to one of the "brood" of children as "it." Lawless's novel is everywhere inflected with the discourse of racial degeneracy. Surveying both "scientific" tracts on race and the imagery of commercial advertisement and political cartoons, Anne McClintock has linked the discourse of degeneracy with a triangular formation of race, class and gender. Positioning the Irish within this triangle, she powerfully argues that:

> The iconography of domestic degeneration was widely used to mediate the manifold contradictions in imperial hierarchy—not only with regard to the Irish but also to the other "white negroes": Jews, prostitutes, the working-class, domestic workers, and so on, where skin color as a marker of power was imprecise and inadequate. (1995, 53)

An initial example cited by McClintock is an 1882 Puck cartoon entitled "The King of a Shantee," in which "an Irishman is depicted lazing in front of his hovel—the very picture of domestic disarray."[13] McClintock's analysis begs the question of the extent to which borderline groups, but particularly white natives such as the Irish, fulfilled an important function in *maintaining* distinctions of race and class at the imperial center. Their function was to represent domestic disarray and underlying sexual disorder as foreign even when they manifested themselves locally.

In the Puck cartoon analyzed by McClintock, the simianized husband sits on an upturned washbasin, a cooking pot on his head, his equally unprepossessing wife stands in the doorway, "the boundary between private and public."[14] The domestic scene in this cartoon is turned inside out: an instrument of hygiene becomes a site of idleness, the maternal cooking pot is absurdly misappropriated, housekeeping and husbandry are in chaos. In a number of important respects the earlier scene from

Granía more subtly reproduces these stereotypes of domestic degeneracy. The cabin's inhabitants are dehumanized; the woman of the house is unable to nurture, maintain order or to properly maintain the boundaries between private and public, as a proper Victorian mother should; the brutish, incoherent drunk recalls the simianized King of a Shantee; the imagery of a neglected hearth locates the source of this poverty internally, in a lack of proper care and domestic industry, not in the external worlds of social and economic life. Yet, the subject of address in this scene is radically different, for the mediating consciousness is that of one who could become the thing she sees and dreads, not one who can recoil and find reassurance in her difference from the scene. (On more than one level: retrospectively, it is impossible to ignore Lawless's own addiction to heroin, though its exact genesis and trajectory remain unclear.) Consequently, instead of establishing boundaries, this confrontation with domestic degeneracy challenges though it ultimately cannot subvert them. McClintock notes that "the so-called degenerate classes were bound in a regime of surveillance."[14] Here the surveillance is from the inside. Granía's authenticity, her rootedness in the island, her relationship with the sea, her status as "atavistic throwback"[15] are precisely what distances her from the degenerate present of these "Celtic Calibans."[16]

Uncomfortable Prosperos

Granía's affinity to landscape and alienation from her native community echoes earlier nineteenth-century women's fiction, where nature takes the side of heroines like Maggie Tulliver and Catherine Earnshaw against a corrupt society. More alienated in the drawing room than on the desolate moor, Catherine Earnshaw is the epitome of the type. But if Granía has affinities to her, she singularly lacks a Heathcliff. Murdough Blake, whom she loves from childhood, is the opposite of rugged authenticity: "Murdough had nothing to sell and nothing to do, but any opportunity of escaping for a few hours from Inishmaan, any prospect of stir, bustle, and life was welcome to him" (104). Integrity in the novel is associated with having only one, native language: "I've got no English either, and I don't want any of it," she [Granía] answered proudly; "I had sooner have only the Irish" (131). Murdough, who is talking while idly watching Granía work, despises his own language and craves a multiplicity of languages, a desire that is the very substance of all his ambitions, and, like those ambitions, is defined by impracticality and excess and a repudiation of work and struggle (he craves languages more than a horse, for example):

> I wish that I knew all the languages that ever were upon this earth since the days of King Noah, who made the Flood. Yes, I do, and more too, than ever there were on it! Then I could talk to all the people and hold my head high with the best in the land. (131–32)

Language is power and wealth to Murdough, but his language is without referent or structure. His loquacity is an effect of impotence, not creativity or power:

> It was a torrent to which there was apparently no limit, and which, once started, could flow as readily and continue as long in one direction as another.
>   Granía was hardly listening. She wanted—she hardly knew what she wanted—but certainly it was not words. (139–40)

The other figure of cultural continuity in the text is the storyteller with no audience, Old Durane. His memory is largely a matter of words, but of unuttered or private ones. His rich language is not a communal one and is used for recollection, not communication. He is described sitting alone for hours:

> muttering over and over some cabbalistic word—a word which, for the moment, had the effect of recreating for him the past, one which, even to himself, had grown almost spectrally remote, so dim and far away was it. A queer old ragged Ulysses this, whose Ithaca was that solitary islet set in the bleak and inhospitable Atlantic! (77)

This queer old ragged Ulysses is all that remains of the spectrally remote traditions elegized by Lawless in *Maelcho*. "Senachies, such like beings—big talkers and little doers,"[17] are despised by Hugh Gaynard, the English youth who is the initial hero of that novel. But just such a big talker comes to occupy the central role. Maelcho, with his stories about "the Fear Gortach, a giant who eats up children and animals and drops their bones from the sky and about three young men who conquered the world and then HyBrasil, along the way defeating three giants, Gom, Gum and Groggertnabognach"[18]—is on one level an icon of native strangeness. He is part of a culture of linguistic excess that is identified with violence and the absence of culture. At one point, the crowd is stirred by an incantation:

> Never had they so closely resembled a company of wolves, such a company as one might imagine resting for a moment in the shadow of some wood, before sweeping on to tear down everything it met with on its path, leaving only a few red and mumbled fragments to tell the tale. (54)

Yet Maelcho becomes, in Lawless's powerfully contradictory novel, not Caliban but his master. When Gaynard begins to function as messenger for Sir James, his duties "liberated him from having to act as Caliban to such an uncomfortable Prospero as Maelcho the senachie" (162).

In *Grania*, Murdough's verbosity is modern and restless, but also native. It is a very tattered remnant of the storytelling tradition culture Maelcho eventually loses in madness, silence and defeat. This decline and loss is characteristic of all aspects of native culture in the novel: the Claddagh fishermen "fish less and worse than their father did, and let the lion's share of the yearly spoil fall into the hands of strangers" (79–80). Murdough represents the degeneration of a race, the pure, archaic version of which is represented in Grania, who can see no point in the continuation of life and whose own life ends in a reckless bid to ease her sister's death. (Honor is intensely religious and Grania's death by drowning in a futile attempt to bring her a priest from the mainland can be seen as a suicidal act of self-assertion or her final defeat by the community that refuses to help her and by the church, distant and all powerful.)

Lawless's own anxieties, biographical and historical, pervade her fiction and historical works. Personal anxiety about the role of heredity must have played heavily on the mind of a daughter of a notorious madman. The suicide of Lord Cloncurry, Emily's father, was sensationally reported in the media and fear of hereditary madness (a prevalent concept in the society as it was in the literature of the time) was an inevitable legacy. The kindest thing that Lawless's mentor, the Scottish novelist Margaret Oliphant, could do in her warm obituary for her old friend Lady Cloncurry was simultaneously to obliterate all mention of her husband and laud the achievements of her daughter as the new Edgeworth.

A broader historical anxiety also haunts Lawless's fiction and the Irish gothic tradition that influenced it. Lawless lampooned the alliance of Irish nationalism and American novelty in her weakest and most reprinted novel, *Hurrish*. Yet there and elsewhere an uneasy suspicion surfaces that the peasant life Lawless can chart with extraordinary sympathy and insight is the locus of progress and possibility. In all her contradictions, Lawless was an Irish Victorian; belief in and anger at progress were tempered for her by the fear of elimination by it. Class affiliation complicated and perplexed her desire for reform in social and sexual relations. Perhaps for this reason, contemporary commentators had difficulty classifying her. Swinburne admired *Grania*, another reviewer compared it to Gissing ("But Grania is more poetical and less sordid"). Her poetry was first appropriated by nationalism and then dismissed as mere patriotic verse. Perhaps precisely because of these difficulties, *Grania* is a startling, powerful and still relevant exploration of the conflict between communal identity and feminine individuality. The conflict is cast within the narrative of degeneracy, yet at key points it challenges that narrative.

DESIRING INDEPENDENCE

Katherine Cecil Thurston's sensational tales celebrate self-invention to a dizzying degree. Paradoxically, she is now best known for the one novel where life fails to live up to the fantasies of its protagonist. Thurston's *The Fly on the Wheel* is close to *Granía* in its exploration of the social and psychological restrictions on a young woman of independent mind in turn-of-the-century Irish society. Isabel Costello faces not the perils of the Atlantic, however, but those of middle-class Munster, respectable society. *The Fly on the Wheel* ends, like *Granía*, with the death of the heroine.

Like her contemporary Emily Lawless, Thurston came from a political family. Her father was a Home Rule Mayor of Cork and an associate of Parnell's. Unlike Lawless, Thurston herself strictly avoided national politics in her writing, though the sexual politics of the younger woman's work were spectacularly more radical and overt. While never successful in the complete separation of national and sexual politics, Irish women's writing has consistently tended to be much more adventurous with regard to the possibilities of sexual freedom outside of Ireland. Like Kate O'Brien, for whom she is a significant predecessor, Thurston's fiction set in Ireland is more pessimistic about the possibility of social, sexual and personal change than that set elsewhere. Ireland is nonetheless romanticized in Thurston's fiction, in the rural landscapes of *The Gambler* and the finally irresistible Irish lover for whom Max becomes Maxine. Its society is dreaded, however. Thurston's reputation now rests on *The Fly on the Wheel*, the only one of her novels reprinted by Virago. An excerpt was also included in Colm Tóibín's anthology of Irish fiction.[19] It is the closest Thurston comes to sober realism, despite its melodramatic conclusion. The fatally headstrong protagonist was so far identified with Thurston in her lifetime that her death in a Cork hotel at the age of thirty-six was widely speculated to have been a suicide despite the coroner's verdict of natural causes. The speculation left the realm of gossip and became literary biography when it was repeated by the prurient Stephen Brown in his *Ireland in Fiction*.[20] This confusion of scandalous life and sensational art is not unusual for woman writers, but it has a particular irony in Thurston's case. She was, without doubt, a celebrity constantly on the verge and often in the realm of notoriety. Her divorce from novelist E. Temple Thurston was reported in great detail and the case was in effect fought by him as one between the claims of decadent art and those of the New Woman, attributing the desertion and adultery of which she accused him to their conflicting careers as novelists:

> it was necessary for his literary work that he should descend into the depths of society. He complained that she was making more money from her books than him, that her personality dominated his, and said that he wanted to leave her.[21]

Thurston's novels celebrate the freedom of art everywhere, the right to independence of feeling and thought and the facility of self-invention. Where these are missing, as in the Waterford of *The Fly on the Wheel*, life is simply not worth living. The novel's main male protagonist, Stephen Carey, finds initially that "even for me—the respectable citizen, the cut-and-dried lawyer—there's life to be lived" (281) and seems ready to turn from "sitting in my office, living the petty routine, playing the eternal game" (281) to run away with the novel's heroine, Isabel Costello. When he fails to do so, he is depicted returning to his reading room: "its very barrenness, its very coldness suited him on this day" (311). Isabel, who, in true sensational fashion, finally commits suicide with the poison she had intended for him, is presented as more alive in her death: "her eyes caught the warmth, the redness, the glory of the sun" (327).

There is something incorrigibly youthful about the anger, energy and passionate optimism of most of Thurston's work. Interestingly, *The Fly on the Wheel*, which was her fourth novel, did seem to indicate a turn to social realism and pessimism, but *Max*, published just two years later, can be read as an emphatic recovery from both afflictions. Set in a Paris of fantastically glamorous possibility, *Max* epitomizes the adventurous spirit of much decadent and New Woman fiction in its presentation of gender as role-play, its exploitation of the homoerotic and its exploration of the relationship between sexual and aesthetic freedom. The central character lives as a man in order to become an artist, making out of the loss of sexual identity the very material of her art. Published eighteen years after *Granía*, it indicates the extraordinary reimagining of gender that occurred in the interim. The contrast between its audaciousness and its current obscurity is salutary. Nothing in Irish culture will approach its exuberant gender play until Neil Jordan's *The Crying Game*. Like the latter, the novel turns upon a scene of sexual revelation that is also a scene of sexual transformation. The publisher's advertisement for *Max* linked it to Thurston's enormously popular first novel: "Like *John Chilcote M.P.* it deals with a masquerade, but one planned upon entirely different lines, for it is the heroine and not the hero who masquerades." The successful reinvention of identity was at this point the trademark and selling point of Thurston's fiction. In *John Chilcote M.P.* the impoverished impostor turns out to be a better man than the drug-addicted politician who hires him as a convenient double. The permanent replacement of the real Chilcote by his double, both in the public eye and in his previously ailing marriage, is presented as a happy and even morally appropriate ending. The enormous popularity of this novel, which successfully transferred to the stage and later to cinema, indicates something of the popular appetite for such freedom to reinvent the self. In *Max*, this freedom is linked to art and to the release of a creativity more authentic than the accidents of society, sex and personality that constitute one's "real" identity.

For the first twenty chapters of the novel, Max is consistently referred to as "he" and, though a mystery linked to the disappearance of a Russian lady is hinted at, there are no real clues within the novel that the boy is anything other than that. He then retrieves his long, feminine hair, and is discovered looking at himself in the mirror by Jacqueline, the neighbor who has already guessed his/her secret. This episode constitutes the moment of crisis in the novel, when an incident in a nightclub awakens Max to the sexual possibilities of his/her relationship with Edward Blake, the Irishman whom s/he has cultivated as a friend and mentor. This sexual awakening precipitates an artistic one. Max's femininity does not emerge as a natural, real identity, but is constructed, first by the addition of hair, next by the skills of Jacqueline, finally by Max's artistic "materialization" of it in the painting of his supposed sister, Maxine, with which he, without understanding quite what he is about, seduces Blake. The transformation occurs gradually in the latter part of the novel and is resisted by Max himself (Thurston refers to her protagonist as "him" when dressed as a man and "her" when dressed as a woman, throughout). Initially, Max loses rather than gains sexual and indeed all identity:

> Max looked and, looking, lost himself. The boy with his bravery of ignorance, his frankly arrogant egoism was effaced as might be the writing from a slate, and in his place was a sexless creature, rarely beautiful, with parted, tremulous lips and wide eyes in which subtle, crowding thoughts struggled for expression. (193)

The idealist boy seeks to rationalize and stabilize his identity in a pose of artistic androgyny: "We have all of us the two natures—the brother and the sister! Not one of us is quite woman—not one of us is all man!" (198). Max does not wish to acknowledge that his difficulty in maintaining this position stems from his growing attraction to Blake. He displaces his unease onto a "little human play, where real people played real parts" (199), witnessed between lovers in the restaurant where he had dined with Blake. Jacqueline is more astute, however, and produces an image of the femininity that Max has lost for him in the mirror, taking on the role of artist herself in the process:

> Excitedly, and without permission, she began to free Max of the boy's coat, while Max yielded with a certain passive excitement. "Ah!" She gave a cry of delight and ran to the bed, over the foot of which was thrown a faded gold scarf—a strip of rich fabric such as artists delight in, for which Max had bargained only the day before in the rue André de Sarte.
> "Now the tie! And the ugly collar!" She ran back, the scarf floating from her arm; and Max, still passive, still held mute by conflicting sensations, suffered the light fingers to unloose the wide black tie, to remove the collar, to open a button or two of the shirt.
> "And now the hair." With lightning-like dexterity, Jacqueline drew a handful of hairpins from her own head, reducing her short blonde curls to confusion, and in a moment had brushed the thick waves of Max's clipped hair upwards and secured them into a firm foundation.

"Now! Now, madame! Close your eyes! I am the magician!"
(200–201)

It is not undressing but dressing that makes Max a woman, and while the
description of this process is erotic and obviously sexually charged for
Jacqueline, it is the opposite for Max:

> Max's eyes closed, and the illusion of dead hours rose again, more
> vivid, more poignant than before. With the familiar sensation of deft
> fingers at work upon the business of hairdressing, a thousand rec-
> ollections of countless nights and mornings—countless preparations
> and weariness—countless anticipations and disgusts, were born with
> the placing of each hairpin, the coiling of the unfamiliar—familiar—
> weight of hair. (201)

Femininity as masquerade is hard labor, but also art:

> "Now Madame! Is it not a picture?"
> With the gesture and pride of an artist, Jacqueline cast the wide
> scarf round Max's shoulders and stepped back.
> Max's eyes opened, gazing straight into the mirror, and once again
> in that night of contrasts, emotion rose paramount.
> It was most truly a picture; not the earlier puzzling sketch—the
> anomalous mingling of sex—but the complete semblance of the wom-
> an—the slim neck rising from the golden folds, the proud head, seem-
> ing smaller under its coiled hair than it had ever appeared in the
> untidiness of its boy's locks. (201)

Max seeks the only possible way out of the dilemma. He tries to exorcise
this image of himself as woman by painting it. His success suggests that the
previously struggling and frustrated artist must find a way to channel his
femininity into his art rather than deny it. Aesthetic success intensifies his
personal dilemma, however, for the man he loves falls in love with his picture. Max seeks Blake's critical approval of his art: "But Blake's eyes were
for the picture; the portrait of a woman seated at a mirror" (209). If the
romantic Irishman is an old type, he is in Max also a new man, a creature
that even the New Woman occasionally found difficult to imagine. When
he finally witnesses the transformation of the woman in the portrait into
his young male friend, he only pauses very briefly to say "'God!' very softly
to himself. 'God!'" (321) before rushing into his arms and acknowledging,
"I never treated Max as a common boy . . . I always had a queer—a queer
respect for him" (323). Blake is nonetheless relieved when the transformation is reversed and his love for Maxine finally proven and accepted. Maxine argues:

> I know all the specious things that love can say; the talk of indepen-
> dence, the talk of equality! But I know the reality, too. The reality is
> the absolute annihilation of the woman—the absolute merging of her
> identity. (326)

Thereafter she briefly reverts to Max and art before art itself, in the form
of a love song, convinces her she has lost more than she gained. It is easy
today to dismiss Max's final "ardent and eager" (337) repudiation of his
masculine identity and flight to Blake as a compromise, reinstating the heterosexual couple. In the context of 1910, such an ending was also a celebration of the force of desire itself and an insistence that aesthetic and sexual
freedom are not separable.

Max was published at the end of an era and at the end of Thurston's
short life and represents a kind of apotheosis. It epitomizes the particular
achievement of decadents and New Women: to make the artifice of identity,
particularly sexual identity, into art, to counter the terrible pseudoscientific
certainties of their age with regard to gender and race with that art and to
develop an aesthetics that was very much more ethical and subversive than
the moralists who condemned it could imagine.

PENELOPE, OR, MYTHS UNRAVELING: WRITING, ORALITY AND ABJECTION IN *ULYSSES*

Myth, History and Adultery

The nineteenth-century realist narrative modes disrupted by decadents and
New Women were structured by an understanding of time as an infinite
succession of distinct, unrepeatable moments, self-contained but causally
linked. Yet imprinted in this linear story, in the trajectories of biographical and familial development, was another, organic sense of time, time on
the human and biological scale of cycles of birth and death. Stephen Jay
Gould, in his work on the emergence of a concept of geological time as
infinite and expansive, has argued that there persists in Western thinking,
even in scientific and empirical thinking, two models of time: time's arrow,
purposeful and unrepeatable, and time's cycle, organic and repetitious.[22]
Time's arrow corresponds to the time of history and science. The model
of time represented by time's cycle becomes, after the Enlightenment, the
space of myth and mythic thought. The first becomes the realm of progress;
the second has been increasingly identified as conservative, presenting certain aspects of human experience as unchanging and hence unchangeable.
Precisely because it is linked with the organic and the life of the species,
this space seems particularly at odds with the claims of autonomy and individuality, especially if they are made by women or "others." Frederic Jameson's highly influential reading of *Ulysses* as an example of "Third-World

modernism"[23] foregrounded Joyce's use of the "spatial properties" of *The Odyssey* "whose closure is that of the map."[24] The spatial dimension of Ulysses, its mapping out of its own internal space, is crucial to the novel's relationship not only with the classic text with which it corresponds. It is also indicative of the relationship between myth and history, that is to say Greece and Dublin, in the text.

History is the nightmare from which Stephen Dedalus wishes to wake, but history, linear temporality, cannot be interrupted within its own terms. In a context where groups find themselves radically alienated from history—as happened in the aftermath of the world wars, to colonial peoples, to women—the space of myth presents itself as a place from which to question and redefine history.[25] In the context of the literary subversion of history, it is important to remember that recourse to myth has the consequence of reinitiating the nightmare, if the mythic space is used as an evasion of difference and dissent. Homi Bhabha's contention that women and colonial peoples are currently producing new maps of "nation-space," while it does not foreground myth, suggests the possibility that even myths of national identity can be founded on difference.[26] Bhabha's association of these two groups in this project provides a context for a reading of *Ulysses*'s use of myth in terms of its engagement with the inextricable issues of gender and national identity.

Adulteration and Sexual Politics

Joyce's use of myth is necessarily parodic, distinguishing itself from the earnest, authenticating recourse to myths of Mother Ireland and essential Irishness that characterize Irish cultural nationalism. David Lloyd has argued that *Ulysses* is an "adulterative" fiction, a contagion at the site of the attempt to culturally produce Irish nationality as pure, total and homogenous. *Ulysses* deliberately dismantles "the ideological verisimilitude of cultural nationalism."[27] The "Cyclops" episode in the novel, according to Lloyd, is a passage of "intercontamination" (108) where the Citizen's attempt at monologic national self-representation is infected and its fragility and violent instability betrayed by "the internal heterogeneity, the adulteration of discourses . . . the ceaseless interpenetration of different discourses"[28] that constitute Ulysses. Lloyd's reading implicitly identifies Joyce and Molly Bloom: his stylistic adulterations are "the exact aesthetic correlative of adultery in the social sphere."[29] The promiscuous text is subsequently aligned with female sexuality:

> For if adultery is forbidden under patriarchal law, it is precisely because of the potential multiplication of possibilities for identity that it implies as against the paternal fiction, which is based on no more than legal verisimilitude. If the spectre of adultery must be exorcized by nationalism, it is in turn because adulteration undermines the stable formation

of legitimate and authentic identities. It is not difficult to trace here the basis for nationalism's consistent policing of female sexuality by the ideological and legal confinement of women to the domestic sphere.[30]

It is not difficult to trace here a gendering of "social" adultery as feminine and literary adulteration as masculine, which leaves women once again confined to the domestic sphere. Nevertheless, the alliance implied between the feminine, the sexual and the maternal and the aesthetic rupture of totalizing nationalisms is one well worth exploring.

In "Cyclops" the complicity of the revivalists in Catholic hegemony, their misogyny and their sexual Puritanism are presented as inextricable from their anti-Semitism and xenophobia. Rejecting Bloom's more than dual identity as a Jew and an Irishman, the Citizen makes this very explicit:

> We want no more strangers in our house . . . Our own fault. We let them come in. We brought them. The adulteress and her paramour brought the Saxon robbers here. (420)

The Citizen's logic, or rather the unconscious underpinnings of his logic, corresponds to that elaborated in Julia Kristeva's *Strangers to Ourselves*:

> a foreigner seldom arouses the terrifying anguish provoked by death, the female sex, or the "baleful" unbridled drive. Are we nevertheless so sure that the "political" feelings of xenophobia do not include, often unconsciously, that agony of frightened joyfulness . . . ? In the fascinated rejection which the foreigner arouses in us, there is a share of uncanny strangeness in the sense of the depersonalization that Freud discovered in it, and which takes up again our infantile desires and fears of the other—the other of death, the other of woman, the other of uncontrollable drive. The foreigner is within us.[31]

Kristeva has been rightly criticized for concentrating exclusively on imperial national identities and ignoring the different agendas and possibilities of insurgent nationalities. *Ulysses* is, however, very emphatic about the extent to which insurgent Irish nationalism is formed in the image of its imperial other, cracked though the looking glass might be. In the figure of the outsider, Bloom, the novel offers:

> an invitation (a utopic or very modern one?) not to reify the foreigner, not to petrify him as such, not to petrify us as such . . . To discover our disturbing otherness, for that indeed is what bursts in to confront that "demon," that threat, that apprehension generated by the projective apparition of the other at the heart of what we persist in maintaining as a proper, solid "us." By recognizing our uncanny strangeness we shall neither suffer from it nor enjoy it from the outside. The foreigner

is within me, hence we are all foreigners. If I am a foreigner, there are no foreigners.[32]

The correlative of this of course is that there are no natives either. This argument releases the postcolonial people from the polarity of identity imposed by the relation to the former colonizer, but it offers no ground from which the colonized people can lay claim to autonomy. Kristeva recognizes and repeatedly refers to Joyce as a precursor of her vision of a "paradoxical community."[32] Setting "the difference within us in its most bewildering shape" and presenting "it as the ultimate condition of our being with others,"[33] Joyce of necessity must map out a different nation-space, one predicated on inter/intranationalism, but one that cannot be translated into an imitation of the imperial mode. The concentration on the city, always problematic and difficult for Irish nationalism to assimilate (as Lloyd points out), is a necessary part of this project, not least because it is both inalienably itself, local and particular, and also very like any other city in important respects. Mapping *The Odyssey* onto Dublin, Joyce writes "the nation's modernity as the event of the everyday and the advent of the epochal,"[34] writes Ireland as a modern, Western nation with all the paradoxes implied by that conjunction of terms. This is also mismapping, however, and if Joyce inhabits such concepts of nationality and modernity, it is only as a migrant, an exile and stranger, one of "the marks of a shifting boundary that alienates the frontiers of the modern nation,"[35] one who is spectacularly successful in making all "cultural languages 'foreign' to themselves."[36] In effect, he unravels the myth and history of nationality, creating space and materials for its reconstitution in different terms.

Unraveling

Identification of *Ulysses*'s textual strategies with Molly Bloom's infidelities begs identification between Joyce and Penelope. Like Molly, Penelope is an artist and like Joyce she is an artist primarily concerned with undoing. Weaving and unweaving, making decision and desire wait upon an achievement she constantly undoes, Penelope is more than a figure for the novel's "adulterations" of tradition. She provides a myth of writing that will supersede Dedalus to become central to *Finnegans Wake*.

The representation and subversion of the eternal feminine and her relation to Mother Ireland is a key site of cultural unraveling, enacted early in *Ulysses* and recurring until it is defined and completed in Molly's monologue. The encounter between Stephen, Haines and Mulligan and the milk woman at the very beginning of the novel prefigures all of the contradictions and paradoxes that will be resolved, however unsatisfactorily, by Molly. The milk woman, defined by giving nurture and "her woman's unclean loins" (16) is a stereotypic figure of the maternal, needed and feared. She takes the narrative place of Athene, but never achieves mythic status, for she is mocked even before her entrance by Mulligan's recounting of an old Dublin saying[37]:

> When I makes tea I makes tea, as old Mother Grogan said. And when I makes water I makes water . . . so I do Mrs Cahill, says she. Begob ma'am, says Mrs Cahill, god send you don't make them in the same pot. (13–14)

This is Molly's meditation on her breasts' fascination for the men in her life and her excretions and effusions prefigured and condensed. The old woman's voice is mimicked by Mulligan: Molly's will be constructed by Joyce.

Sayings are the most fragmentary aspect of the oral tradition, the very opposite to the complex but highly coherent set of images implied by myth, particularly the myth of the eternal feminine. No simple opposition is posited here between the local and folkloric and the conservative and universal myth, however. The old woman is also very specifically Mother Ireland: "Silk of the kine and poor old woman names given her in old times" (15). And Stephen prefigures the Citizen's paranoid logic in describing her (which he reprises in "Oxen of the Sun"): "A wandering crone. Serving her conqueror and gay betrayer" (15). The mythic burden of this figure is comically overloaded when the milk woman mistakes the Irish addressed to her by the Englishman Haines for French. Her mistake oddly aligns her with Stephen even as he scorns her for he, not willing to wait for her milk, wanted lemon in his tea: "damn you and your Paris fads," comments Mulligan (13). This perplexity of national identities does not simply debunk the myth of Mother Ireland. That is left to Mulligan who is heartily despised for his crudity here. The residual power of the myth is evident in Stephen's recoil from this woman's subservience and understanding of the encounter in mythic terms, an understanding that neatly removes from the men the responsibility for an understanding of economic terms and full payment of the bill. At the heart of the exchange between the old stereotype and the modern parodists is an ironic sense that "Ireland is just another of those modern places, where there is no there any more."[38]

The confrontation between Bloom and the Citizen provides another scene of unraveling identities. The latter's comment that a faithless wife was "the cause of all our misfortune" (240) applies so aptly to Leopold Bloom's personal predicament that this Irish myth of betrayal becomes in the same gesture personalized, depoliticized and repoliticized. It undermines Bloom's exclusion from the group, since their myths have relevance for him. It unmasks the insecurity of pure forms of identity and the wellsprings of the need for scapegoats. The assembled company in this scene might laugh at the idea that they are strangers to themselves, but the suspicion that their wives are strangers to them surfaces uneasily.

Alice Jardine has argued that modernism makes articulation of the feminine a legitimizing strategy.[39] Forays into this dangerous territory become touchstones of daring, and authenticity is claimed through recycling an old myth of immanent reality, organic life through the feminine. At the same time, modernism is haunted by the fear that the other knows herself better and may have something more interesting to say. This sense of another voice, not defined by the myth or admitted to history, surfaces in "Nausicaa." Gerty's fantasy of the dark stranger is one that Gilbert and Gubar identified as recurrent in nineteenth-century women's literature and that they describe as "female fantasies that are much more concerned with power and authority than romance."⁴⁰ The language Gerty borrows from such fantasies and the other languages of popular culture that surface in the novel constitute frustrated protomyths that seek universal significance for the everyday in ways that correspond to Joyce's strategies. Though these protomyths fail, they are not treated altogether unsympathetically. The pulp romance voice of Gerty benefits by contrast with the immediately preceding spleen of the Cyclops narrator and a highly inflated passage describing Bloom in the jaunting car as ben Bloom Elijah transfigured. There is considerable poignancy in the contrast between her style and the reality of her family's impoverishment and brutalization as a result of her father's alcoholism, and the record of beatings followed by reference to piety (460–61). Her romantic musings may be conventional and hypocritical, but her attraction to Bloom's foreignness is a version of that alliance of the sexual and alien that the Citizen feared. Gerty's romantic prose and devotional pieties mingle into an eroticization of and identification with the Virgin Mother, an unraveling of the myth at the textual level, but also an unwitting personal subversion of its repressive power. Gerty, like Molly, "loved to read poetry" (473), even if her taste is sentimental and satirized.⁴¹

The authority of the author is always perilous and self-parodic in *Ulysses*, but the encounter with feminine self-articulation does seem to raise particular anxieties. Stephen is teased (by John Eglinton) in the National Library about dictating a new version of *Paradise Lost* to six medics "The Sorrows of Satan he calls it" (235). The title is that of a novel by Marie Corelli and the comment is followed by a false smile from Stephen. Stephen and the despised popular woman writer are associated in their illegitimate relation to a tradition defined in terms of Goethe, Shakespeare and Lyster's sense of criticism as "A great poet on a great brother poet" (235). Later, Eglinton will comment, "Vining held that the prince [Hamlet] was a woman. Has no-one made him out to be an Irish-man?" (254), indicating he is subliminally aware of the connection. In daring as well as resenting such an association, Joyce's fascination with popular, despised or corrupt cultural forms (advertising, street ballad) and his colonial's sense of exclusion from a masculine realm of cultural authority fuse. Stephen's response is conventionally "feminine," telling himself to smile at this mockery of his intellectual pretensions. Eglinton's next comment indicates that Stephen lacks something necessary to become part of the great brotherhood of poets, whether of the old imperial cultures or the emerging "legitimate" Irish tradition, epitomized by Yeats and Synge—"I feel you would need more for Hamlet." And after Stephen meditates on his sympathy for and alienation from Cranly's quest to free Ireland, here ambiguously gendered ("sireland" but also "gaptoothed Kathleen"), Eglinton "censured" that: "Our young Irish bards . . . have yet to create a figure which the world will set beside Saxon Shakespeare's Hamlet though I admire him, as old Ben did, on this side idolatry." Eglinton's idolatry is the desire of the colonized to culturally rival the colonizer by reproducing the colonizer's forms, and it will lead others like him to censure/censor the writing of a new generation of writers that does not serve this purpose. His association of himself with Ben Jonson is ironic. Joyce implies Ireland's literary "renaissance" is crippled by seeing itself in terms determined by English cultural myths. Yet Jonson's "On inviting a friend to dinner" invokes a defiant conviviality and the social paranoia induced by the presence of informers in a way that is close to Bloom's earlier musing on this subject.

Writing perhaps is always in danger of being on the wrong side of power. Nonetheless, a patrilinear, authoritative Western cultural tradition has been produced in the image of political imperatives of nation, state and empire and it is from this tradition that these Irish literary sons seek recognition. It is a tradition presented with homoerotic overtones by Joyce, in the reference to Aristotle as Plato's "schoolboy" and in the overemphatic denial by Stephen of the possibility of a sexual betrayal of the father–son relationship. "They are sundered by a bodily shame so steadfast that the criminal annals of the world . . . hardly record its breach" (266). The possibility having been raised, it is difficult to ignore the ambiguity of "He is in my father. I am in his son" (248). Such overtones subvert the polarity of body and mind, culture and materiality, sexuality and purity necessary to maintain the notion of an objective, universal aesthetic and cultural standard.

Mulligan mocks Yeats's ecstatic description of Lady Gregory's Poets and Dreamers, "One thinks of Homer" (278), but the comment also anticipates similar mockery of Joyce's own pretensions. The alliance or identification that I am arguing for here between Joyce and the woman writer is attested to some degree in Angela Carter's use of him as a resource in *Wise Children*, for example,[42] and in the readings of Joyce by Kristeva and Cixous that see him as a writer who "gets something by" of woman and as an ally in the feminine attempt to renegotiate the symbolic. Those aspects of language identified by Stephen Dedalus as the source of language's attraction in *Portrait of the Artist as a Young Man* correspond startlingly with Kristeva's semiotic and symbolic:

> Words. Was it their colors? He allowed them to glow and fade, hue after hue: sunrise gold, the russet and green of apple orchards, azure of waves, the grey fringed fleece of clouds. No, it was not their colors: it was the poise and balance of the period itself. Did he then love the rhythmic rise and fall of words better than their associations of legend

and color? Or was it that being as weak of sight as he was shy of mind, he drew less pleasure from the reflection of the glowing sensible world through the prism of a language many colored and richly storied than from the contemplation of an inner world of individual emotions mirrored perfectly in a lucid supple periodic prose?[43]

Bloom is more succinct: "Words? Music? No: it's what's behind" (354). While Bloom leans more toward the semiotic than Stephen does, both men express a preference for that referentiality that is a property of the symbolic order.

Oralization

It has become commonplace to regard Molly's monologue as not only the essence of feminine writing,[44] but also as the novel's final attempt to produce in writing a form of, or fusion with, the oral. Declan Kiberd makes a more radical assertion:

> *Ulysses*, judged in retrospect, is a prolonged farewell to written literature and a rejection of its attempts to colonize speech and thought. Its mockery of the hyper-literary Stephen, of the writerly talk of librarians, of the excremental nature of printed magazines, is a preparation for its restoration of the human voice of Molly Bloom; and, in a book where each chapter is named for a bodily organ, the restoration of her voice becomes a synecdoche for the recovery into art of the whole human body.[45]

A site of recovery from literature, a textual embodiment of the negation of literature, Molly becomes the pre-Oedipal regained by the son *in his own words*. The anxieties and loss implicit in national and sexual differences are lost in a utopian passage to language before its fall from senses to sense. Such euphoric identifications indicate *Ulysses*'s success in consummating the perilous modernist romance with the phallic mother. Lack is lost in the embodied word. For Molly's soliloquy is, after all, not oral, but a masterpiece of oralization:

> a reunion with the mother's body which is no longer viewed as an engendered, hollow and vaginated, expelling and rejecting body, but rather as a vocalic one—throat, voice and breasts; music rhythm, prosody . . . the Oedipus complex of a far off incest. This oralization restrains the aggressivity of rejection through an attempted fusion with the mother's body, a devouring fusion . . . A return to oral and glottal pleasure combats the superego and its linear language. Suction or expulsion, fusion with or rejection of the mother's breast seem to be at the root of this eroticisation of the vocal apparatus and through it, the introduction

into the linguistic order of an excess of pleasure marked by a redistribution of the phonetic order, morphological structure and even syntax;
portmanteau words in Joyce, syntax in Mallarme.[46]

Or to use the language of Molly's soliloquy, "like some kind of a big infant
I had at me they want everything in their mouth all the pleasure they get
out of a woman" (893). Seamus Deane, in his analysis of Joyce's "mapping
of sexual and national identity," asks:

> Is this the language of emancipation or merely its phantom? Is it the
> language of the emancipated or merely its phantom?[47]

Kristeva's answer appears to be that it is, in fact, revolutionary. Devouring
the mother in combat with the Name of the Father, this revolution does not
achieve a redistribution, however, least of all of power. On the contrary, it
provides narrative closure, the victory of myth as the opposite of history,
essentially of a myth of the feminine as history's other. Only the first three
and last three books of *Ulysses* follow Homer's narrative, the "historical"
dimension of *The Odyssey*. The intervening sections reorder the "original"
events and encounters, a strategy that renders them episodic and puts the
focus on mythic figures rather than the heroic tale. It is in these intervening books that semiotic turbulence comes closest to doing violence to the
symbolic order and where unraveling is the primary textual mode. *Ulysses*'s conclusion marks a return to a myth that puts an end to that process,
though it does not foreclose the possibility for other (hi)stories that had
opened up along the way.

Adulteration may institute "a multiplication of possibilities for identity,"[48]
but its multiplicity is defined in terms of binary polarities (Ireland or England, Molly or Bloom, dialogic or adulterative, pure or hybrid, myth or
history) that reassert themselves at the novel's end. Like the cultural nationalists he challenged, Joyce finally made a version of the feminine a guarantor of his new (literary) order, but, like Wilde's Sphinx, Molly Bloom is
an eternal mystery, an artist and a willful woman. Bloom comes home to
quite a strange place. The space of oralization becomes, in Kristeva's later
work, the space of abjection, the gesture of revulsion against the outside of
self that is the first step in the constitution of a sense of inside self and the
threshold of language. A vortex of summons and repulsions, abjection is an
unraveling that writing only approaches at great cost and danger of madness or worse (witness the anti-Semitism of Celine). In *Finnegans Wake*,
"that nightmare production,"[49] Joyce moves beyond Molly, toward a version of the feminine prefigured in the milk woman who was not Mother
Ireland. Anna Livia Plurabelle is another universal and particular myth of
the feminine, but she is also "full of sillymottocraft" (623) and she imagines alternatives; "how the wilde amazia . . . she would seize to my other
breast" (627). Her closing lament, "And its old and old its sad and old its

sad and weary I go back to you, my cold father [sea] . . . and I rush my only into your arms," echoes the lament of the Cailleach Bheara, a mythic and prototypical Mother Ireland poem, but "in the fluid world of the Wake"[50] sovereignty is divorced from ownership: "How can you own water really? It's always flowing in a stream, never the same."[51]

Anna Livia Plurabelle's acronym offers another figure for writing, of folkloric rather than mythic origin. The Alp Luachra in Irish folklore gets into the stomachs of men who lie down in cut grass and breeds there. She and her children can only be expelled through regurgitation over a stream. The story, in Douglas Hyde's *Beside the Fire*, would have been available to Joyce, as it was published in 1910.[52] Hyde was satirized by Joyce and famous for sanitizing these stories, but the impregnating maternal Alp Luachra is a scandalous figure, confusing as tea and water in the same pot, crossing genders and eliciting an abject regurgitation that parallels Joyce's compulsive quotation, appropriation and reproduction. Anna Livia surrenders to the sea: "End here. Us then. Finn, again!"[53] In the combat between "oral and glottal pleasure" and "the superego and its linear language," however, this surrender is also the momentary victory of the maternal. "By a commodious vicus of recirculation,"[54] the end can only reinitiate the struggle and symbiosis of semiotic and symbolic. In Alp's end is not closure, but a beginning.

REGENDERING MODERNISM: THE WOMAN ARTIST IN IRISH WOMEN'S FICTION

The period between 1922 and 1960 is often characterized as one of social and cultural stagnation in Ireland. Irish fiction was dominated by an *avant-garde* writing in exile and the local dominance of the short story. Attention to the noncanonical fiction of women during the period, however, reveals a literature that exceeds this paradigm. The focus of this section is on two novels—*The Troubled House* (1938)[55] by Rosamond Jacob and *As Music and Splendour* (1958)[56] by Kate O'Brien—that feature women as artists. This figure provides in both cases a mode of combining a commitment to narrative realism with a self-reflexive exploration of the role of art, thus evading the fictional polarities of the period. The woman artist as fictional character also offers an opportunity to explore the relationship between gender, sexuality, politics and art.

The linkage between sexual dissidence and aesthetic freedom is a persistent trope of modernism in the Irish context, even if it is often critically submerged under the theme of exile. Both *The Troubled House* and *As Music and Splendour* might be considered to be supplements to Irish modernism in the Derridean sense, "an originary necessity and an essential accident."[57] Through the figure of the woman artist, both of these marginal novels transgress the configurations of gender at the heart of that modernism's aesthetic project.[58] Both link transgressive sexuality with artistic production. In doing so they posit a very different relationship between sexuality, aesthetics and politics.

Art, Politics and Sexuality: The Troubled House

While women have not figured prominently in the histories of Irish literary modernism, they were central to the development of modernism in the visual arts in Ireland. Rosamond Jacob aspired to be an artist herself as a young woman and she moved in artistic circles.[59] A woman artist figures prominently in her 1938 novel *The Troubled House*. Resolutely modernist, Nix is also the primary erotic object for the troubled Cullen family at the novel's center. The novel is stylistically realist, a historical novel set during the War of Independence. The story is told from the perspective of Margaret Cullen, who returns from nursing a sick relative abroad to encounter an almost unrecognizable Dublin, where a guerrilla war is raging in which her three sons are variously involved. Her relationship with her sons is infinitely more intense than that with her husband, who is initially outraged by the new militancy of the nationalist movement. The eldest son, Theo, is in principle a republican pacifist who in practice cannot avoid involvement in political and military activities, rather like Jacob herself. Theo's active involvement in the campaign against the British military is precipitated by the willful middle son, Liam, a figure of considerable authority though also impetuous and somewhat ambivalently the mother's favorite. He also risks the involvement of the youngest son, Roddie, who remains a fairly vague presence, as befits his role as emblem of the future.

The story of the War of Independence in *The Troubled House* is both a form of revolutionary nostalgia for the state that might have been, and a challenge to the appropriation of the rebellion by a conservative and pietistic mythology. Religion does not figure at all in Jacob's account and the importance of women at least in hiding fugitives and sending messages is foregrounded, though typically there is no woman character as politically active as was Jacob herself. Moreover, the inclusion of the voice of southern unionism in the character of James Cullen is highly unusual. He may be represented as misguided, but he is certainly not a villain. His alienation from his sons and the shattering of his sense of security is treated highly sympathetically. It is the mother of the Cullen family who brings them into contact with two women artists, who live and work together in their apartment in Merrion Square. Margaret is invited to visit by the older of the two artists, Josephine Carroll, whom she has met on the journey back to Ireland and who has offered to show her new friend her paintings. There Margaret and Theo meet Nix Ogilvie, an altogether more exciting artist, who also introduces them to her work. Her cubist paintings, in Mrs. Cullen's view, resemble nothing so much as "a proposition in Euclid," and it is her more representational art that most impresses mother and son:

Now the fifth picture was on the easel. It showed a young man, naked, just poised to dive from a plank into dim green water. You could not tell if it was the sea or a swimming-bath; everything was vague except the slim tense figure. Even the face was indistinct. There was a strange effect of violence, as if it had been painted with blows and thrusts instead of strokes of the brush, but the beauty of it was blinding.[60]

Later presented with an extraordinary portrait of her two sons playing chess, Margaret Cullen accuses Nix of a form of witchcraft, her powers of observation are so acute. Nix observes, "I'm only an artist who has the advantage of working in a new field." Asked if this new field is cubism, Nix responds:

"No—men. The possibilities of men."
"Oh. Is that a new field?"
"Well," said Nix, resuming her brush and setting to work at theoverhead lamp, "it's not a new field in sculpture, of course, but in painting it's been pretty well let alone. Once in a blue moon you get a picture that really gives you a glimpse, but compared with women or landscapes or animals or children, or even buildings, nobody, paints men. They come into a picture sometimes, but that's not painting them. Take portraits, for instance. You must have noticed. Portraits of men are painted because the subject is successful or important in some way, mostly very tiresome-looking old gentlemen, and the artist is commissioned. Sir John So-and-so, with a lot of letters after his name, a famous doctor, or the head of some business concern, or a professor, and painted conventionally, with great respect. But practically never will you see a man's portrait that looks as if it was done for the love of any kind of beauty—for the sake of the picture. Whereas portraits of women are painted to show how nice someone looks lying on the floor in her petticoat, or how well an orange jumper goes with black hair. Or what grand pearls some rich man's wife has got, of course. But though the beauty motive is overdone and exploited with women, to the point of vulgarity, it's right in principle, and ought to be applied just as much to men. When I paint a man, I paint him to show the various kinds of charm I see in him—the things that made me want to paint him—and to show how interesting that charm is, and for nothing else."[61]

Such transgressive looking, while it may occur within the sexual dynamic of heterosexuality, has a queer edge to it. For one thing, these paintings of men are an object of exchange between two women and the scene has an aura of seduction. For another, Nix's painting from the perspective of her own desire is identified by her as opposition to a canonical tradition that refuses to look, except in one way and at one thing.

The link between audacity in sexual and artistic practice is even more evident in the intriguing opening chapters of an unpublished and unfinished novel entitled *Nix and Theo* that Jacob wrote in 1924.[62] The action appears to take place after that of *The Troubled House*: Nix refers to Theo's grief for his father and to his torture, imprisonment and escape from execution during the War of Independence. While *The Troubled House* in its current form was not published until 1938, Jacob describes writing "the Cullen story" in March 1924.[63] Jacob also describes reading an extract from "the Cullens" to her friend, the historian and novelist Dorothy Macardle (discussed in Chapter 3), on June 21, 1924. Macardle, Jacob remarks, "very much admired" the chapters describing Bloody Sunday during the War of Independence, and the day of the massacre figures prominently in the published novel. The genesis of *Nix and Theo* and *The Troubled House*, then, are probably concurrent.

The unfinished novel concerns the relationship between Nix and Theo after Theo's release from wartime imprisonment, or rather it concerns an "experiment" that Nix undertakes, inviting him to "honey-moon" with her while refusing any long-term commitment to him. The influence of D.H. Lawrence—whom Nix refers to in the story—on Jacob's style is apparent in *Nix and Theo*, and there is a distant echo of George Egerton. The lovers wander around Rathdrum in the Wicklow mountains,[64] painting, endlessly discussing sex and art, and making love in the heather (given the climate, the latter probably explains why Theo is on the verge of serious illness at the conclusion of the fragment). However, the story inverts almost all of the conventions of modernist representations of the relationship between gender, art and sexuality. It is Nix who takes all of the sexual and aesthetic initiatives. She books the room in her name and Theo must become "Mr. Ogilvie" for the duration of their stay at a highly respectable village hotel. She mocks Theo's virginity and, after they first make love, she thinks "how interesting and stimulating it would be, when this fortnight was over, to have another week or two with Theo's young brother, Liam, in the same Glen." Nix is a more ambivalent character in this story than in *The Troubled House* and the nature of her artistic freedom is questioned. Her interrogation of Theo about the details of his torture in prison is described as sadistic. Her sexual manipulation of him frightens Theo, not because he is prudish or his masculinity is threatened, but because he understands that she is willing to experiment with a sadomasochistic dynamic he sees as inimical to equal relations between the sexes. (The characters' explicit engagement with the terminology of psychoanalysis as well as feminism is slightly startling given the context of composition.) Theo is occasionally bewildered and sometimes mortified by Nix's treatment of him as a delightful erotic and aesthetic object. "God knows I've seen enough naked models—or nearly naked," she tells him, "but seeing you, here, is different." Any illusions he might have that this is a preface to a declaration of love or even commitment are dispelled by her immediate explanation of it in technical, artistic and even scientific terms:

"The curve of your deltoid muscle and the way the light shows the modeling of your back are the two loveliest things in the world," she said, releasing him for a moment to kiss his shoulder blades. "Maybe so," said Theo, "but you make me shy."

Here the distance between erotic and aesthetic pleasure is erased. While Nix's language objectifies Theo, her hands as well as her eyes are involved in this act of appreciation that both takes and gives pleasure. "'You've even got the semi-antique iliac line!' Her fingers traced it. 'I've hardly ever seen that, thanks to those beastly little loin clothes models wear.'" There follows a discussion between the two on the injunction on the representation of the penis in Western art, which refers to the difficulties Nix has had with the art establishment. Theo argues:

> "It may be sculpted, but it can never be painted whatever suggestive stratagem has to be resorted to. And all because it's obtrusive without being handsome."
> "I paint it," said Nix.
> "You do, and you had a picture refused by the RHA [Royal Hibernian Academy of Art] for no other reason."
> "Yes—wasn't it grand!", said Nix with a little spurt of laughter.

Nix and Theo is much more daring in relation to sexuality than anything Jacob published in her lifetime. While the political engagement of her female fictional characters always falls short of Jacob's own, the ability to laugh at censorship indicates Nix has a far greater freedom in this regard than her author. *Nix and Theo* is an untellable tale, at least in the public domain of 1920s Ireland.

Nix's new way of looking at things is not easily contained within any single form of sexual "identity" any more than it is within one gender. Nor does it accommodate symmetrical oppositions of masculine and feminine, active and passive, subject and object. Rather extraordinarily, *The Troubled House* offers a glimpse of a dissident form of female desire for a different sex. In this regard, Jacob's novel can be regarded as utopian in the sense proposed by Stephen Maddison, "characterized by a radical inclusion of resistant identities."[65] This heterosocial space for Maddison includes "gay, woman, any force of sexual dissidence, but also a community and indeed a utopian social space as yet only imagined": he cites Pedro Almodóvar's *All about My Mother* (Spain/France, Pathé, 1999). Such a space arguably can only be established in cultural margins that are quickly co-opted or disappear. (Maddison points to the art house appropriation and neutralization of Almodóvar as a case in point.) Jacob's work calls for more than celebration of the instability of identity, however, for it is grounded in a very particular, if historically marginalized, identity. That identity is both culturally and historically specific, gendered and political, that of lifelong feminist activist, a category too easily deconstructed precisely as resisting the free play of gender instability. *The Troubled House*, situated in a historical context that recent years have made archivally visible, both invites and resists interpretation as part of a subaltern culture in opposition to the hegemony of right-wing, state, Catholic nationalism. In the case of Jacob, there is considerable evidence of a social and cultural context, far from the center of power in Irish political and social life yet culturally vibrant, that even at the height of social and sexual repression in Ireland bred dissident fictions, but that has never featured in political, social or cultural histories of the period.

Jacob, with the former suffrage leader Hannah Sheehy-Skeffington, was involved in an organization called the Women's Social and Progressive League. No history of the league or its activities has yet been undertaken. One of its aims was to promote the election of more independent women, public representatives outside the mainstream political parties.[66] A fascinating pamphlet on Emily Lawless, based on a lecture given to the members of the Women's Social and Progressive League in November 1944, included an account of the discussion that took place after the lecture.[67] It offers a glimpse of the context in which Jacob wrote and was read. "The chairman, Miss Rosamond Jacob, the distinguished authoress, thanked Mr. Fenton." Thereafter there was a series of interventions from the floor. Mrs. Nicholls, who might have been irritated by Fenton's appropriation of Lawless to a nationalist tradition, "said that her chief recollection of Emily Lawless was that she had always been a supporter of the struggle of women for the vote, and was a warm friend of the Irish Women's Franchise league and for every just cause."[68] Hannah Sheehy-Skeffington "recalled the admiration of the late Thomas Kettle . . . for Emily Lawless's verse and also that Mary Lawless, Emily's sister, offered the hospitality of Lyons to the locked-out children of the Dublin workers in 1913." Sheehy-Skeffington's emphasis on the pro-worker activities of Lawless's sister is a useful corrective to the emphasis on her grandfather's and great-grandfather's pro-nationalist ones in almost all late twentieth-century biographies. What is evident from the account of this meeting is that a countercultural presence existed in the period that extends beyond *The Bell* and its contributors, though that journal was undoubtedly a major source for the dissemination of its ideas.

Another Irish women's organization that awaits historical research is the Women Writer's Club. The only published account of the club's history appears to be that contained in the *Dublin Evening Mail* on the occasion of the club's silver jubilee in 1958.[69] This account mentions that the club was founded by the poet Blanaid Salkeld and lists Patricia Lynch, Kate O'Brien, Winifred Letts, Teresa Deevy, Constantia Maxwell and Maura Laverty among its well-known members. (There are other records: correspondence between Hannah Sheehy-Skeffington and the poet Blanaid Salkeld in relation to the nomination of the Book of the Year for 1936 has also been preserved among Sheehy-Skeffington's papers in the National Library of

Ireland, for example.) Perhaps more intriguingly, the *Irish Press* of December 10, 1958, includes a photograph of Jacob, Kate O'Brien and Madeline Ross, the organization's vice president, at the jubilee banquet. Jacob was guest of honor, her novel *The Rebel's Wife* being the club's Book of the Year for 1958. Dorothy Macardle, who was the club president, was too ill to attend. The longevity and invisibility of the club in literary records is equally striking. Jacob's involvement extended beyond cultural organizations. She was a prominent member of the Women's Prisoners Defense League. One of the small treasures of the correspondence between Jacob and Sheehy-Skeffington is a draft of antivivisection arguments on the back of promotional material (for the 1936 election) for an independent republican called George Gilmore, who campaigned, among other things, "for free school books and for school meals and for proper school accommodation."[70]

Jacob's woman artist in *The Troubled House* is situated in history and has to make political and practical decisions from which her artistic life cannot be separated. The novel's sense of historical possibilities lost is epitomized in the fate of Nix Ogilvie's paintings. Raided because she has been sheltering Liam while he is wounded, she finds her work destroyed by the Black and Tans.[71] The artistic deconstruction of identity politics does not free one from its consequences. School meals, political argument, civil strife and Irish history are the conditions out of which Jacob's marginal texts emerge.

ORPHEUS AND VIOLETTA

Kate O'Brien's last novel, *As Music and Splendour* (1958), is her most complex meditation on the relationship between life, art, sex and politics. The novel traces the development of two Irish opera singers, Clare Halvey and Rose Lennane, from disorientated scholarship girls to mature artists. As is so often the case in O'Brien's novels, her protagonists discover themselves by becoming strangers to themselves and their homeland. "Supposing we'd been left where we were," Clare speculates as they sit drinking wine and discussing their lovers and careers and the prospect of La Scala:

> You'd still be Rose Lennane, your exact, born self, the very girl who was sent to France . . . And I'd be Clare Halvey, as sure as I *am* Clare Halvey. But that Rose Lennane and Clare Halvey there at home, our identical twins, wouldn't be recognizable to us now; to us, I mean, who are trying to imagine them, here in Rome at this minute.[72]

Rose, less introspective and more comfortable with her role as diva-in-the-making, responds, "but that's true about anyone who, well, who was once definitely parted from herself, her obvious self, at any kind of crossroads. Isn't it?"[73]

Remade into "Chiara Alve" and "La Rosa d'Irlanda," respectively, by their training and profession, the two women also remake themselves and, especially in Clare's case, their art. Clare is, for much of the novel, defined both artistically and sexually by her performance in Gluck's *Orfeo ed Euridice* with her lover Luisa:

> The music they both loved had carried them far tonight, together and above themselves. Their descent was slow and reluctant, and their hands did not fall apart when they paused in Clare's doorway. Still Orpheus and Eurydice, their brilliantly made-up eyes swept for each the other's face, as if to insist that this disguise of myth in which they stood was their mutual reality, their own true dress wherein they recognized each other, and were free of that full recognition and could sing it as if their very singing was a kind of Greek, immortal light, not singing at all.
>
> "Thank you, thank you," they both said, and then they laughed at this reciprocal gratitude that always swept through them after they had sung together. And in their laughter they became at once, Clare and Luisa; so, lightly they kissed, and turned away to wash and cold-cream themselves back into the ordinary Roman night.[74]

The contrast with Roman ordinariness reinforces the Greek and immortal value of extraordinariness. That "Greek immortal light" is, of course, symptomatic of the association of poetry, culture and transgressive eroticism epitomized by Shelley's "We are all Greeks."[75] Marjorie Garber argues that while Shelley's remark was a "claim of heritage it was also an erotic claim in the life and writing of Shelley's friend and contemporary Lord Byron."[76] This association of the exploration and challenging of cultural heritages with transgressive sexual and gender identities is central to *As Music and Splendour*. Garber notes that a contemporary reviewer of *Childe Harold's Pilgrimage* warned Byron against the fate of Orpheus.[77]

Orpheus is a pervasive image in O'Brien's novel and the image is chronically overdetermined. Renowned for his love of Eurydice, Orpheus, having lost her twice in Ovid's account, went on to prefer the love of young men.[78] Because of this, he was torn apart by the Ciconian women, his head and lyre drifting, still murmuring music, to Lesbos.[79] That island thereafter became associated with the Orphic mysteries, but its relationship with Sappho and with the origins of lyric poetry are obviously now much better known. To this heady mix of mythic significance, O'Brien adds the identification of Clare with Gluck's opera. She learns the part of Eurydice, plays Orpheus and Alceste, is addressed on several occasions as Orpheus and eventually as Alceste. *Orfeo ed Euridice* is generally regarded as a milestone in the reform of opera and the shift toward greater dramatic realism and lyrical intensity in the eighteenth century, a reform Clare seeks to emulate in the nineteenth.[80] Even at sixteen, "cross, uncertain and at bay," she wonders: "Why can we only sing about what isn't true?"[81] By the time she realizes the nature of her affection for her former school friend Luisa, and the truth of myth, she has come to find Verdi tiresome and to develop a far less mainstream operatic career than Rose. Clare functions in O'Brien's novel as Orpheus does in Gluck's opera, "not merely a plaintive human being, but also a symbol of the singer's most exalted art, transcending all that is personal wherever it finds expression in regular forms."[82] In the figure of Clare, particularly in her artistic collaborations with Luisa and with Luisa's male lover Duarte, *As Music and Splendour* explores a utopian, heterosocial space that is also the space of artistic production. Playing Orpheus, Clare takes on not an unambiguously male role, but one originally written for a castrato. Yet, as the passage quoted earlier shows, the two women's performance is highly sexualized. Duarte, whom Luisa takes as a lover in an initial attempt to fend off her feelings for Clare, trains both women in a more ascetic musical direction than Rose's triumphs at La Scala, with a particular emphasis on church music. Clare and Luisa's performance in Pergolesi's *Stabat Mater* under Duarte's direction, however, is summarized by Clare's admirer, Thomas Evans, as "unusual—wrong, maybe?—but not musically."[83] The performance takes place the day after a scene in Clare's apartment in which Duarte has revealed that Luisa, unfaithful to both of them, has a new lover, Julie, a young concert pianist. Paradoxically, Clare, who strives to retain some hold on the absolutism of her childhood Catholic morality, has a far more labyrinthine personal life than Rose, who finds the idea of reinventing herself in Italy "soothing": it "makes it easier to waive certain questions that would be immoveable at home."[84] Clare's love for Luisa is spectacularly unconditional. When Thomas Evans, himself in love with Clare, proclaims his disgust with her relationship with Luisa, he points to the latter's promiscuity. Clare responds: "It may be for that alarming honesty that I love her."[85] Moreover, this emotion, temporarily at least, seduces her into identification with the operatic personae she had initially feared: "love shows me how to sing the greatest imbecilities!! [*sic*] . . . Because I've lost my bearings, I suppose, like all those cracked sopranos!"[86] But Clare does not lose her bearings for long. She may love promiscuous, volatile and amoral Luisa, but she does so as an opposite. When Duarte, inevitably, switches his affections from Luisa to Clare, she thought "how perverse and strange it would be to kiss a mouth that Luisa had known and kissed—had kissed by habit and goodwill even when she was Clare's sworn lover. Would I find her there, the villain? Would I find any trace of you, Luisa, in so wrong a place?"[87] Perhaps the structural weakness of this remarkable novel's conclusion lies in its final unwillingness to go to so wrong a place, an unwillingness entirely understandable in resisting, as Clare does with a series of suitors, the replacement of her excessive love for Luisa with a more moderate and compromised heterosexual relationship. This is in keeping with Clare's identification with artistic truth and personal integrity throughout. The gradual elevation of Clare's strenuous artistic efforts above Rose's more relaxed deployment of her talents creates a more problematic imbalance by the end of the novel:

It had been observed of Rose by many experts and from her earliest ordeals that nothing, no agitation, no underlined instruction, no first-night terror, no shouting *vis-à-vis*, could get her to force or fuss her singing voice. She could not be made to exaggerate whatever she had to sing. For this she was often in trouble—with bad acoustics, with imperious conductors or uncertain orchestras—and also with her fellow-singers.[88]

This "musical intelligence" has parallels with Rose's personal life, in which she defers her grand passion for one tenor in order to "learn love" with another, a beginner in music and love, as she is herself.[89] "Italy and music had educated her temperament and her talent."[90] Yet the adventurousness, self-preservation skills and sophistication of this "Italianate self"[91] are eventually compromised: she is forced to live an operatic plot. When Antonio, the singer who becomes her grand passion, returns to his aristocratic roots and honors his arranged betrothal to another aristocrat, he assumes their relationship will be unaffected: "Marriage is marriage. It's not everything."[92] The shock of this resurrects her "plain Catholic scruples,"[93] if a little operatically. She cries herself to sleep thinking, "I do nothing else but commit mortal sins—for sentimental reasons."[94] It is as if the novel itself cannot let go of the framework of sin, guilt and retribution that is the legacy of the girls' childhood religion. Neither can it propose this framework as remotely adequate to the world of adult relationships, art, work and Europe. Rose thinks of both her French and Italian lovers as "Catholic pagans,"[95] acknowledging that the problem is not one of belief, but of the inescapability of her Irish origins. In effect, Ireland is both the place Clare and Rose must leave to become artists, but also the certainty they must leave behind to become adults. The exasperating aspect of Ireland is figured throughout in Paddy, a former aspirant to the priesthood who latches on to Clare but is increasingly alienated by what he perceives as her bohemian lifestyle. As Clare moves further away from her roots, she tells Thomas Evans she likes Paddy on the basis that he is "wild and unusual. And he has brains. Oh, he reminds me of home, and forgotten things . . . he's very Irish."[96] This liking gradually cools to toleration. Eventually, when Paddy refuses to write to Rose on the basis of his disapproval of her love life, Clare concurs with Evans's dismissal of him as "a sort of under-done Savonarola."[97]

The inconclusiveness of the novel's ending is indicative that it cannot choose absolutely between Ireland and Italy, Catholicism and opera. (Interestingly, the first and last scenes of *As Music and Splendour* are set in Paris.) Rose comments to Clare: "I've played enough *Traviata*, pet . . . excepting the hacking cough—I play Violetta too much these days."[98] Her sentimentality, if not her scruples, still powerful, she last appears in the novel setting out to cross "the Atlantic before Antonio took his marriage vows. . . . [on] a long and splendidly paid tour of the chief cities of America and South America," with a besotted American millionaire in tow.[99] Clare is left alone in Paris, singing Thomas's musical setting of *As Music and Splendour* to herself: "The Place de la Concorde struck exaggeratedly against the sad quiet of her heart."[100] The contrast between the two singers could be described as that between the sublime Clare and the beautiful Rose. O'Brien's own work is consistently concerned with the aesthetics of the sublime. As John McGahern has astutely commented, she was "a poet working in prose."[101] This suggests that Clare is an author surrogate. Yet Rose, the "absolutely honest artist,"[102] who manages to live life to the full, is in some ways closer to O'Brien's own artistic practice. Indeed, O'Brien's novels, employing the conventions of popular genres of women's fiction and the realist mode, are closer to Rose's operatic preferences than the poetic and mythic preferences of Clare. When Clare complains that their pampered operatic existences have nothing to do with life, Rose is robust in contradicting her: "We have to do with life—that's why we sing. Singing is about life. And we can't help having stomachs and senses."[103] "I write in praise of personal pleasure," said O'Brien at the beginning of that most political travel book, *Farewell Spain* (1937):

> A book, a hand, a first-rate joke; a prayer to God, or the birth of a child; an escape into solitude or a wild night out; a fit of hard work, an attack of romantic love or of marital peace; a visit to the play; a glass of good brandy or good beer. Or a trip abroad—away from it all, as we say.[104]

Rose sails away to glory: Gluck seems to be perpetually leading Clare into the underworld. There is undoubtedly a struggle at the heart of O'Brien's work to honor life while aspiring to exceed its terms in the sublime: "To generate a form imbued with the art of living"[105], to borrow a phrase from her contemporary Katherine Arnold Price. Perhaps Clare's final artistic encounter, not her personal narrative, is more significant in this context. She brings a parting gift from Thomas Evans back home to Ballykerin, for a "cold, lonely summer" awaiting her beloved grandmother's death.[106] "She was shocked at how difficult she found the primitive life of her own people,"[107] and in the isolation consequent upon that realization she teaches herself Evans's songs, for once without guidance in either singing or musicianship:

> They were difficult to get into outline at first; their design seemed too arbitrary . . . She could find no reason in the music, or between each other, for the poems Thomas had made into songs for her. A verse from here—rarely the first or last verse of anything; half a verse from there; two songs set to Welsh, without translation; one prose passage about a swan that seemed like a translation from the German; one verse from Goethe. Lines from John Clare, from Shelley, from Poe, from Tennyson, from Landor.[108]

Evans leaves his own language untranslated: the rest initially appear to be the orts and fragments of the legacy of Romantic poetry. The lines that are most specifically identified have a certain thematic consistency despite Clare's puzzlement. "'A shadow flits before me . . . ' one song began," we are told.[109] This is the second verse of Tennyson's "O that 'twere possible," which echoes the theme of Orpheus and establishes the theme of impossible or lost love that runs through the verses:

> O that 'twere possible
> After long grief and pain
> To find the arms of my true love
> Round me once again!
> A shadow flits before me,
> Not thou, but like to thee:
> Ah, Christ! that it were possible
> For one short hour to see
> The souls we loved, that they might tell us
> What and where they be!

The next song begins "Stand close around, ye Stygian set,"[110] and presumably includes all four lines of Landor's "Dirce," which concerns another ghostly love object. Seeing Dirce, Charon "may forget / That he is old and she a shade." The songs that most appeal to Clare, however, are the settings of John Clare and Shelley. Those from Shelley's "The Flight of Love" link the themes of love and art as does O'Brien's novel:

> As music and splendour
> Survive not the lamp and the lute,
> The heart's echoes render
> No song when the spirit is mute—
> No song but sad dirges,
> Like the wind through a ruin'd cell,
> Or the mournful surges
> That ring the dead seaman's knell.
> When hearts have once mingl'd,
> Love first leaves the well-built nest;
> The weak one is singl'd
> To endure what it once possesst.
> O Love! who bewailest
> The frailty of all things here,
> Why choose you the frailest
> For your cradle, your home, and your bier?

Thomas and Clare are identified in their loss of the possibility of fulfillment in love, but this is also a continuation of his argument against her tendency toward asceticism and his insistence that there is no song without the warmth of living. This song "disturbed her very deeply,"[111] as, understandably, did the setting of John Clare's "Written in Northampton County Asylum":

> I am the self-consumer of my woes;
> They rise and vanish, an oblivious host,
> Shadows of life, whose very soul is lost.
> And yet I am—I live—though I am toss'd
> Into the nothingness of scorn and noise,
> Where there is neither sense of life, nor joys,
> But the huge shipwreck of my own esteem
> And all that's dear. Even those I loved the best
> Are strange—nay, they are stranger than the rest.

Clare's final role is as Alceste. The role identifies her with a female figure this time, breaking apart the identification of her self-aware and strenuous artistry with a masculine role. Duarte, loving and losing her, ceases to call her Orpheus and bids her good-bye as Alceste. Alceste, volunteering to go into the underworld in place of the man she loves, rescued by the man who has loved her, is much closer to the mutable tangle of desire and displacement that characterize romantic relationships in O'Brien's novel than the excessively faithful Orpheus. The original story of Alceste can be seen to complete the project of Orpheus successfully. The heroine this time does come back and death itself is defeated. *Alceste* completes Gluck's project too: it is the ultimate achievement of his attempt to renew opera, more demanding and more self-aware than *Orfeo ed Euridice*. The composer's famous preface outlined the aims of his operatic reforms:

> I sought to reduce music to its true function, that of supporting the poetry, in order to strengthen the expression of the sentiments and the interests of the situations, without interrupting the action or disfiguring it with superfluous ornament ... I have thought, again, that my main task should be to seek a noble simplicity ... there is no rule I have not thought it my duty to sacrifice willingly in order to make sure of an effect.[112]

This chimes with Evans's songs in its sparseness and insistence on the unity of poetry and music. The songs define Clare's art as an art of absence, of longing, in effect an art of desire for the lost object. Defined by the incommensurability of representation and reality, hers are songs of a melancholy sublime. While *As Music and Splendour* is not stylistically modernist, there is no doubt that its self-reflexive meditation on art and the relationships between aesthetic and personal freedom are among the central thematic concerns of modernism.

Dissent, Marginality and Persistence

The traces of cultural, political and social agitation excluded from existing histories of Ireland between 1922 and 1960 are crucial to a reappraisal of the "minor" fiction of the time. One does not really need to see photographic and newspaper evidence (though it helps) of Jacob, O'Brien, Macardle and Sheehy-Skeffington sitting down to dinners and awards ceremonies together to postulate a critical culture that was woman centered, dissident, active and well aware of its political limitations. For the cultural hegemony of Catholic nationalism and social conservatism was unflurried by these uncomfortable presences on its margins. O'Brien was censored and her work made unavailable in Ireland whenever she became too daring. The publication history of both these novelists and women poets in this period indicates what dominant historical forces do to dissident cultural spaces. *The Troubled House* remains out of print. Salkeld's poetry is increasingly reappearing in anthologies and critical accounts, but awaits a new edition of any or all her volumes. The feminist publishing houses, Arlen House and Virago, revived O'Brien's reputation in the 1970s and 1980s, and she is now acknowledged as part of the canon of Irish fiction. There have been four full-length studies of O'Brien to date.[113] *As Music and Splendour* returned to of print in 2005. This delay must have been influenced by the fact that the novel contains O'Brien's only account of a mature lesbian relationship. One of the more striking similarities between *Nix and Theo* and *As Music and Splendour* is their use of poetic quotation. Evans's songs are settings of well-known poems: Nix and Theo play a game of "verse capping" in which they lob quotations from English and Irish poetry in both languages back and forth at each other in a spiral of disagreement about the nature of love and sexuality. The complex and enchanting patterns of quotation and allusion in both texts range from classical literature to opera, Renaissance to Romantic to modernist poetry and, in Jacob's case, Gaelic literature to cubist painting. This self-reflexive referentiality constitutes an effort to lay claim to a broader tradition and to intervene in mainstream cultural and canonical formations. In effect, O'Brien and Jacob are quoting into existence a context for the reading of their work that bridges the gap between the marginality of the identity "Irish woman writer" and the center of cultural production represented by the conjunction of modernist and national literatures. The self-consciousness and difficulty of the enterprise, however, produces an effect close to postmodern *bricolage*. Their intervention precludes the cohesion of the traditions they lay claim to. Whatever utopias *The Troubled House* recalls imagining did not come to pass. Nevertheless, the trace of the supplement is surprisingly strong. The extraordinary level of textual output of this marginal group compensated to some degree for their poverty of political resources. The Jacob and Sheehy-Skeffington papers and the abundant correspondence between women in this period has been making its way into the archives over the last two decades, offering seductive territory for further scholarship and a different view of the period.

5   Haunting James Joyce
Invisible Bodies

> When she was young, in a world now lost and gone, one came across
> people who still believed in art.
>
> (J.M. Coetzee, *Elizabeth Costello*, 207)

THE LOCAL BOY MADE GOOD

In assessing Joyce's place in contemporary culture, there appear to be two
strands, distinct but interwoven. The strongest, international and most
overt strand is that of Joyce the revolutionary enabler, the author of *Ulysses*
and *Finnegans Wake*, after whose intervention the horizons of the novel
form were infinitely expanded and the duties of the critic a grand adventure. The second strand, recently fueled by deconstructions of institutional
modernism, is that of Joyce as disablingly difficult. These two attitudes to
Joyce can coexist even in the work of a single writer or critic, but the second
had something of a resurgence in Ireland in reaction to the Bloomsday Centenary. Joyce was repeatedly praised in the Irish media for the lucid perfection of his early work, while impatience and distrust was apparent for the
linguistic exuberance of his late epics. This was perhaps inevitable given
that, at least until recently, the mainstream of Irish fiction seemed to share
a genealogy with Joyce's early work but remained comparatively untouched
by the later novels. The popularity of Irish fiction with readers and a certain generation of critics owes much to its filiation to the realist mode,
while *Ulysses and Finnegans Wake* remain touchstones of the avant-garde
in writing, twin pillars of modernist aesthetics and postmodern interrogation of the novel, form and language itself. While Joyce is enthusiastically
claimed as evidence of the quality and stature of twentieth-century Irish
writing, an uneasy suspicion hovers on the edge of literary consciousness
that he might have thoroughly disliked a great deal of it. Perhaps inevitably
then the sense of freedom and adventure in Joyce's writing is something
that Irish commentators seem to miss. Both the institutionalization of Joyce
as an icon of Irish cosmopolitanism and the simultaneous commodification of him as an aspect of the heritage industry have potentially made
Joyce a cultural monument, not a cultural resource. He still attracts reverence (never liberating) and suspicion. He is simply too clever by half. The
Bloomsday Centenary celebrations were a popular success, but they did
elicit the hostility of radio phone-ins and tabloid newspapers on the basis

that since *Ulysses* is difficult and we all know difficulty is no more than pretentiousness, then *Ulysses* was merely pretentious. Simmering under the surface was a more erudite variation on this theme, a preference for the formal economy and frequent despair of the early fiction. This was most apparent in the *Irish Times* commentary on their reader's poll of the "greatest Irish novels." *Ulysses* inevitably topped this poll, but the journalistic commentary that accompanied the results suggested *Portrait of the Artist as a Young Man* was a better novel. In an interview on the subject of the Davy Byrne's Short Story Competition (held in Joyce's honor) in the same paper, Tobias Woolf suggested that "The Dead" was an instance of formal perfection no novel could equal.

There were a number of intricately connected critical precepts at work in Woolf's evaluation. One is that formal perfection is the ultimate artistic achievement. Another is a suspicion of opacity and, finally, a preference for the tragic rather the comic mode. (Hugh Macdiarmid, whose appraisal of Joyce is discussed below, with his great, baggy monsters of long, late poems, his hopeful political interventions and outbursts of optimism about the future, could be savaged by such standards far more thoroughly than Joyce.) Form in Woolf's formulation here becomes more than its own justification. It becomes a mode of self-limiting excellence. This image of Joyce the novelist as god paring his fingernails while his creation revolved on the axis of its own formal perfection has come to predominate over that of cultural revolutionary in the popular media, as part of Joyce's extraordinarily transition from "heretic to heritage in one generation," noted by Edna Longley. This chapter examines this transition from two parallel perspectives, first that of representations of Joyce in contemporary writing, looking at three Irish and one intriguing South African example. The second looks at the critical construction of Joyce, focusing on the institutionalization of Irish cultural studies as a form of postcolonial criticism.

ON THE BORDERS OF REALISM

Perhaps appropriately, the most obvious contemporary rewrite of Joyce does not exist: "Elizabeth Costello made her name with her fourth novel, *The House in Eccles Street* (1969), whose main character is Marion Bloom, wife of Leopold Bloom, principal character of another novel, *Ulysses* (1922) by James Joyce."[1] Costello is the eponymous heroine of J. M. Coetzee's 2003 novel. Self-reflexively commenting on its own recourse to a "shouted conversation"[2] in a hotel gymnasium between Elizabeth Costello's son and the chairman of a panel of literary judges awarding her a prize, the novel observes:

> Realism has never been comfortable with ideas. It could not be otherwise: realism is premised on the idea that ideas have no autonomous existence, can exist only in things. So when it needs to debate ideas,

as here, realism is driven to invent situations—walks in the country-side, conversations—in which characters give voice to contending ideas and thereby in a certain sense embody them. The notion of *embodying* [Coetzee's italics] turns out to be pivotal. In such debates ideas do not and indeed cannot float free: they are tied to the speakers by whom they are enunciated, and generated from the matrix of individual interests out of which their speakers act in the world, for instance, the son's concern that his mother not be treated as a Mickey Mouse post-colonial writer, or the chairman Wheatley's concern not to seem an old-fashioned absolutist.[3]

Elizabeth Costello herself comments very directly on *Ulysses*, describing Bloom as a man of "infirm identity, of many shapes,"[4] for example. Her son comments obliquely on it through his consideration of his mother as artist: "*Eccles Street* is a great novel; it will live, perhaps, as long as *Ulysses*; it will certainly be around long after its maker is in the grave. He was only a child when she wrote it. It unsettles and dizzies him that the same being that engendered it engendered him."[5] Elizabeth Costello enables Coetzee to deal with Joyce and the not always compatible demands of realism and modernism at a distance. When Coetzee imagines a writer bold enough to rewrite *Ulysses*, he makes that writer an Irish-Australian woman. It appears to be Irish women writers in the twenty-first century who have the most robust relationship with Joyce's work. An interviewer for the London *Times*, commenting on Anne Enright's Booker win for *The Gathering*[6] in 2007, commented:

> Evidence of her voracious reading life, too, shines out in *The Gathering*. She imagines, for instance, the 1920s Dublin of Veronica's grandparents—a place and time for ever associated with James Joyce, whose work has inspired her own. Was she nervous about comparisons? "No, and, if you don't mind me saying, that's quite a masculine way of looking at it," she says. "There are writers in Ireland who think Joyce threw a great shadow, who are in awe of him. I think that's all bollocks. He cast a great light."

Enright's contempt for Bloomian agonistics is bracing, but literary journalism has been relentless in its application of a Joycean standard by which to measure her novel. When it is praised, the stylistic similarities to *Dubliners*[7] are foregrounded. Denigrated as it was in a particularly virulent set of contributions to online blogs, Joyce is once again a reference point. Given Enright's comment that Joyce cast a great light for Irish writing, the extent to which her work has been attacked in terms that replicate the original condemnation of Joyce is thought provoking: "When Robert Harris, bestselling author of *Fatherland* and *Pompeii*, launched his invective against the Booker last week, saying agents put pressure on authors to write 'Booker-winning' novels that were 'grim and unreadable and utterly off-putting to many readers,' he might have had it [*The Gathering*] in mind."[8] The unofficial literary media repeatedly referred to Enright as "sex obsessed," referring back to her earlier novel *The Pleasure of Eliza Lynch.*[9] In the twenty-first century, respectable literary reviewers cannot thus deprecate a novel, but the brave new world of literary blogging and internet "communities" provides ample evidence that such views persist. Joycean liberation to write beyond the boundaries, to admit the subconscious recesses of the mind to literature, is a prerogative literary fiction cannot afford to take too much for granted. Enright's scrupulous mapping of the silences across which her brave new Dubliners skate unsteadily from past to future, bewildered by the present, reminds us that the borders of the sayable still need to be breached. The phrasing and rhythm of *The Gathering*'s prose replicates that tension in *Dubliners* between what is said and what is known. The alternation of the stark embodiment of ideas in things and the observation of the rules for realism spelled out in *Elizabeth Costello* with the exploration of subjective experience in a rush of lyricism is perhaps the most Joycean element of Enright's style. It also situates it back at the borders, across the borders, of realism:

> I would like to write down what happened in my grandmother's house the summer I was eight or nine, but I am not sure if it really did happen. I need to bear witness to an uncertain event. I feel it roaring inside me—this thing that may not have taken place. I don't even know what name to put on it.[10]

The Gathering indicates that the current level of direct engagement with Joyce's work is part of a reappraisal of the novel form itself at the site where it looks for the names to put on things. The need to bear witness and the uncertainty of the event have a renewed urgency in the twenty-first century as anxiety replaces ennui as the postmodern condition. Enright's novel takes a story that has become a cliché, "yet another miserable Irish childhood," and makes it unbearable. On the fault line between the word and the wordless, where the novel defines and redefines itself, Joyce's work remains unavoidable.

REVISITING NESTOR

Roddie Doyle caused a minor cultural fracas during 2004 when he remarked that *Ulysses* might have benefited enormously from a good editor. Phillip Ensher's remarks were typical:

> From any normal position—the academic's, the ordinary reader's— Roddy Doyle is wildly eccentric to say that Jennifer Johnston is a better writer than Joyce. She is a very good writer indeed, but very few people would place her books above *Ulysses*. What Doyle really means

is that he would himself like to write a book like Johnston's: domestic, tender, full of undisclosed pain. He has no desire whatever to write an enormous book full of allusions to myth and arcane knowledge, and for the sake of his own books cannot afford to understand why anyone at all should want to do such a thing.

It is a perfectly respectable and, indeed, inevitable attitude for a good writer to take. Wrestling with forebears is at the heart of what it means to write fiction in an ambitious way. In this case, everything is made more complex because Joyce has, quite unfairly and almost inexplicably, come to take on an emblematic and suffocating status in Irish writing. With fetes, sponsored readings, and the endorsement of the Irish government, he has stopped being just another writer, and become a monument.[11]

Not the least burden here is that Irish literature be continued in masculine terms. Doyle's preference for Jennifer Johnston over James Joyce is the ultimate rebellion against the masculinist hierarchy of the Irish literary canon. (No Irish male writer has yet publically stated a preference for Virginia Woolf, to the best of my knowledge.) John MacGahern and even Kate O'Brien opted for Proust as their way around the Joycean edifice toward a different relation with modernist style and sensibility. Edna O'Brien's enthusiastic embrace of Joyce's influence seems to indicate that Irish women writers can, however, share the sense of Joycean possibility expressed by Angela Carter, for example.

As the same commentator noted, "nobody apparently checked whether he [Doyle] had any particular liking for Joyce. It was just assumed that he would,"[12] and nobody seems to have asked Doyle what he thought of Joyce before he was invited to speak in his honor, presumably on the assumption that any Irish writer would be glad to do so. A careful survey of Doyle's work might have warned the organizers that the contemporary novelist had a less than reverential attitude toward literary tradition. Doyle wrote the screenplay and coproduced one of the few Irish forays into the romantic comedy genre, *When Brendan Met Trudy,* in 2001 (directed by Kieron J. Walshe, Deadly Films 2, Ireland). Brendan is an English teacher, seduced into a wild double existence by Trudy, a professional thief, in a film that is somewhere between an homage to and a parody of *Au Bout de Souffle.* Brendan's profession and cultural pursuits offer numerous opportunities for comedy in the film. His musical and cinematic tastes have attracted considerable comment by critics,[13] but Brendan's abysmal attempts to teach literature offer comic insight into contemporary Irish culture's relationship with the literary past and are as dependent on insider knowledge as the film's cinematic in-jokes involving *Au Bout de Souffle* and *The Searchers.*

The culmination of the literary in-jokes occur in a scene where Brendan is called from his classroom for an interview with the headmaster in the aftermath of his televised participation in an anti-deportation demonstration, where he has been filmed in violent scuffles with police. The scene parodies the "Nestor" episode in *Ulysses* in considerable detail. Brendan's resistance to his friend's deportation has been as ultimately ineffective as that of Pyrrhus at the Battle of Tarentum, about which Stephen Dedalus quizzes his students at the beginning of "Nestor." Where Joyce presents schoolboys comically struggling with recitation of "Lycidas" and Stephen Dedalus agonizing over his relation with the tradition Milton represents, Doyle presents Brendan teaching in front of a schoolroom poster representing great figures from the literary past, including Shakespeare, George Eliot and, of course, Joyce. The schoolboys again intervene in the relationship, this time by answering the question posed by the poster, "What do all these writers have in common?" with the graffiti comment, "They never said fuck." The schoolboy humor has a certain Joycean ambiguity to it, raising the possibility that the lack of explicitness in literature is actually a lack of meaning. While the literary canon is derided in this scene, the next proposes a popular culture text as transformative and revolutionary. "Do you ever listen to Iggy Pop at all?" the headmaster inquires of Brendan, "He changed my life, I'll tell you that for nothing." Thereafter "I am the passenger" becomes a recurrent motif on the soundtrack.

Both the conversation between Stephen Dedalus and Mr. Deasy in "Nestor" and that between Brendan and the headmaster in *When Brendan Met Trudy* center on questions of race, migration and identity. An anti-Semitic diatribe on Deasy's part culminates in his famous remark that, "'Ireland,' they say, 'has the honour of being the only country which never persecuted the jews. Do you know that? No. And do you know why? . . . Because she never let them in'" (44). For Deasy, migratory status is a special affliction visited upon the Jews, "wanderers on the earth to this day" (41), in retribution for their role in the crucifixion. Doyle's headmaster remarks in contrast, "Aren't we all refugees?" The film concedes his view is a minority one in contemporary Ireland. He tells Brendan he has received numerous complaints from pupils' parents but ends, "I told them all to feck off." In its constant and interlinked referencing of *nouvelle vague* and John Wayne, *When Brendan Met Trudy* positions itself between Europe and America, between high art and popular culture, between a very postmodern version of modernism and Hollywood as the last great apparatus of realism. This intertextual web also positions its central male protagonist in terms of (but outside of) two very different modes of masculinity, Wayne and Belmondo, the patriarchal authority he can only inhabit as parody and the role of outlaw already played with far more conviction by the female lead. In revisiting Joyce through "Nestor" in the specific context of contemporary immigration policy, the film foregrounds the political dimension of modernism. Deasy defines himself in terms of his forefathers: "We are all Irish, all kings' sons" (38). Doyle's headmaster defines himself in contrast in terms of his daughters, themselves migrants. The headmaster's respect for his daughter's choices is a utopian moment, a reversal of Deasy's xenophobic misogyny: "A woman brought sin into the world . . . A faithless wife first brought the strangers to our shore here." (43) The film's major weakness is in its ultimate trivialization of the deportation issue, with Brendan's deported friend being sent to Berlin where he initially entered the EU, not back to Nigeria where he is facing imprisonment and torture.

A NEW ODYSSEY?

One of the most self-consciously Joycean of contemporary Irish novelists is Sean O'Reilly. In *The Swing of Things*[15] O'Reilly appears to have set out to write a novel of the new Dublin, one that engaged with its street life and its underclass in a manner that emulates Joyce. Bloom as outsider and Dedalus as errant son of the city are combined in the figure of Boyle, a Northerner released under the terms of the Good Friday agreement. Boyle had been caught up in the fringes of IRA activity and is at the novel's outset fleeing both his past and the politics it implies as a mature student at Trinity College: "Yes, say he is a man who has had enough of the past."[16] Boyle has even less chance than Stephen Dedalus of awaking from the nightmare of history. In effect he wakes into it at the novel's end: "To whom it may concern, I am guilty of murder. I came down here hoping to change myself, no, not even that, to alter the things around me . . . I was resigned to myself" (246). Boyle tries to make his self-destruction into an epiphany: "At last he had shed the burden of himself . . . Things can be known. Everything is achieved at a price. This bright empty calm" (247). The calm does not last, however: "Then the sudden surge of dread like there are wings sprouting through the flesh from your backbone. Littler ones higher up at the neck a-flutter. Some people go to hell and come back having learned nothing, without even a memento or a good story. Empty handed" (247).

In *The Swing of Things*, Joyce, modernism, the Revival and the attempt to imagine the future into existence have become part of the nightmare from which it is impossible to wake. This dreadful dream of the past is materialized in the figure of the street performer, Fada:

> Poetry on tap, the great classics of Irish literature. Joyce and his chamber pots. Wilde and his twilight balconies. Yeats and his randy ghosts. I'll take you turf cutting with Heaney or onion eating with Jonathan Swift, lamenting the earls with O'Leary, into the monasteries and out on the misty hills, I've got Sam the merciless, and brawling Behan, poets from the North and rednecks, dreamers and believers, wasters and wantnoters, scavengers and squanderers, a poem for everybody alive from the new Spanish armada and the Russian angsters, your mammy in heaven and your daddy in bed all the livelong day. (17)

Fada initially appears here to put a literary feast democratically at the disposal of the new Dublin and new Dubliners. This is not a gift, however, but a sale. Fada busks Irish literature on Grafton Street, reciting for money and scavenging for coins to support his precarious existence:

> some tourists stopped, Italians, then a few Americans, and he fired words at them, sometimes putting on actions: pleading, slapstick fury starving peasant, man against the wind, dying warrior, and hunting around the sandwich board where the names were written in gold paint on a white background scrolled with green Celtic snakes and birds. (17)

High culture and national myth is performed here at the same level and in the same street as dancing leprechauns, Guinness T-shirts, Gucci handbags and Manolo shoes are sold. As Fada sells/tells it, literary tradition ceases to be a luxury that can deny its own status as commodity, may even be just another shoddy souvenir. The scene spirals from satire to madness and the grotesque, as if the novel itself cannot sustain this insight sanely. Another street vendor teases Fada:

> The flower girl threw a coin high in the air, a livelier one come on please, a funnier thing, lighten it up, and the reciter went after it, wings a-flapping, skinny pinions, his tongue hanging out, but he made a mess of the catch and the coin disappeared under the feet of the crowd. Shocked, fascinated too, Boyle watched the lunatic go after it, a dog now on his hands and knees scuttling between the legs. He seemed immune to any type of shame. Some of the passers-by found it funny but most wanted to kick him out of the way. The barking grew more desperate and was broken by howls; going round in circles, sniffing, the reciter was licking at the feet of those who had stopped to watch. (17)

Boyle, *The Swing of Thing*'s new Bloom, is shadowed by a portrait of the artist as a mad peddler. O'Reilly's work is in terrible contrast to the exuberant claims of literary fellowship with Joyce in Hugh Macdiarmid and Angela Carter. "If Joyce had been a singer, as his wife, Nora, had wanted," Carter once proclaimed, "I, for one, as a writer in post-imperial Britain, would not even have had the possibility of a language."[17] In contrast to this sense of liberating possibility, in Ireland it can seem that Joyce is a burden to be carried, a challenge to be met. The commodification of Joyce in the heritage industry, his recruitment to sell not just Irish products, but to sell Dublin to others as a tourist destination and to itself as a cosmopolitan success story, all of this contributes to the anxiety, not least because it calls into question the relationship between art and commerce. Irish culture has until very recently zealously guarded the boundaries between high and popular culture, to the considerable advantage of a flourishing industry in middlebrow, "quality" entertainment and commentary. Fada scrabbling after his coins in the street for the sale of his only possession, literature, is an uncomfortable, worried image of the contemporary literary marketplace and Ireland's place in it.[18] Ultimately Fada proves fatal to Boyle's attempt to live from "each instant of self-awareness to the next. I now to me now" (261). *The Swing of Things* invokes the very Joycean trope of betrayal in the end, casting the reciter of other's words as a teller of tales too compellingly terrible to be disbelieved when he condemns Boyle by turning a fight gone wrong into a tall tale of willful murder.

Doyle, Enright and O'Reilly have found their literary reputations forged in the unstable and contingent space where media, academia and ideology meet to define the standards of literary culture and their relation to the national. Even Coetzee can only imagine a writer brave enough to directly rewrite Joyce. No matter how comprehensively deconstructed from the academy's margins, the understanding of Irish literature in Oedipal terms, with the modernists as overbearing forebearers to be outgrown or surpassed retains a surprisingly strong hold on journalistic and scholarly imaginations. The centenary of Bloomsday marked the culmination of Joyce's transition from avant-garde margin to popular icon. The annual celebration changed irrevocably from an amiable conjunction of scholarship, fandom and eccentricity to slick tourist attraction. In doing so, it foregrounded *Ulysses*'s extraordinarily detailed snapshot of the quotidian life of Dublin on that day. Precisely because *Ulysses* tells you what its protagonists had for breakfast, it is amenable to reconstruction at the level of food, drink and costume. Such reconstruction of the domestic is the mainstay of the heritage industry. Because that industry excels in the marketing of the past as nothing more than a lost lifestyle, however, it radically changed the meaning of the detail of the lifestyles of 1904 as it realized them. Joyce the rebel became the local boy made good and the city he understood too well to live in was remembered in a haze of nostalgia quite at odds with his fiction's ample recording of the poverty, squalor and prejudice simmering under its surface and swelling through its streets.

While *Ulysses* has a fundamentally comic vision, it is a dark, urban comedy, the laughter always shadowed by the possibility of despair, often deriving from it. It maintains its comic equilibrium only insofar as Bloom maintains his optimism in the face of sexual betrayal, anti-Semitism, death, poverty, illness, prostitution, alcoholism and the company of that disturbed young Dedalus. The novel knows his optimism is in itself comic: "And they beheld Him even Him, ben Bloom Elijah, amid clouds of angels ascend to the glory of the brightness at an angle of forty-five degrees over Donohoe's in Little Green street like a shot off a shovel". (299) *Ulysses* laughs at its protagonists and itself. A degree of self-mockery was also once a key quality in Bloomsday's tradition of dressing up and strutting out. This Joycean camp–style was wonderfully harmonious with *Ulysses*'s status as an icon of the oppositional avant-garde. In the context of corporate-sponsored events that use the novel to sell everything from sausages and stout to the creative city, the camp became kitsch, though the kitsch now teeters at times back toward farce, as in the James Joyce plaques on "olde Dublin" pubs built in the late 1990s. The farce has its own harmony: it is oddly appropriate for a novel whose chief protagonist sells advertising for a living. Concurrent with this popularization of *Ulysses* as icon is a critical return to the early work and the emergence of one story as a different type of icon.

THE DEAD AND THE CRITICS

In a letter dated June 29, 1914, Arthur Symons wrote to Joyce, "I find a great deal to like in *Dubliners*—unequal as the stories are—but original, Irish, a kind of French realism, of minute detail, sordid; single sentences tell . . . But the best is the last: the end imaginative."[19] In the twenty-first century, "The Dead" has come to occupy a central position in the overcrowded, overheated territory where Irish cultural criticism seeks to define itself and Ireland. It has become the cornerstone of postcolonial readings of Joyce as an anti-imperialist whose impatience with the narrow nationalism epitomized in *Ulysses*'s Cyclops should not be read as impatience with Irish nationalism in its more progressive manifestations. "The Dead" has attained exemplary liminal status, a text on the unstable border between tradition and modernity (Gibbons), between the memory of past trauma and cultural amnesia (Whelan), between folk song and literature (Henigan), between naturalism and modernism (Cleary). These borders have been renegotiated in a flurry of twenty-first-century articles, falling thicker and faster than the snow on the streets of the story. That redefinition has been mediated through two discordant elements within the petit bourgeois life of the story's main protagonists; the servant girl, Lily, and the folk song that reminds Gretta Conroy of another life and another world, "The Lass of Aughrim." Gender relations in two very different guises are at the heart of these readings, for, as Marjorie Howes remarks, "Considerations of how 'The Dead' engages with cultural nationalism on the one hand and with gender on the other are not easily separated."[20]

Luke Gibbons's reading of "The Dead" is mediated through John Huston's 1987 adaptation of the story.[21] Huston's film marked the emergence of the heritage film, a genre that flourished in Ireland in the following decade as the Celtic Tiger economy developed. While heritage cinema is often associated with nostalgia and particularly with nostalgia for a secure and marketable sense of national identity, the same decade saw the emergence of what might be called critical costume drama, where the seething repression of the past is a forum for the exploration of the deep anxieties of the present. Scorsese's *The Age of Innocence* (US, Cappa Productions, 1993), Campion's *The Piano* (Australia, New Zealand, France, Australian Film commission, 1993) and Coppola's *Dracula* (US, American Zoetrope, 1992) are cases in point. Huston's film has elements of both, though Gibbons's reading places it more directly in the critical costume drama category, with its emphasis on the implied narrative of exploitation of the servant girl, Lily. As Gibbons observes, the figure of the servant in the novel traditionally marks a point of ambiguity between public and private life. The servant performs domestic labor for money, thus unmasking the euphemism of "domestic duties" to reveal hard work, predominantly performed by women, and the economic basis of family life. Lily's embittered remark that "the men that do be nowadays are only all palaver", also gestures toward the vulnerability of the servant to sexual exploitation and the instability of the boundary between licit and illicit sexuality, as contiguous to each other as wife to housemaid within the early twentieth-century bourgeois household. Gibbons comments that: "Reality is not so much obscured as viewed, in Stephen's famous description in *Ulysses*, through 'the cracked looking glass of a servant,' reflecting a world in which memory finds no refuge in nostalgia and truth itself offers no consolation."[22] In this reading, Joyce's story, refracted through Huston, is the site of the desolation of an artificial and unreal present by the terrible truths of the past. Lily is linked, via Huston's inclusion of the performance of "Donal Og" at the Misses Morkan's annual dance, to the major catalyst of memory in the original story, the last, unsatisfactory party performance, Mr. D'Arcy's rendition of "The Lass of Aughrim." Both ballad's concern the folk staple of the innocent young woman seduced and betrayed. In the case of "The Lass of Aughrim," this narrative has acquired a metaphoric relation to the Battle of Aughrim and the dispossession consequent upon the defeat of Gaelic Ireland. While the singing of "The Lass of Aughrim" is important to Gibbons reading of "The Dead" as "national allegory,"[23] it is central to Kevin Whelan's interpretation of that allegory in terms of the impact of the Great Famine of 1845–1848 in the construction of a national psyche characterized by repressed trauma. Whelan argues that: "the post-Famine condition of Ireland is the unnamed horror at the heart of Joyce's Irish darkness, the conspicuous exclusion that is saturatingly present as a palpable absence deliberately being held at bay."[24] In both Gibbons's and Whelan's readings, "the shallow bourgeois present"[25] quivers on the verge of apprehension of its own unreality. For Whelan, the story eschews the frivolity of hope in any future for it has no mode of recovering its past: "an Irish deep past no longer existed. It had been eviscerated by a dual colonialism—'The English tyranny and the Roman tyranny.'"[26] Imbedded in this reading of Joyce is a (highly partial) intellectual debt to his contemporary, Freud. "The Lass of Aughrim" marks the return of the repressed in "The Dead," but the psychoanalytic narrative of acknowledgment and recovery is forestalled: "The only reality the Irish past bequeathed was a treadmill of brute repetition, the endless circling of Patrick Morkan's horse around King Billy's statue in 'The Dead.'"[27] In this Irish version of trauma theory, there is no recovery from irreversible loss. What then is the function of the "radical memory" Whelan praises for its ability to "deploy[ed] the past to challenge the present"?

In Joyce's story, and more so in Huston's film, it is as if the memory of the dead on the night of the Misses Morkan's party acts as an allegory for an intersection between the shattered remains of a vanquished culture in post-Williamite Ireland, and an incipient modernity from the margins.[28]

National allegory might be assumed to have some tutelary function for the nation: Howes identifies in Gibbons reading, for example, an attempt to postulate a national identity that is not correlative to print capitalism: "In contrast to the abstract national identity offered by print culture, this form of the national—found in fragmented, hybrid bits of oral culture—mixes the personal and political, rather than allegorizing the latter through the former."[29] In spite of this, while these readings unpack an extraordinary intensity of political significance in "The Dead," this significance is both of and *for* the past. "The Dead" was written in 1907. The shattered remains of a vanquished culture and incipient modernity were even then reconfiguring to provide the foundation of a new state. Whelan seems to identify the failures of that state as inevitable even by the time Joyce came to write "The Dead": "An indigenous Irish culture could no longer be resuscitated even by a determined policy of cultural revival. 'Just as ancient Egypt is dead, so is ancient Ireland.' To believe otherwise was to live delusionally in a twilight world of Celtic kitsch, by 'the broken lights of ancient myth.'"[30] For Gibbons, the intensity wrought by the historical and cultural tensions he maps in Joyce's story do have a legacy in the late twentieth century, but it is an aesthetic one: "Huston's *The Dead* gives us a rare glimpse of . . . an epiphanic, or, perhaps—closer to 'the old Irish tonality'—an epi*phonic* cinema."[31] Whelan concludes: "Joyce understood the force of William Faulkner's aphorism: 'The past is not dead. It is not even past.' The scale of his achievement is to weave this complex historical understanding and narrative imagination into what seems at first reading a standard naturalist text."[32] These valorizations of Irish modernism exude precisely the nostalgia for a lost past they collectively decry as symptoms of vacuous bourgeois modernity, though it is not—directly—nostalgia for tradition. The lost past for which these texts mourn is the moment of belief in the politically transformative power of aesthetic complexity and more particularly of modernist aesthetics. The maintenance of that position of mourning (for recovery from mourning is a form of inauthenticity in this critical discourse) depends on radical memory only insofar as it is radically selective memory. The understanding of history in geological terms as igneous rather than stratified, as proposed in Whelan's essay and as attributed by him to Joyce, is a strategy of prioritizing spatial over temporal relations characteristic of postmodernity and symptomatic of the priority of historicity over history in contemporary literary studies. As such, it inhabits an illuminating paradox. In this reading, "The Dead" and perhaps the entire corpus of Joyce's work is haunted by both the reality of Irish history and the loss of that reality. The ghosts of famine, pre-famine and precolonial Ireland stand outside the windows of the ordinary little world of post-famine, post-national and postcolonial Ireland, harbingers of the terrifying Real, figures of a death that has always already happened and has always happened too soon. A frozen relation to history, as transfixed by a deep past as it is oblivious to recent social and cultural change, seems to ground this form of contemporary Irish cultural criticism. It sometimes seems to be a revenant of the intersections of modernism and cultural nationalism, a post-revival. More particular ghosts attend the twenty-first-century reading of "The Dead," however.

"THE LASS OF AUGHRIM" AND "LORD GREGORY": LIVING TRADITIONS

Literary Predecessors

"The Dead" was not the first literary outing for the ballad collected by Childs as "Lord Gregory." Whelan notes the ballad came from Scotland to Ireland and a well-known Scots version by Robert Burns, titled "Lord Gregory" was published in 1793.[33] Burns offers a short narrative of seduction and betrayal and the song is sung from the point of view of the young woman whom Lord Gregory has abandoned. Another version, entitled "The Lass of Lochryan" was published by Sir Walter Scott in 1802.[33] Scott's version is very much longer than Burns's and the narrative is of love tragically thwarted by Lord Gregory's mother. Scott includes a verse that is close to that cited in "The Dead":

> She's ta'en her young son in her arms,
> And to the door she's gane;
> And long she knocked, and sair she ca'd,
> But answer got she nane.
> "O open the door, Lord Gregory!
> "O open, and let me in!
> "For the wind blaws through my yellow hair,
> "And the rain drops o'er my chin."

The existence of versions by Burns and Scott puts the ballad at the heart of Scottish tradition at the point where that tradition was consolidating itself in literary form in English and Scots. Burns's sad common tale of abandonment and Scott's tragic one of young love doomed, embroidered by references to witches and the supernatural, do not map the song's origins neatly, however. Its provenance is more complex.

The English Romantic "peasant poet" John Clare wrote two versions of the ballad. The first, "The Maid of Ocram, or Lord Gregory" is an extended treatment with much in common with Walter Scott's. The second, "The Maid of Ocram II," is a shorter version that, like Burns's, concerns "false love," but unlike Burns's retains the dialogue between the lovers. Both Clare versions contain the lines "The wind disturbs my yellow locks, / The snow sleeps on my skin," which is uncannily reminiscent of "The Dead," though Clare appears to have taken the weather to extremes for the purposes of assonance only—rain is much more consistent in the other versions of the ballad. Clare's version is significant for "The Dead" for two reasons. A selection of Clare's poems was published in 1908, edited by Joyce's then mentor, Arthur Symons, just one year after Joyce wrote his short story. Symons's role in bringing Clare's work back into circulation in the early twentieth century is a reminder that the conjunction of avant-garde modernism and "folk" literature was not an exclusively Irish phenomenon.[35] On the contrary, an appetite for authenticity and authentic tradition might be considered a defining characteristic of high modernism and occasionally a dangerous one.

The proximity of Symons's edition of Clare to Joyce is both less and more than a coincidence. Yeats introduced Joyce to Symons during his sojourn in London in December 1902 and, according to Richard Ellmann, Symons "was to play as important a part in the publication of Joyce's early works as Ezra Pound was to play later."[36] So obvious and profound was the influence of this mentor that George Moore dismissed Joyce's early poems with "the derisive but acute comment, 'Symons!'"[37] In May 1904 Symons placed one of Joyce's poems for him in the *Saturday Review*.[38] Later the same year Symons recommended Joyce to John Baillie and so was instrumental in the publication of two further poems in *The Venture*.[39] Symons even interrupted Joyce's elopement: once again stopping over in London on his most significant migration in 1904, Joyce left Nora Barnacle sitting in a park in London for two hours while he went to see Symons.[40] Joyce asked Symons advice on where to submit *Chamber Music* and got it.[41] Symons continued to solicit publishers to take on *Chamber Music* though 1904–1906[42] and "[t]rue to his word, Arthur Symons wrote the first review when the book was published in May" 1907,[43] the same year as Symons's edition of Clare. Ellmann's remark that while Joyce was grateful for the review, he "was more interested in what his fellow-Dubliners would make of the book"[44] has set the tone in many ways for discussions of *Dubliners* and the prioritization of Joyce's relations with literary Dublin over the point of transition and influence of French symbolism on the emergence of English language modernism represented by Symons. Joyce was still seeking assistance from the stalwart Symons when he went looking for a publisher for *Portrait* in 1915,[45] and the influence of Symons's work on Mallarme on Joyce can be traced, much later, in *Finnegans Wake*.[46] Symons's decline into episodes of madness and ill-health must have made some impression on Joyce, who met his early mentor on one of his late, sad visits to France in 1924. Joyce made a point of his continuing respect for Symons's judgment even when the old man had been forgotten or dropped by a younger generation of poets.[47] Beckson and Munro note a letter from Rhoda Symons in the Featherstone Collection at Columbia University, dated March 26, 1926, where she tells Arthur that Joyce wants to send him some poems to get his opinion on them. In May, Symons wrote to her, "I lunched Joyce yesterday at La P'erouse—he can talk as he did then, wonderful. He also has a fascination of his own—we got on splendidly—the same race for one thing."[48] (Symons was very keen on defining himself as a Celt, thanks to his Cornish and Welsh origins, though paradoxically he admired Joyce's rejection of the Celtic twilight.) As Kevin Whelan points out, according to Joyce's sisters, he "purported to know thirty-five verses of 'The Lass of Aughrim,' so it is quite possible that Joyce . . . knew the long, thirty-five verse Scottish version printed in Francis Child's five volume *The English and Scottish Popular Songs*."[49] It is fruitless to guess if he knew how near at hand was a nineteenth-century literary version at the intersection of English Romanticism and folk song. What Joyce knew of the ballad's history is of limited importance—and I will return to the significance of the construction of Joyce as the-one-who-knows (Ireland) later. I want to focus on what Joyce couldn't know, the future of "The Lass of Aughrim," both as a locus of scholarship and as, quite simply, a song that continued to be sung and so continued to change.

Clare's version of the ballad is again significant here. His use of "Ocram" indicates where the association between the ballad and Aughrim may have originated, in a linguistic slip that Joyce might have appreciated. Clare's title links his version with the earliest broadside versions of the ballad, dating from the mid-eighteenth century, entitled "The Lass of Ocram."[50] Clare's English versions appears to be closer to the Irish, rather than the Scottish, versions of the ballad: Fowler notes, "The nine stanzas from Ireland ([Child] H) are interesting as an illustration of the development of a burden, and as evidence that a form of the original 'Ocram' version ('Aughrim' in H) had survived independently as late as 1830." (561–2)[51] Fowler, writing at the end of the 1950s, argues that:

> All of these correspondences, both in structure and in treatment of the story, lead me to the conclusion that "The Lass of Roch Royal" [an alternative title for the ballad] properly belongs with the extensive lore and literature of the Accused Queen. Whether this conclusion is of any value for fixing the date of origin of the ballad I hesitate to say. If the theory of one recent critic is correct, the story of the Accused Queen goes back ultimately to the Clementine Recognitions of the third century. At the other end of the scale (which is, of course, where ballad scholars now realize they should look), our Queen survives, on the inappropriate level of farce, as "Christian Custance," a wealthy widow in Nicholas Udall's *Roister Doister* (mid-sixteenth century), and, more suitably, as the noble and virtuous Queen Hermione in Shakespeare's *The Winter's Tale*.

The development of folklore as an academic discipline situated the song in a complex set of relations between oral and literary, folk and modernist, traditional and modernizing cultural trends. Fowler's analysis runs very much counter to the tendency in contemporary criticism to trace folk elements in literature back to an originary oral tradition, a tendency that is evident in the equation of "The Lass of Aughrim" with a traumatic history and a lost language in Whelan's reading of "The Dead," for example. Fowler's more old-fashioned folklore studies might be considered a diachronic account of the folk song, where an attempt is made to trace a genealogy, if not an origin, for the song. In contrast, contemporary readings of the significance of "The Lass of Aughrim" in "The Dead" draw the threads of preceding Irish histories and texts into a synchronic web with its center in Dublin in 1907. Folk songs, however, pose particular problems for those who try to fix their meanings along either of these lines. For the ballad known variously as "The Lass of Aughrim," "Lord Gregory" and "The Lass of Loch Royal" continues to be sung and to evolve new meanings long after a couple of its lines were preserved in the aspic of Joyce's prose. It still persists in a wide variety of versions sung by American, Canadian, Irish, English and Scottish singers. Moreover, the way in which the song has evolved within the still thriving folk tradition sheds fascinating light on the way in which contemporary criticism understands Joyce's use of it and why.

Arguing that "it is neither the ballad's lyrics nor narrative that Joyce exploits in his story, but rather, its 'lyric intensity,'"[51] Julie Henigan attributes to folk song the qualities of "immediacy, directness, and emotional intensity" that "have long been identified as characteristic of traditional ballads."[52] Henigan characterizes Gabriel's initial security within "ultimately safe, aesthetic abstraction" as "emotionally deficient": "In contrast to Gabriel, Gretta is spontaneous, direct, and both emotionally honest and accessible."[53] This emotional honesty is linked directly by Henigan to Gretta's ability to respond emotionally rather than aesthetically to the song and while her conclusions are very different to Whelan's, Henigan's article makes explicit the aesthetic value placed on immediacy and the breaking down of civilized defenses implicit in Whelan's reading of the use of the traditional folk song at the middle-class party. Arguing that "Modern Ireland was haunted by the afterlife of that deeper world from which it was permanently estranged", Whelan posits the singing of the song as a form of haunting. "The Dead" does not tell the story of the effect of loss, grief, the history of famine: in this reading, it renders its affects. "Joyce understood the power of music to capture emotion and sought to replicate its effect in his prose". Deferring again the question of the power of Joyce's understanding, it is illuminating to trace the uses to which more recent interpreters of the song have put its ability to invoke "the sense of desolation and loss" noted by Henigan.[54]

The context of these interpretations includes the history of folk music in the twentieth century and its relationship with the category of "world music." The resurgence of the English-language ballad tradition in Ireland from the late 1950s and 1960s onward was part of the emergence internationally of folk music as part of the counterculture of the era. The importance of emigrant Irish communities in this second revival is well attested. It is worth quoting the obituary for one of the leading figures in that revival, Tommy Makem, published by the *New York Times* on August 3, 2007:

> In 1961 the Clancy Brothers and Tommy Makem, the name under which they performed, signed a $100,000 recording contract, a big deal at the time. Mr. Makem and Joan Baez were named the most promising newcomers at the Newport Folk Festival that year.
>
> On March 12, 1961, the group, all of whom were born in Ireland and emigrated to the United States, performed for 14 minutes in front of a television audience of 80 million on "The Ed Sullivan Show," the first of many television appearances.
>
> The next year an Irish radio announcer visiting the United States took some of their albums back to Ireland and played them on his show. They skyrocketed to popularity. By 1964 a third of the albums sold in Ireland were by the Clancy Brothers and Tommy Makem.
>
> In 1963 they performed at the White House at the request of President John F. Kennedy, who was of Irish descent.

In this narrative, Irish America revitalizes and exports this music back to Ireland: the references to iconic American names and events (Newport, Baez, Sullivan, Kennedy and, elsewhere in the same piece, Bob Dylan) indicate how mainstream this music was in the context of 1960s popular culture.

The career of the co-founders of the new ballad tradition is similarly implicated in the unstable relation of commercial media and counterculture in the 1960s. The Dubliners may have begun in informal sessions in O'Donoghue's pub in Dublin, but the continuing impact of their repertoire on bands like The Pogues was a result of a performance at the Edinburgh Festival in 1963, which in turn led to a recording contract, appropriately with Transatlantic Records, which, by 1967, led to airtime for "Seven Drunken Nights" (based on Childs's Ballad 273, sometimes known as "The Goodman") on Radio Caroline, the pirate radio station that was the first major alternative to the state-operated BBC and RTE. The folk ballad and the protest song of the sixties circulated through clubs, coffee shops, records and radio, just as earlier ballads did through taverns, fairs and broadsheets, but they circulated much more rapidly. There is much more continuity than change in the twentieth-century symbiosis of mass and folk culture. The dissemination of "The Lass of Aughrim"/"Lord Gregory"/"The Lass of Loch Royal" through Scotland, England, Ireland and America in the nineteenth century reminds us that these songs never know or have known borders. As Joyce commented of Irish culture, "it is useless to look for a thread that may have remained pure and virgin without having undergone the influence of a neighbouring thread."[55] The song offers not a relation to authenticity or originary trauma, but to life and change: as the versions and their meanings shift from place to place and time to time they trace the ordinariness of the migrant condition.

BUT NONE WILL LET ME IN

Contemporary versions of the ballad known as "Lord Gregory," "The Lass of Aughrim" and "The Lass of Loch Royal" do seem to have come (back) from Ireland to England and persisted in Scotland. Shirley Collins, a major figure in the English folk revival and scrupulous acknowledger of her sources, included "Lord Gregory" "from the singing of Elizabeth Cronin" on her 1964 album, *Folk Roots, New Routes*.[56] Elizabeth "Bess" Cronin, "The Muskerry Queen of Song," was a key figure in the twentieth-century transmission of Irish folk songs, whose repertoire was widely collected, transcribed and broadcast. Her recording of "Lord Gregory" was included in the ur-text of the 1960s folk revival, a series of albums called *The Folk Songs of Britain*, which included versions of *The Child Ballads* collected and still sung in the mid-twentieth century.[57] In the version Cronin passed on to Collins, in contrast to the version that Gibbons and Whelan cite, Lord Gregory remains faithful to his lass and the ballad ends with the death of the lovers and their child as a result of the cruelty of his mother, who tells the girl who arrives looking for Lord Gregory with her dying child, "it's deep in the sea you should hide your downfall." Cursing his mother, Lord Gregory vows, "I'll range over mountains, over valleys so wide / Till I find the girl I love and I'll lay by her side." This version is directly related to attitudes to single mothers and their children in twentieth-century Irish society and the challenge to those attitudes implicit in Cronin and Collin's version becomes more overt as the century progresses.

Maddie Prior, who originally recorded the song on an album she made with June Tabor in 1976, commented in the sleeve notes when she recorded it again with Steeleye Span in 2006 on *Bloody Men*, "I first heard this from the singing of Paddy Tunney, but it is many years since I heard his delicate rendition, and I expect there have been some changes. I don't have the most accurate musical ear, nor the best memory, so the folk process will be at its most evident in my versions of traditional songs. This is a beautifully portrayed picture of a devastating romantic encounter that leaves the girl in despair, given the social mores of the day." This later version is even darker, for no trick is played on Lord Gregory, who really is "gone to bonny Scotland to bring home his new queen" and his lover herself declares, "I'll leave now these windows and likewise this hall, / For it's deep in the sea I will find my downfall." In these and in many current versions the girl is declared to be "from Cappaquin" (sometimes spelled Capakin in English folk song sources),[58] which suggests that the historical significance of

Aughrim is no longer as resonant with either the singers or their audiences. Radically different versions of the narrative persist. In Prior and Tabor's first version, this is not a song of seduction, but rape: "do you remember Lord Gregory that night in Cappaquin / you stole away my maidenhead and sore against my will." The version by Scottish traditional and early music group Distant Oaks is lyrically very close to Prior and Tabor's version and the line between rape and seduction is again blurred, "you stole away my maidenhead." This element seems to surface most often in English, Scottish and Irish versions sung by women and is not a feature of the Appalachian versions, for example. Versions that emanate from the southern US, usually under the title "The Lass of Loch Royal," do not seem to identify any link with Ireland. Neil Morris, who sings it on the album, *The Alan Lomax Collection, Southern Journey, Vol. 1: Voices from the American South, Blues, Ballads, Hymns,* introduces it with the remarks, "My people brought this song from Scotland into this country. Other people might have brought it from other places, I don't know, but I learnt it from my grandmother when I was a very small boy." Interestingly, he ends with the lass's appeal to her lover to "feel his fond embrace" again, so while a certain ambiguity pertains to this version, it remains a love song. These versions often retain the device of the wicked mother: "ye have not been the death of one ye have been the death of three."

Versions of the ballad as allegories of national history are by no means extinct. Treasa Ni Mhaolain introduces the song, which she sings under the title "Lord Gregory," as a song "about an Irish girl who is treated badly by an English lord."[59] When admonished, "it's deep in the ocean you should hide your downfall," she cries, "who will shoe my babe's little feet" and "who will be my babe's father 'til Lord Gregory comes home." In the American versions, this concern for provision for the child is sometimes attributed to the father not the mother, but differences in the order of verses in Ni Mhaolain's version mean that a number of elements attributed to Lord Gregory in the American versions are attributed to the deserted woman, "Saddle me my finest horse . . . And I'll range over mountains and valleys so wide 'til I find Lord Gregory and lay by his side." If the ballad is not understood as a ballad about Irish mistreatment at English hands, a very different narrative emerges. The English folk guitarist and singer Martin Simpson also sings the song under the title "Lord Gregory," beginning "I am a king's daughter that's straight form Cappaquin / Lord Gregory let me in." This version initially closely resembles Treasa Ni Mhaolain's, but then Simpson reverts to an exchange of tokens that does not figure in her version, foregrounding class not nation, and returns the original twist: Lord Gregory curses his mother (and her class consciousness) and goes to lie down by the side of his dead love.

Allegorical interpretations appear to be increasingly in the minority. Prior's reference to the role of "the social mores of the day" in rendering the girl in the ballad's story a tragic one is reflected in the radical shortening of the ballad in some very recent versions where there are important small changes in the lyrics. The last two lines in Prior's 1976 version were: "And I'll leave now these windows and likewise this hall, / For it's deep in the sea I will find my downfall." The 2006 version by the same singer is: "She's took her young son in her arms, turned from that cold hall, / Saying, deep in the sea we will find our downfall." The introduction of the third person indicates the intervention of a new consciousness in the narrative, one in which the death of the child is no longer presented as the work of the weather but a direct consequence of those who refuse to accept his mother. This increased emphasis on the child in the girl's arms in a song the singer associates with the Irish tradition invokes an image that, a century after Joyce wrote "The Dead," is powerfully associated with Ireland in global popular culture, that of the condemned and excluded single mother. Two even shorter versions make this more explicit. In Beth Patterson's much praised 1999 a cappella version she sings, "My babe lies cold in my arms / Lord Gregory, let me in."[60] Susan McKeown's similarly short version, released in 2006, excludes the girl's appeal to Lord Gregory completely, and her third verse ends, "And none will let me in."[61] By the time Patterson, McKeown and Prior record their versions of "The Lass of Aughrim," the dominant image of the history of seduced and abandoned girls in Ireland was that of the woman caught in what James Smith has called "the architecture of containment,"[62] incarcerated in mother and baby homes and Magdalene asylums, excluded from Irish society. In the contemporary mind, the Lass of Aughrim is not just abandoned by her lover but by her whole society. It is striking that Treasa Ni Mhaolain doesn't use the line "none will let me in." In a version where nationality is the primary issue, Lord Gregory and his family are exclusively responsible for the girl's plight. Where gender and sexuality are the primary issues, Irish "social mores" are to blame.

It is important to understand that this critical attitude to the punitive response to single mothers is not a just a characteristic of twenty-first-century versions. In an analysis of the influential version by Elizabeth Cronin, a "dazzling re-casting of *Lord Gregory*,"[63] Fred McCormick indicates the unstable relationship between lyrics and melody for the ballad, "the melody which Mrs Cronin uses is not unique to the present text. It is associated with several versions of *The Shooting of His Dear*." The power of Cronin's version, its inclusion in the influential collection and the championship of Cronin's repertoire in Ireland by the influential musician and broadcaster, Phillip King, have made it the dominant interpretation in Irish folk music circles. McCormick's interpretation of Cronin's version is based on a very different understanding of the function of folk song than that of Whelan, Gibbons and especially Henigan, with their contrast between bourgeois restraint and peasant emotion. He notes, "What is significant . . . is the way the text has been restructured to accommodate the sexual mores of the Ireland Mrs Cronin grew up in," and raises the question of why the ballad is so shortened and why it retains in the Irish tradition these particular verses:

> In its older forms *Lord Gregory* is a very long ballad, which moves through several episodes before culminating in the girl's death by drowning . . . In Mrs Cronin's version, the action centres around just one scene. The girl stands at the castle gates, the illegitimate babe dying in her arms, while she begs and pleads for admission. She is refused by Lord Gregory's mother and she leaves. We do not know what happens to her. We only know that when Lord Gregory discovers his mother's treachery, he vows that he will not rest until he can "find the Lass of Arrams and lie by her side." Why? Why is the ballad so truncated, and why does this version obviate the more usual and more tragic ending? Why is the mother viewed as the traitor, and why, in a ballad which puts out several clues that the subject is a fallen woman, is so much weight, and sympathy, given to her plight?

McCormick's reading negotiates between the functionalist view of folk culture as a conservative means of social regulation, full of "don't stray off the path" morals, and the romantic view still prevalent in Irish cultural studies of folk culture as the trace of the insurgent nation, lost authenticity or age-old class struggle. In the former view, "folksongs existed as integrative mechanisms to reinforce codes of social behaviour" and "remembering the moral climate in which Mrs Cronin's *Lord Gregory* existed, we might expect the ending [where the girl drowns] to be retained intact as an example to others." In the latter, "folk song summons the deep, oral, Irish-language, Jacobite, Gaelic past of the west of Ireland,"[64] "whose ability to move and even transfigure is inherent in its very nature"[65] and "that connects personal with political memory in the Irish popular imagination."[66] Against both extremes, McCormick argues:

> If we try to interpret Mrs Cronin's version of Lord Gregory in normative or didactic terms, it does not make sense. Far from legitimising, or explicating, social codes, it is truer to say that folksongs existed as a means of enabling people to live under those codes. Rural Ireland, until very recently, had harsh canons of sexual conduct. Association between unmarried individuals of opposite sexes was rare and frowned upon. If it happened that a girl found herself pregnant out of wedlock she could expect to be shown the door by her parents. In a land where arranged marriage was common enough to be considered the norm, and where marriage was constrained by inheritance and property rights, she could expect no sympathy from her own family and even less from the family of her seducer. She might as well go and drown herself. The fact that she does not appear to do so, and the fact that Lord Gregory vows to "lie by her side," i.e. to marry her, suggests that Mrs Cronin's version

both dramatises the dilemma of non-marital pregnancy, and offers an emotional solution to the dilemma.

What is extraordinary is the apparent lack of awareness of this aspect of the folk song by contemporary critics of "The Dead." In Gibbons's reading, the lass of Aughrim is representative and part of her community, "not the only victim to be thrown onto the roads by a callous Lord Gregory."[67] Her modern-day counterpart, Lily, "has been emotionally bruised, if not actually sexually exploited, in conformity with the vulnerability of maids, servants or nurses in respectable bourgeois households."[68] For Whelan, "The Lass of Aughrim" is "a folk song which summoned the deep, oral, Irish-language, Jacobite, Gaelic past of the west of Ireland."[69] Whelan, who assumes that Lily, like the heroine of the ballad, is abandoned and pregnant, identifies this with the theme of betrayal.[70] Yet Joyce's choice of excerpt from the ballad is remarkably close to the contemporary short lyric and the three verses that Joyce's letters tell us he definitely learned from Nora Barnacle and her mother are almost identical with Patterson's version, with the sole difference that it is Lord Gregory who leaves the girl out in the cold, rather than "none will let me in."[71] "This form of the national—found in fragmented, hybrid bits of oral culture"[72] is no more willing than any bourgeois household to admit to the ghosts tapping at its window, those whom the nation and the much romanticized traditional community defined itself against.

Is it ahistorical to even discuss the history of women in post-independence Ireland in relation to a text written in 1907? Asserting that this history is certainly relevant to a reading of Huston's film version is to evade that question unnecessarily. The extent to which the ballad of "The Lass of Aughrim" has become a figure for the relation between Ireland's traumatic past and its bourgeois present indicates that while the readings of "The Dead" by Gibbons and Whelan are historicist in relation to the text, they are also responsive to the historical conditions of their own composition in the twenty-first century. Their critique of the upwardly mobile Gabriel Conroy is also a critique of upwardly mobile Ireland. Yet more is needed than this double historicism, for reading "The Dead" raises serious questions about the relationship between historicism and history, about the limitations of historicist critique that can set a text with exquisite complexity within its own time, but cannot account for social and historical change, politically effective action or the relationship between writing, reading and changing. Gibbons, Whelan and Henigan restore a series of interlinked hidden histories and intensities to the reading of Joyce. The history of the women who hid "their downfall" in the sea or were themselves hidden in mother and baby homes and Magdalene asylums and of those women who moved on like Gretta to the city or beyond the borders of the nation is occluded in this paradigm. None will let them in and the exclusion of their history is not incidental: it is a condition of the contemporary revival of cultural nationalism, however hybrid and benign that nationalism appears to be. Historicism offers the literary critic a powerful but partial instrument of interpretation. For to allow oneself to know no more than Joyce did in 1907 is to refuse to acknowledge the history of the nation-state that was to follow and to construct instead utopian versions of the nation that might have been. The inevitability of the process whereby new nation-states operate in remarkably similar ways to their imperial predecessors from the point where they acquire armies, borders and institutions limits the liberationary potential of even the most utopian nationalisms. Macardle is an important precursor to the contemporary critics of "The Dead": haunted by a republic that never came to be and setting the ghosts of those the actual state excluded very far away (see Chapter 3, this volume). But the ghosts do make their presence felt.

WHAT IS A MAN LOOKING AT A WOMAN LISTENING TO DISTANT MUSIC, A SYMBOL OF?

In her thought-provoking reading of the significance of the boardinghouse in the work of the peripatetic Joyce, Julieann Veronica Ulin argues: "In his depiction of the Irish home as always already unstable, Joyce rejects the fundamentally false attitude of romantic nationalism in favor of the residuum of truth about life found in the boarding houses of Dublin."[73] Aligning the moral panic of the cultural nationalist about the "stranger in our house" in the Cyclops episode of *Ulysses* with the sexual terror of Davin in *Portrait of the Artist as a Young Man* when a peasant woman attempts to draw him to her cottage, Ulin shrewdly observes: "To notice the stranger in the house is not only to recognize, as Julia Kristeva articulates, the foreign within oneself but the 'within' as itself a deeply problematic space" (289). Marjorie Howes and Margot Norris's readings of "The Dead" in terms of the impact of the mobile Gretta on the pillars of cultural, social and political authority in early twentieth-century Dublin is relevant here: "it acknowledges that Gretta is from Galway, but emphasizes that she left there."[74] Crossing the country and crossing class lines, Gretta Conroy is both a successful migrant and a woman who remains "within," even if she reveals herself to be foreign there. Michael Furey's old song may penetrate the "health, wealth, long life, happiness, and prosperity"[75] of the party on Usher's Island, like a cold draught of dead history, but it is Gretta who has kept "locked in her heart for so many years that image of her lover's eyes when he had told her that he did not wish to live" (224). Michael Furey was always inside Gabriel Conroy's house. Gabriel's world is revealed to be structured like a set of Russian nested dolls, at the center of which an enigma looks back at him. Is that enigma the boy who went home to die, or Gretta, the woman "packing up" who knew, as Howes reminds us, how to leave Galway and live? "Better pass boldly into that other world, in the full glory of some passion, than fade and wither dismally with age," thinks

Gabriel (224), but Gabriel is the ultimate unreliable narrator and "perhaps she had not told him all the story" (223). The sentimental preference for those who die young and leave a good-looking corpse must be read ironically, coming as it does here from a man who wears galoshes. And Gabriel's seduction by this myth occurs as he looks at his wife's face and realizes "it was no longer the face for which Michael Furey had braved death" (233). He experiences his own mortality vicariously, as her mortality. The act of looking is at the heart of "The Dead" and at the heart of Gabriel's dilemma. He does not understand what he sees and when he is finally told what he should have heard, the meaning is death to him:

> Gabriel had not gone to the door with the others. He was in a dark part of the hall gazing up the staircase. A woman was standing near the top of the first flight, in the shadow also. He could not see her face but he could see the terra-cotta and salmon-pink panels of her skirt which the shadow made appear black and white. It was his wife. She was leaning on the banisters, listening to something. Gabriel was surprised at her stillness and strained his ear to listen also. But he could hear little save the noise of laughter and dispute on the front steps, a few chords struck on the piano and a few notes of a man's voice singing.
>
>   He stood still in the gloom of the hall, trying to catch the air that the voice was singing and gazing up at his wife. There was grace and mystery in her attitude as if she were a symbol of something. He asked himself what is a woman standing on the stairs in the shadow, listening to distant music, a symbol of. If he were a painter he would paint her in that attitude. Her blue felt hat would show off the bronze of her hair against the darkness and the dark panels of her skirt would show off the light ones. Distant Music he would call the picture if he were a painter (211).

Gabriel aspires be look up and find meaning, but instead he is fixated, still, in the gloom. The extent of his enchantment with his wife's image is the extent of his powerlessness.

> In the standard notion of the opposition between subject and object, the subject is conceived of as the dynamic pole, as the active agent able to transcend every fixed situation, to "create" its universe, to adapt itself to every new condition, and so on, in contrast to the fixed, inert domain of objects. Lacan supplements this standard notion with its obverse: the very dimension which defines subjectivity is a certain "exaggerated," excessive *fixation* or "freeze."[76]

It is, of course, this reversal that underpins the dominant concept of theories of film spectatorship (as opposed to audience): that of a subject fixed in the act of looking. Žižek's reading draws attention to the internal contradictions of the theory. If the act of looking freezes the subject, then what happens to the sadistic subject of scopophilia, in a position of dominance over the object of the gaze? Instead the object, medusa-like, has power over the subject's gaze. "Lacan himself uses the metaphor of cinema projection, and compares the ego to the fixed image which the spectator perceives when the reel gets jammed."[77] Film theory has predominantly deployed the Lacanian concept of the imaginary, the relation between the ego and its images, as a mode of understanding the relation between the subject and the cinema screen. However, as Žižek points out, the fixing of the subject by its object also occurs in the registers of the symbolic and the real. "The very plasticity of the process of symbolization is strictly correlative—even grounded in—the excessive fixation on an *empty signifier*."[78] The example he gives of such an empty master signifier is democracy: the term remains constant but its range of application and meanings changes radically over time to include new groups, new freedoms and new equalities, for example, those relating to women, workers and minorities. The example is indicative of Žižek's vertiginous dives into political specifics from theoretical generalities. The elaboration of the way in which "subjectivity is grounded in an excessive fixation" in relation to the "Real" is related implicitly to the politics of gender.

Gibbons argues that in the film adaptation of "The Dead," "when Gabriel apprehends Gretta listening to the ballad on the stairs, his response is to translate sound into spectacle, and music into the still formality of an image" and in contrast to this, "reversing the silence of a still-life, Huston's achievement is to create an acoustic image, infusing the film at key moments with the sound at the top of the stairs."[79] The sound-image restores life, but offscreen, out of the line of vision. Marjorie Howes reads "Gretta and Lily, neither as sexual victims nor as emblems of tradition, but as modern female migrants" and "aligns them with a view of migration that registers the traumas and dangers involved, but that nevertheless finds migration positive and enabling."[80] While noting "Gretta's submission or subjection to various kinds of authority—male, bourgeois, and urban," she draws on Margot Norris's reading of the story, which "foregrounds the fatal effects she has on representatives of such authority." In an implied contrast with the consciously political Molly Ivors, Howes notes, "This gendered construction of Gretta as a modern female migrant depends more on her body and its movements than on her self-awareness or explicit mental processes. Such performances constitute a form of consciousness, but not necessarily self-consciousness."[81] In effect, Gretta is a moving statue. Žižek, in "Fetishism and Its Vicissitudes," calls the "paradox of moving statues, of dead objects coming alive and/or of petrified living objects" that comes into play when "the barrier which separates the living from the dead is transgressed."[82] As Žižek points out, psychoanalytic theory grounds the freedom of the human subject in "the distance between 'things' and 'words'":

Here again, however, a certain excessive fixity intervenes ... a human subject can acquire and maintain a distance towards (symbolically mediated) reality only through the process of "primordial repression"; what we experience as "reality" constitutes itself through the foreclosure of some traumatic X which remains the impossible-real kernel around which symbolization turns. What distinguishes man from animals is thus again the excessive fixation on the trauma (of the lost object, of the scene of some shattering *jouissance*, etc.); what sets the dynamism that pertains to the human condition in motion is the very fact that some traumatic X eludes every symbolization.[83]

What Žižek is doing here is paraphrasing Lacan's theory of subjectivity and with very particular consequences. In Lacan, the impossibility of the symbolization of the Real determines the subject's castration within language, always without the power of the transcendental signifier that would finally and completely recover the lost object into that language. Sidestepping the metaphor of castration allows Žižek to defer the issue of sexual difference to which he eventually and provocatively returns:

the Real as "impossible" is precisely the excess of "immediacy" which cannot be "reified" in a fetish, the unfathomable X which, although nowhere present, curves/distorts any space of symbolic representation and condemns it to ultimate failure. If we are to discern the contours of the Real, we cannot avoid the meanderings of the fetish.[84]

The Real is that which cannot be fetishized and so of course its contours are no more or less than an inversion of the contours of the fetish. The theoretical problem that Žižek sets himself is "how are we to conceive of some 'immediacy' which would not act as a 'reified' fetishistic screen, obfuscating the process which generates it?"[85] Yet the answer is already there. The Real is that which is not—yet—fetishized. The answer is deferred in an attempt at another fixity: Žižek's question fixes the Real in a stable relation of otherness to reality. Within his discussion of fetishism the instability of the boundary becomes apparent and it does so particularly around the question of sexual difference: "The fetish functions simultaneously as the representative of the Other's inaccessible depth *and* as its exact opposite, as the stand-in for that which the Other itself lacks ('mother's phallus')."[86]

Fetishism in its Freudian and Lacanian formulations is a radical disavowal of sexual difference, defined in both of their paradigms as recognition of the castration of the mother in relation to sexuality, power and language and the consequent possibility for the (masculine) subject of just such a castration also. The function of the fetish is to deny the "fact" of castration and reconstitute the infantile fantasy of the phallic mother, who is all powerful, who can make everything all right and who is never separate from or lost to (her) subject. Such a figure is of course both a fantasy and a horror. Žižek's reformulation insists on this ambiguity at the heart of fetishism:

> Contrary to the *doxa*, the fetish . . . is not primarily an attempt to disavow castration and stick to the (belief in the) maternal phallus; beneath the semblance of this disavowal it is easy to discern traces of the desperate attempt . . . to *stage* the symbolic castration—to obtain separation from the mother, and thus obtain some space in which one can breath freely.[87]

Here the subject fixed by the object of the gaze is reunited with the sadistic subject in scopophilic control of its object. But not without a paradigm shift. For Žižek's meanderings around the Real and his insistence on the role of excessive fixation in the constitution of subjectivity amount to a proposal that subjectivity is structurally fetishistic: "This allows us to propose the notion of false activity: you think you are active, while your true position, as embodied in the fetish, is passive."[88] Žižek proposes that "in order to be an active subject, I have to get rid of—and transpose on to the other—the inert passivity which contains the density of my substantial being."[89] It is easy to map onto this structure the pattern of projection onto the feminine other of the functions of display, of object of the gaze and of fetish within the masculine construction of subjectivity. Žižek, in a maneuver that is relevant to theories of fetishism and subject object relations in cinema, argues instead that this fetishistic subject is feminine:

> What if the "original" subjective gesture, the gesture constitutive of subjectivity, is not that of autonomously "doing something," but, rather, that of the primordial substitution, of withdrawing and letting another do it for me, in my place? Women, much more than men, are able to enjoy by proxy, to find deep satisfaction in the awareness that their beloved partner enjoys (or succeeds, or has attained his or her goal in any other way).[90]

The stereotyping is shocking, but deliberately so and veiled in a revolutionary proposal: "What . . . if this cliché nevertheless points towards the feminine status of the subject?"[91] Moreover, Žižek claims that this construction "allows us to complicate the standard opposition of man versus woman as active versus passive: sexual difference is inscribed into the very core of the relationship of substitution—woman can remain passive *while being active through her other*; man can be active *suffering through his other*."[92]

The contrast between remaining passive and being active is alarming. Žižek's position here may appear to support the possibility of a feminine fetishism and a feminine paradigm for subjectivity, but it is implicitly far more conservative in relation to gender than that of Lacan. Within Žižek's (re)construction of fetishism, this revolutionary meta-gaze is merely feminine after all. The woman looks for an other. To identify the pessimism of Žižek's proposition is not, of course, to disprove it. Nor is the Lacanian construction of subjectivity easily assimilable to a feminist project. To paraphrase Judith Butler, that which Lacan identifies as impossible, outside of representation as we know it, is not necessarily beyond representation as it might be.[93] Butler's reading of Lacan's "violent appropriations"[94] of classical texts is in direct opposition to Žižek's celebration of their "breathtaking 'effect of truth.'"[95] Butler argues that the "the limits of the ineffaceable,"[96] which Lacan fetishizes as "the Real," are historically, socially and culturally determinate and moreover subject to change. In short, it is not only possible to move outside established frames of representation, it is possible for the underlying structures of representation itself to change. This, after all, was modernism's great ambition.

The woman Gabriel fetishizes at the top of the stairs ceases to be the other onto which can be transposed "the inert passivity which contains the density of" his "substantial being." The listening woman swells with the density of her own substance, shattering the mirror, the light and dark panels of her skirt crumpled into reality. This is more than an act of memory, however radical. Gretta, mistaken for an aesthetic object, becomes an aesthetic subject, moved by music as she was so many years before. Once a young man sang to her. While the folk song tradition frequently features two or even three speaking protagonists in "The Lass of Aughrim"/"Lord Gregory," "The Dead" quotes only from the woman's point of view. Long ago in Galway, a lover sang in the cold outside his beloved Gretta's window and died as a result. This was no seduced and abandoned girl, but a soon to be abandoned boy. Michael Furey takes the place of the lass in this scenario and Gretta of Lord Gregory, occupying the unstable position of power accorded to that phallic woman, the femme fatale. It is not only sexual fetishism that is at stake here, though "sexuality plays its part in the drama as the site of the symptom, the first sign of the return of the repressed."[97] At this point it is useful to draw on a feminist psychoanalytic reading of a postcolonial text to hold up a different kind of mirror to "The Dead." Laura Mulvey's reading of Ousmane Sembène's *Xala* extolls, like Gibbons's reading of Huston's adaptation of *The Dead*, the power of cinema to generate a new relationship between oral and written cultural traditions:

> The cinema can speak across the divisions created by oral tradition and written language . . . It can perpetuate an oral cultural tradition as spoken language plays a major role in cinema; and it can bring oral traditions into the modernity of the postcolonial.[98]

Just as in Whelan's reading of "The Dead," "in *Xala*, the question of language is at the political centre of the drama."[99] In a reproof to her father's preference for French, the key character of Rama will only speak their native Wolof, a language with no written correlative. (In the novel version of *Xala*, a group of students develop a written version of Wolof and publish the first journal in the language.) This is reminiscent of Molly Ivor's reproach to Gabriel Conroy for his preference for French holidays and the French language over the Aran Islands and "your own language," but Rama's politics are more complex. Like Gabriel Conroy, the central protagonist in *Xala*, El Hadji, "cannot control the narrative." In El Hadji's case this is because he "is unable to understand his own history," while in "The Dead" it is because Gabriel has never known his wife's. The contrast is telling: masculine identity in "The Dead" is vulnerable because it is held in reserve by a feminine subject, shattered when that subject remembers for him the origin of both their stories. Sembène's film maps exactly the "superfetishism" of the postcolonial, capitalist nation-state where his driver insists that only bottled water can be put in the radiator of El Hadji's Mercedes. Gabriel Conroy must make do with a glittering chandelier, foreign holidays and gutta-percha galoshes, but then the national elite he represents had yet to attain precious, compromised independence. As the carapace of Gretta-for-Gabriel dissolves, "the feminine status of the subject"[100] puts much more than Gabriel's sense of self at risk: "Sembène suggests that these fetishised objects seal the repression of history and class and colonial politics under the rhetoric of nationhood."[101] Teshome Gabriel's reading of the end of *Xala* moves beyond a reading of the film as a critique of the neocolonial status of Senegal's hard-won nation-state. At the end of the film, the deflated postcolonial male at its center, El Hadji, asks his clever, modern daughter, Rama, what she needs and is told, "Just my mother's happiness." This mother is both the wife he has neglected and Africa, represented on-screen by a map, but also in Rama's dress: "the color of the map reflects the exact same colors of Rama's traditional *boubou*, native costume—blue, purple, green and yellow—and it is not divided into countries and states."[102] Teshome Gabriel reads this as a pictorial representation of pan-Africanism: for Mulvey it marks the point where meaning "leaps out and breaks the boundaries of the screen."[103] The ending of "The Dead" has been read as just such a point where meaning breaks the bounds of the text. As Gabriel Conroy's "own identity was fading out into a grey impalpable world . . . snow was general all over Ireland . . . falling faintly through the universe and faintly falling, like the descent of their last end, upon all the living and the dead" (223–24).

Emer Nolan's 1994 study made a persuasive case for reading this as the point where Joyce produces his own version of the "rhetoric of nationhood." The readings surveyed earlier of the text's relation to the colonial and postcolonial condition and to the interface of modernity and tradition, print and oral culture, have effectively built on that case. It is worth pursuing the contrast between this conclusion and that of *Xala*, examining the role that oral culture plays in both and the context of the postcolonial history of nation-states. The dead white of Ireland in midwinter is the vision of a disillusioned man, the flowing colors of Rama's dress too easy to contrast as a symbol of life—that would be to fall into Gabriel Conroy's trap, projecting, fetishizing. The final erasure of boundaries is, however, a common feature in both texts. Joyce's paralyzed Dublin is a colonial city, imagined early in a century in which one form of imperialism would dwindle and others rise. Sembène's career as a filmmaker has been exactly correlative to his native Senegal's independence. He knows, on many levels, a great deal better than Joyce could when he wrote "The Dead" the limitations of nationalism as liberationary rhetoric. *Xala*'s fleeting utopian moment "without boundaries and states" comes at the end of a chronicle of the failures of the postcolonial subject and the nation-state. What is striking is the extent to which current readings of "The Dead" occlude such knowledge, so often seeking to reimagine the nation before its inception as state, as if the recuperation of Joyce to a national project that never materialized were the only grounds for the reading of his work in postcolonial terms. To read "The Dead" in the context of the history and diversity of postcolonial cultural production might release it from historicity and restore history to the reading process.

In his "In Memoriam James Joyce," the Scottish poet Hugh Macdiarmid did not so much commemorate Joyce as use him as a starting point for a sustained exploration of the nature of writing, of literary traditions and of the shortcomings of critical evaluation. It is a gloriously eccentric and yet important work, from which one may trace Joyce's ongoing impact on late twentieth-century writing. For Macdiarmid, Joyce was a fellow adventurer in language: "Among the debris of all past literature / And raw material of all the literature to be."[104] The poem celebrates Joyce's achievement in tracing the lineaments of a future consciousness. In this reading, the late novels meet the need of: "A society of people without a voice for the consciousness / That is slowly growing within them."[105] Macdiarmid compares Joyce to Schonberg, arguing that "the problem" is not that the arts have advanced beyond human comprehension, but that human comprehension must catch up with the art.[106] Joyce's so-called experiments are neither excess nor an indulgence in this schema, but a necessary preparation for a new way of seeing the world: "Even as nerves before they function / Grow where they will be wanted."[107] On the one hand, this is a last gasp of the great modernist belief in the future. Radical that he was in many ways, Macdiarmid is by contemporary standards tremendously old-fashioned precisely because he believed not just in the future, but that art might play a role in bringing it into being, "containing within itself an instrument of voice / Against the time when it *will* talk."[108] The urgency of thinking differently and producing an art to match the complexity of the world and exceed it is too easily dismissed as the utopianism of a late Romantic and residual modernist, however. Macdiarmid reminds us that it is possible to read Joyce's work as more than a scrupulous chronicle of the past and once commonplace to regard it as a companion into the future. It is Joyce's futurity that is at stake in the contrast between Mulvey's reading of Sembène's use of oral traditions and the readings of "The Dead" that focus on its relation to the oral tradition. In the former, the technology of the cinema allows oral culture to move into the present and the future, to recover memory and move forward. Sembène's view of the relationship between traditions and modernity emphatically refuses the fetish of authenticity:

> In the traditional society which I come from, when you look at our societies, whether you're talking about the Mandinka, Bambara or Fulani, we have the tradition of the storyteller called the griot and also other kinds of storytellers. Their role was to record memories of daily actions and events. At night, people would gather around them and they would tell those stories that they had recorded. I think there are parallels between myself and these storytellers, because in that traditional society, the storyteller was his own writer, director, actor and musician. And I think his role was very important in cementing society. Now, with new technologies and the tools that we have acquired, I think we can take inspiration from them and do some work.[109]

Sembène's final film used the resources of oral culture and cinematic technology to attempt a radical change in folk tradition. *Moolaadé*'s story of the ordinary heroisim of a woman who challenges the practice of female genital mutilation in her village presents an extreme and urgent case of the necessity to challenge tradition as well as use it. The comments of Fatoumata Coulibaly, who played the lead role of Colle in *Moolaadé*, are worth citing in this regard. Herself an activist who had both worked in Malian villages and made a documentary for Malian television on FGM in a very hostile context, Coulibaly remarked to the British Film Institute that:

> in our society, talking about sex is still a taboo, and of course many village chiefs don't want to hear about that issue. "You are trying to deviate us from our way of life, our traditions." And of course the argument they give is that these traditions date back to before our birth, and actually they accuse us of being funded by the outside world to subvert their way of life. But with persistence we would come back and get our message across.

The necessity of deviation and the destruction of negative traditions are intrinsic in radical cultural practice and political cinema. Sembène's and Joyce's challenging relationships to tradition are very different, but Coulibaly's comments hint at what might be explored in the space between them. Linking the occlusion of the "illegitimate" bodies of mothers and children excluded from Ireland's self definition in readings of "The Dead" and the difficulty in looking at the actual effects of "tradition" on women's bodies described by Coulibaly is neither feminist universalism nor postcolonial analogy. This chapter was written while the complex case of Pamela Izevbekhai, who claimed asylum in Ireland on the basis that her daughters would be subject to female genital mutilation in Nigeria, was going through the Irish courts. Amid the claims, counterclaims and shrill tabloid head-lines generated by this particular case,[110] the Irish government's resistance to such a defense against deportation has been consistent. The national project prioritizes the integrity of the state over the integrity of women and children's bodies. Ireland is no exception to this, but it is unusually insistent on perceiving and presenting itself as a tolerant nation in dramatic contrast to the active policy of the state. "There's an emotional sense of under-standing about what immigrants are going through because of our experi-ence as immigrants," Conor Lenihan, the minister of integration, informed the *New York Times* (February 25, 2008). The article drew attention to the case of Olukunle Elukanlo, a Nigerian student whose deportation was revoked in response to the protests of his schoolmates and community. It did not mention that the Irish state sought to deport him again when his secondary education was complete nor the controversial deportation of sev-eral hundred Nigerian immigrants at the same time.

When El Hadji in *Xala* submits himself to the materiality of folk ritual, "it signals a lifting of amnesia and an acceptance of history": he rejoins his community and his community "resurrects" him. This is the antithesis of the paralyzing trauma that Whelan's reading in particular identifies as the effect of the singing of "The Lass of Aughrim" in "The Dead": "An indig-enous Irish culture could no longer be resuscitated even by a determined policy of cultural revival." The question is what exactly died and needed resuscitation? Certainly not the folk song tradition represented by "The Lass of Aughrim," which continues to be sung, to change, to resonate with political, social and sexual significance. Moreover, the very vitality of that tradition marks it as equally resistant to determined policy and the borders and divisions implicit in the concept of the indigenous. The fragment of "The Lass of Aughrim" in "The Dead" indicates that the sites of intersec-tion between oral and written culture are maelstroms of cultural signifi-cance where official histories and fixed identities are subject to haunting by the excluded, the subjects of expedient amnesia, the specters of change. Now as then these ghosts demand a rearticulation of the boundaries of the sayable. The possibility and necessity of challenging these boundar-ies is one of the lessons postcolonial cultural production could teach Irish cultural commentators, if they would shift their gaze from the fetishized authenticity of the traumatic past. The institutionalized practice of postco-lonial criticism could serve a really radical political function in Ireland if it challenged the fiction of postcolonial solidarity where the expression of "an emotional sense of understanding" is used to obscure the institutional ruth-lessness of "the racial state."[111] Ireland has a tendency to strike a cultural pose of postcolonial sympathy based on a common experience of migra-tion, while its legislation and practice in relation to actual migrants has actually been more inflexible than some of its postimperial neighbors.[112] Ireland's position is complicated by its ability to celebrate its multiculturalism and simultaneously restrict national citizenship on the basis of ethnicity, and this requires real and serious analysis, especially in the volatile context of rapid economic contraction and recent migration. Joyce's most useful legacy is, after all, a national epic that rewrote Ireland from the point of view of an ethnic outsider and a ferocious parody of the one-eyed monster of national certainty.

6 The Sons of Cuchulainn
Violence, the Family, and the Irish Canon

In a 1957 essay questioning the idea of a "national" literature, Janet Mac-Neill recounted the following anecdote:

> I once sat in the Abbey Theatre at a performance of "The Playboy," and beside me was a German Jew who lived in New York. His English was not sufficiently competent to allow him to follow the action of the play, and he asked me to instruct him. This I did, to the understandable annoyance of people in the adjacent seats. I took advantage of excitement on the stage and laughter in the audience to whisper, "He is telling them that he has killed his father." My neighbor's spectacles lit up. "Ah," he exclaimed, "in Ireland it is a joke when you kill your father, it is funny, hein?" I did my best afterwards to correct this impression, but I am afraid that this was, for him, the significant message of the play.[1]

MacNeill deduces from this that comedy does not have the universalist potential of tragedy. The image of the middle-class Northern Protestant novelist and her German, Jewish, American companion irritating and disturbing the Irish National Theatre's most celebrated play at Oedipus is irresistible for a variety of reasons. Not the least of these is the way in which MacNeill calls attention to the importance of the theme of parricide in defining a specifically Irish literature *and* the strangeness of the theme if dislocated from its central cultural position. Martin McLoone, Elizabeth Cullingford and Cheryl Herr have all commented on the remarkable persistence of this theme in contemporary Irish culture.[2] This chapter seeks to explore the nature of that persistence and the construction of the Irish literary canon, specifically the canons of modernist Irish drama and contemporary Irish film, in ways which mirror and refract this central theme.

Commenting on Neil Jordan's *Michael Collins*, Cullingford notes Jordan's production diary entry that de Valera was "a father who will betray" Collins: "If de Valera was the symbolic father and Collins the son, their encounter replicates a theme that has considerable resonance in Irish culture: Cuchulainn's killing of his only son, Connla, and his subsequent battle with the waves."[3] The most influential twentieth-century version of the story of Cuchulainn's battle with his son is Yeats's *On Baile's Strand*, but the source from which Yeats, Synge and others gleaned the story was Augusta Gregory's *Cuchulainn of Muirthemne*.[4] Declan Kiberd includes an extensive discussion of Gregory's text in his *Irish Classics*,[5] proposing it as a major influence on key texts of the revival. The text not only had a direct influence on W.B. Yeats, J.M. Synge, Mary Colum and others, it contains within it a central trope for the emerging Irish canon. Cuchulainn's misguided battle with his son becomes a recurrent paradigm of the impossibility of a national, civil society, that is, one that can bequeath posterity to a new generation. This is, of course, entirely appropriate for a society defined by mass emigration throughout most of the twentieth century. "This is no country for old men," Yeats complained, but it wasn't one the young could stay in either. At least some of the bitterness Cullingford traces in the debunking of de Valera in contemporary Irish culture lies in his identification with Ireland as failed parent, specifically failed father. In her study of Jim Sheridan's *The Field*, Cheryl Herr comments that "if Irish writers of Sheridan's generation are to be believed, the father that 1980s emigrants left Ireland to escape was intolerant, atavistic, irascible, at the same time acute and barbarous."[6] If official nationalism demanded Ireland be loved as a mother and modernist exiles fled it as a suffocating one, there has always been another strand, not far below the surface and often in the same texts, that has hated it as a bad father. In this regard the state that was established in 1922 inherited a fully elaborated complex of signifiers that repudiated the possibility of cultural authority in patriarchal terms.

The exceptions tend to prove the ubiquity of the rule. At the end of Rosamond Jacob's 1938 novel, *The Troubled House* (discussed in Chapter 4), the Oedipal paradigm is invoked and rejected. The novel uses the metaphor of family as nation, with the Troubles of 1916–1922 internalized in the Cullen family home. The father is a unionist; the eldest son, Theo, a republican pacifist; the middle one, Liam, a member of the IRA; and the mother a highly conflicted narrator who sides with the politics of her sons against their father while trying to save her youngest child from politics altogether. At the novel's end, Liam accidentally kills his father during an ambush. His mother forgives him, however, and he escapes Oedipus's tragic fate. In effect, this episode toward the novel's conclusion is Jacob's gesture toward the Civil War. *The Troubled House* enacts the slippage whereby the new social and political dispensation simply inherits the position of illegitimate authority and recipient of the son's violence: middle-class professionals such as Mr. Cullen were to emerge almost seamlessly in exactly the same position they had enjoyed under the colonial regime. This sense of the illegitimacy of social and political authority accounts, at least in part, for the ferocity with which it was wielded by church and state and the pivotal role of the church in investing religious and symbolic significance to the nation. Indeed the Oedipal fantasy of the castrating father has been so closely identified with the historical failures of the father/church/state/ nation that at the heart of the Irish canon there appears to be an arrest of the Oedipal process.

In his strenuous defense of Yeats's position at the center of the Irish dramatic tradition, Christopher Murray asserts:

> Yeats may be called the seminal figure in the growth of modern Irish theatre and drama, not just because he had the energy, skill and authority to establish and maintain the Abbey Theatre but because it was he who first formulated the role of the Irish dramatist as shaman, as the necessary outsider/insider.[7]

At the heart of Yeats's contribution to the development of Irish drama lies the Cuchulainn cycle, spanning twenty-five years and resonating throughout twentieth-century Irish culture. As Cullingford's account of *Michael Collins* and Herr's of *The Field* make clear, the closing image of Cuchulainn fighting the waves after the death of his son in *On Baile's Strand* is a resonant and powerful one. Cuchulainn, the symbolic hero of the revolution, is from the instigation of the national theater to the breakthrough of the national cinema portrayed as a murderous father and failed patriarch, one who seeks to take up the role of paternal authority and finds that in doing so he destroys it.

GREGORY, YEATS AND CUCHULAINN

The residual question that Elizabeth Cullingford identifies at the heart of Neil Jordan's work is "Who is my father?"[8] In choosing between Collins and de Valera the question becomes "Who is my (politically) legitimate father?"—a reversal in itself of the Oedipal emphasis on biological paternity in favor of socially responsible fatherhood. In Gregory's originary Cuchulainn for the twentieth century, it is, in contrast, the identity of the son that is mysterious. Cuchulainn's son Conlaoch[9] is under *geasa* (a combination of curse and taboo) from his mother to conceal his identity and declares, "I will never give in to any man to tell my name, or to give an account of myself."[10] Recognizing his father, Conlaoch "threw his spear crooked that it might pass beside him. But Cuchulainn threw his spear . . . at him with all his might, and it struck the lad in the side and went into his body."[11] Identifying himself to his father as he dies:

> Conlaoch said, "My curse be on my mother for it was she put me under bonds: it was she sent me here to try my strength against yours."
>   And Cuchulainn said: "My curse be on your mother, the woman that is full of treachery: it is through her harmful thoughts these tears have been brought on us."

This coming together of father and son in hostility to the mother is quite at odds with Yeats's adaptation of the story in *On Baile's Strand*. There, Cuchulainn is obviously still enthralled by Aoife.[12] When the king, Conchubar, refers to her as "that fierce woman of the camp,"[13] Cuchulainn is furious:

> You call her a "fierce woman of the camp,"
> For, having lived among the spinning-wheels,
> You'd have no woman near that would not say,
> "Ah! How wise!" "What will you have for supper?"
> "What shall I wear that I may please you, sir?"
> And keep that humming through the day and night
> For ever. A fierce woman of the camp!
> But I am getting angry about nothing.
> You have not seen her. Ah! Conchubar, had you seen her
> With that high, laughing, turbulent head of hers
> Thrown backward, and the bowstring at her ear,
> Or sitting at the fire with those grave eyes
> Full of good counsel as it were with wine,
> Or when love ran through all the lineaments
> Of her wild body—although she had no child,
> None other had all beauty, queen or lover,
> Or was so fitted to give birth to kings.[14]

Cuchulainn's disdain for conventional femininity and love for the warrior queen Aoife is entirely in keeping with his characterization in *On Baile's Strand*, where he himself is reported to have "run too wild."[15] As a consequence, King Conchubar has come to secure his own and his heirs' authority by binding Cuchulainn to an oath of allegiance to him. The parallels with the colonial situation were obvious when the play was first staged in 1904–1906. In accepting the false authority of the king, Cuchulainn betrays his own nature and destroys his descendents in the interests of that king's. On discovering he has killed his son, having overcome an initial liking for the boy at Conchubar's insistence, Cuchulainn blames not Aoife but the king:

> 'Twas you who did it—you who sat up there
> With your old rod of kingship, like a magpie
> Nursing a stolen spoon.[16]

Submission to the paternal and social authority of the king deprives Cuchulainn of a future and, at least temporarily, of his own reason. As Cullingford notes in relation to Jordan, the myth is of a deeply pessimistic nature: "in killing his only son the father destroys the potential dynamism of the as yet uncreated future and dooms the culture he represents to sterile repetition of the past, embodied in his own image."[17] The desolation of a man without progeny in a feudal society is realized in Gregory's text in a form very close to the peasant lament she imitates in her short plays, particularly in *The Gaol Gate*:

> Without a son, without a brother, with none to come after me; without Conlaoch, without a name to keep my strength . . .
>   I am the father that killed his son, the fine green branch; there is no hand or shelter to help me.
>   I am a raven that has no home; I am a boat going from wave to wave; I am a ship that has lost its rudder; I am the apple left on the tree; grief and sorrow will be with me from this time.[18]

In destroying his son, Cuchulainn has destroyed himself. Whereas in Yeats's versions, Cuchulainn's fight with the waves is an impulse of madness, in *Cuchulainn of Muirthemne* it is the result of cunning strategy on the part of Conchubar, who fears Cuchulainn will turn on him and his men in his mad grief and destroy them. Conchubar directs his druid, Cathbad, "to bid him go down to Baile's Strand, and to give three days fighting against the waves of the sea, rather than to kill us all."[19] This is in sharp contrast to Yeats's finally unbiddable if broken Cuchulainn. Declan Kiberd has commented on Gregory's relationship with the hero of her text: "It was as if the Celtic hero were her own undiscovered animus, a secret self which had lain dormant for years beneath the exterior of the Coole wife and widow . . . For Gregory Cuchulainn was a drag act in more ways than one."[20] Gregory undoubtedly ventriloquizes Cuchulainn and the text consequently allow her to speak as a strong man and in the voice of the people. But social restraint is not an exclusive property of the world of the drawing room. To assume Cuchulainn is a figure of liberation and release is to fall into Gregory's cleverly fashioned trap, which proposes heroic intensity and peasant authenticity as the essence of a lost (about-to-be-recovered) Irish national spirit. Kiberd proposes that as well as injecting a novelistic strain in her epic, Gregory may have read *Bleak House* while she worked on it "to remind herself of the world of property and social class, which her book was intended to transcend." The world of Dickens's social novel and Gregory's heroic epic are not quite that far apart. Cuchulainn as the father whose place in a complex society has cost him his son keenly resembles Lady Deadwood, even if Morrigu rather than Inspector Bucket is the harbinger of his fate. The resemblance points to an awareness of the sterility of the heroic code implicit in *Cuchulainn of Muirthemne* as it is, as Kiberd points out, explicit in *On Baile's Strand*.

There is a very marked difference between the two texts in the attribution of blame for Conlaoch's fate and in the focus of Cuchulainn's consequent anger. In *On Baile's Strand*, when Cuchulainn in his madness fights the waves, "He sees King Conchubhar's crown on every one of them."[21] In

Cuchulainn of Muirthemne, Cuchulainn, coming upon a great white stone on the strand, splits it in two saying, "If I had the head of the woman that sent her son to his death, I would split it as I split this stone."[22] Yeats was a much more sentimental Victorian than Gregory could afford to be: he could not present his hero in a murderous rage against the mother of his son. In foregrounding misogyny in her synthesis of the legends of Cuchulainn, Gregory draws attention to the role of rejection of (powerful) women in the relationships of (heroic) men. In her text, Aoife submerges the role of Jocasta in that of Sphinx, hiding the son's true identity and mysteriously controlling the fate of her men, lover and son. Unable to overcome this feminine power and deprived of his son, Cuchulainn cannot beget the future. He remains warrior, never king. Here heroic masculinity is presented as dependent on a complex set of relationships, which can withdraw as well as endow posterity, fame and identity. "Without a son, without a brother," with "no hand or shelter to help me," the great hero of ancient epic becomes a modern lost soul, "a raven that has no home . . . a ship that has lost its rudder."[23]

PLAYBOY OEDIPUS AND THE KING OF SPAIN'S DAUGHTER

The most significant exception to the rule of frustrated Oedipal development in Irish drama is a crucial one. Synge's *The Playboy of the Western World* is a highly contested heart to the canonical enterprise. At stake are the desirability of national development into the position of secure masculinity, the predication of this position as already reached and the establishment of a canon of Irish literature in the same terms. Declan Kiberd has been the most influential exponent of the reading of *The Playboy of the Western World* as a narrative of liberation. "Synge is arguably the most gifted Irish exponent of the three phases of artistic decolonization later described by Fanon," he declares.[24] He persuasively argues that the play is "an occluded parody" of *Cuchulainn of Muirthemne*, a mock-heroic remedy to the sterility of outmoded heroism.[25] In contrast, Seamus Deane has argued, "In Synge, the cause is always lost."[26] The same critic later gave a different inflection to the play's movement toward the creation of an authentically imaginative hero in opposition to an inauthentic community. In Christy Mahon, "the modernist hero of Irish letters—already prefigured in Stephen Dedalus—is born. National character has become national identity; blarney has become eloquence; history, legend. It was as complete a translation as one could wish."[27] At the heart of both Kiberd's and Deane's readings is an acknowledgment that a particular type of masculine identity as national identity is achieved in the play. The dispute is merely over the value of that achievement. In Kiberd's benign reading of it, the play then becomes prototypical, "a sort of blueprint for a new species of Irish artist."[28] In Deane's reading it is a blueprint of artistic failure, or rather of art as a strategic evacuation of politics. In this reading, the play inevitably rehearses the trope of sterility: "male freedom is not accompanied by freedom for women. Rather it is through freedom from women."[29] The final departure of Christy and his father and the desolation of Pegeen Mike are very close indeed to *Cuchulainn of Muirthemne*, where Cuchulainn and Conlaoch are united only in their curses on Aoife. Strangely, this is a sexual and social economy mirrored in the mob who rioted at the play's opening performance, the mention of women in their shifts providing the pretext for a riot against the play's incommensurability with the masculine national identities then perilously new.

David Lloyd reads the history of the novel in nineteenth-century Ireland as anomalous precisely because the diffusive and calming process of identification is impossible in a context where all fictions are already partisan. The history of twentieth-century drama in Ireland is not anomalous insofar as reenactment of the violence that constitutes society is at the heart of the theatrical enterprise in Western culture. Hence the international success of plays so explicitly rooted in local conditions. The anomaly that arises is a more subtle and disturbing one. The independent southern state promulgated an ideology of the idealized family as the basic building block of society, while, in conjunction with the Catholic Church, creating a series of mechanisms of social control that transferred large numbers of children to institutional care, with effects still sending shock waves through Irish society. Finola Kennedy noted, in her study of family change in Ireland, the findings of a government commission on admissions to industrial schools, perhaps the harshest of these institutions, that, "in 1934, 6 per cent of admissions were due to serious offences, 6 per cent were due to failure to attend school, while 88 per cent were due to poverty and neglect."[30] By 1955, a contributor to the Jesuit journal *Studies* estimated that "over 10,000 normal healthy dependent children" were "in institutions and foster homes throughout the state," noting that the return of children to their relations was rare, a child, once he enters this system, has "no normal home life; he has none of those things which matter most in the child's development."[31] Kennedy estimates that more than seventy thousand children were detained by the courts in industrial schools. While a defining feature of the institutionalizing of children was a refusal to recognize any deviation from the two married parents norm as a family as such, "in the case of the Reformatories, over half the children were known to have parents who were alive, married and living together."[32] In other words, church and state valorized the family while persistently intervening to shift large numbers of the population out of family structures in the interests of social control. The church's concern to break the familial ties of recruits to the clergy and religious orders was exemplary in this regard. (Una Troy/Elizabeth Connor's short story, "The Apple," is an extraordinary exploration of the church's restrictions on one elderly nun's return to her family home.)

Meanwhile the nation's theater ritually reenacted and naturalized the violence that instituted society as an extension of the violence that defined and doomed the family. In contrast to the idealization of the family in official discourse, the theater showed explicit scenes of violence as the familial norm. The very prevalence of it, however, seems to make the violence of the domestic scene invisible, even to criticism at the turn of the twenty-first century. The explicitness of the brutality of the family in Irish drama was, it seems, a form of disavowal, shown but not recognized as social or historical fact. For example, both Kiberd's and Deane's most recent readings of *The Playboy of the Western World* place the emphasis on the social and symbolic condition of women. Kiberd reads the play as a drama of Pegeen Mike's incarceration. Deane sees Pegeen as "someone who is ultimately replaced, who becomes historically anachronistic"[33] as the national character is recast in masculine terms. Neither critic comments on the other victim conjured up in his father's description, Christy himself, "the way he'd come from school, many's the day, with his legs lamed under him, and he blackened with his beatings like a tinker's ass."[34] Mahon's violence against his son is clearly connected in the play to a wider social violence, which is not symptomatic of Irish wildness, but of Ireland's attempt to tame and if necessary lame anything "wild." If, as Kiberd argues, Synge was interested in investigating what Ireland would be after colonization, *The Playboy of the Western World* is darkly prophetic of the limitations of postcolonial Irish society. At the play's end the roles of father and son are reversed, but the roles of dominant and dominated persist. The occupier of the position of power may change, but power itself remains and its structure is unaltered.

This sense of unalterable structure is exposed and satirized in Teresa Deevy's own occluded parody of *The Playboy of the Western World*. Deevy's work is in many ways unremittingly bleak and can be too easily read as naive domestic realism. *The King of Spain's Daughter*,[35] first performed in the Abbey Theatre on April 29, 1935, concerns a young woman who is as skilled in the linguistic embroidery of her circumstances as Christy Mahon, those circumstances being just as limited and brutal. Her father bullies her unmercifully and Peter Kinsella's violence against his child is shown onstage in a very different form from the tussles between the Mahons. We see Kinsella beat Annie for being late delivering his dinner to his workplace. Annie is despite—or perhaps because of this—a hopeless romantic, who dreams of "sailin' out into the sun, and to adventure."[37] She initially rejects the advances of her suitor, Jim, who seems to genuinely care for her and tries to intervene with her father to save Annie from the beating, but who is irritated by Annie's flights into fantasy. The relationship between the need for fantasy and the unbearable nature of some realities is foregrounded in the play. Jim is constantly berated for his love of Annie by the appallingly comical Mrs. Marks, who voices local society's moral judgments in the play, "Don't do yourself harm on anyone's account. We get what we merit, and God is good . . . Don't be moved to any foolish compassion. The hard man wins."[38] Jim defies the old woman by going to comfort Annie after her father's beating, and asks, "He hurt you then—did he do you any harm?" but Annie is eager to escape back into her fantasy ("Let us leave that behind us") and begins to describe the bride at a local wedding in elevated language:

> ANNIE. She looked lovely passin' along, her hand restin in his, and her body swaying beside him down the path. The arms of the two families were painted on the launch: the sun was shinin' on it: everything was white or burnin' red, but she was dressed in pale, pale gold and (*hands to breast*) two red flowers were crushed agen her here.
> JIM. (*springs up*) What lies are you tellin'? I saw her myself: she was dressed in grey: she had no flowers.
> ANNIE. (*gentle, bewildered*) Jimmy, what's wrong with you?
> JIM. She was dressed in grey. Tell the truth!
> ANNIE. It was in pale gold I saw her. (30)

Annie resists an arranged marriage to her literal-minded suitor until she is threatened with a five-year contract in a local factory, "I couldn't face it. (*Falters*) Every mornin' walkin' the road, every evenin' back so tired."[39] Her acceptance provocatively echoes Molly Bloom's: "I might as well have you. (*Low*) Who would I ever meet would be fit for me? Where would I ever find a way out of here?"[40] Jim, who offers to throw his sisters out of his house to facilitate the marriage, seems more like her father than initial appearances had suggested. Nonetheless, Annie seems to resign herself to the fact that reality will never be commensurate with her imaginings, until she comes across the notebook in which Jim has kept careful account of the money he has saved every week since she said he had no money: "He put by two shillin's a week for two hundred weeks. I think he is a man that—supposin' he was jealous—might cut your throat. (*Quiet—exultant; she goes.*)"[41] Instead of pretending to be a murderer, Annie Kinsella can ultimately hope only to be interestingly murdered. The stage directions for *The King of Spain's Daughter* specify that the set should be flanked on either side by signs saying No Traffic and Road Closed, respectively, and the plight of Annie Kinsella is that while she can imagine almost anything, she cannot go anywhere.

The King of Spain's Daughter demonstrates that when familial violence is not submerged in the Oedipal framework that sustains *On Baile's Strand* and *The Playboy of the Western World*, it becomes visible as brutal and unavoidable reality. Like Annie, Deevy's play can reference the mythological but not realize it. There is no place beyond the historical particularity of the factory and the forced marriage for it to go. Therein lies the play's strength, but also its marginality. It can parody and even subvert the mythic and canonical conjunction of family, nation and tragic lyricism, but it refuses to mythologize and remains uncanonical.

THE STAGE, THE SCREEN AND THE LAST BUS HOME

Insofar as the conflict of fathers and sons presented on the Irish stage is general to Western culture, it is Oedipal. The general, Oedipal scenario does not fully account for the strength and persistence of the trope, particularly at the heart of the canons of twentieth-century Irish literature, however. That must at least be partly attributed to the very particular social and familial dysfunctions that were the result of a complex of sexual, familial, religious and social structures aimed at controlling population, resources and discontent. In effect, Irish culture was parricidal insofar as Irish social structures were those of a failed patriarchy. Jim Sheridan's version of *The Field* reprises the murderous violence of family relations and the mad sterility of that patriarchy, a reprise that Cheryl Herr has persuasively read as part of the interrogation of Irish identities in the 1980s. The film occupies an important place in the establishment of a canon of Irish film, not least in establishing the relationship between that new formation and its antecedents in Irish literature and drama.[42] Herr argues that "Sheridan creates a homology between that theatre-to-film development and his characteristic theme of father-son relations. In a very real sense, Irish drama fathers the experiential zone occupied by its cinematic offspring."[43] That homology is established by the addition to the story, as told in John B. Keane's original play, of a number of concluding scenes borrowed from or influenced by *On Baile's Strand*. Herr observes that Keane's problematic relationship to the canon of twentieth-century Irish drama is attributable to his work's adherence to older, nineteenth-century, melodramatic and populist forms. Given this, the addition of elements from Yeats's plays to Keane's is a bid for canonical centrality for the preoccupations of the 1980s, which inform Sheridan's deconstruction of a romanticized relation between land and people and his depiction of the relationship between traditional Ireland and social change. *The Field* and *Michael Collins* indicate a high degree of self-conscious continuity between the established canon of Irish literature and the emergent one of Irish film. It is a very Oedipal form of continuity, however. For if theater is to film as Cuchulainn is to Conlaoch, then *The Field* registers the Irish film industry's fear that it will be overwhelmed by its difficult progenitor.

Other versions of the story of Cuchulainn and Conlaoch emerged in the popular culture of the late twentieth century, however. Whereas in the film version of *The Field*, the Ireland of the 1980s interrogated what it perceived to be the legacy of the nineteenth and early twentieth centuries, in *The Last Bus Home* the Ireland of the Celtic Tiger years tries to find its own origins and identifies them in the 1970s. *The Last Bus Home*, rooted in an alternative Ireland, exceeds the murderous pessimism of the Oedipal tangle. While the film's main narrative concerns the relationship between Reena, manger of a punk rock group in 1970s Dublin, and Jessel, the group's charismatic lead singer, their relationship is intertwined and finally destroyed by their different relationships with Petie, the band's drummer. Petie is in many respects a conventional figure of the sensitive and artistic gay man, a college student who designs the group's posters. A sort of anti-*Commitments*, the film offers an insight into the punk scene and the street life of Dublin in the period. Reena and Jessel first make love in front of a television screen showing the Pope's visit to Ireland, the "Young People of Ireland" speech competing for audibility with the lovers and the bass player's strumming. They call their band The Dead Patriots, identifying themselves with the demise of the idea of heroic nationalism. There is an obvious reference to this theme in Irish punk and punk-inflected popular music, specifically the Radiators' "Faithful Departed," which could surely be marketed as the most literary punk rock anthem ever. The song draws on some of the best-known texts in Irish modernism, identifying the punk generation's radical disillusion with the pieties of church and nation with a tradition of critical dissent and fusing it with a parody of a Catholic hymn. It also exhibits the questioning of accepted versions of Irish history characteristic of the period: "Rattled by the glimmerman man, the bogey man, the holyman / And living in the shadows, in the shadows of a gunman." (Punk fused with traditional ballad singing later explicitly linked disillusion with nationalism to subverting the heroic figure of Cuchulainn in The Pogue's "The Sickbed of Cuchulainn."[44]) "Faithful Departed" obviously touched a chord. It was covered by Moving Hearts, a highly successful hybrid of traditional Irish and rock music, and The Pogues and was re-released in 2003 as part of a "best of" Moving Hearts collection.

The Last Bus Home references these innovative and alternative aspects of Irish culture in the seventies and eighties in a way that has some parallels with Sheridan's referencing of the theatrical canon, and the film's narrative does suggest that contemporary Ireland owes much to those questioning decades that broke definitively with the past. Some of *The Last Bus Home*'s milieu is reminiscent of Cathal Black's *Pigs*; however, the film is not concerned with the desperate poor, but the desperately angry children of the middle class. Its sensibility is closer to John T. Davies's exploration of punk culture in *Shellshocked Rock* than the feel-good factor that *The Commitments* associated with the story of a band as that of hope in the face of adversity. The Dead Patriots don't overcome adversity, it overcomes them and it is partly their fault. The atmosphere of violence on the streets during the period permeates the film, with sporadic outbreaks of street fighting between skinheads and punks, the former group also spawning the gay-bashing that became high profile in Ireland with the murder of Declan Flynn in Fairview Park in 1983.[45] On one level, this is another Ireland, which though infrequently presented on-screen or onstage, is highly familiar to a middle-aged, middle-class audience at the beginning of the twenty-first century. These are the scenes of a youth before the Celtic Tiger. The ubiquitous joke of the eighties, "last one to leave, turn out the lights," is recounted on the bus of the title.

The film's climax is the death of Petie, outed by Jessel who is obsessively jealous of Reena's relationship with Steve, an English A&R man, interested in signing the group. Jessel's insecurity, his fear of failing in London, his rivalry with Steve and his failure of both Reena and Petie identify him with the same old (Irish) story. But though he loses Reena, Jessel is ultimately redeemed. Long after the fact, Reena discovers it is neither Jessel nor the chasing skinheads that have caused Petie to pause before the oncoming bus, but, inevitably, his father, who has greeted his son's admission that he is gay with the threat of commitment to a mental hospital.

Critical responses to *The Last Bus Home*, while generally positive, are an interesting indicator of the extent to which the existing paradigms of Irish film history deny and enact the older canonical certainties. Martin McLoone describes the film as "not only one of the most astute comments yet on the smugness of the 'Celtic Tiger' era," but "also one of the first revisionist films about the punk era."⁴⁶ For McLoone, the film is about class, consumerism and self-interest, "Not only is punk seen as a fake rebellion to the bourgeois conformity of society, its rapid recuperation by that society confirms the absence of any political alternative."⁴⁷ Here an apparently Marxist analysis actually recuperates the film for the Cuchulainn paradigm, where the past is an unbearable burden, the future a domain of impossibility. Harvey O'Brien is entirely indicative of the attitudes of some of the emerging voices in Irish film criticism in criticizing the film for not presenting the past as entirely horrific, but his conclusions are nonetheless very similar to McLoone's:

> There is not quite enough anger though, especially for a film set in the punk scene. It harbors a certain affection for traditionalism embodied in the regard shown for the character of Ryan's grandmother, and, in fact, by the film's end, punk is itself shown to be a form of hypocritical, futile rebellion masking a neo-conservative desire for success.⁴⁸

In both these accounts Petie's story is very much peripheral to the film's meaning, though O'Brien criticizes the film for what he sees as a soft-centered approach. Lance Pettitt's brief but highly engaging analysis of the film as a post-gay movie makes Petie's narrative central. Like McLoone he reads the final scene as a questioning of the advances that have been achieved since the seventies: "The film captures a transitional moment in the late-1970s, but it also questions the extent to which 1990s reforms have delivered gays from insidious homophobia."⁴⁹ For Pettitt, "this is less a negative image than a reminder that teenage gays are disproportionately represented in Irish suicide figures, still get 'gay-bashed' and feel compelled to emigrate despite law reform and Ireland's relative economic prosperity."⁵⁰

While acknowledging the qualifications which Pettitt rightly makes, I would argue that the closing scene achieves something more than eulogy, irony or warning. The film eschews the melodrama it moves toward with

Petie's death. The closing scene brings Reena and Jessel tentatively back together, but gives the stage to Billy, Petie's lover and a soul singer. Billy is not a romanticized figure: in trying to keep his lover with him, he helped contribute to his demise. The club where Reena, Jessel and Billy commemorate Petie and celebrate the decriminalization of homosexuality in Ireland represents a future that mourns the death of the son without madness and offers reconciliation in the domain of the heterosocial,[50] which for once isn't mere utopian speculation. Decriminalization is the political and historical correlative of the cultural debunking of the ultimate patriarchal authority in the form of the Pope in the film's opening scenes. It may not have banished homophobia, but it did register the political effectiveness of gay activism. In *The Last Bus Home*, the future has already come to pass. The figure of Billy exceeds the murderous singularity of the Cuchulainn versus Oedipus scenario. In the heterosocial community with which the film ends, relationships of choice supersede those of inevitability and the family metaphor is displaced by the group.

Part III

Race, Masculinity, and Popular Culture

7 The Devil's Own Patriot Games
The Troubles and the Hollywood Action Movie

This chapter analyzes the representation of the Troubles in the mainstream Hollywood action thriller of the 1990s. It focuses on two films, *Patriot Games* (directed by Phillip Noyce, UIP/Paramount, US) from 1992 and *The Devil's Own* (directed by Alan J. Pakula, Columbia, US) from 1997, which elicited very different audience and media responses. *Patriot Games* initiated the highly successful series of films featuring CIA agent Jack Ryan, initially played by Harrison Ford, later by Ben Affleck. The Devil's Own recouped only $42.9 million of its $95 million budget at the US box office and was attacked by the British tabloid media as an apologia for the IRA. Between them the two films sketch the parameters within which the Troubles functioned in the Hollywood action thriller. *Patriot Games* established many of these parameters for the nineties. *The Devil's Own* exceeded them too early, having gone into production in the aftermath of the first IRA cease-fire in 1994, but released after the breakdown of that cease-fire and some months before its renewal in July 1997.

The purpose of this chapter is to locate the films within three interlocking contexts. The first is that of the development of the Hollywood action movie in the nineties. I will briefly sketch out the major critical debates in this area, focusing in particular on the analysis of male relationships of antagonism and friendship within the films and the reasons for the centrality of these relationships. I will draw on the paradigms established in the work of Cynthia Fuchs[1] and Yvonne Tasker[2] at the time, particularly on their analysis of the mediation of racial and social conflict in action films. The centrality of the family and kinship structures in action films dealing with Irish situations and characters will be analyzed in the context of the genre's development and its treatment of masculine roles during the later nineties.

The second context of this discussion is provided by the "Troubles" themselves and political developments in the nineties. These problematized the "myth of atavism" traced, for example, by Martin McLoone[3] through Hollywood representations of Ireland during this period. Here it is important to trace changing US policy and attitudes to Ireland itself, but also to the broader international scene. The third context is the study of ethnicity and neighborhood in contemporary Hollywood, drawing on Diane Negra's (2001) insights into the role of ethnicity in stardom, but also applying models developed by Paula Massood[4] and Vivian Sobchack,[5] which use Bakhtin's theory of the narrative chronotope to analyze the construction of social, cultural and geographical places in contemporary Hollywood film. One purpose of this discussion is to analyze the representation of Northern Ireland in the Hollywood action thriller in the light of this work on the construction of a sense of place in film and to integrate this with the understanding of stardom, characterization and the relationships between characters foregrounded in critical accounts of the action film. Massood and Sobchack are concerned with the narrative construction of very specific American places and genres. The contemporary action thriller raises the possibility that Hollywood's mapping of the relationship between its self and others' troubles is indicative of a global complex of chronotopes that constitutes a cultural map of a worldview. While this map is projected onto US–Irish relations in the films under discussion here, it is motivated by a much broader set of international relations. In this final regard, the fundamental argument of this chapter is that much more is at stake for Hollywood in representing Irish "Troubles" than the representation of Ireland itself. It proposes that Ireland serves a specific function in the reimagining of the boundaries between heroes and villains in 1990s US popular culture and asks why Ireland is able to perform this mythologizing task.

Systematic analysis of the action movie over the last two decades is heavily indebted to the analysis of masculinity and the male body on screen that Steve Neale originated in his 1983 article, "Masculinity as Spectacle."[6] Neale's work took Laura Mulvey's analysis of the woman as object of the gaze and of the masculine structure of film spectatorship[7] as his starting points. His groundbreaking article then developed the premise that the male body as object of the gaze stages a crisis within a structure of spectatorship predicated on the gendering of the gaze as masculine, the object of the gaze as feminine. Heavily Lacanian in its psychoanalytic underpinnings, Neale's argument set the discussion of spectacle firmly within the realm of the imaginary, crucially identifying narcissistic identification as a key component in the relationship between the male spectator and the action hero. The hero represents the Ego Ideal: in other words, in the relationship between the ego and its images, the male spectator finds in the male star the image he wishes to find in the mirror.

There is, however, a less obvious, but equally strong, countercurrent. For the ego will never reach its ideal and the male-to-male gaze is as voyeuristic in Neale's formulation as the male-to-female gaze in Mulvey's. Both the classical Hollywood genres and the action movie mediate the erotic gaze at the male object through spectacles of suffering, especially in scenes of combat. This applies to both male and female spectators. The fight scene in the much-analyzed *Lethal Weapon* (directed by Richard Donner, 1987, Warner/Richard Donner, Joel Silver, US) is a typical case in point. Mel

Gibson's character, Riggs, appears to stop in the middle of a knockdown fight to remove his shirt, thus presenting a more effective display of his musculature—and some relief from the tedium of the protracted fight scene, presumably, for Gibson's female fans. As Neale acknowledged, if the male body as spectacle provokes a crisis of cinematic representation, it is a safely contained crisis. Suffering, torture and violence are visited upon these highly paid and much worked-out male bodies to screen their status as objects of another's gaze. Hence a sadomasochistic dynamic is set up between hero and audience, and also within the relationships between men on-screen. (Here Neale is close to the formulation of the interdependence of the homosocial and homosexual also outlined in the eighties by Eva Kosofsky Sedgewick.[8])

When a 1993 collection reproduced Neale's article as its springboard for a broader analysis of masculinity in cinema, the psychoanalytical critique of masculinity in cinema was modified by historical and social analysis.[9] The interesting question, after all, was why the action movie was such a dominant trend in the cinema of the 1980s that Yvonne Tasker could describe it as cinema of "masculinity."[10] The post-Vietnam crisis of masculinity and of US self-confidence combined with the emergence of the new right were important factors,[11] but internal racial conflict is equally important. As Cynthia Fuchs so persuasively argued, action movies in the eighties consistently invoked a paradigm of male camaraderie, modeled on military camaraderie, which erased both the threat of the homoerotic and of racial conflict in the image of "buddies."[12] "The Buddy Politic" traces the displacement of sometimes nearly blatant homoeroticism in narrative emphasis on interracial partnership. Buddy action thrillers also displaced persistent paranoia about black male sexuality and miscegenation through an image of racial harmony without interracial sex. The imperative "Look, black and white together," forestalled the question, "Why are those men holding hands?" It is in this internal US context that the function of Irish characters and situations in the action thriller needs to be understood.

Racial tension was not the only imperative for change. Changing gender roles also generated significant mutations in the action genre in the 1990s. Not the least of these was the advent of the female action hero, notably in the *Alien* and *Terminator* series of films. Action and masculinity were no longer synonymous. According to Yvonne Tasker, "the emergence of action heroines into the mainstream has necessarily redefined the articulation of gender identity in the action picture."[13] One significant development was the increased tendency of the 1990s action genre to figure the now apparently permanent crises of masculinity *and* society in narrative terms as a crisis of fatherhood. The link between heroic status and regaining the role of good father emerged strongly in the *Die Hard* series. Parallel to the built bodies and seriously deranged masculinities of the 1980s genre, this series evolved another stereotype of masculinity: the wisecracking, flawed, ironic persona played initially by Bruce Willis. This latter stereotype is, of course, more in keeping in many respects with the traditionally understated hero of Hollywood thrillers, whose cunning, skill with weapons and intelligence will always defeat the brute strength of an opponent. The smirk with which Willis played this role has spun off a continuing cycle of comedy thrillers combining humor and special effects. The Hollywood action thrillers dealing with Northern Ireland do not belong to this strain, however, though it is obviously much beloved and aspired to by Irish directors and Irish film. (*Divorcing Jack*[14] is an interesting variant on almost every convention of the genre in the context of pre-cease-fire Belfast.)

Harrison Ford, who stars in both *Patriot Games* and *The Devil's Own*, made his reputation and originally established his star persona by playing the hero ironically in the *Star Wars* and *Indiana Jones* series. It is the aura of his other, later roles as the epitome of ordinary, male American decency that he brings to his two films dealing with the Troubles. This and the downplaying of comic elements are fundamentally connected to the centrality of family in these narratives and the seriousness with which the role of husband and father is treated. Ford's characters in these two films are the opposite of the always almost about to be divorced characters played by Willis. Strong family men with roles in law enforcement and government, the characters of Jack Ryan in *Patriot Games* and Tom O'Meara in *The Devil's Own* are poster boys for benevolent patriarchy. The question "how to be a man" became an ironic question within the action genre from the point where postmodern nostalgia became a major component of the genre in the *Indiana Jones* films, until the aftermath of 9/11. During this period, this question was usually given emotional resonance by extending it to "how to be a (good) father." The predication of the national on the familial and the centrality of fatherhood in both are central to both *Patriot Games* and *The Devil's Own*.

FAMILY, NATION, ACTION

The video release and promotional poster for *Patriot Games* carried the caption, "Not for honor. Not for Country. For his wife and child," above a still of Harrison Ford pointing his gun directly at the onlooker, with a dark image of an eye peering out from a balaclava in the background, an image of rifle gunsights superimposed on both. The violence of Ryan is legitimated by his need to protect his family. The violence of Sean Bean's character, Miller, is also linked to familial ties, however. The contrast between the good nuclear American family and the dysfunctional Irish one is linked to the film's construction of their very different homes. An establishing opening shot identifies Ryan's home as a large and idyllic seaside family residence, respectable and prosperous. The voice-over features Ryan's telephone message, instructing the housekeeper on the care of the family's goldfish. This call and the shots of his empty home establish

Jack Ryan's character: domesticated, responsible, a little humorous and cutely forgetful. He is very concerned to protect his daughter from any unpleasantness that may occur as a result of an oversight on his part. In this case, the unpleasantness is death, which may already have overtaken the goldfish. Ironically of course, the threat of just this unpleasantness will overtake his family as a result of his intervention in a terrorist attack in London.

The film's London is a tourist cliché. The Ryans are shown ensconced in a luxurious hotel playing Monopoly with their young daughter. When she goes to bed, Jack's wife has champagne and candles delivered to the room as a prelude to the film's only love scene. Having established the hero as ideal husband and ideal father, the film immediately cuts from the Ryans' bedroom to Ryan in his role as senior CIA man addressing the British military on their mutual role in the new world order. The specific context is the aftermath of the Cold War:

> We have all watched with a sense of awe the protean events which have taken place in Moscow and the Republics and the enormous changes resulting from these events. In this volatile climate then I conclude we can only speculate about the future of Soviet fleet development and deployment.

Ryan's speech does several things. It presents our hero as a spokesperson for the US and indeed its embodiment. It locates the film in relation to the international political scene in a way that echoes the publicity's elision of Ireland into terrorism. It also reminds us why Jack Ryan is engaging with the Troubles in the first place: the horrible dilemmas presented to thriller writers and to Hollywood studios by the redundancy of the good old Cold War plots. The Russians were not coming, not ever again, and *Patriot Games* is part of a transition toward different kinds of plots, in which the new bad guys are terrorists, who, however marginalized and misled, combine technological resources and military cunning. This new threat was just beginning to be seen as a menace to the US, taking the place of the old enemy.

The sequence following Ryan's speech intercuts scenes of his wife and daughter doing tourist London with a dissident republican cell planning an attack on yet another family unit, this time a neatly nuclear constituent grouping of the royal family. The sequence establishes a strong contrast between right and wrong family values. The dominant family relationship between the IRA men in *Patriot Games* is brotherhood. Excessive desire for vengeance on Miller's part scarcely needs to be attributed to guilt for involving his "little brother" in the fatal attack. Their relationship is implicitly coded as diseased, introduced as it is by the handing of the gun from older to younger brother. The opposite of the Ryans' fertile relationship, this family is constituted by a deathly male-to-male bond.

In the nineties the terrorist attacks carried out on American soil, such as the Unabomber attacks and the Oklahoma City Bombing in 1995, were predominantly by internal dissident groupings and individuals. Hollywood movies occasionally, as in *Arlington Road* (directed by Mark Pellingham, 1999, Sony/Screen Gems/Lakeshore Entertainment, US) for example, mirrored this, but this did not become a major trend. The equation of the foreign and the terrible continued to dominate the popular imagination. The Irish terrorists who feature in *Patriot Games* and *The Devil's Own*, however, do register the cultural impact of these homegrown terrorists. Part of the function of their white foreignness is both to acknowledge and exploit the anxiety that the terrorist is not immediately identifiable by his skin color or strangeness. The Irish as terrorists keep the new threat at a safe distance and appropriately foreign: they might look like regular guys, but they are from a very different place. The ideas of place as a determinant of character and origin as destiny run through both films, though the themes are very differently inflected. (While Northern Ireland is scarcely differentiated from any other terrorist point of origin in *Patriot Games*, the narrative implies that an excess of memory and attachment to the past is a crucial component in Miller's madness.)

The promotional poster and the video blurb for *Patriot Games* never mention the Troubles or Ireland, eliding them in references to "lethal terrorist action" and "a radical terrorist group." Here it is Ireland's metonymic relation to terrorism that gives it its place in the narrative. That relation requires some examination. The Irish terrorist is both the same and different, white and foreign. He lends himself to the paranoid thriller because he can hide so easily, looking just like us, having no particular quarrel with the US as such. In *Patriot Games*, the fact that this terrorist turns to an American target is motivated by revenge for his brother's shooting, with his obsessive pursuit of Ryan and his family in the second half of the film closer to the conventions of psychotic killer and stalker narratives. *Patriot Games'* fusion of the political and serial killer variants of the thriller genre makes a political point: terrorism is merely a particularly crazy variant of criminality. Stemming from excessive devotion to the ties of masculine kinship, its causes are located in the familial and are symptomatic of individual dysfunction. A causal framework in which political violence can be investigated as symptom of broader dysfunctions of social, political, regional or global relations is unimaginable within the conventions of characterization and narrative deployed in *Patriot Games*.

NORMAL PEOPLE IN AN ABNORMAL SITUATION?

Released five years later, *The Devil's Own* configures the relationship of family, nationality and fatality differently. Its opening sequence features the brutal disruption both of family life and of a traditional chronotype of

"Ireland." Before the action starts, so to speak, in a pre-credit sequence we see a small boy helping his fisherman father on their boat, returning home to a scenic rural home presented as nurturing and warm. A fire blazes in the grate as the mother dishes up dinner and the family talk about their day seated around a circular table. There is a sudden jarring cut to a loyalist gunman, who literally breaks the family circle, shooting the father. The scene ends with an extreme close-up of the little boy's eyes, which fades to a grainy close up of the eyes of his adult self. The rest of the credits roll over this picture, which a voice-over identifies as Frankie the Angel, proceeding to list the number of British soldiers, RUC officers and loyalist paramilitaries he has killed. The cut from Frankie's eyes shows a military briefing room that features both Frankie's picture and the sinister owner of the voice identifying him as a target for a military capture operation. The immediate cut from this room to a group of boys playing football in the streets of Belfast indicates a game is afoot and also reinforces the motif of children caught up in violence. Interestingly, it is only at this point, when we cut to the streets of Belfast in 1992, that a caption is deemed necessary, identifying the place and the time. The run down and militarized streets of Belfast are in strong contrast to the rural idyll in which the boy Frankie was introduced. Indeed they represent a chronotype of Irish place neither as firmly established nor as recognizable as the rural one, which, with its landscape dominated by mountains and isolated homes, needed no captions. "Belfast, 1992" is the opposite of the scenic Irish landscape that has featured so persistently in films set in Ireland since the silent era. Interestingly Frankie's escape from the gun battle in a ruined house (where the army ambushers are themselves ambushed by the IRA) involves his disappearance into foliage at the end of the overgrown garden. Nature at this point seems to be his preserve.

In telling the story of how Frankie became a gunman and what motivates his mission in New Jersey, *The Devil's Own* attempts to restore history to the myth of terrorism. The terrorist is a protagonist in his own story, not just a projection of another's fears. "We're normal people in an abnormal situation, fighting a disgusting ugly war which you can't understand because you haven't lived it," Frankie later tells O'Meara. The film, despite the assumptions of condemnatory tabloids on its release, resolutely endorses O'Meara's condemnation of Frankie's actions, telling him he is only ensuring other eight-year-olds will see their fathers die. The film also affords Frankie ample dialogue space to blame the British government for its failures in Northern Ireland, however. At least some of the tabloid fervor was a reaction to the casting: having Brad Pitt in the role of the IRA man indicates from the start that this is a very different characterization than the one afforded to Miller in *Patriot Games*. There Sean Bean cannot possibly counter the moral authority of the A-list Ford. In *The Devil's Own*, two Hollywood leading men are pitted against each other, representing different generations and types of hero, but both with the looks, profile and salary of American heroes. It was not surprising that casting Pitt as

Frankie would evoke resentment of the film's representation of the IRA in the British media. The breakdown of the cease-fire also provoked the actor himself to distance himself from the film as "irresponsible" in a *Newsweek* interview, which generated another controversy in the US media.

Yet *The Devil's Own* shares *Patriot Games* grounding of character development and motivation in the familial and the personal. Numerous shots of children playing in the buildup to the first gun battle and one of a mother trying to shield her small children from gunfire in a recess establish that children are not safe in Belfast. When Frankie, now calling himself Rory, arrives at Tom O'Meara's house in New Jersey it is as if he has returned to the idyllic familial space of his childhood home. A scene where he shares a meal with the O'Meara family reinforces this, echoing the earlier scene of his own family around the table. A son who has lost his father, Frankie/Rory meets in Tom O'Meara a father who has no sons, though he does have three daughters. Ethnic identity here is almost indistinguishable from the familial. It is also linked to a reassertion of masculinity: Tom initially tells the young Irishman that it's good to have someone else in the house who pees standing up. When Tom's wife sends him out for milk, he diverts to a neighborhood bar with Frankie/Rory. Here they exchange insults with a group of local Italian Americans and beat them at pool, with rousing Irish traditional music on the soundtrack. (When the Italians challenge them to the pool game, Tom tells the barman to throw the milk in the cooler.) This triumphant, macho ethnicity is utterly discredited in the film in narrative terms, but its easy conviviality is never matched by the complex, negotiated set of relationships between colleagues that characterize Tom's role as a policeman. Rory tells Tom of the murder of his own father, a story that the hard-bitten cop finds both distressing and moving and one that invokes in him a fatherly protectiveness toward the younger man that ultimately survives even Rory's endangerment of O'Meara's actual family.

Rory's integration into that family seems complete on the day when he participates in celebrating their daughter's confirmation. Accompanying them to church, the camera focuses on Rory's troubled face as the priest repeats the tenets of the Catholic faith. The family party after the confirmation, complete with fiddlers, reprises all of the clichés of Irish ethnic identity and simultaneously marks the high point of Rory's integration into the O'Meara household. It is preceded, however, by scenes of his continued activities acquiring arms for the IRA and succeeded by one of his romantic involvement with a young Irishwoman who is similarly involved. It is she who asks him if he ever feels guilty about what they are doing and elicits the response, "Everyone has ghosts, no one's innocent in this situation." The metaphor of haunting recurs in the film. Frankie is haunted by the death of his father. He himself is a specter of a history elsewhere that haunts not just Irish Americans, but all forms of ethnicity and even the apparatus of law and order itself. Not only is Tom O'Meara a policeman, but the prominent Irish American who has knowingly persuaded him to take in an IRA gunrunner is a local judge.

PARTNERS, FATHERS AND SONS

The Devil's Own's exploration of Irish-American identity is grounded, through a series of scenes portraying Tom's working days on the streets of New York, in a web of interracial and interethnic relationships characterized by misunderstanding and potential violence. Initially O'Meara's police role in this context is coextensive with his paternal one at home. We see him intervene in a commonsensical and compassionate way when a rookie cop mistakenly chases a young African American. O'Meara's relationship with his Hispanic partner, Eddie Diaz (played by Rubén Blades), is also initially a classic buddy partnership, until the latter shoots a suspect. The morally upright O'Meara reports his friend: "We're in the police business, Eddie, not the revenge business." This rupture in what had been a coequal partnership makes O'Meara even more open to and dependent on the paternal relationship he develops with Frankie/Rory. Yet when a group of gunmen raid O'Meara's house and hold his wife hostage while they search for Frankie/Rory's IRA arms money, it is to his former partner that O'Meara turns for help. The intercultural camaraderie of the streets that binds these two proves more reliable than either the ethnic and familial ties that link Tom to Rory/Frankie *or* the codified world of "the force" and the law. Tom needs his old buddy when his family is threatened. When Frankie/Rory kills Eddie while escaping the partners' custody, O'Meara's temporary prioritizing of ethnic affiliation modeled on familial (father–son) relations over equal partnership based on common experience proves to be fatal for his partner. It also isolates Tom and pushes him into an oppositional relation with the system that had previously defined his identity. Sloan, the British agent working with the FBI to apprehend Frankie/Rory, asks O'Meara, "what exactly is your relationship with this terrorist?" commenting, "you *are* Irish." O'Meara responds, "So is Cardinal O'Connor," and refuses to cooperate with an investigation. This British-American cooperative venture is condemned by Ryan, just as he had condemned his own partner, because it operates outside the law: "they're not going to bring him in, they're going to kill him." The refusal of revenge and the upholding of justice define O'Meara as the moral center of the film. This dedication initially costs him his partner, then fails to save his adoptive son. "I've come to bring you in son . . . the killing's got to stop," he tells Frankie/Rory, who replies, "Then you're going to have to kill to stop it. Get's a bit complicated, doesn't it?" This final confrontation both invokes and negates the father–son dynamic between the two. It also epitomizes the trajectory of homoeroticism in the action thriller. The men achieve physical intimacy through violence: their final embrace occurs when they have shot each other. Frankie/Rory's dying explanation of the failure of good intentions throughout the film is that this is "not an American story, it's an Irish one." This is hard to uphold for the film as a whole. Perhaps, however, *The Devil's Own*'s failure as a commercial thriller may derive from its reflection of the complexity of relationships between US security and its others in the film's central "buddies."

IRELAND, THE US AND THE WORLD

These films possess a confidence that history is something horrible that happens elsewhere that is almost eerie in the aftermath of 9/11. The action thriller at the end of the twentieth century appeared to echo the narrative paradigms identified by Stephen Arata[15] in relation to popular adventure fiction at the end of the nineteenth century. Ford in *Patriot Games* is another "occidental tourist" and, even if the British Isles are not so far east as the exotic destinations of Kipling and Rider Haggard, the same pattern of exposure and contamination occurs and the horrible other follows him home. US security, with all the gamut of meaning the phrase implies, is haunted by the shadows of political conflicts that threaten to catch it too in nets of political and social consequence beyond its control. These horrible others, like Stoker's Dracula or the conspirators in Conan Doyle's *The Sign of Four*, are dangerous precisely because they can blend so easily into the anonymity of modern urban environments that are defined by migration, movement and chance. There is a marked shift from *Patriot Games* to *The Devil's Own*. In the former, danger comes from the unseen stalker on the highway and in the street. In the latter, it comes from the refugee you have invited into your home precisely because he is just like you. The hero in the first instance can ultimately recover his family from tragedy, reestablishing the boundaries between them and us, safety and danger, home and abroad. In *The Devil's Own*, he can neither recuperate the former terrorist into the good American son, as he wishes to do, nor return so easily to a bounded identity. "If I was eight years old and saw my father gunned down in front of my family, I'd be carrying a gun too. And I wouldn't be wearing a badge," O'Meara (Ford) claims. *The Devil's Own* ruptures its own narrative boundaries. O'Meara becomes alienated from the police, disregarding orders to cooperate with an implausibly combined FBI and SAS operation that he is convinced aims to kill Frankie/Rory not arrest him. He is equally alienated from the leading figures in the Irish community, who are complicit in Frankie's gunrunning. There is no stereotype quite so indicative of American political morality as that of the one good cop. O'Meara's form of alienation is typical of the end of conspiracy thrillers, a genre that the director of *The Devil's Own*, Alan J. Pakula, did much to define. *The Devil's Own* does not take the radical chances that made films like *The Parallax View* (1974, Paramount/Gus/Harbour/Doubleday, US) and *Klute* (1971, Warner, US) genre defining, however. Faced with the FBI's hostility, O'Meara has the US Constitution to protect him: "Next time you want to talk to me, read me my rights."

The final scene where O'Meara grieves for the man he has regarded as a son, killed and tried to save, mirrors the opening scene where Pitt's character is seen with his father prior to the latter's sectarian murder. Both scenes are connected with the sea and the two men fighting on the boat are sharing the same kind of space as the father and son had shared in the idyllic pre-credit fishing scene. The metaphoric construction of the US as father is hard to miss in these films, even if the special relationship it has with Britain in *Patriot Games* is that of responsible son caring for a parent country in its dotage. (The stereotypes of English characters in both films, as either quaintly ineffectual or despotically ruthless, are considerably more patronizing than the Irish ones, despite their very different views of the Troubles.)

The action movies of the nineties contain within them maps of imagined global relations defined by two opposed chronotopes, the US and Ireland, i.e., home and abroad. Each of these is in turn defined by a series of internal antinomies of urban and suburban, violent ghetto and rural idyll, familial and public spaces. The cinematic construction of these opposing places maps the imaginary relation between the US and its (self) images. The specific role of the Irish Troubles, in this context, is connected to the instability of the boundary between "them" and "us" in the nineties. In *The Siege* (directed by Edward Zwick, 1998, TCF, US), which focused on Arab terrorism, the confrontation with an apparently racially identifiable enemy provokes a confrontation between two very different United States. Denzel Washington's character epitomizes the self-concept of the US as fundamentally democratic, individualist and free speaking: Bruce Willis in contrast plays a kind of sub-Macarthur, with a strutting, patriotic sense of US importance that jeopardizes the nation's values by overzealous defense of the nation's territory. In *The Devil's Own* and *Patriot Games*, the Irish enemy confronted is more like the real terrorist threat that America could not admit to itself in the nineties: white, hard to distinguish, related.

In her fascinating study of the Irish-American 1920s star, Colleen Moore, Diane Negra makes the point that the Irish at that time were the model minority, assimilable advertisements for the immigrant American dream:

> If Irishness connotes transformative potential, such an association carries within it a fundamental dismissal of the desirability of retaining Irish characteristics. . . . Irishness is assimilable in large part due to the fact that it is capable of becoming something else.[16]

In the Hollywood action thrillers of the nineties it was harder to lose the Irish story in a new American one, but Irishness began to connote transformative potential of a different kind. In 1996, just when *The Devil's Own* must have looked like a surefire box office hit in production meetings, Bill Clinton made two speeches that featured Northern Ireland prominently. In an address to the Democratic National Convention on August 30, President Clinton declared that he sought "to build a bridge to the twenty-first century with the world's strongest defense and a foreign policy that advocates the values of our American community in the community of nations." In this context, he surveyed the US role as arbitrator of international political conflict:

> We have helped to bring democracy to Haiti and peace to Bosnia. Now the peace signed on the White House lawn between the Israelis and the Palestinians must embrace more of Israel's neighbors. The deep desire for peace which Hilary and I felt when we walked the streets of Belfast and Derry must become real for all the people of Northern Ireland.
> And Cuba must finally join the community of nations.[17]

Clinton's address to the United Nations on September 24 of the same year reinforced the parallels, again featuring Bosnia and Haiti briefly before linking developments in Northern Ireland and the Middle East even more explicitly:

> In the Middle East and in Northern Ireland, there is progress towards lasting peace, and we are moving in the right direction. Now we must support continued progress between Israel and Palestinians, and we must broaden the circle of peace to include more of Israel's neighbors. We must help to give the children of Belfast a chance to live out normal lives.[18]

The imperative case is differently directed here, this time stressing the obligations on the US rather than the participants in the conflict. Presenting himself to his own party, Clinton constructs the US as in a position to dictate terms to others: addressing the UN, he presents the US as part of an international community subject to the moral imperative of peacemaking. The contradictions between these two positions acquired explosive intensity in the subsequent decade.

If Ireland had a metonymic relation to terrorism for most of the nineties, it had by 1996 acquired an allegorical function. This new configuration established itself in the thriller genre with the box office success of *The Jackal* (directed by Michael Caton-Jones, 1997, Universal/Mutual/Alphaville, US). The casting of Richard Gere as the former IRA man indicates the possibility of moral ambiguity, but by the end he has been so far assimilated as to achieve a form of partnership with the FBI man played with his customary moral authority by Sidney Poitier. In the aftermath of the Good Friday agreement, Ireland became a metaphor for the resolution of apparently intractable political, religious and ethnic conflict. In the aftermath of the events of September 11, 2001, Irishness became a different kind of metonym as a high-profile form of American masculine identity.

8 Masculinity and Ethnicity
The *Wire* and *Rescue Me*

This chapter will examine critical elements within US popular culture that engage with the construction of Irish-American masculinity as embodiment of patriotic, blue-collar masculinity. It seeks to extend the analysis of the way in which Irishness has been crucially deployed, post–September 11, 2001, in the articulation of white, working-class, male identity. Not coincidentally, the 2006 New York St. Patrick's Day Parade was led by the 69th Infantry Regiment of the US Army, recently returned from Iraq. The ceremony at the parade's end in which military medals were bestowed on members of the regiment was accompanied by music from the Wolfe Tones. The regiment has a historical link with Irish America, as have the New York fire and police departments, which have achieved an iconic status in the representation of the 9/11 attacks. In some ways, the conjunction of militarism and republican balladry at the New York parade indicates the enormous gulf that separates the self-representation of Irish America and Ireland. The Dublin parade in the same year came in the aftermath of republican riots and the sound of the Wolfe Tones would probably have cleared the streets of law-abiding citizens in ten minutes (a different strand of the ballad tradition was represented by the Dublin Grand Marshall, Ronnie Drew). The no doubt bemused Powder Springs High School marching band found itself marching in Dublin beside a lone protestor waving a "US troops out of Shannon" banner. (The official antiwar protest was staged on March 18.) The relation between Ireland and Irish America is not that of easy contrasts and opposition, from whichever side of the Atlantic it is viewed. For as the New York parade indicates, Irishness has become part of American self-representation.

IRISHNESS IN US TELEVISION DRAMA

For the purposes of this chapter, I will concentrate on two television drama series featuring Irish-American characters. *Rescue Me* has been a critical success and won audiences for the Fox network[1] while *The Wire* is a prestigious HBO production that has won widespread critical acclaim and features two well-known novelists among its screenwriters (George Pelecanos and, more recently, Dennis Lehane). The main protagonist in *Rescue Me* is that epitome of Irish-American heroism, a New York fireman who has survived the 9/11 attacks, Tommy Gavin. He is also the epitome of all the major Irish stereotypes; hard drinking, impulsively brave but prone to violence, hopelessly in love with his ex-wife, self-destructively having sex with all the other women who find him fatally attractive. These stereotypes also attach to Jimmy McNulty, one of an ensemble of interlinked central characters in HBO's *The Wire*, though McNulty is practically an intellectual by comparison with the foulmouthed Gavin. Unlike Gavin, McNulty also works well with strong, competent women. In fact his working relationships with women in general are much more successful than his sexual ones.

Both characters are emotionally inept, but passionately committed to their work. Both have an intimacy with death that sets them apart from their colleagues. In *Rescue Me*, the central protagonist is literally haunted by his dead partner and by all of those whom he has not, over the years, succeeded in rescuing. Much of the first series concerns his conversations with these dead people. In a striking parallel, McNulty spends much of the second series of The *Wire* carrying around a photograph of a dead Eastern European woman whose body he has retrieved from the bay, seeking to identify her and get her a "proper" burial. In both series, the relationship between Irishness and America is played out as the tension between the incompatible demands of modern masculinity.

ABJECT HEROISM: MASCULINE BODY ANXIETY IN RESCUE ME

The pilot episode of *Rescue Me* (Season 1, Episode 1, "Guts") appears to open with Tommy Gavin going to the bathroom. An overhead shot shows the toilet bowl from Gavin's perspective as it fills with smoke. Just as he appears to be trapped inside the bathroom, Gavin wakes and we realize we have been inside his nightmare. The series repeatedly plays with the boundaries between dream and reality to the extent that it, like the main character, inhabits a psychotic space where such boundaries cannot be drawn. The location of the first such breakdown in the bathroom is telling, at a site where the body separates itself from its waste. The abject vortex where boundaries between inside and outside, food and waste, life and death, are always in danger of breaking down is the very site of this narrative, which tells how difficult it is to maintain one's own proper identity as the man in the heroic story. Tommy wakes from his dream and coughs, as if the smoke from it is still in his lungs. He drinks some juice, goes out the door, all of which is shot in close-up with a rapid sequence of shot and countershot at eye level that puts us unsettlingly close to Tommy. The first words we hear Tommy Gavin speak are "Do you want to know how big my balls are?" in voice-over over a panning shot of new recruits to the fire brigade lined up in a classic military formation, with a panoramic view of New York's skyline visible across the river behind them. Denis Leary maintains in the voice-over commentary on the DVD of the series that the speech that follows was taken almost verbatim from one delivered by a drill instructor in the New York fire department of his acquaintance, whose brother, also a firefighter, died in the 9/11 attacks. (The additional features included on the DVD are very much concerned with authenticating the series, stressing its realism, the casting of actual or former firemen, etc., in contrast to the series' willingness to break the rules of conventional television realism.) The accuracy of this is not undermined by the familiarity of the scene from a dozen films featuring raw army recruits, tough sergeants and the relations of men in combat. The beautifully composed shot, which sets this quintessentially military exchange between men directly in front of the skyline that was changed forever on 9/11, leaves the viewer in no doubt that these men are on the frontline of a new battlefield. Gavin's macho speech, however, is somewhat at odds with the beauty of the scene and the heroic narrative implicit in it. "My balls are bigger than two of your heads duct taped together. I've been in the middle of shit that would make you piss your pants," he informs the new trainees. The purpose of their training, he tells them, is not to make heroes of them, but to find out cowards, because "if you can't take the heat that's what you are, you're a pussy and there ain't no room for pussies in the FDNY." Until this point the scene had effectively disconnected Tommy's voice from his physical presence: the camera pans over the ranks of men so that we don't see the speaker. Voice and body are reunited only in confrontation with a young man who dares to express amusement at all this macho excess and we see Tommy in close-up facing him and standing too close to him until seriousness is restored. At this point the dead men whose photographs are displayed as examples for the recruits are used to validate the form of masculinity needed on this new frontier. "I knew sixty men who gave their lives at Ground Zero, sixty. Four of them from my house. . . . Vito Costello, found him almost whole. Ricky Davis, found him almost whole hugging a civilian woman. Bobby Vincent, found his head. And my cousin, Jimmy Keefe, my best friend, know what they found of him? What they was able to bring back and give to his parents? A finger." Throughout this part of his speech the camera cuts back and forth between Tommy and the photographs of the dead men. The reaction shots, close-ups, of the horrified and chastened recruits are kept until the reference to the finger and then continue to the end of the speech as Tommy tells them, "these four men were better firemen and better human beings than any of you will ever be." At this point the camera pulls back and Tommy's parting salute to the ranks of men heavily reinforce the military overtones.

  This pre-credit speech sets up the central conflicts of the series: the absolute necessity and simultaneous impossibility of emulating the heroes of 9/11; the fascination and horror of "pussy"; the erasure of the trauma of vulnerability in the emphasis on the men who "gave" their lives, rather than having them taken. The language of the speech sets up the tone and atmosphere of the series. Its reliance on the kind of language completely unacceptable on prime-time mainstream television is typical of the increasing subgenre of amoral crime drama aimed at a predominantly male audience, such as *Prison Break*, *The Shield* and *24*, which go far beyond the moral boundaries of traditional prime-time fare. The credits to *Rescue Me* feature the rapid edits of urban scenes, handheld cameras and pounding rock soundtrack signatures of "hard-hitting," i.e., masculine, US television. However, the language of Tommy's speech also reveals the extraordinary difficulty of "holding it together" in the context of the grief, loss, paranoia and post-traumatic stress disorder these series normalize as the masculine condition. Tommy's wife has left him because he can't open up and is emotionally "unavailable," but this extreme psychic closure is accompanied by the language of mental and physical disintegration. The references to the body indicate a crisis of boundaries. Tommy has been "in the middle of shit that would make you piss your pants." The opening dream sequence features an attempt to make water that turns into smoke. A running joke through the first episode culminates in the closing scene when the fire station chief mistakenly drinks a urine sample. The men discuss at length medical tests that involve rectal examinations. These are not the hard bodies of the action movies of the eighties. On the contrary, they are porous, vulnerable to penetration, their fluids seeping from them, their boundaries unstable. Mortality stalks them.

The ultimate expression as well as the explanation of this is there in this pre-credit scene that validates archaic masculine values, but also catalogues the literal decomposition of men. The proud names of the fallen heroes are reduced to their body parts, some almost whole, others only a head or a finger. All that is left is not to be a "pussy." Yet even this is no longer viable. The band of men at the fire station will be penetrated and dispersed by the female therapist sent by the troublingly authoritative and alien "headquarters" before the end of the episode. By the end of the series, there will actually be a woman firefighter among them. Ultimately in this context, the aftermath of 9/11 is no more than a verification of the paranoia that preexisted it. "Where have we seen all this before?" asks Slavoj Žižek in *Welcome to the Desert of the Real*.[2] In the nightmares of our competent men, answers *Rescue Me*. The phallic dilemma, where the masculine ego will never actualize its ideal, reaches crisis proportions in the guilt and anxiety of survivors who will never be the men their dead predecessors were.

The pre-credit section of the first episode of *Rescue Me* has one more twist. After the military salute, Tommy gets back in his truck, which an establishing shot shows us is empty. A rapid shot countershot then cuts from Tommy, unsurprised, to Jimmy Keefe, his cousin and friend killed at Ground Zero. "That was nice, what you said about me," says Jimmy's ghost, though he goes on to point out that they wouldn't think Tommy so tough if they knew he was talking to dead people. When Tommy finally addresses Jimmy, he disappears. Tommy's arrested grieving process and his communications from the dead are, on the one hand, part of the way in which *Rescue Me* deploys the psychotherapeutic narrative its protagonists so strenuously resist. Since Tommy cannot talk about his feelings without becoming a pussy, his feelings are externalized as ghosts and talk to him. (This takes an unexpected turn in the second season when giving up drink results in hallucinations of Jesus Christ who takes on the role of Tommy's internal/external interlocutor.) The series' actualization of Tommy's ghosts goes a step further than the use of dream sequences as an indicator of buried trauma. The device breaks the convention of realist television drama, as do the use of techniques borrowed from body horror. Bobby Vincent's head turns up in Tommy's locker, for example, talking amiably. *Rescue Me*'s combination of such shock tactics, ghosts, humor and tragedy identify it with postmodern gothic television and especially with genre hybrids such as *Twin Peaks*, *The X-Files* and *Buffy the Vampire Slayer*. Fred Botting commented, on postmodern gothic pre-9/11, that the horror at the heart of its narrative games was that there were only narrative games.[3] In other words, it was afraid there was ultimately nothing outside in the dark waiting to pounce. In *Rescue Me*, something has already pounced, but this only serves to make it more unnamable. The terrible other is no longer a luxury of the imagination but an enemy so alien that it cannot enter the narrative at all. For *Rescue Me* so relentlessly focuses on Ground Zero that it never refers to the sky above. What happened and who did it are absent from the narrative, which never admits the agency of the other. Instead the event impacts in the fragmentation of bodies and selves, the breakdown of the boundaries between inside and outside and the living and the dead.

The extraordinary racial and sexual homogeneity of the fire station reflects this sense of tightly drawn boundaries and this community, like the men within it, is under pressure from the start to maintain itself against forces outside and beyond it. Female therapists and bosses and dissatisfied African Americans make demands which the characters and to a large extent the narrative derides, yet cannot resist. In an exchange, which has gained considerably in irony since the series first broadcast, an African American waylays the chief fire officer to complain the rescue services would have responded much more quickly if it was a white neighborhood, a joke far less funny after Hurricane Katrina. The therapist's arrival clears the room, but Tommy stays to tell her how little she understands and ends by explaining himself and breaking down in tears. Women completely undermine the fragile masculine selves to which the characters cling in the series. Tommy's ex-wife makes him feel inadequate in her obvious preference for far less macho men in her choice of new boyfriend. His daughter is almost killed when she goes out in a car with an unsuitable boy whom her father had warned her against. Beyond his daughter's burgeoning sexuality, a much greater threat to Tommy's definition of himself as father is his ex-wife's desire to move and take the children away from him and from the scene of trauma. Tommy's sexual relationships with women other than his wife are desperate; alcohol fueled and, for most of the first season, short lived. The threat of impotence hovers over his investment in a dead relationship and dissatisfaction with sex outside his social role as husband. Jimmy's ghost is banished in the course of the series when Tommy starts sleeping with his widow, but this sublimation of his unhealthy obsession with a dead man in a relationship with a live woman is in fact considered perverse by his colleagues, who see it as an insult to Jimmy's memory. The terms of identity through the homosocial bond at *Rescue Me*'s heart include the priority of the dead past over future living, which in turn has become a key element in the meaning of Irishness in contemporary popular culture. The narrative circles around the originary trauma of 9/11 with the possibility of a different story in the future troped from the start as a form of betrayal, specifically of allowing the dead to be dead.

At the end of the pilot episode, Tommy takes a trip to the ultimate liminal space, the edge of the ocean, accompanied by the ghosts of all those he failed to save. These include his fallen comrades and two children who perished in the more ordinary tragedies of fires in overcrowded apartment blocks. The scene is visually very striking, especially as Tommy leads the procession of ghosts back from the edge of the sea toward the land and ultimately the city. At its beginning and its end, the pilot episode of *Rescue Me* establishes Tommy Gavin as a haunted man and a liminal consciousness, neither mad nor sane, between the living and the dead, nature and the city, land and water. His particular link to the dead, the tragedy of his fidelity to the past and his association with in-between spaces make Tommy Gavin typical of the new image of the Irish American, embodying masculinity as something primal and atavistic, defined by discipline and self-sacrifice, but shadowed by the experience of social and personal fragmentation, random violence and meaningless loss. In effect, Irishness is put to its old work of figuring liminality, while acquiring a new function of mediating death, transforming it from victimization to heroic choice.

RITUAL, RACE AND DEATH: ETHNICITY IN *THE WIRE*

In the first season of *The Wire*, his superior comments that Jimmy McNulty's dogged integrity indicates he is "not Irish enough" for the Baltimore police force. However, in the course of the second season McNulty's Irish ethnicity becomes much more explicit as his professional identity temporarily breaks down. The narrative context for the foregrounding of McNulty's Irishness is his exclusion from the ranks of detective as a punishment for what his immediate superior sees as insubordinate zeal in the pursuit of a case. Jimmy is consigned to the water, the harbor patrol of Baltimore City, an assignment that he hates. *The Wire* has a much more complex ensemble of central characters than *Rescue Me*, however, and his Irishness is part of the season's exploration of white, working-class, masculine identities in which ethnicity is linked to the experience of immigration and assimilation. The central investigation in the series is set in motion by rivalry between two sets of Polish workers, dockers and policemen. When the Dockworkers' Union succeed in getting a stained-glass window in their local church previously intended as a police memorial, a senior Polish policeman starts an investigation into where they got the money out of spite. The discovery of the bodies of fourteen young women in a cargo container, where they had suffocated, makes the issue of immigration one of current desperation, not past heritage. The story's focus on the docks makes it a story of how America was and is made at the point of intersection between it and its others. The anonymous stacks of containers off-loaded in Baltimore Harbor make any hard and fast border almost impossible to maintain. The second season of *The Wire* was broadcast more than a year before the possibility of foreign control of US ports provoked a major political crisis, but it dissects the central dilemma that "business" by which the US defines itself inevitably makes it open to others. The waterfront setting insists on the history of this process. Yet even here openness and borders are a scene of terrible anxiety. The dockworkers are becoming obsolete, the highly organized masculine labor force competing for work that is in terrible short supply. They long for the nurture of a new granary, which promises a more traditional form of labor, but must contend with increased mechanization and computerization, which means the docks require fewer and fewer men. In an exchange between the Polish union boss, Frank Sobotka, and the African-American counterpart with whom he rotates his union job, he comments, "No offense, but without this granary, we are all niggers," to which his counterpart replies, "No offense, but without it we're all Pollacks." In its dissection of the way in which global capital destroys traditional masculine and social roles, *The Wire* engages in an exploration of the causes of crime highly unusual in the television crime genre where good and evil, them and us, are more usually treated as explanatory categories in themselves. It shows the desperation that drives Sobotka's nephew Nick to drug dealing, for example, in order to fulfill the traditional male role of providing a home for his girlfriend and child. While it is predominantly the male role that drives the no longer working class to crime, the women who are strongly identified with ethnicity are also incapable of surviving or providing for themselves in the brave new world. Sobotka's wife has retreated into tranquilized nonentity as the moral universe collapses around her and her role as "good Polish mother" becomes meaningless, Nick's girlfriend pressures him to create their mutual future but has none of her own and the young Eastern European women who die in the container seem to indicate that an American future is no longer available to the new arrivals. When it becomes apparent that the women were suffocated deliberately, it turns out that this is because one of them refused to prostitute herself on board the ship when the "shepherd" charged with getting them to the US turned pimp. Refusing to be an object of exchange, this girl ends up as an unidentified subject. She is the floater whom Jimmy McNulty pulls out of the bay, separated from the other girls who enter the US as damaged goods. His unsuccessful attempts to identify her lead the narrative into an underworld of young women who cannot or will not communicate, moved around by pimps and immigration officers, with no apparent volition of their own, except their desperate desire to stay. These lone female immigrants destined for exploitation counter the history of the successful migration of families and generations of assimilation in Frank Sobotka's stories of the old days and Jimmy McNulty's Irish ballads. The INS tells Baltimore police there are fifty thousand such undocumented girls working in the US, "They need a whole new agency just to police 'em." Russell, a policewoman, responds, "What they need is a union."

Russell, the patrolwoman who investigates but eventually weeps for Frank Sobotka, has found police work to be a way out of the economic dead end in which her husband's departure left her, though we are shown that her prospects for the kind of detective work that she enjoys are severely restricted by the fact that she is a responsible and competent parent. The incompatibility of work and family is a recurrent theme of *The Wire* and an implicit theme in a vast array of crime fiction. For the male characters the incompatibility of the demands of work and the demands of contemporary fatherhood mean that it is structurally impossible to fulfill the male role required of them. However, even Jimmy McNulty's eventual partner, Keema, finds herself following in his dysfunctional footsteps when she and her lesbian partner have a baby. Only work confers identity in the society *The Wire* maps out, but the identity it confers is sterile, limited, itself deathly.

In the character of Jimmy McNulty, as with Tommy Gavin, this is intensified to the point where fidelity to the dead prevents them from living. Other detectives in the series are strongly associated with new technologies: it takes its name from wiretapping after all, and Lester Freamon, an African-American detective who shares a history of being punished for doing his job too honestly with McNulty, rediscovers himself as a detective through the application of technology to intelligence gathering. McNulty is a much more traditional detective. Like the dockworkers whose sense of themselves is corrupted by lack of work and the traditional social networks it supports, McNulty disintegrates when his identity is not fixed by the job. He tells his partner, Bunk, that he "*needs to get off that boat. I need to do a case*" (Season 2, Episode 8, "Duck and Cover"). When he is not a detective, McNulty becomes much more stereotypically Irish. "Duck and Cover" opens with him stumbling around a bar, trying to talk to his wife on the phone, failing, demanding more drink. He then drives away with The Pogues' "Transmetropolitan" blaring on the car stereo: "This town has done us dirty / This town has bled us dry." The song's nihilism links Jimmy's despair, his Irishness and self-destruction. He doesn't burn the city down, but he does drive his car quite deliberately at a wall. As Bunk tells their captain to persuade him to take McNulty into his detail, "Jimmy McNulty, when he ain't policing, he is a picture postcard of a drunken self-destructive fucker . . . but on a good case, that's the closest the man comes to being right." The drunken self-destruction is linked via the soundtrack to McNulty's Irishness, though the choice of "Transmetropolitan" hints that it is the migrant condition and not the accident of origin that defines Jimmy's insecure identity. The phrase "homeland security" is routinely derided by the police in *The Wire*, signifying a shift of resources away from regular policing: they are reduced to pretending a drug dealer's first name is Ahmed in order to secure a wiretap on him. "Homeland" transparently doesn't include West Baltimore.

Jimmy McNulty's drunken driving spree is shown in a sequence of alternating close-ups of Jimmy in his car with The Pogues blaring and long shots of his car driving at high speeds through deserted, broad and unmistakably American streets that have been part of the visual repertoire of American alienation since film noir. His old-fashioned-looking car hints more at the seventies than the forties though, and the streetscape is more reminiscent of *Taxi Driver* than *The Maltese Falcon*. At the point when he is most forlornly Irish, Jimmy is most quintessentially American.

NOT QUITE AMERICAN HEROES

Music works as in important signifier of ethnicity and sometimes as commentary on the narrative throughout *The Wire*. McNulty's soundtrack signature is the use of The Pogues and their music signals the occasions when Irishness serves as metonym for blue-collar masculinity. In an extraordinary wake scene, in the third series of *The Wire*, the ritual mourning of a dead colleague involves laying him out at Kavanagh's Irish Pub, an oration, a great deal of drink and the singing of The Pogues "Body of an American" by a group of colleagues that is at least half composed of African-American officers. The scene mirrors the songs mock-heroic: the dead man, Ray Cole, has died not from a bullet but a heart attack in the gym. "We're police," says his erstwhile boss, Landsman, "so no lies between us. He wasn't the greatest detective and he wasn't the worst. He put down some good cases and he dogged a few bad ones. But the motherfucker had his moments. Yes, he fucking did." Characteristically ambivalent, the scene both mocks and celebrates the archaic masculine values of heroic camaraderie. That this male bonding through shared work and experience is archaic is very clear. The second series of *The Wire* was declaredly an analysis of the "death of the American working class," figured through the masculine occupation of dockers and longshoremen, though often seen through the eyes of the policewoman, Russell. Gavin and McNulty configure Irish-American masculinity as a combination of heroic resistance and traumatized survival.

The Irish inheritance of emigration and struggle is recruited to express both the sense of loss and the requirements of survival. Tommy Gavin and Jimmy McNulty bear the traces of troubled migration, not triumphant assimilation. The care both lavish on the dead identifies Irishness and the past: their failures as fathers indicate they have more trouble connecting to the future.[4] These characters tend to self-deconstruct. It is tempting to read their limitations and the failures of their attempts at heroic patriarchy as national allegories, with their Irishness functioning as a protective distance (they are not quite American heroes). They certainly reflect a renewed pre-occupation with ethnicity at a time when fear of terrorism was generating both a desire for closed borders and for clear lines of demarcation between "them" and "us" in the US. The two characters reflect difference responses to this. Gavin cannot imagine working with Chinese, women or little green men[5]; McNulty finds that the drowned immigrant girl he cannot name is turning up in his dreams.

Ethnicity, because it is a matter of family history, is part of the fabric of domesticity, determining food and music and conversational practice ("Four Pollacks, six opinions," Frank Sobotka reminisces fondly.) Because of this intimacy, ethnicity makes the history of immigration personal, immediate. It invokes the security of home(land), but the homeland is always already lost in the process of becoming American. In this context, the figure of the tragically Irish American in keynote television series at the beginning of the twenty-first century expressed the desire for unity and the terror of disintegration in a divided nation.

9 The Undercover Irishman
Extimating National Anxiety

Now ain't it strange that I feel like Philby,
There's a stranger in my soul.

(Rory Gallagher, "Philby," *Top Priority*, Chrysalis Records, 1979)

BETWEEN ENGLAND AND AMERICA:
TROLLOPE'S GORGEOUS IRISHMAN

When Anthony Trollope's Phineas Finn arrives as a Liberal MP by various parliamentary machinations at "his gorgeous apartment in the Colonial Office," he finds "the walls of the room were bright with maps of all the colonies. And there was one very interesting map,—but not very bright,—showing the American colonies, as they used to be." Phineas is very impressed to find that an "Earl's nephew, his private secretary" thinks that "it was all very gorgeous. Often as he looked round upon it, thinking of his old bedroom at Killaloe, of his little garrets at Trinity, of the dingy chambers in Lincoln's Inn, he would tell himself that it was very gorgeous. He would wonder that anything so grand had fallen to his lot."[1] Such grandeur does not fall to his lot for very long, for he finds he has uncomfortably real political principals and a vote for tenant right in Ireland puts him out of office, though this is by no means the end of his career or his interest to Trollope, who weaves Phineas's story in and out of his Palliser series. That Trollope places Phineas Finn among the Colonial Office's interesting maps in his first major appointment is significant. Serial publication of the second of Anthony Trollope's Palliser novels began in *St. Paul's Magazine* in October 1867, some seven months after the Fenian Rising began in Tipperary and one month after an attempt to rescue Fenian prisoners resulted in the death of a policeman on the streets of Manchester. The prisoners were hanged and became the Manchester martyrs by the time Trollope's next installment came out in November 1867, in which month twelve people died and 120 were injured in the Clerkenwell explosion. In December 1867 *Punch* published its famous cartoon of the Fenian guyfawker, an apelike Irishman sitting on a smoking keg of gunpowder in the middle of a group of children while a mother nursed her infant nearby; Millais's elegant illustration of *Phineas Finn* in the same month shows a handsome young man of impeccable taste and manners, the image of metropolitan success. These conflicting images indicate the profound and persistent ambiguity of English attitudes to the Irish. In 1868 Gladstone's liberal government came to power, determined to solve the Irish question, and Trollope tried and failed to be elected as MP for Beverley. By the time the serial version of *Phineas Finn* came to a conclusion in May 1869 and the two-volume novel was published, a high-profile campaign was under way for a general amnesty of Fenian prisoners that raised serious concerns about the treatment of the prisoners and the conditions under which they were held. The maps in Phineas Finn's office reminded the Colonial Office that the borders of empire could contract as well as expand, obliquely identifying US history and Irish potential. Trollope would later both prescribe American energy as a restorative to a decline in English liberal tradition at the end of the Palliser series of novels and decry Irish unrest as a mere proxy for American ideas in *The Landleaguers*.

This complex of associations provides a starting place for this chapter's analysis of the shifting function of Irish identities in the construction of masculinity and its relation to English and US national identities. Phineas represents what Joseph Valente has described as the metrocolonial status of the successful Irishman in late nineteenth-century England.[2] By the beginning of the twentieth century, the opposed images of this almost-assimilated Irish hero and the explosive Fenian villain might be considered to have found synthesis and sublimation in the figure of Dracula, the offspring of Irish gothic and British *Grand Guignol*. The extraordinarily enduring power with which Stoker's novel focused the sexual, social and national anxieties of the twentieth century has been variously linked with imperial anxiety, capitalist guilt and sexual repression. According to Franco Moretti, "Dracula is a refined attempt by the nineteenth century mind not to recognize itself."[3] In that respect this displaced Irishman's nightmare represented an uncanny double, the extimate of Englishness. Extimacy is more than the projection on to another of what we fear we are, argues Joan Copjec, "they are in us, that which is not us."[4] Identity can only be established "through the inclusion within ourselves of this negation of what we are not."[5] It is worth considering in general terms whether the "intimate enmity" of imperial powers and their colonies is transformed by late twentieth-century patterns of immigration to the old imperial centers into relations of extimacy. Anglo-Irish cultural relations have a somewhat different trajectory. Joe Valente has argued that:

> with the Act of Union in 1800 . . . Ireland ceased to be a distinct if colonized geopolitical entity and assumed the unique and contradictory position of a domestic or "metropolitan" colony, at once a prized if troublesome colonial possession and a despised but active constituent of the greatest metropole on earth, the United Kingdom. From that point in time until the founding of the Free State (1922), the Irish people at large found themselves at once agents and objects, participant-victims as it were, of Britain's far-flung imperial mission—in short, a "metrocolonial people". (Valente, *Dracula's Crypt*, 3)

However, this is to define Irishness in terms of Ireland's political sovereignty. The Irish were also the largest immigrant group in Britain from the nineteenth century onward and this Irish presence within England and its longevity is an often overlooked but powerful factor in Anglo-Irish cultural relations. At least one reason for the persistence of Stoker's nightmare of the insidious vampire (who can make his way in everywhere, replicate himself, consuming and corrupting all around him) is that it is grounded in a fear of foreigners, immigrant populations, taking up a position at the metropolitan center. At the time of *Dracula*'s publication the two largest immigrant groups in London were the Irish and Eastern European Jews, one driven eastward by poverty, the other driven westward by a wave of late nineteenth-century pogroms. Neither had anything to go back to and both possessed the characteristics of being visually indistinguishable from the local inhabitants, but alien in religion, all the more suspect because they were so uncannily similar to their English neighbors. In the Irish case, this immigrant population was associated with Fenian violence on English soil in the nineteenth century, IRA bombing campaigns in the 1940s and again from 1969 to 1997, so the longevity of Irish immigration did not dissipate British unease, but it did normalize it. Irishness was a (sometimes dangerously) contiguous national identity. In the US narratives discussed in the preceding chapters, male Irish characters perform the role of the internal outsider who affirms proper masculinity by negating it. In contemporary English narratives, both Irish and US plots and protagonists can function as extimates of English identity. This chapter examines two radical and radically different explorations of Anglo-Irish extimacy, one written in full and one in part by Howard Brenton, the first set along the fault lines of old empires, the second in the anxious interval between the September 11, 2001, attacks and the beginning of the Iraq War in 2003.

THEATER AND TELEVISION, BRENTON AND IRELAND

The title of Howard Brenton's 1980 play, *The Romans in Britain*,[6] inevitably brings to mind the famous moment in Conrad's *Heart of Darkness* when Marlow, standing on his ship on the Thames, "thinking of very old times, when the Romans first came here, nineteen hundred years ago," says suddenly, "And this also . . . has been one of the dark places of the earth."[7] This contemplation of the historical reversal of polarities of civilization and power is dramatized in Brenton's play along two timelines, one set in ancient Britain and another in 1970s Northern Ireland. Ancient history and contemporary politics converged on the national stage as two narratives of brutal culture clashes intersected. A recent reappraisal of the play's status in English culture by the high-profile journalist Mark Lawson is an interesting indication of its reception history:

The Romans in Britain case has come to be regarded as a standoff between filth and decency, but the real battle-line was Ireland v Christ. Whitehouse, who seems scarcely to have noticed the play's politics, was pursuing a puritanical interpretation of Christian values. The dramatist and the artistic director, who intended no particular offence to God, were both energised by the ease with which the British public and politicians accepted the presence of the British army in Northern Ireland. It may surprise Hall's enemies and even some of his friends, but he insists that he regarded the lack of plays about Ireland as one of the failures of late 20th-century British theatre . . . So, although *The Romans in Britain* is doomed to be remembered as a play about the buggering of a druid, Hall and Brenton were much more interested in a later metaphor for colonial invasion: a coup de théâtre in which, after a long section set in 54BC during Caesar's second invasion of Britain, a modern tank rolls across the stage, triggering a sequence set in modern Ulster.[8]

The tanks were obscured by what turned out to be the actor Peter Sproule's thumb, mistaken for a public erection. This version of the narrative of the significance of the staging—and silencing—of *The Romans in Britain* came in the context of the revival of Brenton's play in the Sheffield Crucible Theatre in 2006. As Brenton has pointed out, the play had been performed over the years by student groups and the occasional small company, but controversy had kept it from the professional stage for twenty-five years. That long interval indicates that censorship of the play was very effective, but also that the combination of the Northern Ireland peace process and ongoing debates about religious censorship had made the tanks rolling across the stage visible, perhaps because they were now in their turn a metaphor, chronologically closer than Roman Britain but nonetheless consigned to history.

By this time, Brenton himself had returned to the subject of Northern Ireland with a narrative set in the context of a different conflict, but with the urgent articulation of contemporary politics that characterized *The Romans in Britain* in 1980. Brenton contributed to the scripts of the BBC series *Spooks* (broadcast in the US under the title *M.I.5*) created by David Wolstonecraft. The series began in 2002, returning annually. Made by independent television company Kudos, *Spooks* is a signature series for high-quality drama on the British national broadcaster's main channel. *Spooks* indexes the shocks a post September 11, 2001 world registered in the British—and more particularly the English—political psyche and provides a kind of map of paranoid fantasy. The obvious point of comparison on US television is *24*, but *Spooks* also maps out the differences between English and US paranoia and politics. In bringing radical playwrights, like Brenton and Zinnie Harris, into the writing team along with popular fiction writers, such as Raymond Khouri, the series has tended to deconstruct itself from within, a spy thriller with a high degree of critical self-awareness. It has consequently attracted considerable controversy, especially in the right-wing media. However, it has also attracted considerable audience share, an indicator that it does in fact tap into widely felt fears and fantasies. Its imagined threats were initially often criticized in the press as inaccurate or implausible, but the series performs the cathartic function definitive of the twenty-first-century paranoid thriller not because it accurately maps geopolitics but because it dramatizes cultural nightmares. A plotline where Mossad agents impersonated Arab terrorists was widely criticized for its inaccuracy about the nature of Mossad's operations, for example, but such a plot illuminates the ambivalent nature of the fear of the eruption of Middle East politics into central London. The assassins in the episode are both Arab and Israeli, devious, ruthless, a fusion of Islamophobia and residual anti-Semitism. Despite or perhaps because of such occasional lapses into national atavism, the series' critical instincts have remained fairly consistent, with the fairly constant moral that the greatest threats to a nation's security are the things done precisely in the name of national security.

Brenton's contributions to the series have been, as might be expected from his theatrical career, controversial, including his depiction of the recruitment of British Muslim suicide bombers at a mosque in an episode called "Nest of Angels," broadcast in June 2003. At the end of series one (Episode 6), Brenton co-wrote, with series creator David Wolstonecraft, an episode entitled "Mean, Dirty, Nasty" (US: "Lesser of Two Evils") that originally aired on the BBC on June 17, 2002. The episode concerned an extreme form of Anglo-Irish rapprochement in the face of a mutual threat, that of Asabiyah, an Al Qaeda–inspired group's attack on the Sefton B (formerly Sellafield, formerly Windscale) nuclear power station on England's west coast. The power station name changes signify unsuccessful attempts to generate pubic amnesia of its shortcomings on safety. Its emissions into the Irish Sea have been a cause of persistent tension between Ireland and the UK. The fear of a Chernobyl-style accident at Sellafield prompted one of Ireland's very few notable science fiction novels, Eilis Ni Dhuibhne's haunting *The Bray House* in 1990. Unease about Sellafield contributed to the election of Green party MEP's in the 1999 European parliamentary elections: this evidence of a strong environmental protest vote rapidly made it a more pressing issue for the mainstream political parties. Widespread anxiety accompanied the lead up to the extension of the plant's facilities to include a MOX processing plant in 2002. A protest campaign backed by both high-profile media personalities and politicians in Ireland in 2002 was criticized by the British Home Secretary as an undue intervention by Ireland in Britain's internal affairs, and a drama, *Fallout*, on the Irish national television channel RTE in 2006, itself attracted negative comment from members of the Irish cabinet. Environment Minister Dick Roche, a prominent advocate of the closure of Sellafield, proclaimed on RTE radio: "it was bizarre. They were suggesting there would be riots on the streets of Dublin. We have a very sophisticated society here in Ireland . . . We don't automatically descend into barbarity. It was a slur on the Irish people."

In an interview with *The Guardian* newspaper on April 21, 2002, at the height of the postcard campaign and less than two months before the broadcast of "Mean, Dirty, Nasty," environmental campaigner Ali Hewson crystallized the new urgency and unease with which Ireland viewed its nuclear neighbor. "'This is a nuclear-free land and yet if anything happens to that plant, the east coast of Ireland is straight in the firing line,' she says. 'The Irish nation is not even in the debate; we have no choice and yet we take all the risks. . . . After 11 September, everyone is questioning their own personal safety and their children's safety, and, when the people of Ireland look at their vulnerability, Sellafield sticks out like a sore thumb. The plant has to be on top of any terrorist's list." Hewson in Ireland is well known for her charity work with children affected by the Chernobyl nuclear disaster, but her identity as wife of U2's Bono gave her access to the mainstream British media unlikely to be afforded Irish Green party members of the European parliament or local environmental groups on the Irish east coast. "Mean, Dirty, Nasty," then, takes a recurrent Irish nightmare to a prime-time slot on the British national television station. It weds this nightmare with an ongoing anxiety that dissident Irish republicans would launch a bombing campaign on the British mainland, having already launched a devastating attack in Omagh in Northern Ireland in August 1998. The possibility that Sellafield would be at the top of any terrorist's list is once again raised in an Irish accent, but one with a very different resonance than the cool Green Dublin tones of Hewson, that of an "evil bastard," dissident republican Patrick McCann. McCann's group, suffering a "temporary corporate cash-flow problem" in the aftermath of the September 11, 2001, attacks, has "diversified" into "consultancy" projects. McCann's use of corporate language is of course darkly humorous, but it also draws attention to the contradictory signification of Ireland in the English popular consciousness in 2002 as both residually dangerous, with violent atavisms always in danger of shattering an uneasy peace, and almost unrecognizably transformed into the essence of confident late capitalism. "Never underestimate Patrick McCann," the senior officer, Harry Pearce tells his bemused subordinates when McCann succeeds in locating an MI5 safe house, walking in with a grenade and communicating with them through their own surveillance equipment.

Brenton and Wolstonecraft's screenplay explore the sense of transition from one world order to another prevalent in the early twenty-first century and the paradox at the heart of the concept of domestic security. The episode begins with Tom Quinn, the key male character in season one, trying to create a secure home environment for his girlfriend, Ellie, and her daughter, Maisie. Ellie has been threatening to leave him on the grounds that his occupation as a spy has caused him to lie to her and put her daughter at risk. This romance plot links Tom's character in *Spooks* with the paradox of masculinity faced by Jack Ryan in *Patriot Games*, Tom O'Meara in *The Devil's Own*, Tommy Gavin in *Rescue Me* and

Jimmy McNulty in *The Wire*. Like them he finds that the fulfillment of the heroic role demanded by the exigencies of contemporary social and political crisis jeopardizes his aspiration to the traditional male role of father and husband. It is notable that the emergence of a critical female voice, demanding a compromise of the social role and threatening to make the sexual and familial one redundant, is a feature of all of the television series. In *Spooks* the gender dynamic is complicated by the fact that, on the one hand, the hero's love interest is a woman who has a daughter from another relationship and to whom she has a preceding loyalty, and, on the other, that his female colleagues rarely succeed in maintaining any life beyond work and a perilous public world. It is Tom in the first two seasons who aspires to domesticity and romance and fails to achieve them. The pre-credit sequence of "Mean, Dirty, Nasty" leaves the viewer in no doubt that the narrative is situated at the intersection of boundaries between private and public, safety and danger, them and us, known and unknown. It features three doors, first Tom's being fortified, then Ellie's being opened to admit Tom, who gives her the key to the first door ("Fort Knox"), and pleads with her to come home. The third door is observed through a surveillance camera as McCann arrives at the MI5 safe house to make his offer of information. The security of home is the overt concern, but the repeated opening of doors situates the story in a liminal space, where home opens to admit an other, but a recognizable other. Surveillance technology on all but Ellie's flat means identities and histories are assigned before the door is opened. Danny communicates McCann's record to the safe house "keeper" while observing him on a webcam, for example.

This other's history is a site of contagion. Harry Pearce, the senior officer who has served in Northern Ireland, initially objects to dealing with McCann, "this is not the truth, this is their truth," and reacts to his information about a planned Al Qaeda splinter group attack on Sefton B nuclear power station derisively, "This is contaminated truth." The word *contamination* carries a certain additional resonance in the context of a threatened nuclear disaster. Harry talks of the need to "sterilize" the safe house system after McCann's breach of its security. His remark that the expense of such an undertaking will use up most of MI5's budget is a humorous reference to debates about the resource implications of counter-terrorism and a reminder that spies are also civil servants. It is also a reminder that doing deals with those you previously demonized threatens good housekeeping on many levels. The identification of McCann as a contaminant of security processes conflates the metaphors of surveillance and infection and indirectly others the female space occupied by Ellie and Maisie. Their insecure flat is not a viable living space, "You can't stay here," Tom tells her. Maisie has become ill because it lets in the damp and of course the fact that her door opens to the world means Ellie finds it hard to keep Tom himself out. His initially unwelcome entry is analogous to McCann's. Tom is also a source of contagion, who entangles Ellie's domestic world with the web of dangerous connections between Al Qaeda cells, IRA splinter groups and US and UK security services that can at any time generate terrifyingly unexpected contingencies.

While this plot bears no surface resemblance to *The Romans in Britain*, it does contain a series of interlinked allusions. The British senior officer in both cases is called Tom. The scene in *Romans* is set on the northern side of the Irish border: the Dublin-born actor Lorcan Cranitch plays the character of McCann in *Spooks* with an accent that identifies him to those familiar with Irish accents with the southern border counties, particularly Cavan. This is partly a question of verisimilitude (the main pockets of dissent from the IRA cease-fire were widely reported to be in the border county of Armagh and among southern republicans), but beyond their relationship with historical time, the play and the program also share a preoccupation with liminal space. Doors, rivers and borders are in-between places and Brenton's work enacts the dynamics of Anglo-Irish relations in the space where the foreign haunts the native, the present disrupts the past and proximity and familiarity intensify threat. Both *Romans* and *Spooks* stage aborted intercultural understandings by the side of a river. In the play, the undercover SAS man, Tom Chichester, is mistaken for an IRA man by the British army, discovered as a British agent by the IRA. Waiting at sunset, the time in between, to kill a man named O'Rourke, he tires of killing and lying and challenges his quarry to spare him. This mad gesture simply changes who is killed however and Tom gives his blood to the field that so resembles the field on his mother's farm in Colchester, figured in the other timelines and scenes of violence. The extreme repetition of acts of sacrifice in *Romans* is a sustained assault on the function of sacrifice in traditional tragedy. One more death brings no catharsis: the action could only progress if Tom Chichester's mad offer of friendship were taken up. Instead, the relentless bloodletting dissolves history itself into a chaos of bloodied fields. The field and the Celtic goddess buried in it and fed by blood are deromanticized and in the process the role of theater as substitute for the sacrifice that binds society together is questioned. Sacrifice represents the opposite of progress in this play and it stages this by disconnecting death and dramatic resolution.

The matriarch of the Celtic tribe and "the Irish woman" played by the same actress confound any idea that female power might be gentler or wiser than imperial patriarchy. The "mother" of the Celtic tribe represents a form of tribal politics that makes her people more, not less, vulnerable to the Romans. She participates in blood sacrifice and in keeping slaves. The similarly nameless woman played by the same actress in part 2 of the play insists O'Rourke kills Tom Chichester, rebuking the utopian idea of peace with her litany of past wrongs. She is a somewhat tentative British version of a bloodthirsty Mother Ireland: her grievances are valid, but she prohibits the possibility of a rational understanding between men beyond the logic of blood sacrifice and the apparently eternal cycle of conflict and death in which power changes hands, but never changes. Despite this alignment of female stereotypes with a particularly brutal form of immanence, the play's principal figures of resistance are also female. The slave girl who kills her rapist is followed in the sixth-century episode by a pair of abused daughters who take the opportunity of the Saxon invasion to kill their father and escape. Even if Brenton takes the Mother Ireland stereotype on board, he spectacularly refuses another cliché of colonial metaphor. The slave girl's rape and the sexual abuse of Corda and Morgana are mentioned but not described in detail by them and take place offstage. Roman penetration of Britain is represented in a male rape and the outcry against the explicit depiction of this form of rape, as opposed to rape of a woman, became definitive of the play's reception. *Spooks* makes two allusions to this definitive scene, which achieve more than an in-joke, but only to those who are in on the joke. The extent to which the episode works on two levels, one of which is only available to a theatrically literate audience, raises the question of how subversive a popular culture text can be for its mass audience. The script of the episode included on the DVD material is not identical to the final program, especially in the opening sequences, but it describes the first meeting of McCann and Quinn in almost identical terms to those in which it was shot. This meeting is almost a parody of the homoerotics of Anglo-Irish relations as described by Cullingford[9]:

> The two men stop about twenty feet from one another. And then do a strange thing. They start undressing efficiently. They continue until both men are completely naked. They examine each other briefly. Satisfied neither is wired, they start to put their clothes on again.
>
> PATRICK.
> (*Irish—subtitled*)
> Davy Crockett I presume.
>
> TOM.
> (*Irish—subtitled*)
> King of the wild frontier.
> (*beat—English*)
> Keep it English. No use drawing more attention to ourselves.
>
> PATRICK.
> Are you joking? Anyone seeing that would think we're in some fecky farmer's porn video.

McCann's information maps out the contours of the new world order, which neatly encapsulates the mutual hostility of the new forms of terrorism and the emergence of new necessary alliances between old enemies:

PATRICK.
We've had a minor corporate cash flow problem thanks to certain recent events. So we've been freelancing. Bit of management consultancy.
Few hard lads in Columbia. The odd mercenary in Somalia. And then
we got a call from some hard nuts in Sudan. Needed a swift how-to
on some anti-tank weaponry they'd just acquired. State of the art, the
dog's bollocks. Our lads went over there, but we weren't taking any
chances and we had them all checked out. Bastards would kill you soon
as look at you.

TOM.
You could disincentivise them.

PATRICK.
Kill them, you mean? Great minds think alike, Davy. Sadly my branch
chief had other ideas. Wanted his money first. By the time he realised he
was an eegit they had a couple of lads already on their way. And I had
to come crying to yous. (*spitefully*) For help.

McCann's linguistic register is a combination of corporate and military
jargon with a regional accent. His conversation is colorful, highly local-
ized, obscene, given to extravagant metaphor and highly seductive. This is
a dangerous seduction, which jeopardizes and breaks up Tom's family and
eventually leads to McCann's murder (he is executed by his comrades for
warning Tom about the bomb, his body left with a tag on its toe, "Property
of MI5"). The information that Tom needs to stop the terrorists attack-
ing Sefton B is contained on a laptop that McCann gives him, but that
the latter's comrades have packed with explosives. This combination of
information technology and hidden violence neatly crystallizes the dominant images of Ireland in early twenty-first-century English popular imaginings. McCann, in classic IRA form, phones a warning, telling Tom the
plan was for him to bring the laptop to MI5 headquarters. Instead Tom has
brought it home. His house, now a virtual fortress, equipped with every
possible high-tech surveillance and security device in order to secure his
family, proves a trap. The technology is vulnerable to Maisie, whose fingers
become sticky as she bakes with her mother, coating the swipe card that
opens the door with a sticky mess and rendering it inoperable. A series of
such mishaps lead up to the series cliff-hanger finale when the laptop is
about to explode inside the house, where mother and daughter are imprisoned by the technology installed to keep them safe, while Tom is locked
outside. An extended suspense sequence features the process that leaves
Tom helpless and his family vulnerable.

   Brenton's 1989 preface to *Romans* identifies the play's curious temporal
structure: "The scenes of the past are haunted by the 1980s with another
army, the British, blundering around in another foreign country, Ireland."[10]

The present haunts the past. In *Romans in Britain*, the relationship between the two temporalities is mediated through the figure of the slave girl, the object of everyone's violence, who becomes a very ambivalent icon of liberation: "The men from the ship burnt my home. Now home is wherever I have a stone in my hand."[11] The stone in her hand in 1980 identified her uneasily with the young men seen on the nightly news throwing stones at tanks on the streets of Northern Ireland. Originally a "thing" owned by the Celts, the slave girl flees with the Irish outlaw Conlag, only to be raped by him. Her moment of bloody liberation, when she takes up a stone and kills him, is immediately followed by Brenton's coup de théâtre, accompanied, the stage directions tell us, "in the distance" by "the sound of an approaching helicopter": "From the back the Roman Army advances in British Army uniforms and with the equipment of the late 1970's."[12] She throws her stone without speaking a word and is immediately killed by retaliatory gunfire: the stage directions specify this comes from an automatic weapon, emphasizing the disparity of her native stone and the technology at the disposal of her opponents, but also filling the theater with explosive and repetitive sound in contrast to her silence. Her corpse is kicked by a Roman soldier, who addresses it as "fucking bogshitting mick!" The dead girl is mistaken for the descendants of the Celts who enslaved her.

Between season one and season two, *Spooks*'s version of the new and yet known old Irish story leaves its protagonists similarly suspended between two narratives. The first season ends with a flash that may be the bomb exploding inside Tom's house, but that also shatters linear temporality. The resolution is deferred until the beginning of the next series. When that series begins, the information that Ellie and Maisie have survived is again deferred until after the scene setting up the rest of the episode. This structure in effect creates a double narrative, one with an ending that is tragic but dramatically satisfying, one that is much more complex. In this latter narrative that continues into the next season, Ellie refuses to support the hero and removes herself and her child from the contagion of his exposure to geopolitical necessity. This in turn propels him from the relationship with Ellie, a chef by profession, who promises and then withholds nurture, to one with an accident and emergency doctor, who in turn promises and then withholds a caring relationship between equally stressed professionals. Tom has to be rescued from the doctor's eventual insanity by his CIA counterpart, Christine, who inevitably betrays him. These romance narratives are intimately connected with the hero's roles as embodiment of national identity. Tom, who cannot maintain the role of patriotic patriarch embodied by Jack Ryan in *Patriot Games*, for example, plays out the collapse of a particularly English form of cultural authority. A series of verbal clues in "Mean, Dirty, Nasty" link Tom with the US, despite his often expressed frustration in season one of the unequal nature of the "special relationship" between the US and UK secret services. Having installed a state-of-the-art security system in Tom's house, his colleague Danny tells him, "You wanted Fort Knox. You got it." McCann, telling Tom to dress for the country for their first meeting, gives him a code name of Davy Crockett. It is tempting to transpose Arata's comments on Dracula and his monstrous contemporaries, "In the marauding invasive Other, British culture sees its own imperial practices mirrored back in monstrous form."[13] However, the possibility of another empire and a different monster provide the backdrop to the narrative. Asabiyah, the name of the Sudanese terrorist group in *Spooks* season one, refers directly to the theory of social cohesion developed by the fourteenth-century Islamic philosopher, Ibn Khaldun, which he attributed particularly to the necessities of nomadic life in desert conditions. "Mean, Dirty, Nasty" invokes this concept to describe a twenty-first-century terror cell in the Sudanese desert that is impenetrable to outside intelligence ("How do you get between brothers who never write anything down?" asks Tom Quinn) that arrives in England with what Patrick McCann describes as "a very detailed aerial schematic of a . . . nuclear power station." It is the Irishman who spells out the implications:

> They do what I think they're gonna do and most of Ireland's uninhabitable for the next two hundred years. Not to mention everything north of Bristol. Not that we'd miss Wales.
>
> TOM looks at him—scepticism in his eyes—
>
> PATRICK (CONT'D).
> Don't look at me like that. It's a holy war. These lads are serious. And when a man with my experience tells you that, you should listen. (*beat*) They scare the shit out of me.

McCann's "experience" gives him access to the authentic information that is unavailable to MI5 and geographical proximity pushes him into an unwelcome alliance ("It's not easy for us either you know," he tells Tom). Irish characters and references repeatedly offer object lessons from history in *Spooks*, suggesting that actions undertaken in conditions of combat cast long shadows on the peace that follows. The complex relationship between Patrick McCann and Tom Quinn does, in this very popular format, serve as a reminder that policy shifts constantly reposition the line dividing demonized terrorists from assets and allies. In season four, in an episode called "The Innocent" written by playwright and director, Ben Richards, an Algerian called Nazim Malik is wrongfully imprisoned and kept in solitary confinement as a serious security risk due to an administrative error confusing him with another man of the same name. The episode was first aired on October 13, 2005, as controversy was raging on the Blair administration's proposal to extend the term for which terror suspects could be detained without charge from fourteen to ninety days (the parliamentary defeat of this proposal with a backbench revolt on November 9, 2005, was the first of the administration). The part of the Algerian was powerfully played by Jimi Mistry, a high-profile British actor who has spoken in interviews about his dual heritage as the son of an Indian father and Irish mother. The casting of Mistry makes the character of Malik a salutary proxy for a very broad range of immigrants and children of immigrants who might be mistaken for someone or simply excite suspicion. (The British media featured prominently a case in 2003 where Israeli authorities blamed a tip-off from British intelligence for their arrest on the West Bank of an Irish language activist on a cultural program, mistaken for a dissident republican of the same name.) Malik's transformation from innocent internee to potential recruit for extremists might pass for a very brief history of the consequences of internment in Northern Ireland. An oblique hint is given that the Maliks will be the future Birmingham Sixes and Guildford Fours when the Irish government offers him a passport. The unsettling familiarity of Anglo-Irish conflict defamiliarizes and clarifies the new war and old response.

As well as formulating the concept of Asabiyah, Ibn Khaldun is often credited as the first sociologist and historiographer, best known for his observation and theorization of the process by which dynasties and civilizations rise and fall, in a cycle, as a result of psychological, economic, environmental and social, as well as political, factors. Brenton, commenting on the rehearsals for *The Romans in Britain*'s revival, suggested the wheel of imperial fortune had taken a new turn and wondered if an audience in 2006 might "see contemporary parallels. Is America our Rome? The Trinovantes, a powerful tribe in what is now Essex and Suffolk, were in an abject alliance with the Romans, just as we are with Washington today. All the way from here to the Iraq-Iran border, an imperial power is barging around the world believing that it alone holds the keys of 'civilization,' as dangerous as Caesar's legions."[14] In series six of *Spooks,* a much more conventional Irish plot resurfaces at a point of tension in just this alliance in another episode written by Richards. The character of Davey King is described as "a walking ghost with a death wish." He is both the synthesis of every IRA psychopath stereotype known to thriller writers and a former MI5 asset. King is contracted to get rid of the "good" spies just when one of them is about to go public with information about American activities in Iran. The labyrinthine plot involves a derided New Labour functionary bringing in King to kill off MI5 agents as part of a deal with Iran to give them industrial nuclear capacity with no military potential, thus preventing a hawklike US administration launching attacks on Iran and a potentially apocalyptic new phase of the war on terror. (This was aired in December 2007: looking back from the vantage point of 2009, Ibn Khaldun's cycle of four generations for cyclical rotation of power looks very slow.) In effect, the IRA man enacts a dangerous form of British independence.

Brenton himself has argued that the revolution he sought to achieve in *The Romans in Britain* was primarily a matter of theatrical form, but it is clear he identifies formal and political revolution. The *Spooks* episodes are more properly described as subversive than revolutionary, but they do seek to alter popular perception. The thriller is an extraordinarily powerful ideological apparatus. Usually this power is conservative, predicated on the latent nature of its political content. The question then arises if manipulation of, for example, the meaning of Irishness in English popular consciousness in the thriller form constitutes a genuinely critical popular culture. The exploration of historical dynamics that configures Brenton's cultural map of Anglo-Irish relations indicate that this chronotope is much more unstable than the Irish-American ones found in the Hollywood action thrillers' engagement with the Troubles or the reinvention of the blue-collar Irish-American hero in television drama. If Ireland is an extimate of England, Irishness is also a difference at the center of Englishness.

Conclusion

IRISHNESS ABROAD

Traditionally, Irish Studies defined itself in terms of the study of culture emanating from Ireland itself, defending the authenticity of its subject against the continuum of stage Irishry and Blarney characterized as first by London's, then Hollywood's, failure to represent either the complexities of Ireland's history or the reality of its people. While there is a significant body of scholarship on the negative stereotyping of the Irish in nineteenth- and twentieth-century British and American media, there was until Negra (2006) little on the production of positive (or at least attractive) cultural stereotypes of Irish ethnicity and their functions in the discourses of race, gender and "homeland."[1] My focus in the preceding analysis of the representation of Irish men in the Hollywood action movie, US and English television drama and English theater has been on the function of these representations at specific crises in the articulation of English and US national identities. "The invisibility of whiteness as a racial position in white (which is to say dominant) discourse is of a piece with its ubiquity"[2]: the analysis of Irishness in English and US popular culture examined the consequences of the invisibility of Irish whiteness. The role of liminal white identities in the vortex of race, class and gender continues to change and to perform an important role, particularly in mediating the shifting power relations of Anglo-American identities. Drawing on the work of Joan Copjec, I have proposed that Irishness has come to occupy an extimate space in relation to dominant masculinities. It will be interesting to see if this continues in the new cultural self-concept of the post-Obama US. There are signs that the significance of Irishness for Americans is changing. A story line in the cult series *Heroes* that involved Irish locations and a story line involving an Irish woman immigrant and an apocalyptic virus were dropped. The most prominent Irish actor on US television in the 2008–2009 season was Gabriel Byrne playing a psychotherapist in HBO's *In Treatment*. Byrne, against the recent trend of European actors learning American accents to get parts on US television, plays the part with a Dublin accent without any explanatory backstory. Paul's profession puts him at radical odds with the values of Tommy Gavin and Jimmy McNulty, but interestingly he has the same conflict of interest between professional commitment and family life.

Canons and Conflicts

The three chapters on "Writing, Bodies, Canons" investigated the relationship between cultural authority, gender and modernist innovation. The chapter on modernism and the gender of writing focused initially on the challenges to aesthetic and sexual proprieties of the late nineteenth and early twentieth century. Running through the analysis of the work of Katherine Cecil Thurston, Emily Lawless, Kate O'Brien, Rosamond Jacob and James Joyce in this chapter is the theme of how artistic practice and cultural authority are officially gendered. This gendered construction of the role of writers and artists is challenged in the figure of the woman artist as she appears in the fiction of Thurston, Lawless and O'Brien, but also in that of Penelope as she is stitched into the fabric of *Ulysses*'s concept of writing as performance. In all of these texts the relationship between aesthetic, political and sexual expression is explored within the complex interrelationship of cultural and political authority. Chapter 6 traced the mythic conflict of Cuchulainn and his son Conlaoch in works by Yeats, Synge, Gregory, Deevy, Sheridan and Gogan, exploring the paradox of a society imagined as an extension of the patriarchal family in which no patrimony was secured for future generations and in which the family was apparently venerated but the integrity of family and kinship was routinely violated by church and state in the interests of social control. Perhaps appropriately, the most striking exploration of the interlinked themes of Irish intergenerational conflict, patriarchal failure and the violence on which society is found in the work of an American director, Martin Scorsese.

In a prophetic scene in John Boorman's *The General* the Irish criminal boss Martin Cahill refuses a comradely hug from his closest lieutenant with a derisive, "What are we, fucking Italians?" The scene was primarily self-reflexive at the time of the film's release. In telling the story of Irish society in the eighties through the story of its most well-known crime boss, Boorman was importing a set of generic conventions that were at the time overwhelmingly associated with the Mafia, and Italian America was overwhelmingly associated in the global cinema-going mind with the work of Francis Ford Coppola and Martin Scorsese. The question resonates rather differently now, with Scorsese taking Irish-American gangs and gangsters as his theme and Irish filmmakers engaged in complicated homages to Scorsese in films such as *In Bruges*. Scorsese's interest in Irish themes was established as intimately linked to his interest in American urban history with the release of *Gangs of New York*. The timing of that release, despite the long gestation of the film and its making, linked its project of social archaeology with the interest in working-class Irish-American New Yorkers in the aftermath of the September 11, 2001, attacks, prompting the *New York Times* to compare Scorsese's film with Spike Lee's *25th Hour*, released around the same time:

> Both films portray the events of Sept. 11, 2001 as a historical watershed. Mr. Scorsese's 19th-century epic culminates with the 1863 Civil War Draft Riots, which reduced much of the city to a smoking ruin, then fades out with a photomontage of the soaring downtown skyline that emerged out of those ashes only to be defaced on Sept. 11. Mr. Lee's movie, steeped in paranoia, has a moment in which the camera solemnly pauses to contemplate the desolation of ground zero. To be sure, Mr. Scorsese's film, inspired by Herbert Asbury's chronicle of 19th-century gang warfare, was in the planning stages long before the twin towers' collapse. And its vision of the city's streets awash in blood is a variation on the urban violence that runs through many of his films. But what distinguishes "Gangs of New York" from previous Scorsese bloodbaths is its apocalyptic tone. The movie, which is nothing less than Mr. Scorsese's "Birth of a Nation," reminds us that the American empire, for all the lofty principles embodied in the Constitution, was born through conquest and came of age in a civil war.

"America was born on the streets" was the tagline for the film's publicity and the streets in *Gangs of New York* repeatedly run with blood. Scorsese's historical epic is concerned with the violence on which society is founded in a manner so close to the Cuchulainn motif at the heart of Irish theater and film that it is not surprising that Irish characters have come to dominate his recent explorations of American history and culture. Despite Scorsese's well-known interest in Joyce and the inclusion of a reference to *Portrait of the Artist as a Young Man* in *The Departed*, these films are closer to Yeats's social vision than Joyce's. *Gangs of New York* and *The Departed* mirror the Yeatsian construction of the nation as a crisis-ridden Oedipal family, where the only birthright appears to be bloodshed.

In contrast, Claire Kilroy's novel *All Names Have Been Changed* satirizes the formation of canons in Oedipal terms and of literature in national ones. Her protagonist's efforts to live the Irish literary life are rudely punctured. His tenancy of a bedsit in Mountjoy Square sets him in the middle of quite another story, that of urban deprivation, the Dublin of the heroin epidemic of the 1980s and the brutality of inner-city life at the time. *All Names Have Been Changed* critically rehearses a central theme of 1980s Irish writing, the unraveling of myth and the assertion of historical realities. In the process it constructs a very different genealogy of Irish fiction.

Blood, Science, and Monsters: Blood of the Irish

It would be wonderful to conclude that the synergy of racial thinking, unease with the maternal and the desire to establish an *a priori* Irish identity that precedes history and delimits the future analyzed in the first chapter of this book has now abated, but it bubbles just under the surface of twenty-first-century popular culture. I want to look briefly at a popular documentary broadcast in 2009 by the Irish National broadcaster, RTE, as an indicator of the way in which the lack of a self-critical impulse in relation to race keeps profoundly essentialist versions of Irish identity in circulation. *Blood of the Irish* purported to be an exploration of what modern genetics can tell us about the first inhabitants of Ireland and it obviously understood its mission in those terms, but it offers a fascinating insight into the continued conflation of race, nation and gender in Irish popular culture. The pre-credit sequence opens with a series of aerial shots, beginning with an establishing shot zooming in from the pylons of the Pigeon House electricity generating stations, which sets the series in the context of contemporary Dublin. The focus shifts further inland and narrows to a general view of Dublin at its most densely urban center, zooming in on O'Connell Street, the capital's main thoroughfare. The Spire, one of the few landmark pieces of public architecture of the Celtic Tiger era, features prominently. At this point, the voice-over begins with the comment, "Never in history have the Irish been so varied." The cut to a vertical camera angle is accompanied by a fast-forward of the city's contemporary citizens walking under the columns of the GPO, Irish nationalism's iconic Dublin site. As the film speed becomes standard, these citizens come into focus. The voice-over declares, "Our population today is a blend of many races, colors and creeds," but the screen shows only one black woman among the throng, whose bright pink sweater makes her stand out from the crowd quite as much as her skin color. When the voice-over asks, "But who were the very first people to set foot on this island?" there is a cut to two elderly white people, each isolated in close-ups, as is the very conventionally Irish-looking young woman with red hair and umbrella who is the next visual focus. The camera pulls back but faces continue to be picked out amidst a series of rapidly alternating shots of people, buses and trams as the voice-over continues, "Up to now all we could do was wonder about the origins of the first Irish. But new science if beginning to resolve this age-old mystery."

At this point, the visual register of the program changes dramatically. The presenter speaks directly to the camera from a wind- and wave-swept beach. There is a very strong visual contrast, from rainy streets where the distortion of images by flickering lights from shops and vehicles was intensified by the use of dissolves and alternation between close and medium shots, to a high-angled, long, establishing shot of the beach in sunshine, with characteristic green cliffs behind. Rural elemental Ireland comes dramatically into view and the voice-over is replaced by the personification of the program's quest in the reassuringly nonscientific and nonpolitical presenter, Diarmuid Gavin (a celebrity landscape gardener whose television career had its roots in the English enthusiasm for gardening and home improvement programs). Later in the program, Gavin, rowing a boat at sea, again speaking directly to the camera, remarks, "Many of us are directly descended from the first waves of settlers who made Ireland home." As we are shown a family of prehistoric settlers land and unload their boat on the Irish shore, the voice-over continues, "These are our ancestors and, for me, the most extraordinary discovery is that their blood still flows in our veins." The personal element in the narration ("for me") is accompanied by an extraordinary visual sequence in which the father cuts his hand with a knife and then places the bloody imprint on his son's forehead. The blood flow here is from father to son and, despite all the references to genetics, symbolic and social ties of kinship are what are at stake here. The transmission of blood is represented as a ritual between fathers and sons, not a mere matter of giving birth. A birth scene on the shore would have had at least as much visual and dramatic impact, but this would represent a very different concept of heredity and a very different politics. A man marking his son as his own is a settler and a forefather. A woman giving birth as she arrives might evoke the image of the immigrant mother, of the mother's body as active originator of life and of the fluid borders of identities marked by journeys, crossing, landings.

In *Blood of the Irish* infants are not represented at all, nor do any of these families of ancestors appear to have had any daughters, which poses certain practical difficulties for the survival of the species. The image of these ancestral families is centered from the start on boys on the verge of adolescence. Despite the insistence on Africa as the common home of the human species and the references to cultural diversity, the series indicates that the understanding of Irish national identity in racial terms is quite mainstream in Irish popular culture. The use of frequent crosscuts between contemporary white Irish and ancient Africans may be read as an attempt to forestall the identification of the program's presumption that genetics can tell us "who we are" as racist. If this was the case, the reception of the program indicates that in general this attempt was successful. More troublingly, the device seems to indicate a genuine lack of understanding of racism and in particular that to construct Irish identity in terms of genetic inheritance, visually recognizable physical characteristics and relation to the island's original inhabitants is to construct it in racial terms. The second program in the series indicates that the construction of Irish identity in masculine terms is equally mainstream and equally unconscious. The elements of *Blood of the Irish* that received most comment were not the lack of genetic evidence for a Celtic invasion, which might have been anticipated to challenge perceived notions of Irish identity, but the identification of strong genetic links between the populations of the Basque country in Spain and the western seaboard of Ireland and of a common male ancestor, identified very tenuously with the legendary Niall of the Nine Hostages, for 20 percent of the male population of northwest Ireland. Ireland is no longer a

Virgin Mother, but Irishness at home and abroad remains resolutely linked to a particular form of masculinity.

It is important to see *Blood of the Irish* in the contradictory context of Irish disbelief in racism as intrinsic to Irish society and the casual racism of the Irish popular media. In the same issue that a national newspaper, the *Irish Independent*, reviewed the series as "the laboured efforts of Diarmuid Gavin in *Blood of the Irish* (RTE1) to explain where we all came from," the television reviewer complains: "On the first All-Ireland Talent Show (RTE1), judge Shane Lynch was the arbiter for the Dublin region and . . . plumped for five to remain in the contest. Most of these were either black or East European. I'm all for multiculturalism, but are there no authentic jackeens left in Dublin?"[3] While the resurgence of cultural nationalism in Ireland in response to economic development and the end of the northern conflict has attracted some comment, contemporary popular media in Ireland indicate that this resurgence is both uneasily and deeply felt.

In contrast, in contemporary English popular culture, representations of Irishness have become fragmented, with an increasing tendency for roles associated with traditional troublesome or troubled Irishness to be gendered masculine, those associated with the new, successful Ireland to be feminine and glamorous. (Claire Bracken and Emma Radley's analysis of the star personae of Colin Farrell and Deirdre O'Kane indicates the changing role of gender in determining the meaning of Irishness in global media.[4]) So the undercover policeman in *Murphy's Law* is played by James Nesbit, as an unstable, disillusioned Northern Irishman. *Murphy's Law* resolves the conflict of familial and professional values typical of these types of characters, for Murphy's family has been assassinated before the narrative begins when he refused to carry a bomb for the IRA. In contrast, the Irish woman barrister played by Dervla Kirwan in *55 Degrees North* is both impeccably professional and an apparently excellent single mother. In *28 Days Later*, it is precisely the instability of identity of the Irish survivor, played by Killian Murphy, that enables him to mimic inhuman behavior and even death, which allows him not only to live, but to ally himself with the surviving women against both extremes of barbarism and dictatorship and form a new surrogate family.

Writing the Future

In Eilis Ní Dhuibhne's *Fox, Swallow, Scarecrow*, published in 2007, Anna, the main protagonist and modern-day version of Anna Karenina, attends a book launch in the old Irish parliament building, now the headquarters of the Bank of Ireland:

> The topic of the book was Irish identity, an old chestnut that continued to fascinate—though perhaps the word is too strong—as many people as it had recently begun to repel. But although the rebels declared that

Ireland was no different from England or America, and insisted on locating their stories in anonymous places representative of the modern globe, some readers still wanted poems and stories about bogs and farms and derelict market towns in Leitrim and Laois and Limerick. They expected the leading writers to explore the tired old topics. They would be grateful to the Nobel laureate for attempting to satisfy their insatiable thirst for literature about the subject they loved best—themselves.[5]

Implicit here is the view that Ireland is the figment of its own fond imagination. These satirical jabs at the nation's narcissism are timely, even if the prosperous confident Dublin Ní Dhuibhne chronicles has collapsed in an orgy of debt, corruption, incompetence and recrimination. Ni Dhuibhne has always drawn on both her training as a folklorist and her acute observation of a rapidly changing Ireland to generate narrative spaces that are neither anonymously modern nor determinedly rural. Perhaps because she works in both the English and Irish language and is published by small independent Irish publishers, Ní Dhuibhne is relatively little known outside of Irish Studies circles, but she has been a consistently interesting voice in Irish fiction. *Fox, Swallow, Scarecrow* paints an acerbic picture of a literary Dublin where writing has become just another luxury commodity, but it ends with a sense of possibility. Like her Russian prototype, Anna loses her lover and is run over by a train, in her case the LUAS tram, named for speed, symbol of change and Dublin's fondest aspirations. Unlike Anna Karenina, she survives. Like Henry O'Connor in Johnston's *Foolish Mortals*, discussed in the Introduction, Anna Kelly Sweeney has problems with memory after her collision. "Anna was trying to remember a name, but it would not come to her. It was very frustrating, like trying to get the internet connection to work when the link has broken."[6] Like Henry, Anna sets out to live with a permanently fractured relation to the past. This is appropriate, for Ni Dhuibhne has shattered her novel's parallels with *Anna Karenina* by imagining a different, new life for her Anna:

Anna writes, tries to write, writes, tries to write. Lets the words float to the top like spawn on the water, lets the words sit like a hare on the track, lets the words leap like a trout in the lake, lets the words sing like the finches. Lets the words. Lets the words. Lets the words.[7]

Having forgotten her traumatic breakup and the new life she had thought would be hers, Anna literally writes herself another future. Narrative is the mode in which culture maps what Homi Bhabha memorably calls "the space of the perplexity of the living."[8] In that space, after the train wreck of the national economy, profoundly regressive forces still tug Ireland and Irishness toward certainty, toward authenticity, toward an identity secured by a known and knowable relation to the past. Those very certainties, authenticities and identities have, as we have seen, always been haunted by the unaccountable past, the ghosts of those whose history the living do not want to own as part of their inheritance. Now tapping at the window with them, cracking the glass and letting in a storm of possibility, are the shades of a different future.

Notes

NOTES TO THE INTRODUCTION

1. *Verbal* 9 (December 2007).
2. Jennifer Johnston, *Shadows on Our Skin* (London: Hamish Hamilton, 1977), 66.
3. Ibid., 67.
4. March 1902, from the Preface to Lady Augusta Gregory, *Cuchulainn of Murithemme* (London: John Murray, 1902).
5. Act 2, scene 3.
6. Jennifer Johnston, *Foolish Mortals* (London: Headline Review, 2007), 127.
7. Ibid., 128.
8. Ibid., 160.
9. Ibid., 306–7.
10. Ibid.
11. Ibid., 127.
12. Ibid., 311.
13. See, for example, the work of emerging scholars such as Mary McCarthy and Cliona Rattigan.
14. Maria Luddy, *Prostitution and Irish Society, 1800–1940* (Cambridge: Cambridge University Press, 2007), 2.
15. Deepika Bahri, "Telling Tales: Women and the Trauma of Partition in Sidhwa's Cracking India," *Interventions: International Journal of Postcolonial Studies* 1, no. 2 (1999): 219.
16. Diane Negra, ed., *The Irish in Us* (Durham, NC: Duke University Press, 2006).
17. *Irish Times*, April 15, 1971, quoted in R.F. Foster, *Luck and the Irish: A Brief History of Change 1970–2000* (Harmondsworth: Penguin, 2007), 42.
18. *Irish Times*, May 7, 1997. The quotation comes from John Waters, an *Irish Times* columnist and media personality whose persona developed from nostalgia for rural life to apologist for de Valera's Ireland during the period.
19. Wanda Balzano, Anne Mulhall and Moynagh Sullivan, eds., *Irish Postmodernisms and Popular Culture* (London: Palgrave Macmillan, 2007). See also Borbola Farago and Moynagh Sullivan, eds., *Facing the Other: Interdisciplinary Studies on Race, Class and Gender in Ireland* (Newcastle: Cambridge Scholars Press, 2008).
20. Joe Cleary, *Outrageous Fortune: Capital and Culture in Modern Ireland* (Dublin: Field Day Publications, 2007), 7.

NOTES TO CHAPTER 1

1. Anne McClintock, "Family Feuds: Gender, Nationalism and the Family," *Feminist Review* 44 (Summer 1993): 61.
2. Shelley Feldman, "Feminist Interruptions: The Silence of East Bengal in the Story of Partition," Interventions: *International Journal of Postcolonial Studies* 1, no. 2 (1999): 177–78.
3. Miroslav Hroch, "From National Movement to the Fully Formed Nation: The Nation-Building Process in Europe," *New Left Review* 1, no. 198 (March/April 1993): 15.
4. McClintock, "Family Feuds," 62.
5. Peggy Watson, "The Rise of Masculinism in Eastern Europe," *New Left Review* 1, no. 198 (March/April 1993): 75.
6. Contributors to the 1999 special issue of *Interventions* 2, no. 1 consistently remarked on the process whereby, in the Indian context, relatively liberated women in the eighties and nineties became metaphors for secularism and modernity and a constituency to be targeted by the religious right.
7. Luke Gibbons, "Race against Time: Racial Discourse and Irish History," in *Transformations in Irish Culture* (Cork: Cork University Press, 1996), 149.
8. For an account of this process in the context of US immigration history, see Noel Ignatieve, *How the Irish Became White* (New York and London: Routledge, 1997).
9. See, for example, Diane Negra, ed., *The Irish in Us* (Durham, NC: Duke University Press, 2006).
10. Richard Dyer, *White* (London and New York: Routledge, 1997), 74.
11. Bryan Fanning, *Racism and Social Change in the Republic of Ireland* (Manchester and New York, Manchester University Press, 2002).
12. Ronit Lentin, "Black Bodies and Headless Hookers: Alternative Global Narratives for 21st Century Ireland," *Irish Review* 33 (Spring 2005): 7.
13. Ibid., 9.
14. For the historical and social context of these cultural developments, see James Donnelly, "A Church in Crisis." *History Ireland* 8, no. 3 (2000); "The Peak of Marianism in Ireland." In *Piety and Power in Ireland*, ed., Stewart Brown and David Miller. Bloomington: University of Notre Dame Press, 2000; 'Opposing the "Modern World": The Cult of the Virgin Mary in Ireland, 1965–85, *Éire-Ireland*, Volume 40: 1 & 2, Spring/Summer 2005, 183–245.
15. See John Turpin, "Visual Marianism and National Identity in Ireland: 1920–1960," in *Art, Nation and Gender: Ethnic Landscapes, Myths and Mother-Figures*, ed. Tricia Cusack and Sighle Bhreathnach-Lynch, 72 (Aldershot, Hampshire and Burlington, VT: Ashgate, 2003).
16. Turpin, "Visual Marianism," 70.
17. Yeats in *Samhain: An Occasional Review*. Dublin, Maunsel and Co. and A.H. Bullen, 1905; New York, Hard Press, 2009.
18. Freda Laughton, "The Woman with Child," *The Bell* 9, no. 4 (January 1945): 289.
19. Freda Laughton, "When You Were with Me," *The Bell* (August 1944): 287.
20. "The Poems of Freda Laughton," *The Bell* 9, no. 4 (January 1945): 249–50.
21. Ibid., 249.
22. Ibid., 250.
23. Patricia Harrison, Letter to the Editor, *The Bell* (August 1945): 446.
24. Laughton, "The Woman with Child," 289.

25. See also Eily O'Horan, "The Rustle of Spring," *The Bell* 13, no. 5 (February 1948): 28–39.
26. Mary Daly, *The Slow Failure: Population Decline and Independent Ireland, 1920–73* (Madison: University of Wisconsin Press, 2006).
27. Daly, *Slow Failure*, 4. She draws on work by Michael Anderson and Donald J. Morse, "High Fertility, High Emigration, Low Nuptiality: Adjustment Processes in Scotland's Demographic Experience, 1861–1914, pt. 1," *Population Studies* 47, no.1 (1993): 5–25 and pt. 2, *Population Studies* 47, no. 2 (1993): 319–43; Enda Delaney, *Demography, State and Society: Irish Migration to Britain, 1921–1971* (Liverpool: Liverpool University Press, 2000): 5–21; Delaney, "Placing Post-War Irish Migration to Britain in a Comparative European Perspective, 1945–81," in *The Irish Diaspora*, ed. Andy Bielenberg (Harlow: Pearson Education, 2000); Timothy V. Guinnane, *The Vanishing Irish: Households, Migration and the Rural Economy in Ireland, 1850–1914* (Princeton, NJ: Princeton University Press, 1997), xv; Silvana Patriarca, *Numbers and Nationhood: Writing Statistics in Nineteenth Century Italy* (Cambridge: Cambridge University Press, 1996), 1–3.
28. Maria Luddy, *Prostitution and Irish Society, 1800–1940* (Cambridge: Cambridge University Press, 2007).
29. Clair Wills, *That Neutral Island: A Cultural History of Ireland during the Second World War* (London: Faber and Faber, 2007).
30. Patrick Noonan, "Why Few Irish Marry," in *The Vanishing Irish: The Enigma of the Modern World*, ed. John A. O'Brien, 48 (New York: McGraw Hill, 1954). Also Daly, *Slow Failure*, 36.
31. Clair Wills, "Representations of Women, Marriage and Modernity in the 1950s" (paper presented at the Inventing and Reinventing the Irish Woman Symposium, Humanities Institute of Ireland, University College Dublin, October 10–11, 2008).
32. Daly, *Slow Failure*, 36.
33. See Bernadette Whelan, "Ireland, the Marshall Plan, and U.S. Cold War Concerns," *Journal of Cold War Studies* 8, no. 1 (Winter 2006): 68–94.
34. Daly, *Slow Failure*, 265.
35. See Daly, *Slow Failure*, 285–89; Louise Ryan, "Irish Newspaper Representations of Women, Migration and Pregnancy Outside the Marriage in the 1930," in *Single Motherhood in 20th Century Ireland: Cultural, Historical and Social Essays*, ed. Maria de la Cinta Ramblado-Minero and Auxiliadora Perez-Vides (Ceredigion: Edward Mellen Press, 2006).
36. Julia Kristeva, "Stabat Mater," in *The Kristeva Reader*, ed. Toril Moi (Oxford: Blackwell, 1986).
37. Vincent Cheng, *Inauthentic: The Anxiety Over Culture and Identity* (New Brunswick, NJ, and London: Rutgers University Press, 2004), 27.
38. Declan Kiberd, *The Irish Writer and the World* (Cambridge: Cambridge University Press, 2005), 303.
39. Colin Graham, *Deconstructing Ireland: Identity, Theory, Culture* (Edinburgh: Edinburgh University Press, 2001), 109–10.
40. Sean O'Reilly, *The Swing of Things* (London: Faber and Faber, 2004).
41. The volume includes an excellent contextualizing essay on Hardy by Sarah Smith, "Ireland in the 1940s and 1950s: The Photographs of Bert Hardy," 133–56.
42. Seamus Deane, "Edward Said (1935–2003): A Late Style of Humanism," *Field Day Review* 1, no. 1:199.
43. "Engendering the Sublime: Margaret Corcoran's *An Enquiry*," *Circa* 107 (Spring 2004).
44. Ibid.

NOTES TO CHAPTER 2

1. "The Theater of Irish Cinema," *Yale Journal of Criticism* 15, no. 1 (2002): 23.
2. Fidelma Farley, "Aisling: The Female and National Body in Films about Ireland" (PhD dissertation, University College Dublin, 1999); Luke Gibbons, *Transformations in Irish Culture* (Cork: Cork University Press, 1996).
3. Gibbons, "Romanticism, Realism and Irish Cinema," in *Cinema and Ireland*, ed. Kevin Rockett, Luke Gibbons and John Hill, 203 (New York: Syracuse University Press, 1988).
4. Claire Johnston, "Maeve," *Screen* 24 (1981): 61.
5. See Fidelma Farley, "Screening the Irish Mother/Land," in *Into the Shadows: The University of Limerick Women's Studies Collection*, vol. 2 (Limerick: University of Limerick Women's Studies Collection, 1996). In "Hibernia and Cinema: Romance and Anglo-Irish Politics in Post-War British Cinema" (paper presented at "To the Other Shore: English Views of Ireland and the Irish" Conference, LSU College of Higher Education, Southampton, June 1995), Farley offers a detailed analysis of the influence of this tradition on British films' representation of Irishwomen and Ireland itself. Farley traces the relationship between these representations and the history of Anglo-Irish relations, particularly in the immediate postwar period.
6. See Antonia Lant, "The Female Spy: Gender, Nationality and War in *I See a Dark Stranger*," in *Resisting Images: Essays on Cinema and History*, ed. Robert Sklar and Charles Musser (Philadelphia: Temple University Press, 1990).
7. Lady Morgan, *The Wild Irish Girl* (London: Phillips, 1806).
8. See Lant and Farley for an analysis of Kerr's Irish roles in this film and in *Black Narcissus*.
9. Gibbons, *Transformations in Irish Culture*.
10. Barry Lopez, *Arctic Dreams: Imagination and Desire in a Northern Landscape* (London: Pan, 1987), quoted in Kevin Whelan, "The Power of Place," *Irish Review* 12 (Spring/Summer 1992): 20.
11. See Terry Eagleton, *Heathcliff and the Great Hunger* (London: Verso, 1995) for an account of this process in literature.
12. See Suruchi Thapar, "Women as Activists, Women as Symbols: A Study of the Indian Nationalist Movement," *Feminist Review* 44 (Summer 1993): 81–96, for an account of parallel developments in Indian nationalism.
13. Catherine Nash, "Remapping and Renaming: New Cartographies of Identity, Gender and Landscape in Ireland," *Feminist Review* 44 (Summer 1993): 39–57; Cheryl Herr, "The Erotics of Irishness," *Critical Inquiry* 17, no. 1 (Autumn 1990): 1–34.
14. Nash, "Remapping and Renaming," 50.
15. During the "land war" of the 1870s, those who moved into farms from which the previous tenants had been evicted were called land-grabbers. One of the most effective tactics of the Land League was to make eviction unprofitable by discouraging land grabbing through a combination of communal solidarity, boycotting and intimidation.
16. Herr, "The Erotics of Irishness," 33.
17. Nash, "Remapping and Renaming," 50.
18. Nash, "Remapping and Renaming," 54.
19. Nash, "Remapping and Renaming," 51.
20. Released in Ireland as *Waking Ned*.
21. Kevin Rockett, "Irish Cinema: The National in the International," *Cineaste* 24, nos. 2–3 (1999): 24.

22. Ruth Barton, "Feisty Colleens and Faithful Sons: Gender in Irish Cinema," *Cineaste* 24, nos. 2–3 (1999): 44.
23. Rockett, "Irish Cinema," 24.
24. Martin McLoone, "Reimagining the Nation: Themes and Issues in Irish Cinema," *Cineaste* 24, nos. 2–3 (1999): 33.
25. Thomas Elsaesser, "Tales of Sound and Fury: Observations on the Family Melodrama," *Monogram* 4 (1972): 2–15; references are to the reprint in *Home Is Where the Heart Is: Studies in Melodrama and the Woman's Film*, ed. Christine Gledhill (London: British Film Institute, 1987), 43–70.
26. The description is offered in the film by the local bishop when he wishes to dissociate himself from it. Played by John Kavanagh in much more sinister vein than the psychopathic IRA commanders he has played so frequently elsewhere on-screen, this Machiavellian character, more than the dangerously bumptious parish priest played with great subtlety by Tony Doyle, is indicative of changing attitudes to the Catholic Church in Ireland.
27. Elsaesser, "Tales of Sound and Fury," 50.
28. Ibid.

NOTES TO CHAPTER 3

1. Eavan Boland, *A Kind of Scar: The Woman Poet in a National Tradition, Lip Pamphlet* (Dublin: Attic Press, 1989), 13.
2. Clair Wills, "Contemporary Irish Women Poets: The Privatisation of Myth," in *Diverse Voices: Essays on Twentieth-Century Women Writers in English*, ed. Harriet Devine Jump, 254 (Hemel Hempstead: Harvester Wheatsheaf, 1991).
3. Ibid.; Wills acknowledges that her analysis relies on quite early work by Heaney and his comments on it in the 1970s, but points out that the cultural centrality that work has attained "goes some way to prove the strength of the rural, organicist nostalgia" (270).
4. Seamus Deane, ed., *Field Day Anthology of Irish Writing*, 3 vols. (Derry: Field Day, 1991).
5. Boland, *A Kind of Scar*, 11.
6. Two British feminist imprints, Virago and Pandora, have been responsible for most of the republication of Irish women's work, though Pandora's list, which included previously long out of print work by Lady Morgan and Maria Edgeworth, now appears to be unavailable. The Dublin publishers, Wolfhound, published an anthology of Irish women's poetry that included many "lost" poets in 1988, see the following. There have been reprints of individual women's work, notably Mercier's reprint of the popular romantic novelist, Annie M.P. Smithson.
7. Marina Carr, interview, *Women and Words*, Lyric FM, 2008.
8. Boland, *A Kind of Scar*, 11.
9. A.A. Kelly, *The Pillars of the House: An Anthology of Verse by Irish Women from 1690 to the Present* (Dublin: Wolfhound, 1987), 46.
10. Julia Kristeva, "Women's Time," in *The Kristeva Reader*, ed. Toril Moi, 193 (Oxford: Blackwell, 1986).
11. Kelly, *The Pillars of the House*, 46.
12. Benedict Anderson, *Imagined Communities: Reflections on the Origin and Spread of Nationalism* (London: Verso, 1983), 10.
13. Anderson, *Imagined Communities*, 11.
14. Irigaray, *Speculum. De L'autre Femme*, trans. Gillian C. Gill (1974; repr. Ithaca, NY: Cornell University Press, 1985); "The Necessity for Sexuate

Rights," in *The Irigaray Reader*, ed. by Margaret Whitford, 198–203 (1987; repr., Oxford: Blackwell, 1991).

15. G.W.F. Hegel, *The Phenomenology of Mind*, 2nd ed., ed. J.B. Baillie (1807; repr., London: George Allen and Unwin, 1931), 466–67.
16. Ibid., 481.
17. It was not the custom in peasant families for women to take their husband's name on marriage until this century.
18. Lady Augusta Gregory, *Selected Writings*, ed. Lucy McDiarmid and Maureen Waters (Harmondsworth: Penguin, 1995 [1906]), 358.
19. Ibid., 357.
20. Dympna McLoughlin, "Workhouses and Irish Female Paupers, 1840–70," in *Women Surviving: Studies in Irish Women's History in the Nineteenth and Twentieth Centuries*, ed. Maria Luddy and Cliona Murphy, 117 (Dublin: Poolbeg, 1990). McLoughlin's research suggests that Mary Cahel's understanding of going into the workhouse as a desperate stratagem, but a stratagem nonetheless, was characteristic of wider practices.
21. See Betty Cahill "Vocal Expression in Oral Traditions and Theatrical Performance with Particular Reference to the 'Caoineadh,'" *Irish Theatre Forum* 2, no. 3 (1998): 8, for an account of the influence of this form on Irish theatrical traditions.
22. See Angela (Bourke) Partridge, *Caoineadh Na Dtrí Muire: Téama Na Páise I Bhfílocht Bhéil Na Gaeilge* (Dublin: An Clóchomhar, 1983).
23. Gregory, *Selected Writings*, xxxi.
24. Irigaray, *Speculum. De L'autre Femme*, 215.
25. Ibid., 217.
26. Irigaray, "The Necessity for Sexuate Rights," 199.
27. Acting rights for the play were reserved for the women's militant nationalist organization, *Inghinidhe na hEireann*, see Antoinette Quinn, "Cathleen Ni Houlihan Writes Back: Maud Gonne and Irish Nationalist Theatre," in *Gender and Sexuality in Modern Ireland*, ed. Anthony Bradley and Maryann Gialanella Valiulis (Amherst: University of Massachusetts Press, 1997), 40. The organization's name translates as Daughters of Ireland.
28. Quinn, "Cathleen Ni Houlihan Writes Back," 55.
29. Quinn, "Cathleen Ni Houlihan Writes Back," 52.
30. See Margaret Kelleher, *The Feminization of Famine* (Cork: Cork University Press, 1997), for an account of "the feminization of famine," i.e., the representation of famine and its effects through images of women and "the prevalence of figures of mother-and-child" (2). Kelleher's comparative analysis of fictional representations of famine in Ireland and Bengal offers an illuminating context for analysis of the relationship between gender and national identities in diverse colonial contexts.
31. Maud Ellman, *The Hunger Artists: Starving, Writing and Imprisonment* (Boston: Harvard University Press, 1993).
32. Irigary, *Speculum. De L'autre Femme*, 224.
33. Ibid, 221.
34. Irigaray, "The Necessity for Sexuate Rights," 199.
35. See Luke Gibbons, *Transformations in Irish Culture*, for an extended discussion of *Anne Devlin* in this context.
36. Dorothy Macardle to de Valera, May 21, 1937, quoted in T.P. Coogan, *de Valera: Long fellow, Long shadow* (New York and London: Random House, 1993), 497.
37. Coogan, *de Valera*, 497.
38. Boland, *A Kind of Scar*; Edna Longley, *From Cathleen to Anorexia: The Breakdown of Irelands*, *Lip Pamphlet* (Dublin: Attic Press, 1990).

39. *Earthbound* (Worcester, MA: Harrigan, 1924), 92. Page references in text hereafter.
40. Mangan's original reads: "I could scale the blue air, / I could plough the high hills, / Oh, I could kneel all night in prayer / To heal your many ills!" Mangan's version fuses two previous readings of the poem, one by Hardiman, which emphasizes its status as national allegory, another a literal translation by Ferguson that reads it as an account of a priest's forbidden love for a woman. See Deane, *Field Day Anthology of Irish Writing*, vol. 2, 26–27.
41. Mangan, "Roisin Dhubh," in *Field Day Anthology of Irish Writing*, ed. Deane, vol. 2, 27.
42. Ibid.
43. W.B. Yeats, *The Rose*, in *Collected Poems*, ed. Augustine Martin (1893; repr., London: Vintage, 1990).
44. Gonne, 1895, in *The Gonne-Yeats Letters 1893–1938: Always Your Friend*, ed. Anna MacBride White and A. Norman Jeffares (London: Hutchinson, 1992).
45. "The Man and the Echo." He continues, "Did words of mine put too much strain / On that woman's reeling brain?" *Collected Poems*, 361.
46. See, for example. D.E.S. Maxwell's introduction to the play in *Field Day Anthology of Irish Writing*, vol. 2, 597.
47. Margaret Ward, *Unmanageable Revolutionaries: Women and Irish Nationalism*, rev. ed. (London: Pluto, 1995).
48. Senate Debates 1925: 245.
49. Senate Debates 1925: 245–46.
50. Dorothy Macardle, "Letter to Eamonn de Valera," in *The Field Day Anthology of Irish Writing, Volume 5: Women's Writing and Traditions*, ed. Bourke and others (1946; repr., Cork: Cork University Press, 2002).
51. *Fantastic Summer* (London: Peter Davies, 1946). Published in the US as *The Unforeseen* (New York: Doubleday).
52. *Uneasy Freehold* (London: Peter Davies, 1942). Published in the US as *The Uninvited* (New York: Doubleday, Doran, 1942). Page references in text.
53. Macardle, *The Irish Republic* (London: Victor Gollancz, 1937).
54. Macardle, *The Irish Republic*, 29.
55. Sigmund Freud, "The Uncanny," in *Standard Edition of the Complete Psychological Works*, vol. 17, trans. James Strachey (1919; repr., London: Hogarth, 1986), 340.
56. It is only at this point, where the myth of Mary's goodness is at its strongest in the story, that we learn from the priest that Roddy and Pamela are half-Irish like him. Macardle, *Uneasy Freehold*, 94.
57. My thanks to Maria Luddy for this information about the history of the site.
58. Judith Butler, *Antigone's Claim: Kinship between Life and Death* (New York: Columbia University Press, 2000), 40.
59. Fanning, *Racism and Social Change in the Republic of Ireland* (Manchester and New York: Manchester University Press, 2002), 1.
60. Critical reevaluation of O'Brien has proceeded apace in the last fifteen years with a number of significant publications by Eibhear Walshe. See particularly Eibhear Walshe, *Kate O'Brien: A Writing Life* (Dublin: Irish Academic Press, 2006); Walshe, ed., *Ordinary People Dancing: Essays on Kate O'Brien* (Cork: Cork University Press, 1993); Walshe, ed., *Sex, Nation and Dissent in Irish Writing* (Cork: Cork University Press, 1997).
61. See Emma Donoghue, "'Out of Order': Kate O'Brien's Lesbian Fictions," in *Ordinary People Dancing*, 36–58.

62. Not just of Irish existence. O'Brien's *Distinguished Villa; A Play in Three Acts* (London: Benn, 1926) presents lower-middle-class English society as equally stifling, with "refinement" and respectability performing similar repressive functions to Catholicism. The *Ante-Room*'s tripartite structure relates it to the earlier "play in three acts" and both end with a suicide.
63. O'Brien, *The Ante-Room* (1934; repr., Dublin: Arlen House, 1980).
64. O'Brien, *That Lady* (1946; repr., London: Virago, 1985).
65. Page references to *The Ante-Room* are given in text.
66. Julia Kristeva, "Stabat Mater," in *The Kristeva Reader*, ed. Toril Moi (Oxford: Blackwell, 1986), 161.
67. Hélène Cixous, "The Laugh of the Medusa," trans. Keith and Paula Kohn, *Signs* 1, no. 1 (1976): 882.
68. Jacques Lacan, *Écrits: A Selection*, trans. Alan Sheridan (New York: Norton, 1977), 287.
69. Michel Foucault, *The History of Sexuality, Volume 1: An Introduction* (New York: Pantheon, 1978), 8–9.
70. I am using this term in the Lacanian sense, while acknowledging the limitations of such an approach both in itself and in reading this particular novel.
71. Julia Kristeva, *Powers of Horror* (New York and Surrey: Columbia University Press, 1982), 4.
72. O'Brien, *Mary Lavelle* (1936; repr., London: Virago, 1984).
73. Hélène Cixous, "Castration or Decapitation," trans. Annette Kuhn, *Signs* 7, no. 1 (1981): 41–55.
74. Clíona Murphy, *The Women's Suffrage Movement and Irish Society in the Early Twentieth Century* (Philadelphia: Temple University Press, 1989), 200.
75. O'Brien, *That Lady*.
76. Murphy, *The Women's Suffrage Movement*, 57.
77. Page references in text.
78. Aintzane Legarreta Mentxaka, "Kate O'Brien's *Mary Lavelle*: Sex, Art, Politics, and the Fiction of Identity" (PhD dissertation, University College Dublin, 2007).
79. Kiberd, *Inventing Ireland* (London: Verso, 1995), 405.
80. My thanks to O'Brien's friend and biographer, Lorna Reynolds, for confirming that the author was interested in George Santayana's work on the aesthetics of the sublime.
81. It was only in her last novel, *As Music and Splendour* (London: Heinemann, 1958) that O'Brien dealt with a fulfilled lesbian relationship, again associating it with the aesthetic, in this case the singing and operatic training of the lovers.
82. For a very different reading of this text and this scene, see Anne Fogarty, "'The Business of Attachment': Romance and Desire in the Novels of Kate O'Brien," in *Ordinary People Dancing*, 101–19.
83. Kristeva, "Word Dialogue and Novel," in *The Kristeva Reader*, ed. Toril Moi (Oxford: Blackwell, 1986), 36.
84. See David Lloyd, *Anomalous States: Irish Writing and the Post-Colonial Moment* (Dublin: Lilliput, 1993), for an extremely relevant exposition of the adulterative strategies of Joyce's fiction.
85. Homi K. Bhabha, "DissemiNation: Time, Narrative, and the Margins of the Modern Nation," in *Nation and Narration*, ed. Homi K. Bhabha, 99–301 (London: Routledge, 1990).
86. Kristeva, "Word Dialogue and Novel," 36.
87. Kristeva, "Women's Time," 193–94.

88. Irigaray, *Speculum*, 221.
89. Kristeva, *Nations without Nationalism*, trans. Leon S. Roudiez (New York: Columbia University Press, 1993), 35.

NOTES TO CHAPTER 4

1. Sandra Siegel, "Literature and Degeneration: The Representation of Decadence," in *Degeneration: The Dark Side of Progress*, ed. J. Edward Chamberlin and Sander L. Gilman, 209 (New York and Guildford: Columbia University Press, 1985).
2. Katherine Cecil Thurston, *Max* (London: Hutchinson, 1910), 324–25.
3. Elaine Showalter, *Daughters of Decadence* (London: Virago, 1993), xi.
4. Teresa Mangum, "Style Wars of the 1890s: The New Woman and the Decadent," in *Transforming Genres: New Approaches to British Fiction of the 1890s*, ed. Nikki Lee Menos and Meri-Jane Rochelson (Basingstoke: Macmillan, 1994), 55.
5. Karl Beckson, *London in the 1890s: A Cultural History* (New York and London: W.W. Norton, 1992), 139.
6. Emily Lawless, "A Note on the Ethics of Literary Forgery," *Nineteenth Century* (1897): 90–91.
7. Synge, John Millington. *Collected Works. Volume II. Prose*, ed. Alan Price. London: Oxford Univ. Press, 1966, 102–3, n. 1.
8. See Yeats' commentary on his list of 30 best books, *Daily Express* (27 Feb. 1895); also 'Contemporary Irish Writers', *The Bookman* (Aug. 1895); review of *Hurrish* in *New York Times* (21 March 1886).
9. Ibid., 92.
10. Emily Lawless, *Maria Edgeworth* (London: Macmillan, 1904), 38.
11. Page references in text.
12. William Greenslade, *Degeneration, Culture and the Novel, 1880–1940* (Cambridge: Cambridge University Press, 1994), 38.
13. Anne McClintock, *Imperial Leather: Race, Gender and Sexuality in the Colonial Context* (London and New York: Routledge, 1995), 53.
14. Ibid., 53.
15. Ibid., 56.
16. Ibid.
17. Ibid., 52.
18. Emily Lawless, *Maelcho* (London: Metheun, 1895), 185.
19. Ibid., 152–53.
20. Colm Tóibín, ed., *Penguin Book of Irish Fiction* (Harmondsworth: Penguin, 2000).
21. Brown, *Ireland in Fiction: A Guide to Irish Novels, Tales, Romances and Folklore* (Dublin and London, Maunsel, 1916; Dublin, Irish Academic Press, 1969).
22. *The Times*, p. 3, col. 5, April 8, 1910.
23. Stephen Jay Gould, *Time's Arrow, Time's Cycle: Myth and Metaphor in the Discovery of Geological Time* (Boston: Harvard University Press, 1987).
24. Frederick Jameson, "Modernism and Imperialism," in *Nationalism, Colonialism and Literature, Field Day Pamphlet No.14* (Derry: Field Day, 1988), 23.
25. Gould, *Time's Arrow*, 22.
26. In a letter of October 14, 1921, to his aunt Josephine, Joyce described the then current state of the country as a "slaughterhouse." His novel negates, through painstaking recreation of 1904 Dublin, the destruction wrought

upon the city by 1922. Joyce's Dublin is mythic, but this can be read as an attempt to revive the marginal and rapidly disintegrating city, not a denial of historical change.

27. Homi K. Bhabha, "DissemiNation: Time, Narrative, and the Margins of the Modern Nation," in *Nation and Narration*, ed. Homi K. Bhabha, 291–322 (London: Routledge, 1990).

28. David Lloyd, *Anomalous States: Irish Writing and the Post-Colonial Moment* (Dublin: Lilliput, 1993), 109.

29. Ibid., 107.

30. Ibid., 109.

31. Ibid.

32. Julia Kristeva, *Strangers to Ourselves*, trans. Leon S. Roudiez (Hemel Hempstead: Harvester Wheatsheaf, 1991), 191.

33. Ibid., 192.

34. Ibid., 195.

35. Ibid., 192.

36. Bhabha, "DissemiNation," 293.

37. Ibid., 315.

38. Ibid. Bhabha is elaborating Walter Benjamin's concept of the "foreignness of languages for "a theory of cultural difference."

39. The folklorist Patricia Lysaght has noted that this saying is recorded in the National Folklore Archive at University College Dublin, which indicates it was a folk saying in popular usage.

40. Declan Kiberd, *Inventing Ireland: The Literature of the Modern Nation* (London: Verso, 1996), 337.

41. Alice Jardine, *Gynesis: Configurations of Woman and Modernity* (Ithaca, NY, and London: Cornell University Press, 1985). Emer Nolan has convincingly applied this critique of modernism's deployment of the feminine to Joyce's work in *James Joyce and Nationalism* (London: Routledge, 1995), 164.

42. Sandra Gilbert and Susan Gubar, *The Madwoman in the Attic: The Woman Writer and the Nineteenth Century Literary Imagination* (New Haven, CT: Yale University Press, 1979), 136.

43. See Gerardine Meaney, *(Un)Like Subjects: Women, Theory, Fiction* (London: Routledge, 1993), for a discussion of the relation between Bloom's masturbatory fantasy and Joyce's authorial distance from Gerty.

44. Carter, *Wise Children* (London: Chatto and Windus, 1991).

45. Joyce, *A Portrait of the Artist as a Young Man* (1916; repr., London: Granada Panther, 1977), 151–52.

46. See Nolan, *James Joyce and Nationalism*, 163–81, for a critique of this tendency in feminist readings of Joyce.

47. Kiberd, *Inventing Ireland*, 355.

48. Julia Kristeva, *The Revolution in Poetic Language*, trans. M. Waller (New York: Columbia University Press, 1984); first published as *La Révolution du langage poétique* (Paris: Editions du Seuil, 1974).

49. Seamus Deane, *Strange Country: Modernity and Nationhood in Irish Writing since 1790* (Oxford: Clarendon Press, 1997), 97.

50. Lloyd, *Anomalous States*, 109.

51. Stanislaus Joyce, letter to James Joyce, August 7, 1924; *Letters of James Joyce*, vol. *III*, ed. Richard Ellmann (London: Faber and Faber, 1966), 102.

52. Seamus Deane, *A Short History of Anglo-Irish Literature* (London: Hutchinson, 1986).

53. *Ulysses*, 193.

54. There is warm reference in *Ulysses* to the Gaelic poet, Raftery, whose work became available again through Hyde's translations.

55. James Joyce, *Finnegans Wake* (London: Faber and Faber, 1939), 628.
56. Ibid., 4.
57. Jacob, *The Troubled House* (Dublin: Browne and Nolan, 1938).
58. O'Brien, *As Music and Splendour* (London: Heinemann, 1958).
59. Jacques Derrida, *Of Grammatology*, trans. Gayatri Spivak (New York: The Johns Hopkins University Press, 1976), 200.
60. See Moynagh Sullivan, "The Woman Poet and the Matter of Representation in Modern and Postmodern Poetics" (PhD thesis, University College Dublin, 2001) for an exploration of these themes in poetry.
61. For example, diary entries describe visits from Jack Yeats and visits to Sarah Purser: see MS Diaries, November 1923–June 1924, pp. 3–5: Jacob Papers, National Library of Ireland, Dublin, MS 32,582 (45).
62. Jacob, *The Troubled House*, 60; also in Bourke and others, eds., *The Field Day Anthology of Irish Writing, Volume 5: Women's Writing and Traditions* (Cork: Cork University Press, 2002), 1008.
63. Jacob, *The Troubled House*, 122; also in Bourke and others, *The Field Day Anthology*, 1010–11.
64. Jacob Papers, National Library of Ireland, Dublin, MS 33,117 (the MS of *Nix and Theo* is unpaginated).
65. MS Diaries, March 3, 1924, p. 86: Jacob Papers, National Library of Ireland, Dublin, MS 32, 582 (45).
66. The diaries indicate that Jacob went to Rathdrum with her friend Helen Chevenix in May 1924, where they attended a dance in a hotel very like the one described in *Nix and Theo*. The area and the hotel were obviously very familiar to Jacob by 1924.
67. Stephen Maddison, "All about Woman: Pedro Almodóvar and the Heterosocial Dynamic," *Textual Practice* 14, no. 2 (Summer 2002): 282.
68. Sheehy-Skeffington Papers, National Library of Ireland, Dublin, MS 24, 140.
69. The lecture was given by Seamus Fenton, a retired deputy chief inspector of schools, and was published as a pamphlet by the *Leinster Leader* newspaper in response to "many requests of readers."
70. There is some historical evidence that the "always" at least was inaccurate. Possibly under pressure from her mentor, Margaret Oliphant, Lawless appears to have signed a declaration opposing women's suffrage in her youth; see "An Appeal against Women's Suffrage," *Nineteenth Century* (June 1889).
71. *Dublin Evening Mail*, p. 3, November 26, 1958.
72. Sheehy-Skeffington Papers, National Library of Ireland, Dublin, MS 24, 140.
73. This incident may have been based on one in which the rooms Dorothy Macardle rented from Maud Gonne were raided and her papers destroyed.
74. O'Brien, *As Music and Splendour*, 189.
75. Ibid.
76. Ibid., 113.
77. Katherine O'Donnell examines the identification of Mary Lavelle's beauty with classical Greek sculpture to argue for a new understanding of that novel: "'But Greek . . . Usually Knows Greek': Recognizing Queer Sexuality in Kate O'Brien's *Mary Lavelle*" (paper presented at the Queer Studies/Irish Studies Seminar, University College Dublin, February 2002).
78. Marjorie Garber, *Vice Versa* (New York: Simon and Schuster, 1995), 323.
79. Ibid.
80. Ovid, *Metamorphoses*, trans. Mary M. Innes (Harmondsworth: Penguin, 1955), 227.
81. Ibid., 246–47.

82. The novel opens in 1886.
83. O'Brien, *As Music and Splendour*, 24.
84. Alfred Einstein, *Gluck*, trans. Eric Blom (London: Dent, 1936). Einstein's book *Gluck*, in "The Master Musicians" series, was reprinted regularly until the early 1960s.
85. O'Brien, *As Music and Splendour*, 299.
86. Ibid., 190.
87. Ibid., 211.
88. Ibid., 212.
89. Ibid., 334.
90. Ibid., 191.
91. Ibid.
92. Ibid., 134.
93. Ibid., 135.
94. Ibid., 320.
95. Ibid., 312.
96. Ibid., 320.
97. Ibid., 312.
98. Ibid., 157.
99. Ibid.
100. Ibid., 341.
101. Ibid.
102. Ibid., 346.
103. John McGahern, lecture, University College Dublin, February 17, 1999, quoted in Kiberd, *Irish Classics* (London, Granta, 2000), 574.
104. O'Brien, *As Music and Splendour*, 155.
105. Ibid., 139.
106. O'Brien, *Farewell Spain* (1937; repr., London: Virago, 1985), 15; also in Bourke and others, *The Field Day Anthology*, 1084.
107. Katherine Arnold Price, "Curithir and Liadain—II," *The Dubliner* 2, no. 1 (Spring 1963).
108. O'Brien, *As Music and Splendour*, 343.
109. Ibid., 343.
110. Ibid., 342. All of the poems identified, with the exception of Shelley's, are included in Arthur Quiller-Couch, *Oxford Book of English Verse 1250–1918* (Oxford: Oxford University Press, 1919).
111. O'Brien, *As Music and Splendour*, 342.
112. Ibid.
113. Ibid., 343.
114. *The Essence of Opera*, ed. by Ulrich Weisstein. (nNew York: W. W. Norton, 1969), 106.
115. Adele M. Dalsimer, *Kate O'Brien: A Critical Study* (Dublin: Gill and Macmillan, 1990); Lorna Reynolds, *Kate O'Brien: A Literary Portrait* (Gerrards Cross: Smythe, 1987); and Eibhear Walshe, *Ordinary People Dancing: Essays on Kate O'Brien* (Cork: Cork University Press, 1993).

NOTES TO CHAPTER 5

1. J.M. Coetzee, *Elizabeth Costello* (London: Secker and Warburg, 2003), 1.
2. Ibid., 8.
3. Ibid., 9.
4. Ibid.

5. Ibid., 11.

6. Anne Enright, *The Gathering* (London: Cape, 2007).

7. James Joyce, *Dubliners* (1914; repr., London: Granada, 1977).

8. *Sunday Times*, October 21, 2007.

9. Anne Enright, *The Pleasure of Eliza Lynch* (London: Cape, 2002).

10. Enright, *The Gathering*, 1.

11. Philip Hensher, "No One Has to Pretend to Like James Joyce," *The Independent*, February 12, 2004.

12. Ibid.

13. Dervila Layden, "Discovering and Uncovering Genre in Irish Cinema," in *Genre and Cinema: Ireland and Transnationalism*, ed. Brian McElroy (London and New York: Routledge, 2007).

14. Sean O'Reilly, *The Swing of Things* (London: Faber and Faber, 2005).

15. O'Reilly, *The Swing of Things*, 5. Further page references in text.

16. Quoted in Smith, *The Guardian*, p. 44, Review, May 15, 2004.

17. It is interesting that as O'Reilly more and more self-consciously engages with Joyce's work that he also (re)moves his work to the edge of that marketplace. His most recent novel, *Watermark*, is an attempt at a twenty-first-century Penelope, published with independent small Irish publisher, The Stinging Fly.

18. MS Cornell, published in Beckson and Munro, *Arthur Symons: Selected Letters, 1880–1935* (Iowa City: University of Iowa Press, 1989), 235.

19. Howes, "Tradition, Gender, and Migration in 'The Dead,' or How Many People Has Gretta Conroy Killed?" *Yale Journal of Criticism* 15, no. 1 (2002): 149.

20. Luke Gibbons, "'The Cracked Looking Glass' of Cinema: James Joyce, John Huston, and the Memory of 'The Dead,'" *Yale Journal of Criticism* 15, no. 1 (2002): 127–48.

21. Ibid., 131.

22. Ibid., 145.

23. Kevin Whelan, "The Memories of 'The Dead,'" *Yale Journal of Criticism* 15, no. 1 (2002): 67.

24. Ibid., 69.

25. Ibid., 65.

26. Ibid.

27. Gibbons, "'The Cracked Looking Glass,'" 145.

28. Howes, "Tradition, Gender, and Migration," 149.

29. Whelan, "The Memories of 'The Dead,'" 65.

30. Gibbons, "'The Cracked Looking Glass,'" 146. "In his search for a cinematic technique that would do justice to the task of filming *Ulysses*, Eisenstein wrote of the need for polyphonic images, envisaging a use of the camera that would visualize 'the syntax of inner speech as distinct from outer speech. The quivering inner words that correspond with the visual images."

31. Whelan, "The Memories of 'The Dead,'" 87.

32. Thomson's *Scottish Airs*, 1798, j8. "Written for this work by Robert Burns. Air, *Lord Gregory*. Among the Dalhousie MS in Brechin Castle. The tragic ballad of *Lord Gregory*, containing about sixty stanzas, better known as *Fair Annie of Lochryan*, is the foundation of Burns's verses. The earliest printed fragment is in Herd's *Scottish Songs*, 1776, i. 149, entitled *The Bonny Lass O' Lochryan*. Two double stanzas, with the tune, were engraved in the *Scots Musical Museum*, 1787, No. 5. This was one of the few historical ballads that made an Impression on Burns. Thomson had informed him that Dr. Wolcot had written a song on the subject, and he replied on January 26, 1793, by enclosing a copy of the verses in the text.

A few weeks before his death, Burns touched up the song, and sent a copy to his friend Alex Cunningham. The tune is not in print before the *Scots Musical Museum*, 1787. According to Stenhouse, it is an old Gallwegian melody. The music is also in Urbani's *Scots Songs*, 1792, 1; and Dale's *Scotch Songs*, 1794."

33. Scott notes, "This edition of the ballad obtained is composed of verses selected from three MS. copies, and two from recitation. Two of the copies are in Herd's MSS.; the third in that of Mrs Brown of Falkland. A fragment of the original song, which is sometimes denominated *Lord Gregory*, or *Love Gregory*, was published in Mr Herd's Collection, 1774, and, still more fully, in that of Laurie and Symington, 1792. The story has been celebrated both by Burns and Dr Wolcott."

34. Stephanie Kuduk Weiner, "The Aesthetes' John Clare: Arthur Symons, Norman Gale and Avant-Garde Poetics," *English Literature in Transition 1880–1920* (Fall 2008).

35. Ellmann, *James Joyce*. 115. "Like everyone else in 1900, Joyce was eager to find a style, and turned for this, perhaps in part as a result of Arthur Symon's *The Symbolist Movement in Literature* published the year before, to the French" (Ellmann, 79).

36. Ibid., 140.

37. Ibid., 155.

38. Ibid., 171.

39. Ibid., 185.

40. Ibid., 183.

41. Beckson and Munro, Arthur Symons, 181–83.

42. Ellmann, *James Joyce*. 270.

43. Ibid., 271.

44. Ibid., 413. Symons was one of the 167 signatories to the protest against a US pirate copy of *Ulysses* in 1927 (Ellmann, 599).

45. David Hayman, "Joyce et Mallarme," *Paris* 1 (1956): 27–34; James S. Atherton, *The Books at the Wake* (New York: Viking 1960), 49; Beckson and Munro, *Arthur Symons*.

46. Ellmann recounts that it was Rhoda who suggested to Joyce that he should get *Pomes Penyeach* published.

47. Sunday, May 31, 1925, Paris, MS Munro, in Beckson and Munro, *Arthur Symons*, 253.

48. Whelan 2002, 83

49. David C. Fowler, "An Accused Queen in 'The Lass of Roch Royal' (Child 76)," *Journal of American Folklore* 71, no. 282 (October–December 1958): 553.

50. Ibid., 558.

51. Julie Henigan, "'The Old Irish Tonality': Folksong as Emotional Catalyst in 'The Dead,'" *New Hibernia Review* 11, no. 4 (2007): 145.

52. Ibid., 142.

53. Ibid., 146.

54. Ibid., 143.

55. James Joyce, *Occasional, Critical, and Political Writing*, ed. Kevin Barry (Oxford: Oxford University Press, 2008), 165.

56. *Folk Roots, New Routes*, Shirley Collins, Davy Graham, Decca LP 4652 (LP, UK, 1964); Righteous Records GDC001 (LP, UK, 1980); Topic Records TSCD819 (CD, UK, 1999); Fledg'ling Records FLED 3052 (CD, UK, July 25, 2005).

57. Cronin's "Lord Gregory" is on *The Folk Songs of Britain*, vol. 4., *The Child Ballads 1* (2–95). Original issue Caedmon (US, 1961).

58. ee, for example, http://www.traditionalmusic.co.uk/folk-song-lyrics/Lord_ Gregory.htm.
59. On *The Very Best of the Original Irish legendary Folk Festivals*, vol. 1.
60. On *Hybrid Vigor* (Little Blue Men Records).
61. McKeown then sings the first verse again. Her version is a little over three minutes long, Patterson's just one minute and twenty-three seconds.
62. James Smith, *Ireland's Magdalen Laundries and the Nation's Architecture of Containment* (Notre Dame, IN: Notre Dame University Press, 2007).
63. See http://www.mustard.org.uk/articles/cronin.htm, Article MT062, 25.8.00. McCormick is reviewing *The Songs of Elizabeth Cronin, Irish Traditional Singer: The Complete Song Collection*. Dáibhí Ó Cróinín, editor, Four Courts Press, Dublin, 2000.
64. Whelan, "The Memories of 'The Dead,'" 69.
65. Henigan, "'The Old Irish Tonality,'" 147.
66. Gibbons, "'The Cracked Looking Glass,'" 140.
67. Ibid., 133.
68. Ibid.
69. Whelan, "The Memories of 'The Dead,'" 69.
70. Ibid., 82.
71. Ellmann, *Selected Letters of James Joyce*, 240; Ellmann, *Joyce*, 295.
72. Howes, "Tradition, Gender, and Migration," 149.
73. "Fluid Boarders and Naughty Girls: Music, Domesticity, and Nation in Joyce's Boarding Houses," *James Joyce Quarterly* 44, no. 2 (Winter 2007): 263–89.
74. Howes, "Tradition, Gender, and Migration."
75. Joyce, *Dubliners*, 205. Page references in text.
76. Slavoj Žižek, *The Plague of Fantasies* (London: Verso, 1997), 292.
77. Ibid., 94.
78. Ibid.
79. Gibbons, "'The Cracked Looking Glass,'" 146.
80. Howes, "Tradition, Gender, and Migration," 151.
81. Ibid.
82. Žižek, *The Plague of Fantasies*, 89, 88.
83. Ibid., 95.
84. Ibid., 98.
85. Ibid.
86. Ibid., 103.
87. Ibid., 104.
88. Ibid., 115.
89. Ibid., 116.
90. Ibid., 118–19.
91. Ibid., 118.
92. Ibid., 199.
93. In *Antigone's Claim: Kinship Between Life And Death* (New York: Columbia University Press, 2000), Butler challenges Lacan's reading of the story of Antigone. Lacan interprets Antigone in terms of "the pure and simple desire of death as such"; *The Seminar of Jacques Lacan, Book 7: Ethics of Psychoanalysis, 1959–60*, ed. Jacques Alain Miller (London: Routledge, 1992), 282. Butler counters that "this position outside life as we know it is not necessarily a position outside life as it must be" (55).
94. Žižek, *The Plague of Fantasies*, 95.
95. Ibid.
96. Butler, *Antigone's Claim*, 50.
97. Laura Mulvey, *Fetishism and Curiosity* (Bloomington, Indiana University Press, 1996), 130.

98. Gibbons, "'The Cracked Looking Glass,'" 120.
99. Mulvey, *Fetishism and Curiosity*, 120.
100. Žižek, *The Plague of Fantasies*, 118.
101. Mulvey, *Fetishism and Curiosity*, 134.
102. Teshome H. Gabriel, '*Xala*: A cinema of wax and gold', *Jump Cut*, no. 27, July 1982, pp. 31–33.
103. Mulvey, *Fetishism and Curiosity*, 136.
104. Hugh Macdiarmid, *Selected Poems* (1955; repr., Manchester: Carcanet, 2002), 278.
105. Ibid., 294.
106. Ibid., 295.
107. Ibid.
108. Ibid., 296; Macdiarmid's italics. The relationship between the utopian and the uterine here is a topic for another book. For its context in modernist aesthetics, see Sullivan, "The Woman Poet and the Matter of Representation in Modern and Postmodern Poetics" (PhD thesis, University College Dublin, 2001).
109. See guardian.co.uk, Sunday, June 5, 2005, and http://www.guardian.co.uk/film/2005/jun/05/features for the interviews with Sembene and Coulibaly.
110. Izevbekhai admitted in early 2009 that she had forged papers relating to the death of her eldest daughter as a result of FGM, but refuted claims this daughter never existed.
111. Ronit Lentin, "Pregnant Silence: (En)Gendering Ireland's Asylum Space," *Patterns of Prejudice* 37, no. 3 (2003): 301–22.
112. The European Court of Justice ruled in July 2008, for example, that Ireland's requirement that non-EU spouses of EU citizens have lived in another EU member state before obtaining residency in Ireland was incompatible with the European Directive on the free movement of European citizens.

NOTES TO CHAPTER 6

1. Bourke and others, eds., *The Field Day Anthology of Irish Writing, Volume 5: Women's Writing and Traditions* (Cork: Cork University Press, 2002), 1100.
2. Martin McLoone, *Irish Film: The Emergence of a Contemporary Cinema* (London: BFI, 2000); Elizabeth Cullingford, *Ireland's Others: Gender and Ethnicity in Irish Literature and Popular Culture* (Cork: Cork University Press, 2001); Cheryl Herr, *The Field, Ireland into Film* (Cork: Cork University Press, 2002).
3. Cullingford, *Ireland's Others*, 231. Cullingford lists five further texts dealing with this motif: Yeats's poem "Cuchulainn's Fight with the Waves," his play *On Baile's Strand* and his dance drama *Fighting the Waves*; Bernard McLaverty's novel *Lamb*; and Jim Sheridan's film *The Field*.
4. W.B. Yeats, *On Baile's Strand*, in *Field Day Anthology of Irish Literature*, ed. Seamus Deane, 602–13 (Derry: Field Day, 2000); Gregory, *Cuchulainn of Muirthemne* (London: John Murray, 1902).
5. *Irish Classics*.
6. Herr, *The Field*, 63.
7. *Twentieth-Century Irish Drama: Mirror Up To Nation* (Manchester and New York: Manchester University Press, 1997), 15.
8. Cullingford, *Ireland's Others*, 232.
9. Also appears as Connla.
10. Gregory, *Cuchulainn*, 315.

11. Ibid., 316.
12. In Gregory's text, Aoife is motivated by sexual jealousy, when she hears of Cuchulainn's marriage to Emer shortly after he has left her in her own kingdom in Scotland. In Yeats's version, Emer doesn't appear and Aoife seems to be motivated by a desire for revenge for defeat in battle by Cuchulainn. It is only in *The Death of Cuchulainn* (1939) that Aoife, acknowledged as having the right to kill Cuchulainn, is presented as a deserted lover.
13. Yeats, *On Baile's Strand*, 606.
14. Ibid.
15. Ibid., 603.
16. Ibid., 612.
17. Cullingford, *Ireland's Others*, 231.
18. Gregory, *Cuchulainn*, 318–19.
19. Ibid., 319.
20. Kiberd, *Irish Classics*, 408.
21. Yeats, *On Baile's Strand*, 612.
22. Gregory, *Cuchulainn*, 319.
23. Ibid., 318–19.
24. *Inventing Ireland* (London: Cape, 1995), 186.
25. Kiberd, *Irish Classics*, 413.
26. *Celtic Revivals: Essays in Irish Literature, 1880–1980* (London and Boston: Faber and Faber, 1985), 53.
27. Seamus Deane, *Strange Country: Modernity and Nationhood in Irish Writing Since 1790* (Oxford: Clarendon Press, 1997), 143.
28. Kiberd, *Inventing Ireland*, 187.
29. Deane, *Strange Country*, 143.
30. Finola Kennedy, *From Cottage to Creche: Family Change in Ireland* (Dublin: Institute of Public Administration, 2001), 137.
31. C.J. Barrett, "The Dependent Child," *Studies* 44 (1955): 419–28.
32. Kennedy, *From Cottage to Creche*, 138.
33. Deane, *Strange Country*, 143.
34. J.M. Synge, *The Playboy of the Western World and Other Plays* (Oxford: Oxford University Press, [1907] 1995, 132.
35. *The King of Spain's Daughter and Other One Act Plays* (Dublin: New Frontiers Press, 1946), 25–35.
36. Ibid., 31.
37. Ibid., 30.
38. Ibid., 31.
39. Ibid., 33.
40. Ibid., 35.
41. While films were made in Ireland from the silent era onward, the concerns of contemporary filmmakers such as Sheridan and Jordan have been at the forefront of both critical definitions and commercial marketing of Irish film, with new and younger filmmakers often defining themselves against their work.
42. Herr, *The Field*, 55.
43. The Radiators' Phillip Chevron was a member of The Pogues at the time.
44. The case was a major impetus to gay rights activism in Ireland and was the subject of Aodhan Madden's play, *Sea Urchins* (Project Theatre, Tivoli Theatre, Irish National Tour, 1988).
45. McLoone, *Irish Film*, 174.
46. Ibid.
47. See http://homepage.eircom.net/~obrienh/1bh.htm (accessed December 15 2009).
48. *Screening Ireland: Film and Television Representation* (Manchester: Manchester University Press, 2000), 273.

49. Ibid.
50. I am borrowing this term from Stephen Maddison, "All about Woman: Pedro Almodóvar and the Heterosocial Dynamic," *Textual Practice* 14, no. 2 (Summer 2000): 265–84; Maddison, *Fags, Hags and Queer Sisters* (New York: St. Martin's Press, 2000).

NOTES TO CHAPTER 7

1. Steven Cohan and Ina Rae Hark, eds., *Screening the Male: Masculinities in Hollywood Cinema* (London and New York: Routledge, 1993), 194–213.
2. Yvonne Tasker, *Spectacular Bodies: Gender, Genre and the Action Cinema* (London and New York: Routledge, 1993).
3. McLoone, *Irish Film: The Emergence of a Contemporary Cinema* (London: BFI, 2000), 65–69.
4. Paula J. Massood, "City Spaces and City Times: Bakhtin's Chronotope and Recent African-American Film," in *Screening the City*, ed. Mark Shiel and Tony Fitzmaurice (London and New York: Verso, 2003).
5. Vivian Sobchack, "Lounge Time: Postwar Crises and the Chronotope of *Film Noir*," in *Refiguring American Film Genres: Theory and History*, ed. Nick Browne, 129–70 (Berkeley: University of California Press, 1998).
6. Steve Neale, "Masculinity as Spectacle," *Screen* 24, no. 6 (1983); reprinted in Cohan and Hark, *Screening the Male*, 9–20.
7. Laura Mulvey, "Visual Pleasure and Narrative Cinema," *Screen* 16, no. 3 (1975): 6–18; "Afterthoughts . . . Inspired by *Duel in the Sun*," *Framework* 15–17 (1981): 12–15.
8. Eva Kosofsky Sedgewick, *Between Men: English Literature and Male Homosocial Desire* (New York: Columbia University Press, 1985).
9. Cohan and Hark, *Screening the Male*.
10. Tasker in Cohan and Hark, *Screening the Male*, 132.
11. Ibid., 91–108.
12. Fuchs in Cohan and Hark, *Screening the Male*, 194–212.
13. Tasker in Cohan and Hark, *Screening the Male*, 33.
14. Directed by David Caffrey (1998, BBC/Winchester/Scala, GB/France). The script was adapted by Colin Bateman from his novel of the same name.
15. Stephen D. Arata, "The Occidental Tourist: *Dracula* and the Anxiety of Reverse Colonisation," *Victorian Studies* 33, no. 4 (Summer 1990): 621–45.
16. Diane Negra, *Off-White Hollywood: American Culture and Ethnic Female Stardom* (London and New York: Routledge, 2001), 45.
17. William Clinton, "Clinton Address to Democratic National Convention," United Center, Chicago, August 26, 1996, usinfo.state.gov/journals/itps/1096/ijpe/ clinI.htm.
18. William Clinton, "Remarks by President Clinton in Address to the 51st General Assembly of the United Nations," United Nations, New York, September 24, 1996, http://www.jfklibrary.org/clinton_un_address.html.

NOTES TO CHAPTER 8

1. It debuted to almost 4.1 million viewers in the US, among the highest figures for any new series in 2004 on basic cable and, according to the television

station, FX, its fourth season viewership was still a healthy average of 2.8 million total viewers.
2. Slavoj Žižek, '*Welcome to the Desert of the Real*' (London: Verso, 2002).
3. Fred Botting, *Gothic* (London and New York: Routledge, 1996).
4. See Gerardine Meaney, "Dead, White, Male: Irishness in *Angel* and *Buffy the Vampire Slayer*," in *The Irish in Us*, ed. Diane Negra (Durham NC: Duke University Press, 2006) for another example of this.
5. *Rescue me* (Season 1, Episode 1, "Guts").

NOTES TO CHAPTER 9

1. Anthony Trollope, *Phineas Finn: The Irish Member* (1869; repr., Oxford: Oxford World Classics, 1982), 129.
2. Joseph Valente, *Dracula's Crypt: Bram Stoker, Irishness, and the Question of Blood* (Champaign: University of Illinois Press, 2001).
3. Franco Moretti, "The Dialectic of Fear," in *The Horror Reader*, ed. Ken Gelder (London and New York: Routledge, 2000), 156.
4. Joan Copjec, "Vampires, Breastfeeding and Anxiety" in *The Horror Reader*, 59.
5. Ibid.
6. Howard Brenton, *The Romans in Britain*, in *Brenton Plays: 2* (London: Methuen, 1990).
7. Joseph Conrad, *Heart of Darkness* (1899; repr., Harmondsworth: Penguin, 1995), 20.
8. Mark Lawson, *The Guardian*, October 28, 2005.
9. Cullingford, *Ireland's Others*:
10. Brenton, *Romans*, ix.
11. Ibid., part 1, scene 7, 56.
12. Ibid.
13. Stephen D. Arata, "The Occidental Tourist: Dracula and the Anxiety of Reverse Colonisation," *Victorian Studies* 33, no. 4 (Summer 1990).
14. Howard Brenton, "Look Back in Anger," *The Guardian*, January 28, 2006.

NOTES TO THE CONCLUSION

1. See Diane Negra, ed., *The Irish in Us* (Durham, NC: Duke University Press, 2006).
2. Richard Dyer, *White* (London and New York: Routledge, 1997), 3.
3. John Boland, "RTE Comedy? You're Having a Laugh ... " January 10, 2009, http://www.independent.ie/entertainment/tv-radio/rte-comedy-youre-having-a-laugh-1597863.html.
4. In Balzano, Mulhall and Sullivan, eds., *Irish Postmodernisms and Popular Culture* (London: Palgrave Macmillan, 2007).
5. Eilis Ni Dhuibhne, *Fox, Swallow, Scarecrow* (Belfast: Blackstaff Press, 2007), 6.
6. Ibid., 349.
7. Ibid., 354.
8. 'Dissemination: Time, Narrative and the Margins of the Modern Nation' in *Nation and Narration* (London: Routledge, 1990), 307.

Bibliography

25th Hour, Directed by Spike Lee. US: Gamut, 2003

55 Degrees North. Created by Timothy Prager. UK: Zenith North, 2004–5.

Age of Innocence, The. Directed by Martin Scorsese. US: Cappa Productions, 1993.

All about My Mother. Directed by Pedro Almodóvar. Spain and France: Pathé, 1999.

"An Appeal against Women's Suffrage." *Nineteenth Century* (1889).

Anderson, Benedict. *Imagined Communities: Reflections on the Origin and Spread of Nationalism*. London: Verso, 1983.

Anderson, Michael, and Donald J. Morse. "High Fertility, High Emigration, Low Nuptiality: Adjustment Processes in Scotland's Demographic Experience, 1861–1914, Pt. 1." *Population Studies* 47, no. 1 (1993): 5–25.

———. "High Fertility, High Emigration, Low Nuptiality: Adjustment Processes in Scotland's Demographic Experience, 1861–1914, Pt. 2." *Population Studies* 47, no. 2 (1993): 319–43.

Andrew, Dudley. "The Theater of Irish Cinema." *Yale Journal of Criticism* 15, no. 1 (2002): 23–58.

Arata, Stephen D. "The Occidental Tourist: Dracula and the Anxiety of Reverse Colonisation." *Victorian Studies* 33, no. 4 (Summer 1990): 621–45.

Arlington Road. Directed by Mark Pellingham. US: Sony/Screen Gems/Lakeshore Entertainment, 1999.

Arnold Price, Katherine. "Curithir and Liadain—Ii." *The Dubliner* 2, no. 1 (Spring 1963); reprinted in Bourke and others. *The Field Day Anthology of Irish Writing, Volume 5: Women's Writing and Traditions*. Cork, Cork University Press, 2002, 1026.

Atherton, James S. *The Books at the Wake*. New York: Viking, 1960.

Bahri, Deepika. "Telling Tales: Women and the Trauma of Partition in Sidhwa's Cracking India." *Interventions: International Journal of Postcolonial Studies* 1, no. 2 (1999): 219.

Balzano, Wanda, Anne Mulhall and Moynagh Sullivan, eds. *Irish Postmodernisms and Popular Culture*. London: Palgrave Macmillan, 2007.

Barrett, C.J. "The Dependent Child." *Studies* 44 (1955): 419–28.

Barton, Ruth. "Feisty Colleens and Faithful Sons: Gender in Irish Cinema." *Cineaste* 24, nos. 2–3 (1999): 44.

Beckson, Karl. *London in the 1890s: A Cultural History*. New York and London: W.W. Norton, 1992.

Beckson, Karl, and John M. Munro. *Arthur Symons: Selected Letters, 1880–1935*. Iowa City: University of Iowa Press, 1989.

Bhabha, Homi K. "DissemiNation: Time, Narrative, and the Margins of the Modern Nation." In *Nation and Narration*, edited by Homi K. Bhabha, 291–322. London: Routledge, 1990.

Blessed Fruit. Directed by Orla Walsh. Ireland: Roisin Rua, 1999.
Blood of the Irish. Produced and Directed by Brian Hayes. Ireland: Crossing the Line, 2009.
Bogwoman. Directed by Tom Collins. Ireland: Hindsight Films Ltd., 1998.
Boland, Eavan. *A Kind of Scar: The Woman Poet in a National Tradition, Lip Pamphlet.* Dublin: Attic Press, 1989.
Botting, Fred. *Gothic.* London and New York: Routledge, 1996.
Bourke, Angela, Siobhan Kilfeather, Maria Luddy, Margaret McCurtain, Gerardine Meaney, Mairin Ni Dhonnchadha, Mary O'Dowd and Clair Wills. *The Field Day Anthology of Irish Writing, Volume 5: Women's Writing and Traditions.* Cork: Cork University Press, 2002.
Bracken, Claire and Emma Radley. "A Mirror up to Irishness: Hollywood Hard Men and Witty Women." In *Irish Postmodernisms and Popular Culture.* Eds. Wanda Balzano, Anne Mulhall & Moynagh Sullivan. Basingstoke, Hampshire: Palgrave Macmillan, 2007. 157–168.
Brenton, Howard. *The Romans in Britain.* In *Brenton Plays: 2.* London: Methuen, 1990.
Brewer, Betty Webb. "'She Was Part of It': Emily Lawless (1845–1913.)." *Éire-Ireland* 18, no. 4 (1983): 122–23.
Brown, Stephen. *Ireland in Fiction A Guide to Irish Novels, Tales, Romances and Folklore. Dublin and London, Maunsel,* 1916; Dublin, Irish Academic Press, 1969.
Burns, Robert. "Lord Gregory." In *A Select Collection of Original Scottish Airs for the Voice,* edited by George Thomson. London, Preston and Son, 1793.
Butler, Judith. *Antigone's Claim: Kinship between Life and Death.* New York: Columbia University Press, 2000.
Cahalan, James. "Forging a Tradition: Emily Lawless and the Irish Literary Canon." *Colby Quarterly* 27, no. 1:27–39.
Cahill, Betty. "Vocal Expression in Oral Traditions and Theatrical Performance with Particular Reference to the 'Caoineadh'" *Irish Theatre Forum* 2, no. 3 (1998).
Captain Boycott. Directed by Frank Launder. Britain: Individual Pictures, 1947.
Carter, Angela. *Wise Children.* London: Chatto and Windus, 1991.
Cassidy, James F. *The Old Love of the Blessed Virgin Mary, Queen of Ireland.* Dublin: Gill, 1933.
Cheng, Vincent. *Inauthentic: The Anxiety over Culture and Identity.* New Brunswick, NJ, and London: Rutgers University Press, 2004.
Cixous, Hélène. "Castration or Decapitation." Translated by Annette Kuhn. *Signs* 7, no. 1 (1981): 41–55.
———. "The Laugh of the Medusa." Translated by Keith and Paula Kohn. *Signs* 1, no. 1 (1976): 882.
Cleary, Joe. *Outrageous Fortune: Capital and Culture in Modern Ireland.* Dublin: Field Day Publications, 2007.
Clinton, William Jefferson. "Clinton Address to Democratic National Convention." United Center, Chicago, August 26, 1996. usinfo.state.gov/journals/itps/1096/ijpe/ clinI.htm.
———. "Remarks by President Clinton in Address to the 51st General Assembly of the United Nations." United Nations, New York, September 24, 1996. http://www.jfklibrary.org/slinton_un_address.html.
Coetzee, J.M. *Elizabeth Costello.* London: Secker and Warburg, 2003.
Cohan, Steven, and Ina Rae Hark, eds. *Screening the Male: Masculinities in Hollywood Cinema.* London and New York: Routledge, 1993.
Collins, Shirley, and Davy Graham. *Folk Roots, New Routes.* 1964. Reprint, Righteous Records, 1980.
Concannon, Helena. *The Queen of Ireland: An Historical Account of Ireland's Devotion to the Blessed Virgin.* Dublin: M.H. Gill and Sons, 1938.

Connor, Elizabeth (pseud. of Una Troy), "The Apple", *The Bell*, Oct. 1942
Conrad, Joseph. *Heart of Darkness*. 1899. Reprint, Harmondsworth: Penguin, 1995.
Coogan, T.P. *Devalera: Long Fellow, Long Shadow*. London and New York: Random House, 1993.
Copjec, Joan. "Vampires, Breastfeeding and Anxiety." In *The Horror Reader*, edited by Ken Gelder, 52–64. London and New York: Routledge, 2000.
Crackenthorpe, B.A. "Sex in Modern Literature." *Nineteenth Century* 37 pp. 607–16 (1895).
Cronin, Elizabeth (Bess). *The Songs of Elizabeth Cronin, Irish Traditional Singer: The Complete Song Collection*. Edited by Dáibhí Ó Cróinín. Dublin: Four Courts Press, 2000.
Crying Game, The. Directed by Neil Jordan. Britain: Palace Pictures/Channel Four Films, 1992.
Cullingford, Elizabeth. *Ireland's Others: Gender and Ethnicity in Irish Literature and Popular Culture*. Cork: Cork University Press, 2001.
Dalsimer, Adele. *Kate O'Brien: A Critical Study*. Dublin: Gill and Macmillan, 1990.
Dalton, Louis. *This Other Eden. A Play in Three Acts*. Dublin: P.J. Bourke. c. 1954.
Daly, Mary. *The Slow Failure: Population Decline and Independent Ireland, 1920–73*. Madison: University of Wisconsin Press, 2006.
Deane, Seamus. *Celtic Revivals: Essays in Irish Literature, 1880–1980*. London and Boston: Faber and Faber, 1985.
———. "Edward Said (1935–2003): A Late Style of Humanism." *Field Day Review* 1, no. 1:189–202, Spring 2005.
———, ed. *Field Day Anthology of Irish Writing*. 3 vols. Derry: Field Day, 1991.
———. *A Short History of Anglo-Irish Literature*. London: Hutchinson, 1986.
———. *Strange Country: Modernity and Nationhood in Irish Writing since 1790*. Oxford: Clarendon Press, 1997.
December Bride. Directed by Thaddeus O'Sullivan. Ireland: Little Bird, 1990.
Deevy, Teresa. *The King of Spain's Daughter and Other One Act Plays*. Dublin: New Frontiers Press, 1946.
Delaney, Enda. *Demography, State and Society: Irish Migration to Britain, 1921–1971*. Liverpool: Liverpool University Press, 2000.
———. "Placing Post-War Irish Migration to Britain in a Comparative European Perspective, 1945–81." In *The Irish Diaspora*, edited by Andy Bielenberg, 331–56. Harlow: Longman, 1999/New York: Longman, 2000.
Departed, The. Directed by Martin Scorsese. US: Warner, 2006.
Derrida, Jacques. *Of Grammatology*. Translated by Gayatri Spivak. New York: The Johns Hopkins University Press, 1976.
Devil's Own, The. Directed by Alan J. Pakula. US: Columbia, 1997.
Divorcing Jack. Directed by David Caffrey. UK: BBC/Winchester/Scala, 1998.
Donnelly, James. "A Church in Crisis." *History Ireland* 8, no. 3 pp. 12–17 (2000).
———. 'Opposing the "Modern World": The Cult of the Virgin Mary in Ireland, 1965–85,' *Éire-Ireland*, Volume 40: 1 & 2, Spring/Summer 2005, 183–245.
———. "The Peak of Marianism in Ireland." In *Piety and Power in Ireland*, edited by Stewart Brown and David Miller. Bloomington: University of Notre Dame Press, pp. 252–83 2000.
Donoghue, Emma. "'Out of Order': Kate O'Brien's Lesbian Fictions." In *Ordinary People Dancing: Essays on Kate O'Brien*, edited by Eibhear Walshe, 36–58. Cork: Cork University Press, 1993.
Dracula. Directed by Francis Ford Coppola. US: American Zoetrope, 1992.

Dyer, Richard. *White*. London and New York: Routledge, 1997.

Eagleton, Terry. *Heathcliff and the Great Hunger*. London: Verso, 1995.

Egerton, George, and Mary Chavelita Dunne. *Keynotes*. Edited by Elkin Matthews and John Lane. 1893. Reprint, London: Virago, 1980.

Einstein, Alfred. *Gluck*. Translated by Eric Blom. London: Dent, 1936.

Ellman, Maud. *The Hunger Artists: Starving, Writing and Imprisonment*. Boston: Harvard University Press, 1993.

Ellmann, Richard. *James Joyce*. Rev. ed. Oxford: Oxford University Press, 1993.

———. *The Hunger Artists: Starving, Writing and Imprisonment*. Boston: Harvard University Press, 1993.

———. *Selected Letters of James Joyce*. Harmondsworth: Penguin, 1975.

Elsaesser, Thomas. "Tales of Sound and Fury: Observations on the Family Melodrama." *Monogram* 4 (1972): 2–15.

Enright, Anne. *The Gathering*. London: Cape, 2007.

———. *The Pleasure of Eliza Lynch*. London: Cape, 2002.

Fanning, Bryan. *Racism and Social Change in the Republic of Ireland*. Manchester and New York: Manchester University Press, 2002.

Farago, Borbola, and Moynagh Sullivan, eds. *Facing the Other: Interdisciplinary Studies on Race, Class and Gender in Ireland*. Newcastle: Cambridge Scholars Press, 2008.

Farley, Fidelma. "Aisling: The Female and National Body in Films about Ireland." PhD dissertation, University College Dublin, 1999.

———. "Hibernia and Cinema: Romance and Anglo-Irish Politics in Post-War British Cinema." Paper presented at To the Other Shore: English Views of Ireland and the Irish Conference, LSU College of Higher Education, Southampton, June 1995.

———. 'Interrogating Myths of Maternity in Irish Cinema: Margo Harkin's "Hush-a-Bye Baby", *Irish University Review*, Vol. 29, No. 2 (Autumn - Winter, 1999), 219–237.

Feldman, Shelley. "Feminist Interruptions: The Silence of East Bengal in the Story of Partition." *Interventions: International Journal of Postcolonial Studies* 1, no. 2 167–82 (1999).

Field, The. Directed by Jim Sheridan. Britain: Granada, 1990.

Fogarty, Anne. "'The Business of Attachment': Romance and Desire in the Novels of Kate O'Brien." In *Ordinary People Dancing*, edited by Eibhear Walshe, 101–10. Cork: Cork University Press, 1993.

Foster, R.F. *Luck and the Irish: A Brief History of Change 1970–2000*. Harmondsworth: Penguin, 2007.

Foucault, Michel. *The History of Sexuality. Volume 1: An Introduction*. New York: Pantheon, 1978.

Fowler, David C. "An Accused Queen in 'The Lass of Roch Royal' (Child 76)." *Journal of American Folklore* 71, no. 282 553–63 (October–December 1958).

Freud, Sigmund. "The Uncanny." In *Standard Edition of the Complete Psychological Works*. Translated by James Stachey. 1919. Reprint, London: Hogarth, 217–53 1986.

Gabriel, Tshome H. 'Xala: A cinema of wax and gold', *Jump Cut*, no. 27, July 1982, 31–33.

Gangs of New York. Directed by Martin Scorsese. US: Miramax, 2001.

Garber, Marjorie. *Vice Versa*. New York: Simon and Schuster, 1995.

Garner, Steve. "Guests of the Nation." *Irish Review* 33 (2005): 78–84.

General, The. Directed by John Boorman. Ireland: Merlin Films, 1998.

Gentle Gunman, The. Directed by Basil Deardon. Ealing, Britain: Michael Balcon Productions, 1952.

Gibbons, Luke. "'The Cracked Looking Glass' of Cinema: James Joyce, John Huston, and the Memory of 'The Dead.'" *Yale Journal of Criticism* 15, no. 1 (2002): 127–48.

———. "Engendering the Sublime: Margaret Corcoran's an Enquiry." *Circa* 107 32–38 (Spring 2004).

———. "On the Beach." *Artforum* 31.2 (October 1992), 13–16.

———. *Transformations in Irish Culture. Critical Conditions: Field Day Essays.* Edited by Seamus Deane. Cork: Cork University Press, 1996.

———. "Romanticism, Realism and Irish Cinema." In *Cinema and Ireland*, edited by Kevin Rockett, Luke Gibbons and John Hill. New York: Syracuse University Press, 1988, 194–274.

Gilbert, Sandra, and Susan Gubar. *The Madwoman in the Attic: The Woman Writer and the Nineteenth Century Literary Imagination.* New Haven, CT: Yale University Press, 1979.

Gledhill, Christine, ed. *Home Is Where the Heart Is: Studies in Melodrama and the Woman's Film.* London: British Film Institute, 1987).

Gonne, Maud. 'Dawn', in Robert Hogan & James Kilroy, eds., *Lost Plays of the Irish Renaissance.* Delaware: Proscenium, 1970), 72–84.

Gould, Stephen Jay. *Time's Arrow, Time's Cycle: Myth and Metaphor in the Discovery of Geological Time.* Boston: Harvard University Press, 1987.

Graham, Colin. *Deconstructing Ireland: Identity, Theory, Culture.* Edinburgh: Edinburgh University Press, 2001.

Grand, Sarah. *The Beth Book: Being a Study of the Life of Elizabeth Caldwell Maclure, a Woman of Genius.* 1897. Reprint, London: Virago, 1980.

Greenslade, William. *Degeneration, Culture and the Novel, 1880–1940.* Cambridge: Cambridge University Press, 1994.

Gregory, Lady Augusta. *Cuchulainn of Muirthemne.* London: John Murray, 1902.

———. *Selected Writings.* Edited by Lucy McDiarmid and Maureen Waters. Harmondsworth: Penguin, 1995.

Griffin, Gerald. *The Collegians.* 1829. London: Saunders and Otley; electronic edition   http://mockingbird.creighton.edu/english/micsun/IrishResources/Collegians/collcont.htm.

Grubgeld, Elizabeth. "Emily Lawless's *Granía*: The Story of an Island." *Éire-Ireland* 22, no. 3 (1987): 115–29.

Guiltrip. Directed by Gerry Stembridge. Ireland: Temple, 1995.

Guinnane, Timothy. *The Vanishing Irish: Households, Migration and the Rural Economy in Ireland, 1850–1914.* Princeton, NJ: Princeton University Press, 1997.

Harrison, Patricia. "Letter to the Editor." *The Bell* (August 1945): 446.

Hayman, David. "Joyce Et Mallarme." *Paris* 1 (1956): 27–34.

Hegel, G.W.F. *The Phenomenology of Mind.* 2nd ed. Edited by J.B. Baillie. 1807. Reprint, London: George Allen and Unwin, 1931.

Henigan, Julie. "'The Old Irish Tonality': Folksong as Emotional Catalyst in 'The Dead.'" *New Hibernia Review* 11, no. 4 (2007): 136–48.

Hensher, Phillip. "No One Has to Pretend to Like James Joyce." *The Independent*, February 12, 2004.

Herr, Cheryl. "The Erotics of Irishness." *Critical Inquiry* 17, no. 1 (Autumn1990): 1–34.

———. *The Field, Ireland into Film.* Cork: Cork University Press, 2002.

Hogarth, Jane. "Literary Degenerates." *Fortnightly Review* 63:586–92.

Howes, Marjorie. "Tradition, Gender, and Migration in 'The Dead,' or How Many People Has Gretta Conroy Killed?" *Yale Journal of Criticism* 15, no. 21 149–171 (2002).

Hroch, Miroslav. "From National Movement to the Fully Formed Nation: The Nation-Building Process in Europe." *New Left Review* 1, no. 2 3–20 (1993).

Hungry Hill. Directed by Brian Desmond Hurst. Britain: Two Cities, 1947.

Hush-A-Bye-Baby. Directed by Margo Harkin. Ireland: Derry Film and Video Workshop, 1989.

Hutcheon, Linda. "Kosovo, Ulster and How Research Goes Awry." *Textual Practice* 14, no. 1 (2000): 1–5.

Hyde, Douglas, ed., *Beside the fire: A collection of Irish Gaelic folk Stories.* Translated and annotated by Douglas Hyde, additional notes by Alfred Nutt. London: Dabvid Nutt, 1910.

I See a Dark Stranger. Directed by Frank Launder. Britain: Individual Pictures, 1946.

I Went Down. Directed by Paddy Breathnach. Ireland: Treasure Films, 1997.

Ignatieve, Noel. *How the Irish Became White.* New York and London: Routledge, 1997.

In Bruges. Directed by Martin McDonagh. UK: Universal Pictures, 2008.

In Treatment. Created by Hagai Levi et al. US: HBO, 2008.

Infernal Affairs (trilogy). Directed by Andrew Lau Wai-Keung, Alan Mak. Hong Kong: Media Asia, 2002–3.

Informer, The. Directed by John Ford. US: RKO Radio Pictures, 1935.

Inglis, Tom. *Global Ireland: Same Difference.* New York and Oxford: Routledge, 2008.

Iremonger, Valentin. "The Poems of Freda Laughton." *The Bell* 9, no. 4 (January 1945): 249–50.

Irigaray, Luce. *The Irigaray Reader.* Edited by Margaret Whitford. Oxford: Blackwell, 1991.

———. *Sexes Et Parentés.* Paris: Minuit, 1987.

———. *Speculum. De L'autre Femme.* Translated by Gillian C. Gill. Ithaca, NY: Cornell University Press, 1985.

Islandman, The. Directed by Patrick Heale. Ireland: Irish National Film Corporation, 1938.

Jackal, The. Directed by Michael Caton-Jones. US: Universal/Mutual/Alphaville, 1997.

Jacob, Rosamond. "MS Diaries." In *Jacob Papers.* Dublin: National Library of Ireland, 1923–1924.

———. *Nix and Theo.* In *Jacob Papers.* 1924. Dublin: National Library of Ireland.

———. *The Troubled House.* Dublin: Browne and Nolan, 1938.

Jameson, Frederick. "Modernism and Imperialism." In *Nationalism, Colonialism and Literature, Field Day Pamphlet No.14.* Derry: Field Day, 1988.

Jardine, Alice. *Gynesis: Configurations of Woman and Modernity.* Ithaca, NY, and London: Cornell University Press, 1985.

Johnston, Claire. "Maeve." *Screen* 24 (1981): 24–71.

Johnston, Jennifer. *Foolish Mortals.* London: Headline Review, 2007.

———. Interview, *Verbal* 9 (December 2007).

———. *Shadows on Our Skin.* London: Hamish Hamilton, 1977.

Joyce, James. *Dubliners.* 1914. Reprint, London: Granada, 1977.

———. *Finnegans Wake.* London: Faber and Faber, 1939.

———. *Letters of James Joyce.* Vol. 3. Edited by Richard Ellmann. London: Faber and Faber, 1966.

———. *Occasional, Critical, and Political Writing.* Edited by Kevin Barry. Oxford: Oxford University Press, 2008.

———. *A Portrait of the Artist as a Young Man.* 1916. Reprint, London: Granada Panther, 1977.

———. *Ulysses*. Harmondsworth: Penguin, 1922.

Joyriders. Directed by Aisling Walsh. Britain: Little Bird, 1988.

Kelleher, Margaret. *The Feminization of Famine*. Cork: Cork University Press, 1997.

Kelly, A.A. *Pillars of the House: An Anthology of Verse by Irish Women from 1690 to the Present*. Dublin: Wolfhound, 1987.

Kennedy, Finola. *From Cottage to Creche: Family Change in Ireland*. Dublin: Institute of Public Administration, 2001.

Kiberd, Declan. *Inventing Ireland: The Literature of the Modern Nation*. London, Jonathan Cape, 1995; London, Vintage, 1996.

———. *Irish Classics*. London: Granta, 2000.

———. *The Irish Writer and the World*. Cambridge: Cambridge University Press, 2005.

Kilroy, Claire. *All Names Have Been Changed*. London: Faber, 2009.

Klute. Directed by Alan J. Pakula. US: Warner, 1971.

Kosofsky Sedgewick, Eva. *Between Men: English Literature and Male Homosocial Desire*. New York: Columbia University Press, 1985.

Kristeva, Julia. *Nations without Nationalism*. Translated by Leon S. Roudiez. New York: Columbia University Press, 1993.

———. *Powers of Horror*. New York and Surrey: Columbia University Press, 1982.

———. *The Revolution in Poetic Language*. Translated by M. Waller. New York: Columbia University Press, 1984.

———. "Stabat Mater." In *The Kristeva Reader*, edited by Toril Moi, 61. Oxford: Blackwell, 1986.

———. *Strangers to Ourselves*. Translated by Leon S. Roudiez. Hemel Hempstead: Harvester Wheatsheaf, 1991.

———. "Women's Time." In *The Kristeva Reader*, edited by Toril Moi, 187–213. Oxford: Blackwell, 1986.

———. "Word Dialogue and Novel." In *The Kristeva Reader*, edited by Toril Moi, 36. Oxford: Blackwell, 1986.

Lacan, Jacques. *Écrits: A Selection*. Translated by Alan Sheridan. New York: Norton, 1977.

———. *The Seminar of Jacques Lacan, Book 7: Ethics of Psychoanalysis, 1959–60*. Edited by Jacques Alain Miller. London: Routledge, 1992.

Landleaguers, The. London: Chatto and Windus, 1884

Lant, Antonia. "The Female Spy: Gender, Nationality and War in *I See a Dark Stranger*." In *Resisting Images: Essays on Cinema and History*, edited by Robert Sklar and Charles Musser. Philadelphia: Temple University Press, 1990 173–99.

Laughton, Freda, "When You Were With Me." *The Bell* (August 1944): 287.

———. "The Woman with Child." *The Bell* 9, no. 4 (January 1945): 289.

Lawless, Emily. *Granía: The Story of an Island*. 2 vols. London: Smith Elder and Co., 1892.

———. *Hurrish*. 1886. Reprint, Belfast: Appletree Press, 1992.

———. *Maelcho*. London: Metheun, 1895.

———. *Maria Edgeworth*. London: Macmillan, 1904.

———. "A Note on the Ethics of Literary Forgery." *Nineteenth Century* (1897): 85–95.

———. *With Essex in Ireland*. London: Smith Elder and Co., 1890.

———. 'After Aughrim', *With the Wild Geese*. London, Ibister, 1902.

Layden, Dervila. "Discovering and Uncovering Genre in Irish Cinema." In *Genre and Cinema: Ireland and Transnationalism*, edited by Brian McElroy. London and New York: Routledge, 2007 27–44.

Lethal Weapon. Directed by Richard Donner. US: Warner, 1987.

Lentin, Ronit. "Black Bodies and Headless Hookers: Alternative Global Narratives for 21st Century Ireland." *Irish Review* 33 1–12 (Spring 2005).

———. "Pregnant Silence: (En)Gendering Ireland's Asylum Space." *Patterns of Prejudice* 37, no. 3 (2003): 301–22.

Lloyd, David. *Anomalous States: Irish Writing and the Post-Colonial Moment.* Dublin: Lilliput, 1993.

Longley, Edna. *From Cathleen to Anorexia: The Breakdown of Irelands, Lip Pamphlet.* Dublin: Attic Press, 1990.

Lopez, Barry. *Arctic Dreams: Imagination and Desire in a Northern Landscape.* London: Pan, 1987.

Love Divided, A. Directed by Sydney McCartney. Ireland: Parallel Films, 1999.

Luddy, Maria. *Prostitution and Irish Society, 1800–1940.* Cambridge: Cambridge University Press, 2007.

Macardle, Dorothy. *Earthbound.* Worcester, MA: Harrigan, 1924.

———. *Fantastic Summer.* London: Peter Davies, 1946.

———. *The Irish Republic.* London: Victor Gollancz, 1937.

———. "Letter to Eamonn de Valera." In *The Field Day Anthology of Irish Writing, Volume 5: Women's Writing and Traditions*, edited by Angela Bourke, Siobhan Kilfeather, Maria Luddy, Margaret McCurtain, Gerardine Meaney, Mairin Ni Dhonnchadha, Mary O'Dowd and Clair Wills, 1937. Cork: Cork University Press, 2002.

———. *Uneasy Freehold.* London: Peter Davies, 1944.

MacBride White, Anna, and A. Norman Jeffares, eds. *The Gonne-Yeats Letters 1893–1938: Always Your Friend.* London: Hutchinson, 1992.

Macdiarmid, Hugh. *Selected Poems.* 1955. Reprint, Manchester: Carcanet, 2002.

Madden, Aodhan. *Sea Urchins.* Project Theatre, Tivoli Theatre, Irish National Tour, 1988.

Madden-Simpson, Janet. *Women's Part: An Anthology of Short Fiction by and About Irishwomen 1890–1920.* Dublin: Arlen House, 1984.

Maddison, Stephen. "All About Woman: Pedro Almodóvar and the Heterosocial Dynamic." *Textual Practice* 14, no. 2 (Summer 2000): 282.

———. *Fags, Hags and Queer Sisters.* New York: St. Martin's Press, 2000.

Maeve. Directed by Pat Murphy and John Davies. Britain and Ireland: British Film Institute and RTE, 1981.

Mangan, James Clarene. *Roisin Dhubh.* In *Field Day Anthology of Irish Writing*, Vol. 2, edited by Seamus Deane. 1846. Reprint, Derry: Field Day, 1991 26–27.

Mangum, Teresa. "Style Wars of the 1890s: The New Woman and the Decadent." In *Transforming Genres: New Approaches to British Fiction of the 1890s*, edited by Nikki Lee Menos and Meri-Jane Rochelson. Basingstoke: Macmillan, 1994 47–66.

Massood, Paula. "City Spaces and City Times: Bakhtin's Chronotope and Recent African-American Film." In *Screening the City*, edited by Mark Shiel and Tony Fitzmaurice. London and New York: Verso, 2003 200–215.

McClintock, Anne. "Family Feuds: Gender, Nationalism and the Family." *Feminist Review* 44 61–79 (Summer 1993).

———. *Imperial Leather: Race, Gender and Sexuality in the Colonial Context.* London and New York: Routledge, 1995.

McClintock, Letitia. *A Boycotted Household.* 1881. London, Smith, Elder.

McCormick, Fred. "The Songs of Elizabeth Cronin." *Musical Traditions* (2000) ejournal, http://www.mustard.org.uk/articles/cronin.htm.

McLoone, Martin. *Irish Film: The Emergence of a Contemporary Cinema.* London: BFI, 2000.

———. "Reimagining the Nation: Themes and Issues in Irish Cinema." *Cineaste* 24, nos. 2–3 (1999): 33.

McLoughlin, Dympna. "Workhouses and Irish Female Paupers, 1840–70." In *Women Surviving: Studies in Irish Women's History in the Nineteenth and Twentieth Centuries*, edited by Maria Luddy and Cliona Murphy, 117–47. Dublin: Poolbeg, 1990.

Meaney, Gerardine. "Dead, White, Male: Irishness in *Angel* and *Buffy the Vampire Slayer*." In *The Irish in Us*, edited by Diane Negra 254–281. Durham, NC: Duke University Press, 2006.

———. "Sex and Nation." In *The Irish Women's Studies Reader*, edited by Ailbhe Smyth. Dublin: Attic Press, 1993.

———. *(Un)Like Subjects: Women, Theory, Fiction*. London: Routledge, 1993.

Mentxaka, Aintzane Legarreta. "Kate O'Brien's *Mary Lavelle*: Sex, Art, Politics, and the Fiction of Identity." PhD dissertation, University College Dublin, 2007.

Michael Collins. Directed by Neil Jordan. Ireland: Warner Bros., 1996.

Moolaadé. Directed by Ousmane Senbene. Senegal: Filmi Doomireew, 2004.

Morgan, Lady/Sydney Owenson. *The Wild Irish Girl*. London: Phillips, 1806.

Moretti, Franco. "The Dialectic of Fear." In *The Horror Reader*, edited by Ken Gelder, 148–61. London and New York: Routledge, 2000.

Morris, Neil. *The Lass of Loch Royal. The Alan Lomax Collection, Southern Journey, Vol. 1: Voices from the American South, Blues, Ballads, Hymns*, Rounder Select, U.S.

Mulvey, Laura. "Afterthoughts . . . Inspired by Duel in the Sun." *Framework* 15–17 (1981): 12–15.

———. "Visual Pleasure and Narrative Cinema." *Screen* 16, no. 3 (1975): 6–18.

Murphy, Clíona. *The Women's Suffrage Movement and Irish Society in the Early Twentieth Century*. Philadelphia: Temple University Press, 1989.

Murphys Law. Created by Colin Bateman. UK: BBC, 2003–7.

Murray, Christopher. *Twentieth-Century Irish Drama: Mirror up to Nation*. Manchester and New York: Manchester University Press, 1997.

Nash, Catherine. "Remapping and Renaming: New Cartographies of Identity, Gender and Landscape in Ireland." *Feminist Review* 44 (Summer 1993): 39–57.

Neale, Steve. "Masculinity as Spectacle." *Screen* 24, no. 6 2–17 (1983).

Negra, Diane. *The Irish in Us*. Durham, NC: Duke University Press, 2006.

———, ed. *Off-White Hollywood: American Culture and Ethnic Female Stardom*. London and New York: Routledge, 2001.

Nephew, The. Directed by Eugene Brady. Ireland: Irish Dream Time, 1998.

Newman, Kate. *Dictionary of Ulster Biography*. Belfast: Institute of Irish Studies, Queen's University Belfast, 1993.

Ní Dhuibhne, Éilís. *The Bray House*. Dublin: Attic Press, 1990.

———. *Fox, Swallow, Scarecrow*. Belfast: Blackstaff Press, 2007.

Nolan, Emer. *James Joyce and Nationalism*. London: Routledge, 1995.

O'Brien, Kate. *The Ante-Room*. 1934. Reprint, Dublin: Arlen House, 1980.

———. *Distinguished Villa; A Play in Three Acts*. London: Benn, 1926.

———. *Farewell Spain*. 1937. Reprint, London: Virago, 1985.

———. *The Land of Spices*. London, Toronto, Heineman, 1941; London, Virago, 2006.

———. *Mary Lavelle*. 1936. Reprint, London: Virago, 1984.

———. *As Music and Splendour*. London: Heinemann, 1958.

———. *That Lady*. 1946. Reprint, London: Virago, 1985.

O'Donnell, Katherine. "'But Greek . . . Usually Knows Greek': Recognizing Queer Sexuality in Kate O'Brien's *Mary Lavelle*." Paper presented to Queer Studies/Irish Studies' Seminar, University College Dublin, 2002.

O'Horan, Eily. "The Rustle of Spring." *The Bell* 13, no. 5 (February 1948): 28–39.

O'Reilly, Sean. *The Swing of Things*. London: Faber and Faber, 2005.
——. *Watermark*. Dublin, The Stinging Fly, 2005.
Odd Man Out. Directed by Carol Reed. Britain: Two Cities, 1947.
Oliphant, Margaret. "A Noble Lady (Lady Cloncurry)." *New Review* 14, no. 82 (1896): 241–47.
Ordinary Decent Criminal. Directed by Thaddeus O'Sullivan. Ireland: Little Bird, 2000.
Ovid. *Metamorphosis*. Translated by Mary M. Innes. Harmondsworth: Penguin, 1955.
Parallax View, The. Directed by Alan J. Pakula. US: Paramount/Gus/Harbour/Doubleday, 1974.
Partridge, Angela. (Angela Bourke) *Caoineadh Na Dtrí Muire: Téama Na Páise I Bhfílocht Bhéil Na Gaeilge*. Dublin: An Clóchomhar, 1983.
Patriarca, Silvana. *Numbers and Nationhood: Writing Statistics in Nineteenth Century Italy*. Cambridge: Cambridge University Press, 1996.
Patriot Games. Directed by Phillip Noyce. US: UIP/Paramount, 1992.
Pettitt, Lance. *Screening Ireland: Film and Television Representation*. Manchester: Manchester University Press, 2000.
Phineas Redux. London: Chapman and Hall, 1874.
Piano, The. Directed by Jane Campion. Australia, New Zealand and France: Australian Film Commission, 1993.
Playboys, The. Directed by Gillies McKinnon. Britain: Green Umbrella Films, 1992.
Quiet Man, The. Directed by John Ford. US: Republic, 1952.
Quiller-Couch, Arthur. *Oxford Book of English Verse 1250–1918*. Oxford: Oxford University Press, 1919.
Quinn, Antoinette. "Cathleen Ni Houlihan Writes Back: Maud Gonne and Irish Nationalist Theatre." In *Gender and Sexuality in Modern Ireland* edited by Anthony Bradley and Maryann Gialanella Valiulis, 39–60. Amherst: University of Massachusetts Press, 1997.
Reynolds, Lorna. *Kate O'Brien: A Literary Portrait*. Gerrards Cross: Smythe, 1987.
Rockett, Kevin. "Irish Cinema: The National in the International." *Cineaste* 24, no. 2–3 (1999): 24.
Rory O'More. Directed by Sidney Olcott. US: Kalem Company, 1911.
Ryan, Louise. "Irish Newspaper Representations of Women, Migration and Pregnancy Outside the Marriage in the 1930." In *Single Motherhood in 20th Century Ireland: Cultural, Historical and Social Essays*, edited by Maria de la Cinta Ramblado-Minero and Auxiliadora Perez-Vides. Ceredigion: Edward Mellen Press, 2006.
Scott, Sir Walter. *Complete Poetical Works*. Edinburgh: William T. Amies, 1878.
Senate Debates 1925, *Parlimentary debates - Dáil Éireann: official report*. Dublin: Stationary Office, 1922–. http://historical-debates.oireachtas.ie/en.toc.dail.html.
Sembène, Ousmane. "Guardian/Nft Interview by Bonnie Greer." *The Guardian*, June 5, 2005.
Sheehy-Skeffington, Hannah. *Sheehy Skeffington Papers*. Manuscript collection. Dublin: National Library of Ireland.
Showalter, Elaine. *Daughters of Decadence*. London: Virago, 1993.
Siege, The. Directed by Edward Zwick. US: TCF, 1998.
Siegel, Sandra. "Literature and Degeneration: The Representation of Decadence." In *Degeneration: The Dark Side of Progress*, edited by J. Edward Chamberlin and Sander L. Gilman. New York and Guildford: Columbia University Press, 1985 199–219.

Smith, James. *Ireland's Magdalen Laundries and the Nation's Architecture of Containment*. Notre Dame, IN: Notre Dame University Press, 2007.

Smith, Sara. "Ireland in the 1940s and 1950s: The Photographs of Bert Hardy," *Field Day Review* 1, no. 1: 133–56.

Snakes and Ladders. Directed by Trish MacAdam. Ireland: Livia Films, 1996.

Snapper, The. Directed by Stephen Frears. Britain: BBC, 1993.

Sobchack, Vivian. "Lounge Time: Postwar Crises and the Chronotope of Film Noir." In *Refiguring American Film Genres: Theory and History*, edited by Nick Browne, 129–70. Berkeley: University of California Press, 1998.

Some Mother's Son. Directed by Terry George. Ireland: Hell's Kitchen, 14 1996.

Spooks. Created by David Wolstonecraft. U.K.: Kudos, 2002–10.

Sullivan, Moynagh. "The Treachery of Wetness: Irish Studies, Seamus Heaney and the Politics of Parturition." *Irish Studies Review* 13, no. 4 (2005): 451–68.

———. "The Woman Poet and the Matter of Representation in Modern and Postmodern Poetics." PhD thesis, University College Dublin, 2001.

Symons, Arthur. *Arthur Symons: Selected Letters, 1880–1893*. Iowa City: University of Iowa Press, 1989.

———. *The Symbolist Movement in Literature* [1899] Rev. ed. New York: Haskell House, 1971.

Synge, John Millington. *Collected Works. Vol. II.* Edited by Alan Price. Oxford: Oxford University Press, 1966.

———. *The Playboy of the Western World and Other Plays*. Edited by Anne Saddlemeyer. Oxford: Oxford University Press, [1907] 1995.

Tasker, Yvonne. *Spectacular Bodies: Gender, Genre and the Action Cinema*. London and New York: Routledge, 1993.

Thapar, Suruchi. "Women as Activists, Women as Symbols: A Study of the Indian Nationalist Movement." *Feminist Review* 44 (Summer 1993): 81–96.

This is the Sea. Directed by Mary McGuckian. Ireland: Pembridge, 1996.

This Other Eden. Directed by Muriel Box. Emmet Dalton Productions. Ireland, 1959.

Thurston, Katherine Cecil. *The Fly on the Wheel*. 1st ed. Edinburgh: Blackwoodl, 1908.

———. *The Gambler*. New York: Grosset and Dunlap, 1905.

———. *John Chilcote M.P.* London: Blackwood, 1904.

———. *Max*. London: Hutchinson, 1910.

Tóibín, Colm, ed. *Penguin Book of Irish Fiction*. Harmondsworth: Penguin, 2000.

Trollope, Anthony. *Phineas Finn: The Irish Member*. 1869. Reprint, Oxford: Oxford World Classics, 1982.

———. *Phineas Redux*. London: Chapman and Hall, 1874.

———. *The Landleaguers*. London: Chatto and Windus, 1884.

Troy, Una. (Elizabeth Connor), 'The Apple', *The Bell*, Oct. 1942.

Turpin, John. "Visual Marianism and National Identity in Ireland: 1920–1960." In *Art, Nation and Gender: Ethnic Landscapes, Myths and Mother-Figure*, edited by Tricia Cusack and Sighle Bhreathnach-Lynch. Aldershot, Hampshire and Burlington, VT: Ashgate, 2003, 67–79.

Ulin, Julieann Veronica. "Fluid Boarders and Naughty Girls: Music, Domesticity, and Nation in Joyce's Boarding Houses." *James Joyce Quarterly* 44, no. 2 (Winter 2007): 263–89.

Una (pseud. Elizabeth Connor), "The Apple", *The Bell*, Oct. 1942.

Valente, Joseph. *Dracula's Crypt: Bram Stoker, Irishness, and the Question of Blood*. Champaign: University of Illinois Press, 2001.

Vicious Circle. Directed by David Blair. Ireland: BBC Northern Ireland, 1998.

Visit, The. Directed by Orla Walsh. Ireland: Roisin Rua Films, 1992.

Waking Ned Devine. Directed by Kirk Jones. Britain: Fox, 1999.

Walshe, Eibhear, *Kate O'Brien: A Writing Life.* Dublin: Irish Academic Press, 2006.

———, ed. *Ordinary People Dancing: Essays on Kate O'Brien.* Cork: Cork University Press, 1993.

———, ed. *Sex, Nation and Dissent in Irish Writing.* Cork: Cork University Press, 1997.

Ward, Margaret. *Unmanageable Revolutionaries: Women and Irish Nationalism.* Rev. ed. London: Pluto, 1995.

Watson, Peggy. "The Rise of Masculinism in Eastern Europe." *New Left Review* 198 (March/April 1993): 71–83.

Weiner, Stephanie Kuduk. "The Aesthetes' John Clare: Arthur Symons, Norman Gale and Avant-Garde Poetics." *English Literature in Transition 1880–1920* 243–65 (Fall 2008).

Weisstein, Ulrich, ed. *The Essence of Opera.* New York: W. W. Norton, 1969.

Whelan, Bernadette. "Ireland, the Marshall Plan, and U.S. Cold War Concerns." *Journal of Cold War Studies* 8, no. 1 (Winter 2006): 68–94.

Whelan, Kevin. "The Memories of 'The Dead.'" *Yale Journal of Criticism* 15, no. 1 (2002): 59–97.

———. "The Power of Place." *Irish Review* 12 13–20 (Spring/Summer 1992).

When Brendan Met Trudy. Directed by Kieron J. Walshe Ireland: Deadly Films 2, 2001.

Willie Reilly and His Colleen Bawn. Directed by John McDonogh. Ireland/US: Film Company of Ireland, 1918.

Wills, Clair. "Contemporary Irish Women Poets: The Privatisation of Myth." In *Diverse Voices: Essays on Twentieth-Century Women Writers in English,* edited by Harriet Devine Jump, 254. Hemel Hempstead: Harvester Wheatsheaf, 1991.

———. "Representations of Women, Marriage and Modernity in the 1950s." Paper presented at the Inventing and Reinventing the Irish Woman Symposium, Humanities Institute of Ireland, University College Dublin, October 10–11, 2008.

———. *That Neutral Island: A Cultural History of Ireland during the Second World War.* London: Faber and Faber, 2007.

Xala. Directed by Ousmane Sembene. Senegal: Filmi Doomireew, 1974.

Yeats, W.B. *Collected Poems.* Edited by Augustine Martin. London: Vintage, 1990.

———. 'Commentary on his list of 30 best books', *Daily Express* (27 Fev. 1895).

———. 'Contemporary Irish Writers', *The Bookman* (Aug (895).

———. 'The Death of Cuchulainn' [1939]. In *The Plays: The Collected Works of W. B. Yeats* Vol. 2. Eds., David R. Clark and Rosalind E. New York and Basingstoke: Palgrave, 2001; New York: Scribner, 2001.

———. "Irish National Literature: Contemporary Prose Writers." *The Bookman* (1895): 12–15.

———. *On Baile's Strand* [1904]. In *Field Day Anthology of Irish Literature,* edited by Seamus Deane, 602–13. Derry: Field Day, 2000.

———. 'Review of Hurrish', *New York Times* (21 March 1886).

Žižek, Slavoj. *The Plague of Fantasies.* London: Verso, 1997.

———. *Welcome to the Desert of the Real.* London: Verso, 2002.

Index